TO MAKE A
FORTUNE IN
MISSOURI

TO MAKE A

MEREDITH MILES MARMADUKE
1791-1864

SANTA FE TRADER, SURVEYOR, MERCHANT,
GOVERNOR, FARMER, LAND SPECULATOR,
PILL PEDDLER

BY LEE M. CULLIMORE

Copyright ©2021 by Lee M. Cullimore
Design Copyright ©2021 by Missouri Life, Inc.

All rights reserved.

Published by Friends of Arrow Rock, Inc.
310 Main Street, Arrow Rock, MO 65320

Library of Congress Control Number: 2020952732
ISBN 978-0-9753577-1-2
Printed in the United States of America by Walsworth.

Editing: Copy Editor Kathy Casteel
Friends of Arrow Rock, Editorial Consultant Sandy Selby
Book and Cover Design: *Missouri Life* Creative Director Holly Kite
Missouri Life Project Manager Rebecca French Smith

To Dan and Debbie

*In deepest gratitude to
Zemula Pierce Fleming*

CONTENTS

List of Illustrations	ix
Foreword	xi
Acknowledgments	xiii
Introduction	xv
Chapter 1: From the Ashes of Her Sires	1
Chapter 2: Years of Preparation	9
Chapter 3: The Move West	17
Chapter 4: A Star of No Inconsiderable Magnitude	27
Chapter 5: People of High Standing	35
Chapter 6: Concealed Intentions	47
Chapter 7: A Long and Lonesome Travel	61
Chapter 8: Trouble on the Return	75
Chapter 9: A Partner for Hymoon's Altar	87
Chapter 10: All in the Family	99
Chapter 11: Tasting the Political Bone	115
Chapter 12: The Bone Turns Bitter	133
Chapter 13: If Life and Health Last	143
Chapter 14: An Elusive Empire	163
Chapter 15: Dirt is Destiny	197
Chapter 16: Missouri and No Restrictions	215
Chapter 17: A Rising Generation	233
Chapter 18: Marmaduke's Confliction	247
Chapter 19: Divided Loyalties	267
Epilogue: Journey's End	285
Bibliography	291
Index	303

ILLUSTRATIONS

Map of the Booneslick region	181
Meredith Miles Marmaduke	182
Lavinia Marmaduke	183
Dr. John Sappington	184
Jane Breathitt Sappington	185
Claiborne Fox Jackson	186
Eliza Sappington Jackson	187
Marmaduke homestead	188
20th-century remains of the Marmaduke home	190
Thomas Hart Benton	191
Governor Meredith Miles Marmaduke	192
Marmaduke brothers	193
George Caleb Bingham house, Arrow Rock	194
J. Huston Tavern, Arrow Rock	195
Map of the Sappington/Marmaduke neighborhood	196

FOREWORD

As children, we learned history in simple, easy-to-digest bites: George Washington never told a lie. Abraham Lincoln freed the slaves. Rosa Parks refused to give up her seat. The Friends of Arrow Rock was founded by people who recognized that history should be more like a banquet. There are meaty pieces, delicious details, and some unappetizing bits, too. When it's all laid out for us, we can make informed decisions about what history offers to us today.

It was in that spirit of serving up the whole, unfiltered truth that author Lee Cullimore took on this biography of Meredith Miles Marmaduke. A conflicted and complicated 19th-century man, Marmaduke spent more than half his life in the Arrow Rock area, where his influence increased along with his wealth. He eventually ascended to the Missouri governorship, yet he couldn't even manage to unite his family. Cullimore, through his exhaustive research, gives us a portrait of a man who was neither an admirable saint nor an irredeemable villain but who left a lasting mark on Missouri history.

Since its founding in 1959, the Friends of Arrow Rock has remained committed to two missions: historic preservation and history education. The organization has restored and continues to maintain 13 historic buildings in the beautiful village of Arrow Rock, Missouri. The organization's history education efforts include programs for children and adults, tours, and publications like this one.

Friends of Arrow Rock is proud to publish this biography, the first known history of Governor Marmaduke. This effort would not have been possible without the generosity of Zemula Pierce Fleming, a Friends of Arrow Rock supporter and a Marmaduke descendant. Her gift allowed us to produce the impressive volume you hold in your hands.

We are grateful that author Cullimore, also a Marmaduke descendent, offered us the opportunity to publish his book about one of the Arrow Rock area's most notable citizens. We found the manuscript to be an impressive feat of research and writing, and the result is a compelling and highly readable story we know you will enjoy.

We believe history is at its most valuable when it can be explored fully and from every angle. We are pleased to be associated with a project that does just that.

Sandy Selby
Executive Director
Friends of Arrow Rock

ACKNOWLEDGMENTS

Writing a book of this nature requires involving many other people and they deserve to be recognized for the part they played in its creation.

Mrs. Zemula Pierce Fleming, herself a descendant of Meredith Marmaduke, made possible the book's publication through her support of the nonprofit organization Friends of Arrow Rock, whose mission is stewardship of the historic village so central to Marmaduke's life.

Every writer profits from the critical pencil of a good editor. In my case, I am fortunate that Kathy Casteel, known as "one of the best in the business," agreed to review my work and perform the magic for which she is known. Her eye for style and continuity significantly benefited the manuscript on its way to the printer.

Lynn Morrow, historian and retired director of the Missouri State Archives Local Records Program, and Mike Dickey, historian and administrator of Arrow Rock State Historic Site, are due special recognition for reading the manuscript while in production and offering advice and guidance.

The archive staff members at the State Historical Society of Missouri in Columbia and the Missouri Historical Society in St. Louis aided me greatly with their prompt and courteous responses to my requests for material from the collections their institutions hold.

Joan McPeak, secretary/treasurer of St. Clair County Historical Society, aided in the research of land holdings in that county. Elizabeth Burnes, archivist for the National Archives at Kansas City, searched tract books from the Fayette, Missouri, federal land office. Terry Humphry at the Marshall, Missouri, Public Library, was helpful in finding information about Marmaduke family slaves. Michael-Lee O'Brien Brockhouse, a genealogy research specialist in Blue Springs, Missouri, found photographs of Marmaduke family members and helped secure them for archive retention. Myron Lyman in Westmoreland County, Virginia, provided a copy of his manuscript, *Encounters with the British in Virginia during the War of 1812*. Frances Callaghan sent copies of Marmaduke family documents held by the Mary Ball Washington Museum & Library in Lancaster, Virginia.

If I have failed to acknowledge someone who helped, please know the omission was not intentional.

INTRODUCTION

Talented, ambitious, educated, willing to take risks, 32-year-old Meredith Miles Marmaduke came to Missouri in 1823 hoping to get rich, something he had deemed unattainable in his native Virginia. He could not have picked a better place at this time in the nation's development to seek success for himself. The subsequent four decades he spent in Missouri saw the state transform from a raw frontier community at the junction of the Mississippi and Missouri Rivers into an agricultural and business powerhouse worthy of the title "Gateway to the West." During this time of dynamic social, commercial, and political evolution, Marmaduke's actions as a trader, merchant, businessman, politician, farmer, slave owner, and land speculator influenced the lives of Missouri's citizens and the development of the state's institutions. Following his death in 1864, William B. Napton Jr., in his book *Past and Present of Saline County, Missouri*, took measure of Marmaduke's life. "A man of earnest and purposeful life, he was one to be trusted and his integrity was never impeached nor his character blemished," recalled Napton of his friend and neighbor. "His life was characterized by a constant endeavor to do the right as he understood the right and in his death the community and the state suffered a distinct loss."

The story of Meredith Marmaduke's influence on the development of Missouri from statehood to the Civil War has gone unrecognized by most historians. It is the intent of this book to shed light on a man who deserves better understanding of his accomplishments. Told here also are interesting and often emotional stories about Meredith and his family — both immediate and extended — that illuminate life in Missouri during this period. They range from his search for a bride to a family scandal over bigamy; from political loyalty to intrigue and betrayal; from home schooling to Yale, Harvard, West Point, and Annapolis; and from the high plains of Wyoming to the depths of imprisonment on an island in Lake Erie.

For purposes of clarity, Meredith Miles Marmaduke is usually identified throughout this book as Meredith, with few exceptions. There are numerous other Marmadukes — siblings, children, cousins — whose names appear in the manuscript from time to time. Yet more, during our subject's lifetime there were two other men named Meredith Miles Marmaduke: one a son, the other a nephew.

Between 1820 and 1860, Missouri's location at the center of the nation offered geographical, social, and economic conditions that were essential for entrepreneurship. The state excelled in transportation. Its major rivers brought people and goods from Pittsburgh and New Orleans and provided access to eastern and southern markets for distribution of the abundant natural resources and agricultural commodities its citizens produced. Another aspect of transportation, the prominent trade and migration routes to the West — the Santa Fe, California, and Oregon Trails — began in Missouri and created wealth for those who supplied the needs of westbound trappers, traders, explorers, miners, and pioneer families. An additional asset was Missouri's early banking system. At a time when centralized, federal control of currency did not exist, Missouri banks were required by state statute to be financed by the deposit of "hard" currency — gold and silver coins — rather than paper banknotes for which there was no reliable capitalization. Merchants, farmers, and businessmen could rely on the value of money issued by Missouri's banks remaining stable; it did not fluctuate nor was it subject to the deep discounting that characterized the paper money issued by many other banks in the nation.

Missouri's population quickly expanded during the 40 years that elapsed between statehood and the Civil War. Thousands of people migrated to the state from Virginia, North Carolina, Tennessee, and Kentucky. They came because they wanted to own some of the state's abundant, inexpensive, and — in the right places — highly productive land. As Missouri's population increased, so too did its internal economy. This, coupled with the export of agricultural produce — grains, hemp, tobacco, hams and bacon, horses, mules, and cattle — allowed the state's farmers to move from subsistence to commercial agriculture. For many, that transition was made possible by Missouri's status as a state where slavery was accepted, a social condition of particular appeal to former residents of the Upper South states. The unpaid labor of enslaved black workers added significantly to the wealth of white farmers in the Booneslick counties of central Missouri; Meredith Marmaduke was one of those farmers.

Transplanted from the South, in Missouri Meredith sought to acquire the wealth, political power, and social prestige expected of Southern gentry. The story of his efforts to achieve these traditional goals is told through his relationships with the men and women — farmers, laborers, politicians, merchants, lawyers, bankers, doctors, and slaves — who were his friends, neighbors, political allies and enemies, and business associates. The customs of the plantation-oriented Old South — service as a military officer, agricultural pursuit, slave ownership, and community service — came with Meredith when he relocated to Missouri. But more than these traits marked him as someone who would succeed in life; he also had a generous dose of New England-style, Yankee commercialism, along with common sense reasoning and a willingness to take risks, although he was not so willing to risk losing it all. This is also the story of his broad-reaching and equally interesting family. You'll meet his siblings, wife and children, cousins, and in-laws, and gain insight into how he affected their lives and how they affected his.

Growing up in the Tidewater region of Virginia at the beginning of the 19th century, Meredith was a member of an aristocratic planter society that had evolved on the coastal plain of eastern Virginia during the 200 years since the founding of the colony. The Marmaduke family was not overly wealthy, yet they were successful farmers and managed to retain ownership of their plantation after the early death of Meredith's father. As the second son in a family of four siblings (two sisters), Meredith was not in line to inherit the plantation, and as he matured he lacked the financial resources to purchase enough land to make farming a viable occupation. Serving as a young artillery

Introduction

officer in a Virginia militia unit during the War of 1812, Meredith engaged in numerous skirmishes with British forces along the Potomac River. Rising in rank from ensign to captain (and later colonel), he commanded an artillery company that responded to British foraging incursions into the villages and plantations of the Tidewater region. Service as an officer during the war provided Meredith with leadership skills that would play an important role in his life in Virginia, and later in Missouri. After the war ended, he held a number of local government offices in Westmoreland County, Virginia, and was a chancery court official serving writs and other court documents in eastern Virginia counties.

By 1820, a desire for a more fruitful life had taken hold; yet without formal education in a profession (physician, attorney, engineer, or military officer being the usual vocations), improvement in his status might be a long time coming. Emboldened by the realization that years of civil service lay ahead in Virginia, he decided to look west, beyond the Appalachian Mountains, for his future. Since the Revolutionary War, Virginians had been moving their families, furniture, slaves, and livestock over those mountains, settling on new land in Kentucky and Tennessee. Now, in the early 1800s their descendants were moving to Missouri seeking new land, new trading opportunities, and new resources to exploit. In 1823, Meredith joined them.

From Pittsburgh, Louisville, and New Orleans, people and goods flowed to St. Louis, then a developing midcontinent commercial hub from which routes of transportation radiated in all directions. Arriving in that city during the fall, Meredith did not linger. Some 200 miles up the Missouri River, in what came to be called Booneslick country, the village of Franklin was the tip of a mercantile spear that attracted a growing number of settlers and directed explorers and traders traveling to the Great Plains, the Southwest, and the Rocky Mountains. In Booneslick country, a man with talents and a willingness to work could establish himself and grow with his surroundings. Meredith had taken St. Louis in stride and went on to Franklin; he liked what he saw and never looked back.

Two years earlier, in the fall of 1821, a small group of traders had set out from Franklin to make their way to Santa Fe de Nuevo Mexico. Previously prohibited from trading in Mexico, Americans now were sanctioned to do business there by a newly established Mexican government that desired improved relations with its northern neighbor. A remote provincial capital some 700 miles north of Mexico City, Santa Fe was slated to become a principal entry port for American and European goods. From the small town on the southern edge of the Sangre de Cristo Mountains, merchandise could enter Mexico and be transported directly to the more heavily populated interior of the country. Otherwise, foreign goods brought by ships had to pass through customs at Matamoros on the Rio Grande, near its mouth on the Gulf of Mexico, or at Veracruz farther south along the Mexican coast. Merchandise entering the country at these more southerly ports took longer and cost more to transport inland than goods brought across the border at Santa Fe.

When the Franklin traders reached Santa Fe in 1821, they quickly sold the bundles of personal and household goods they had toted on horseback. Their pockets lined with Mexican silver, they rushed back to Missouri for a new load of merchandise, which in 1822 they sold with similar results. These well-publicized back-to-back successes caught the attention of ambitious men in Franklin and in the spring of 1824, a group met to plan sending the largest-yet selection of trade goods down the Santa Fe Trail to Mexico. Meredith Marmaduke was at that meeting and signed on with Samuel McClure as a partner to join the expedition. Thus began a mercantile venture that in the next few years generated significant profit and marked the onset of his quest to make a fortune in Missouri. His journeys to Santa Fe brought adroit commercial tactics, physical hardship, and dangerous encounters with native tribes who plundered traders, going and returning, occasionally killing some of them. Meredith's experiences in the risk-laden, long-distance Santa Fe trade established him as someone others could rely on for the successful management of complex political and commercial issues, a trait that remained important throughout the rest of his life.

Marriage in 1826 to Dr. John Sappington's daughter, Lavinia, gained Meredith entry into one of the most influential political and commercial-minded families on the Missouri frontier. For nearly three decades, he partnered with Dr. Sappington and other Sappington family members in various business ventures. These commercial activities provided money that Meredith used to buy land in pursuit of his intention to become a wealthy farmer. Much of what he purchased was acquired under terms of the Federal Land Act of 1820, which reduced the minimum amount a farmer had to buy from 160 to 80 acres and lowered its cost from $2 to $1.25 an acre. Economically depressed families in eastern states could now own 80 acres of Missouri land for only $100. The state's population went from 66,500 in 1820 to 1,182,000 in 1860. That year, only 190,500 people (16%) lived in St. Louis, Missouri's largest city. The remainder of the state's residents lived on small to medium-size farms and in towns where the population was less than 2,500.

Meredith was not a small landholder; he had bigger ambitions. Beginning in the late 1820s and over the next three decades, he bought federal land in Saline, Chariton, Pettis, and St. Clair Counties. His holdings in Saline County alone grew to nearly 4,000 acres by 1850. The land policies espoused by Missouri Senator Thomas Hart Benton, who steadily promoted congressional legislation that favored the sale of federal land at low prices, and Meredith's acquaintance with the managers of federal land offices in the state aided him in the acquisition of choice tracts of public land. Although he occasionally speculated on the purchase and subsequent sale of land (usually in partnership with one or more of the Sappingtons or Claiborne Jackson), he was more inclined to view land ownership as a long-term asset. The agricultural land he acquired in Saline County remained unsold throughout his life.

Missouri acquired statehood in 1821, accompanied by the emergence of the state's first political machine, a product of the Democratic Party known as the "Central Clique." Historically, political machines in the United States have been associated with large cities such as New York, Boston, Chicago, Philadelphia, St. Louis, and Kansas City. But the first political machine in Missouri was not urban; rather, it centered in the Booneslick counties along the Missouri River. Wealthy and influential Democrats comprised the Central Clique, men who dominated Missouri's government for more than 20 years during which they controlled the selection of candidates for local and state offices, and promoted legislation that favored their interests. The power of the Clique waned after Senator Benton lost his bid for reelection in 1851, although that

Introduction

was not the only reason for its decline.

Meredith became an influential member of the Central Clique. His political career began in 1827 after he moved to Saline County and married Lavinia Sappington. To bolster his new son-in-law's standing in the county, Dr. Sappington used his influence in Jefferson City to obtain Meredith's appointment as official surveyor. This was followed by service as justice of the peace for Arrow Rock Township and as a judge of the Saline County Court. With the support of the Central Clique, whose influence expanded during the 1830s, Meredith became the Democratic Party's candidate for lieutenant governor in 1840; he won. Three years later, he acceded to the governorship at the death of Governor Thomas Reynolds. In 1844, internal strife within the Democratic Party prompted Meredith to step aside as a candidate for governor in favor of someone the Clique believed more likely to defeat the Whig candidate, thus assuring the machine's control in Jefferson City. Meredith's decision to withdraw for the sake of party unity earned him loyalty among Democrats across the state, and he remained a leading figure in the Clique, holding important positions in several state institutions. Moreover, his term in public office initiated a Marmaduke-Sappington political dynasty that ultimately saw seven members of the two families elected to state offices, three of whom occupied the governor's chair in Jefferson City. The Marmaduke family's influence in Missouri politics only ceased with the untimely death in 1887 of Meredith's bachelor son, John Sappington Marmaduke, while he was governor.

Discord on several fronts plagued Meredith during the 15 years after he left the governor's office. The stress he experienced stemmed from Claiborne Fox Jackson's relentless campaign to further his political career, exacerbated by a growing national sense that slavery should be abolished (which Jackson opposed) and by the nation's drift toward civil war. These two factors collided to create political unrest within Missouri's Democratic Party, fueled in part by Senator Benton's opposition to the extension of slavery into new states. Meredith's choice to remain loyal to Benton and the Clique placed him in opposition to Jackson and led to a fractured relationship between the two men that festered for many years. Jackson's attempt, after he became governor, to bring about Missouri's secession from the Union — something Meredith publicly opposed — further aggravated their conflict.

* * *

Meredith was not a diarist — the only known document of this nature that he authored was an account of his 1824 journey to Santa Fe. Learning his story required the review of hundreds of documents (correspondence, account books, receipts, contracts, bills of sale, etc.) contained principally in three collections in Missouri — the Sappington-Marmaduke Family Papers held by the Missouri Historical Society Library and Research Center in St. Louis and the Meredith Miles Marmaduke Papers and the John Sappington Papers, both housed by the State Historical Society of Missouri in Columbia. Additional Marmaduke-related documents can be found in eight other Sappington-Marmaduke-Hardeman collections held in Columbia. Also investigated during research for this book were the papers of men (not family members) with whom Meredith is known to have corresponded. What characterizes all of these collections is the paucity of letters written by Meredith. Although an avid keeper himself of all kinds of documents (he occasionally made and retained copies of letters sent to friends and relatives), for the most part, his correspondents failed to hold on to most of his letters, or if they did the correspondence has been lost. Thus, in order to tell Meredith's story it frequently became necessary to extrapolate, from letters he received, text attributed to him in a previous letter he had written. In all cases where this was done, the attributed text is supported by the surviving correspondence. Fortunately for the researcher, the style of letter writing at the time required acknowledgment — usually in the lead paragraph — of earlier correspondence between the writers, and this usually included a date and reference to specific subjects contained in the missing letter (for example, "Dear Colonel, Your highly esteemed favor of the 16th July, came to hand on the 19th August informing us that yourself and family were in possession of good health.").

Other primary sources used include the excellent collection of county and state records (court proceedings, tax assessments, land records, legal statutes, legislative proceedings, etc.) in the Missouri State Archives in Jefferson City; United States Census records, including agriculture and slave schedules; United States Bureau of Land Management, General Land Office Records; National Archives and Records Administration (for example, U.S. Provost Marshals' Papers, 1861–1867; Register of Enlistment in the United States Army, compiled 1798–1914; Military Bounty Land Warrants Under the Act of 1812); and documents found in diverse archive collections elsewhere.

In addition to the many published manuscripts that served as secondary sources, the newspaper collection in the State Historical Society of Missouri and past issues of the society's periodical, *Missouri Historical Review,* were particularly valuable references for developing background information about the people, events, and subjects that make up the story of Meredith Miles Marmaduke. Abbreviations used in chapter notes are: SHSMO (State Historical Society of Missouri in Columbia); MHS (Missouri Historical Society Library and Research Center in St. Louis); MHR (*Missouri Historical Review*); SOS (Missouri Secretary of State Archives).

CHAPTER 1

FROM THE ASHES OF HER SIRES

In late August 1619, a 160-ton Dutch ship sailed into Chesapeake Bay after a voyage from the West Indies with a cargo of black slaves obtained in the Caribbean. Aboard was the ship's commander, Captain Jope, his crew, and one Mr. Marmaduke, an Englishman. Sighting Old Point Comfort at the mouth of Hampton Roads some 15 miles into the bay, the crew turned the ship into the James River and rode the tide and winds upstream to the English colony of Jamestown, founded 12 years earlier. There, as colonist John Rolfe reported, Captain Jope traded his cargo of "20 and some odd Negroes, wth [which] the Governor and Cape Marchant bought for Victualle [food] (whereof he was in greate need as he p'tended) at the best and easyest rate they could."[1]

Historians speculate that the Africans aboard this ship, believed to be the first slaves in Virginia, were instead indentured servants. Two versions of their transport to the colony have been put forth. In one, the Dutch man-of-war captured a slave ship bound for the West Indies and took the captive Africans to dispose of them as indentured servants. The other version says the Dutch captain bought the Africans from planters in the West Indies and took them to Virginia, where he sold them as slaves.

Whichever scenario one accepts, ultimately these unfortunate Africans have to be recognized as slaves because, unlike white Europeans who voluntarily came to the colony as indentured servants, they had no voice in determining their fate. They may, or may not, have been freed at some future time. One thing is certain, however: the first Marmaduke to arrive in Virginia (nothing indicates he remained there) was associated with the slave trade and as such was an omen of a future in which Marmadukes and slavery would be affiliated for 245 years, through the end of the American Civil War.

Early Virginia Marmadukes

The next Marmaduke to reach Virginia arrived in the summer of 1637 aboard a ship captained by Christopher Wormeley, who hoped for a comfortable voyage as his small ship left Land's End at the southwestern tip of England in its wake. Scanning the sea ahead, Wormeley undoubtedly envisioned the Virginia plantation he would soon own and the wealth that such property would engender. These thoughts, however, were soon put aside as the perilous voyage demanded his attention if his valuable cargo were to survive. Crowded into a cramped lower deck were men and women, perhaps children as well, he had recruited for the voyage to Virginia by offering them free passage and provisions. In return, his passengers had bound themselves to him for a period of time as indentured servants. Christopher Wormeley was an experienced sailor, having made at least two previous crossings of the Atlantic Ocean. Records of the Virginia Land Office disclose that on an earlier voyage (probably in 1636), he had delivered 16 emigrants to the colony, among them "William Musgrave, his wife and two children, Joe and Samboe, Negroes, and four servants." How many others began that voyage is unknown, but probably some were lost along the way. Captain Wormeley was aware of the dangers his passengers faced on the crossing, seasickness being the first malady to afflict those unable to find their sea legs. Disease, illness, starvation, gales that forced a ship off course and added weeks or months to the journey, and storms that could demast and sink a vessel were constant perils. The first Jamestown colonists, sailing in 1607, lost to disease 39 of the original 144 emigrants who began the voyage. Sometimes the loss was much higher. In 1618, a boatload of colonists en route to Virginia, blown off course by a gale, required six months to reach the colony. Of its 200 passengers, 150 starved to death during the prolonged voyage. In 1637, the second year that Captain Wormeley sailed to Virginia, 25 passengers survived the crossing, among them one woman, Margaret Raw. Another survivor was a Richard Marmaduke, the first of that surname to settle in the colony.[2]

English emigrants to America in the 17th century left their homeland for many reasons, but one motive stands above all others. The subsistence farming economy that had supported England's rural population for centuries began to shift in the 1600s to an industrial model based on fenced pastures, sheep, and wool. As a result, thousands of families were expelled from tenant farms and left indigent. Destitute, roaming the country seeking work, shelter, and food, with no social programs to relieve their suffering, these poor were viewed as surplus population at a time when England was considered overcrowded. How to solve this economic and political problem was a dilemma facing the English king and his ministers. They found their answer in the American colonies where laborers were needed for the production of raw materials the mother country required. In addition, the colonists would become buyers of the plentiful woolen goods and other products produced in England's factories. Thus, two thorny issues — excess population and overproduction — could be resolved with one expedient policy. The promise of free or inexpensive land was used as an inducement to attract impoverished colonists to the scheme. From this grew an industry devoted to the transport and sale of indentured servants, many of whom were transported to Virginia.

To recover the expense of his passengers' transportation to Virginia, Captain Wormeley intended to sell them as indentured servants to the highest bidders among the tradesmen, shopkeepers, and planters already established in the colony. Ship captains usually obtained signed indentures prior to their vessels leaving England. Typical of these is a contract dated November 15, 1698, in which 15-year-old Matthew Evans of Harfordshire "being Destitute of Friends and necessarys ... doth bind and put himself an Apprentice and Servant to ... Thomas Graves to Serve him or his Assignes in the Plantation of Virginia" for a period of four years. In return, young Evans received his passage to the colony and "all necessary Cloathes, Meat, Drink, Washing, Lodging and other necessarys ... according to the custom of said Plantation. ..."[3] Many emigrants to Virginia in the 17th century, including women and children, came under similar terms of bondage to ship captains and were then sold in this manner. Men and women could expect to work for their new masters four or five years before receiving their freedom, and children often worked until they were 18 years old. At the end of an indenture, a worker on a Virginia plantation usually received a plot of land from the former master. This practice became the foundation on which released servants built their future. For many of them it was their first venture as a landowner, something they never could have accomplished in England.

The Reward for Transporting

For his enterprise in transporting 41 colonists in two voyages, Christopher Wormeley received in January 1638 a patent from the royal governor, acting as the king's agent, for 1,420 acres of land in Charles River County (renamed York County in 1642). Land distribution in Virginia at that time was controlled by the king's Privy Council, a group of powerful aristocrats and politicians who served as advisers to the king. Known as the "headright" system, the plan granted 50 acres of land to each person who entered Virginia to settle; in practice, however, the system awarded the land to the person who paid to transport the emigrant. Those who paid their own way could buy 50 acres, and some did. To obtain his patent, Captain Wormeley petitioned the county court with proof that he had transported the emigrants at his expense. Obtaining a Certificate of Importation, he next went to the secretary of the colony, in Jamestown, and received a document called a "right." With this in hand, he had the land surveyed and returned the paperwork to the secretary, who advertised his intention to issue a patent for the land. Since no one disputed Captain Wormeley's claim, his patent was eventually signed by the governor of the colony. This was not always a timely process. A year or more might pass before the governor would issue a patent, although it was possible in the interim for the right to the property to be sold by the person holding it, and this did happen.

A different Captain Wormeley delivered another Richard Marmaduke to Virginia 12 years after the first settled there. The second Richard arrived in 1649 as an indentured servant, along with 63 others brought that year by Captain Ralph Wormeley, brother of the Christopher Wormeley who had transported the first Richard Marmaduke. For his effort in populating the colony, Ralph Wormeley received 3,200 acres of land on the Rappahannock River. Captain Ralph Wormeley, his brother Christopher, and their descendants are remembered today for the establishment of historic Rosegill Plantation in Middlesex County. Unfortunately, as with the first Richard Marmaduke, nothing more is known of the second; presumably he acquired land when he completed his indenture.[4]

Two other Marmadukes, Jacob and William, emigrated from England to Virginia in the year 1663. Jacob arrived as an indentured servant of Daniel Wild and Francis Kirkman, who received a patent for 2,000 acres of land in Westmoreland County (in a region of Virginia known as the Northern Neck) for transporting 40 persons. William Marmaduke's transportation was provided by "David Fox, Gent.," who received 350 acres of land on the north side of Lancaster County (adjacent to Westmoreland County), a property that came to be called Poplar Neck. One suspects these two Marmadukes were related. Nothing is known of Jacob's fortunes in Virginia; however, a William Marmaduke (perhaps a descendant of the William who arrived in 1663) is found in the October 6, 1775, issue of the *Virginia Gazette,* where he placed an advertisement seeking the return of "John Shaw, English convict servant, age 18-19, ran away from Wm. Marmaduke near Westmoreland C. H. [Court House]." Yet another Marmaduke is known to have been an early resident of the Northern Neck; on November 10, 1681, Robert Marmaduke purchased 225 acres in Christ Church Parish of Lancaster County. He sold the tract a few years later.[5]

The Family Prospers

The Mary Ball Washington Museum and Library archives in Lancaster, Virginia, hold the wills of three Marmadukes who were related: Miles, Christopher, and Sarah. The documents prove a line of descent from Miles Marmaduke of the late 1600s to Meredith Miles Marmaduke, who was born in Westmoreland County, Virginia, on August 28, 1791, and migrated to Missouri in 1823. Miles Marmaduke was a tobacco planter in Westmoreland County in the late 1600s. Regarded by his neighbors as an honest man, in the five years before his death he served as an executor for the estates of several deceased county residents, as a juror in civil actions, and for two terms as "grand inquisitor," an office that would be the equivalent of today's grand jury foreman in a criminal court. Miles also sued several people during this period, winning a judgment against Francis Eggleston for a "hogshead [1,000 pounds] of tobacco and parcel of tobacco and the weeding hoe by him attached." Another suit resulted in John Nicholls paying Miles 150 pounds of tobacco and corn and beans to satisfy a debt of 1,000 pounds of tobacco. Miles died in Cople Parish, Westmoreland County, in 1695. His will bequeaths half of his "moveable Estate" to his wife, Jane, and gives the remainder "to my Son Christopher Marmaduke when he arrives to the age of 16 years either in kind and as good now as then [then as now] or tobacco paid according to the appraisment" at the time of his death. He also gave Christopher "all my apparell or wearing Cloaths only one Coat and one hatt Excepted." (One wonders if the one coat and one hat were saved for his burial.)[6]

Grace Marmaduke Sharp, in a monograph titled "The Marmadukes and Some Allied Families," published in *William & Mary College Quarterly,* briefly traces the life of Miles's son, Christopher Marmaduke, writing he was born and died in Westmoreland County. His will, proven July 28, 1761, tells much about Christopher's prosperity and his family's life in the years after the death of Miles, and mentions a son, also named Christopher, who had a son named Vincent:

> Item I give ... unto my Son Christopher Marmaduke my Plantation ... with all the land hereunto ... during his Natural life and after his Decease I give the Plantation to my Grandson Vincent Marmaduke. ...
>
> Item I give ... to [Christopher] my Two Negroes namely James and Nan and the said Nans future increase upon condition that Christopher do pay to my Son Daniel Marmaduke Twenty Five Pounds Current Money. ...
>
> Item I lend to my Daughter Esther Robinson my Negroe girl named Sarah during her Natural life and after her Decease I give ... the said Negroe girl and her increase to my two Grand Daughters ... to be Equally Divided between them.
>
> Item I lend to my Daughter Jemima Sandy my Negroe girl named Hannah for

and during her Natural life and after her Decease I give ... the said Negroe and her increase to my Grand Son Thomas Sandy ... and to his heirs forever.

Item I give ... to my Grand Son Vincent Marmaduke my Negroe Boy named Jack to be delivered to him when he come to the age of Twenty One Years and not before.

The elder Christopher disposed of his remaining estate by directing that his "Still and Worm [coiled tubing] ... be sold and all my large casks ... for Money." His son Christopher received all of his small casks, "three cows and calves, also my mare & colt and cart." Daughter Jemima inherited "one Cow and Calf," and the household furnishings and personal items were divided among the children. Christopher Marmaduke's dispensation of livestock, his cart, his slaves, his land, a whiskey still and a plentiful supply of casks in which to age it, all indicate that he had improved the family's standing and was a prosperous Virginia plantation owner. Grace Sharp records that the family paid taxes on about 1,000 acres of land after the Revolutionary War.[7]

A third document that illuminates the fortunes of Miles Marmaduke's descendants in Virginia's Northern Neck is the will of Sarah Marmaduke, the widow of the "Grand Son Vincent" mentioned in the elder Christopher's will. Vincent had served in the Virginia militia during the American Revolution as an ensign and later as a lieutenant in Captain Thomas Chilton's company organized in Westmoreland County.[8] When he died intestate in 1792, he could not have been more than 46 years old. His wife, Sarah, was left with four children: Vincent, about 12; his younger sister Elizabeth; 1-year-old Meredith Miles; and Molly, an infant. It is believed that Sarah was a midwife in her community and likely had income from that practice. A Spotsylvania District Superior Court of Chancery case recorded in 1818 at Fredericksburg, Virginia, lists Sarah Marmaduke as being paid in 1797 for midwife services to a member of the Elizabeth Steptoe family, who resided near Yeocomico Church not far from the Marmaduke plantation in Westmoreland County. Sarah died 12 years after Vincent and her will, proven in Westmoreland County on October 22, 1804, shows the family had maintained itself fairly well since her husband's death:

Item I give ... to my son Vincent ... one feather bed and furniture, one safe, one small chest, one box, one frying pan, one ram to him and his heirs forever.

Item I give ... to my daughter Elizabeth McClanahan one feather bed and furniture, one chest, one cow and calf, one womans saddle, one ewe and lamb, one dutch oven. ...

Item I give ... to my son Meredith M. Marmaduke one bed and furniture, one white counterpin, one chest, six head of cattle, one small pot, one ewe. ...

Item I give ... to my son in law John Hunter one red cow & calf. ...

Item I give the rest of my cattle not before devised to be equally divided between my son Vincent ... and Elizabeth McClanahan.

Sarah also gave Meredith half of her crop of tobacco and 10 barrels of corn, and directed that the balance of her crops be equally divided among her sons and sons-in-law.[9]

This is not the will of a poor widow. Beds, chests, kitchenware and other furniture, cows, calves, sheep, tobacco, and corn in quantities significant enough to be divided among four persons — all point to a woman who had successfully managed her family's affairs and kept the plantation going. A favorable portion of her estate went to son Meredith, aged 13 at his mother's death, so that he could establish himself independent of his siblings. Neither land nor slaves are mentioned in Sarah's will, although she inherited both when her husband, Vincent, died. Westmoreland County tax rolls from 1787 list Vincent as the owner of four slaves. Prior to her death in 1804, Sarah transferred the plantation and its slaves to her eldest son, Vincent, who managed the property until his death in 1854.[10]

A Land of "Grace and Distinction"

Shaped somewhat like a lopsided rectangle, Tidewater Virginia is a geographical, political and social region bordering Chesapeake Bay on the northeast corner of Virginia. Its ragged eastern edge faces the bay while its western border, along a line anchored by the cities of Fredericksburg on the north and Richmond on the south, faces the Blue Ridge Mountains. Within the rectangle are three fingers of land called "necks," bordered by four large rivers — the Potomac, the Rappahannock, the York, and the James, all flowing southeast to Chesapeake Bay. From north to south, the fingers are known as Northern Neck, Middle Neck, and Virginia Peninsula; the latter was the site of the colony's earliest settlements, Jamestown and Williamsburg. Across Chesapeake Bay is the Eastern Shore, the southern tip of the Delmarva Peninsula, also considered a part of Tidewater Virginia.

Tidewater Virginia's streams influenced the social, economic, and political lives of the people who settled along them, and the lives of their descendants. For more than 300 years these rivers, and Chesapeake Bay itself, served as the region's highways for commerce and the practice of almost all aspects of human social interaction; until the 20th century, there were no bridges that enabled crossing from one neck to another or traveling from the western shore of the bay to the eastern shore. The few roads that did exist ran mainly between adjoining plantations on the necks. In time, roads developed in the western part of the rectangle but distances were great and travel from one neck to another took a long time. For this reason, small boats and coastal ships became the principal means of transportation for colonists. Recognizing their need for accessible transportation, Tidewater planters usually chose tracts of land on the waterfront on which to build their homes.

Author and biographer Paul Wilstach, writing nearly 100 years ago, describes colonial life in the houses along the rivers and bays of Tidewater Virginia as "indeed pleasant and gay ... based on ease and elegance ... it attained grace and distinction." Wilstach characterized Tidewater Virginia as a "region of cousins," and Tidewater aristocracy as a "close corporation,"[11] portraying a colonial and post-Revolution society in which the region's plantation families centered their lives on their extended families — the aunts, uncles, and cousins that derived from multiple marriages within only a few families, often the siblings of one household marrying the siblings of another. These marriages were often consanguineous, first cousin marrying first cousin, their offspring sharing genetics and often the same Christian names. A tradition in England and Europe, such marriages often took place to retain wealth within the involved families.

This close kinship among Tidewater plantation families inevitably led to the development of an aristocratic society comprised of what one historian has called "sanctified cousinhood," relations obliged to indulge their kinfolk whether it was convenient or not.[12] It was also inevitable that these families would produce the colony's professional men — lawyers, doctors, merchants, politicians, and statesmen. Virginia's planters were the ruling class for more than 250 years, drawing from their extended families the men who were elected to colonial (later county, state, and federal) offices as well as those who became officers in the Continental Army and local militias during the Revolutionary War. The planter class also produced the men who served as officers in the War of 1812, and for the Confederacy during the Civil War — the former conflict involved Meredith Marmaduke, and the latter, three of his sons.

Westmoreland County was foremost in the production of Virginia aristocrats. Nowhere was this more apparent than at a memorial ceremony in Montross, Virginia (Westmoreland County seat), on May 3, 1910, to unveil portraits of county residents who had distinguished themselves as "colonial heroes," although the organizers of the event didn't restrict their adulation to the colonial period. After a "delightful luncheon by the ladies of Westmoreland," and a long-winded speech by Dr. Randolph H. McKim of Epiphany Church in Washington, DC (he touted Westmoreland as "the Athens of Virginia ... for the worth, the talents, and the patriotism that once adorned it"), the audience — members of the United Daughters of the Confederacy, the Westmoreland Camp Confederate Veterans, and the Sons of America — listened attentively as the Reverend George William Beale recited the accomplishments of Westmoreland's heroes:

"Richard Henry Lee, a member of the Continental Congress of 1776, offered the memorable resolution for Independence which unsheathed the sword of the Revolution. Another — George Washington — led the colonial armies to victory ... two of them (Washington and [James] Monroe) were elevated to the chief magistracy of the nation. William Lee, Arthur Lee, and James Monroe served as diplomatic agents at the leading courts of Europe; Charles Lee and James Monroe served as U.S. cabinet officers; Henry Lee and James Monroe were Governors of Virginia; Bushrod Washington was a justice of the U.S. Supreme Court; Richard Parker was Justice of the Virginia Court of Appeals; R. H. Lee, Francis L. Lee, Arthur Lee, Henry Lee, John P. Hungerford, Willoughby Newton, R. L. T. Beale, R. M. Mayo held seats in Congress. Robert E. Lee Confederate General. ..."[13]

Some 30 minutes after he began, the Reverend Beale closed his homily with an anecdote about an "aged and shriveled woman" of his acquaintance, a resident of Westmoreland County whose ancestors had served under George Washington, saying that throughout her long life she had drawn her inspirations "from the ashes of her sires."

Growing up in Westmoreland County in the years immediately after the Revolutionary War, with the legacy of such renowned neighbors looking over his shoulder, Meredith Miles Marmaduke undoubtedly was influenced by their accomplishments, and by observing their lives. He saw the successful Virginia plantation owner not as a simple dirt farmer but as a man of abilities who oversaw his lands, his family, and his black servants — his "people," as they were often called — while operating a large agricultural enterprise and advancing his station in life through public and military service. The significance of this style of life was not lost on young Marmaduke; its lessons were observed and remembered, to be later emulated.

Notes

1. Captain Jope traded his cargo of "20 and some odd Negroes": John Rolfe letter to Sir Edwin Sandys, *The Records of the Virginia Company of London*, Vol. 3, 243.

2. Information about Captain Christopher Wormeley and his voyages to North America is from Neal M. Nugent, *Cavaliers and Pioneers,* Book 1, 99.

3. "being Destitute of Friends": Melvin Maddocks, *The Seafarers: The Atlantic Crossing,* 31.

4. A different Captain Wormeley: Nell M. Nugent, *Abstracts of Virginia Land Patents and Grants 1623–1666, Book 2,* 181.

5. Two other Marmadukes: Nugent, *Abstracts of Virginia Land Patents and Grants 1623–1666,* Book 5, 487, 513.

6. The history of Miles Marmaduke is in John F. Dorman, *Westmoreland County, Va., Order Book, Parts I & II, 1690–1698.* 52–91. The wills of Miles, Christopher, and Sarah Marmaduke are in the Marmaduke Family File, Mary Ball Washington Museum and Library. Tobacco was a common medium for payment of debts (and for gambling on horse races) in colonial Virginia, and civil judgments were often awarded in pounds of tobacco. Miles also served on a grand jury impaneled in Westmoreland County in 1715.

7. Will of Christopher Marmaduke: Augusta B. Fothergill, *Wills of Westmoreland County, Virginia, 1654–1800,* 149. Grace Marmaduke Sharp, "The Marmaduke and Some Allied Families," *William and Mary College Quarterly Historical Magazine*, Vol. 15, No. 2 (April 1935), 151–172. "Still and Worm": Christopher's crops included tobacco, raised for export to England, and corn used as feed for livestock and as fermented mash that was made into whiskey he sold or bartered locally.

8. Mention of Sarah Marmaduke as a midwife is found in Barry L. McGhee Archivist, *The Spotsylvania (Virginia) District for the Superior Court of Chancery Abstracts,* Abstract Record ID 262–9.

9. Sarah Marmaduke's will: Fothergill, 178.

10. Neither land nor slaves are mentioned in Sarah Marmaduke's will; Westmoreland County tax rolls: Augusta B. Fothergill and John H. Naugle, *Virginia Tax Payers,* 80. Reference to the Marmaduke plantation: *Historic Places*, Westmoreland County, Virginia, Genealogy Repository; Localized history, stories, documents, books & research for the Northern Neck. Electronic document, np.

11. "indeed pleasant and gay": Paul Wilstach, *Tidewater Virginia,* 92, 100, 137.

12. "sanctified cousinhood": Page Smith, *Trial by Fire,* 11.

13. "delightful luncheon by the ladies": Thomas R. B. Wright, ed., *Westmoreland County, Virginia 1653–1912: A Short Chapter and Bright Day in Its History.* Part 1, 31–33; Reverend William Beale's speech, Ibid., 35–36.

CHAPTER 2

YEARS OF PREPARATION

The opening decades of the 19th century saw the prosperity of Tidewater Virginia's plantations suffer as a general economic depression spread across the states of the Upper South. The cause was threefold. In the years leading up to the American Revolution, the overproduction of tobacco — a leading crop in the Tidewater counties — had caused prices to fall, resulting in reduced income to the colony's planters. Exports to England had grown from 60,000 pounds in 1622 to half a million pounds six years later, and more than 20 million pounds by the end of the 17th century. By 1750, the European market was glutted with cheap tobacco of sometimes dubious quality (in some instances, floor sweepings were added to the packed leaves). In addition, England's unpopular Navigation Acts, enforced by the Royal Navy, required colonial exports to pass through the mother country before they could sell elsewhere; this prevented the colonies from opening new markets for their crops. A third blow fell on the Tidewater economy at the outbreak of the Revolutionary War when the colonial boycott of English products, plus England's blockade of American ports, shut down most trade. Tobacco warehouses in Richmond, Petersburg, and Alexandria on the Potomac River could not ship the Tidewater's primary product throughout most of the Revolution. Virginia's tobacco did, however, play a positive role in the struggle for independence when 5 million pounds of the cured leaves served as collateral for a loan that Benjamin Franklin obtained from France to help finance George Washington's armies. After the war ended in 1783, Tidewater plantations continued to struggle as England exerted policies designed to disrupt the new nation's overseas trade as much as possible.

As the new century dawned, tobacco planters had yet another burden to bear: after nearly 200 years of cultivation, the region's soil was worn out. Tobacco farming was a destructive process that required the continual opening of new ground, and the amount of Tidewater region land suitable for agriculture — not forested or wetland — was limited. The rate of nutrient loss from the soil of a tobacco field was so rapid that a farmer could expect a satisfactory crop for only three years. Then the planter had to abandon the land or sow corn, whose deeper-reaching roots drew upon nutrients unavailable to the shallow-rooted tobacco plants. Unfortunately, corn also robbed the soil of nutrition and after three more years of cultivation a field had to lie fallow for the next 10 to 20 years before it again could produce a profitable crop; there was very little livestock producing manure then and commercial fertilizers would not become available until 1850.

Taken together — years of overproduction followed by decades of depressed exports and a decline in productivity — these conditions created a dismal picture for a young man in the early 19th century who was thinking about his chances for success as a Tidewater planter. Meredith Marmaduke, upon reaching his 20th birthday in 1811, would have looked at the economic conditions surrounding him and wondered about his future. On the horizon that year was the onset of the War of 1812, an event that further depressed Virginia's economy; the war years saw the value of her exports fall from $5 million in 1811 to only $17,000 in 1814.[1]

Gaining Military Credentials

On May 27, 1811, the Westmoreland County Court (the fourth Monday of each month was Westmoreland court day) heard the petition of Meredith Marmaduke for a commission as an ensign in the 111th Virginia Militia Regiment, 14th Brigade, 4th Division, to fill a position recently vacated by the promotion of William Franklin. Meredith was three months shy of his 20th birthday when the court recommended him to Governor George W. Smith in Richmond, who granted the appointment. The rank of ensign, a junior officer equivalent to second lieutenant, was abolished in the United States Army in 1800 but continued to be a designation in state militias for some years. What prompted Meredith to seek the commission is unknown, but it may have been a desire to enhance his standing in his community. It was not unusual for a Southern gentleman of means to gain stature by obtaining a military title. The penultimate form of such recognition (few would become generals) was to be addressed as "Colonel," an honorific that immediately commanded respect and established one's standing among his peers. Virginia's Revolutionary-era statesmen had exemplified the tradition; the commonwealth's representatives to the 1775 Continental Congress to consider a Declaration of Independence "were military men — most ... held the title of colonel in their local militia."[2] Meredith's service in the 111th Militia Regiment eventually provided him with that rank, but first he had to earn it. The War of 1812 supplied the opportunity for him to begin climbing the military ladder.

America's grievances with Britain were renewed in the first decade of the 1800s when England, at war with France, sought to end her enemy's trade with neutral countries — including the United States. To enforce the policy, British naval ships blocked European ports and boarded American merchant vessels on the high seas, impounding ships and cargoes they believed destined for France. Additionally, lacking sufficient manpower to crew its expanded wartime fleet, England impressed American sailors to crew British naval ships. Former British citizens (whose American citizenship was not recognized by England) who were passengers or crew on intercepted American vessels were also pressed into service. Needless to say, Americans were outraged by the British practices. The federal government viewed trade restrictions, ship and cargo seizures, and abduction as violations of national sovereignty, and American citizens thought them an insult to national honor. Despite diplomatic efforts to resolve the issues, Britain remained unmoved by American protestations of its aggressive policies and continued its offensive behavior. Pressured by Congress to end the humiliation of American ships and citizens being seized on the high seas and eager to reopen trade with Europe, President James Madison signed legislation on June 18, 1812, declaring war with England.

For the next 2½ years, commerce in the Chesapeake Bay area was disrupted by activities of the Royal Navy, whose warships generally moved unopposed by the modest American naval fleet. English ships imposed a blockade on the bay, and ships attempting to evade this — either entering or trying to escape to sea — were overhauled and seized or chased back into the outlets from which they came if they were fortunate enough to get away. To stifle trade and communication within coastal Virginia, British warships prowled the Tidewater region, often sending barges manned by marines into the bays, rivers, and inlets to seize schooners and destroy small craft used for local transportation and fishing. The Potomac River, navigable to Alexandria — where warehouses sat stuffed with cotton and tobacco no one could export — and to the nation's capital at Washington City, was of particular interest to the British. They viewed the resources of the Northern Neck counties as a convenient stockpile for the replenishment of depleted supplies. Marines from English ships raided villages and plantations, seizing livestock, food, and fresh water. Sometimes, homes and barns were set afire, crops destroyed, and the residents generally harassed. Slaves were encouraged to abandon plantations and take refuge onboard Royal Navy ships for transport to freedom or were mustered as colonial marines and trained to fight against their former masters. (Planters sometimes attempted to recover their slaves, who were viewed as "property," from ship commanders. In November 1813, planters from Westmoreland County twice boarded the British ship-of-the-line HMS *Dragon* to look for escaped slaves.[3] By the end of the war, several thousand Virginia slaves had gone over to the British.) Not all encounters were violent. Occasionally, a British officer approached with a flag of truce to inform a village's residents that they were subject to a "levy" of whatever could be carried away, promising that the seizure would proceed peacefully unless the villagers resisted. Virginia's militia responding to these random appearances frequently arrived on the scene after the British had reboarded their ships and sailed beyond musket range. Westmoreland County was invaded many times during the war.[4]

In November 1813, the exigencies of war elevated Meredith to the rank of captain and he was immediately assigned to command an artillery company. Numbering 35 to 40 men, such units were equipped with either 6- or 12-pounder cannons, standard guns issued by Virginia's adjutant general, who was responsible for arming militia units. Not all artillery companies were fully equipped or supplied with adequate ammunition, resulting in an inability to contest the enemy on equal terms. Other supplies were also sparse. Tents furnished by the county regiment were usually in short supply. Horses, whether for cavalry or artillery, were provided by the men themselves. As a company commander, Meredith was required to provide blankets, tools, mess gear, and canteens for the men in his unit, at considerable expense.

Meredith's artillery company was mustered for seven consecutive days during the first two weeks of November 1813 when the *Dragon*, with marines aboard, appeared in the Potomac River. No English troops landed, yet their presence demanded close attention. Only a few days earlier, a British ship (probably the 74-gun *Dragon*) had captured and destroyed several American schooners off Northumberland County, which abuts Westmoreland County on the east, and a tender had chased an American ship into the Yeocomico River and captured it when it ran aground.[5] The next call for Meredith's company came five months later on April 26, 1814, a day after British troops landed at Kinsale, a small village on the Yeocomico River, and plundered homes there. One man from a militia detachment observing the enemy's movements was killed. At Yeocomico River four days later, Meredith led his company in a skirmish with British troops during a failed attempt to prevent their landing at nearby Pecatone Plantation. The British later claimed this raid had yielded nearly 100 slaves brought to their ships.[6] Meredith's unit was sent home May 14, only to be called back on July 18 when the British again threatened to invade Westmoreland County.

A skirmish occurred July 20 at the ferry on Nomini Creek when British troops came ashore and drove the 118th Militia, including Meredith's company (his brother, Vincent, and his uncle, William Marmaduke, were also members of the regiment), several miles inland before retiring to their ships for the night.[7] A British chronicler of the event wrote that after destroying everything in the neighborhood, "we returned to the ships carrying with us 135 refugee Negroes — two Captured Schooners, a large quantity of Tobacco, dry goods and cattle and four prisoners."[8] The next morning, more than 1,000 British troops again came ashore and in two days forced their way west for six miles to Montross where they occupied the county courthouse. The Westmoreland County militia engaged the enemy throughout the march, but was forced to retreat before the more numerous English troops. The Yeocomico River again was the target of British raiders on July 23 and 26, and yet again on August 3. Meredith's artillery company was on duty continuously during this time and participated in the defensive effort.

A few days earlier, warships commanded by Vice Admiral Alexander Cochrane had sailed up the Potomac River beyond Alexandria to Washington, where on August 24 British marines burned the nation's Capitol building and the Presidential Mansion. The following day, Cochrane's fleet retired downstream to prepare for an attack on Baltimore. Meanwhile, a British squadron commanded by Captain James Gordon had entered the Potomac River, arriving at Alexandria by August 29. As the squadron sailed upstream, it was followed along the west bank of the river by the Northern Neck county militias, now combined under the command of Brigadier General John P. Hungerford, who would soon be joined by militias from other northern Virginia counties. Hungerford hoped to engage Gordon at Alexandria. Unknown to him, however, the town's council had already surrendered the contents of its warehouses in return for Captain Gordon's promise to not shell the city. Consequently, the gathering Virginia militias were refused entry into Alexandria and during the next three days the British loaded 21 ships with the valuable cargo and sent them down the river. Undaunted, Hungerford moved his force of 1,200 men downriver to a bluff overlooking the Potomac and installed rifle companies and artillery pieces on a hillside, to fire on Gordon's ships as they passed. Meredith's artillery company went into position on the slope and remained there for 10 days while Gordon's ships exchanged cannonade and worked to get by the militia gunfire. The last of the booty-laden vessels escaped to Chesapeake Bay on September 10. Returning to Westmoreland County, Meredith's weary battery was released from duty on September 19 and not recalled for the remainder of the war. By the end of 1814, both the United States and Britain were tired of the conflict and on

Years of Preparation

Christmas Eve representatives of both countries signed a treaty to end the struggle. Although the war provided little gain for either country, Meredith's experience as a battlefield commander brought to maturity an aptitude for leadership that he turned to his advantage for the rest of his life.

Seeking a Future

The decades of the early 19th century were difficult years for Virginia's plantation families whose multiple sons were unable to be accommodated with land and slaves to make their start in life, as had been a tradition for nearly 200 years. Writing about this period, historian Page Smith says that the sons of upper-class families were under pressure to succeed, that "to fail financially was to drop into obscurity. ... The problem was complicated by the limited number of ... career opportunities for upper and middle class males. These were essentially three: law, the ministry, and commerce or business."[9] Looking to his future as he approached his third decade of life, Meredith must have faced some uncertainties. His means of livelihood for three years after the War of 1812 ended is unknown, although he remained in Westmoreland County and stayed in close contact with his family and cousins, of whom there were many. A nephew's newsy letter in 1823 speaks to the breadth of Meredith's kinship: "Uncle V. Marmadukes family are well. Cousin J. Hunter has had an attack of the Billous fever, but has gotten something better. Cousin Sally Hunter & Nancy Jenkings are well. Aunt Porter & Cousin Mary are very sick, the rest of the family are tolerable well; Cousin Sampson Porter is of the same mind as when you left. ... Cousin William and the girls are all well."[10]

In 1817, Meredith appears to have made a decision about his future course, and began to engage in public service. That spring, during the March session of the Westmoreland County Court, he sought and received an appointment as Commissioner of Revenue, a position that required a great amount of diplomacy in dealing with friends, neighbors, and family, for there is probably no local office more difficult to manage than that of tax collector.[11] Not content with his role as the county's collector, that same year he obtained a position as deputy marshal for the Spotsylvania Superior Court of Chancery, working out of an office in Fredericksburg under the direction of John Hanard. Traveling throughout six counties in northern Virginia, for the next six years Meredith delivered legal documents, served warrants and subpoenas, and performed other duties for the civil court, an experience that undoubtedly introduced him to many influential people.[12] In addition to his work as Westmoreland County's tax collector, he was serving as a justice of the peace, and he also found time to become acquainted with the instruments and calculations that were required to be a land surveyor. (In this, Meredith emulated a more famous Virginian, Thomas Jefferson, who as a boy had learned the art of surveying from his father.) In all these endeavors, Meredith was gaining experience and skills that he would use in the future. He also retained his interest in the county militia, rising in rank to major in 1817, accepting the commission after it had been declined by his uncle, Henry Hungerford.[13] Then, in 1820, he was commissioned a lieutenant colonel in the 111th Militia Regiment.

Meredith's interests, though, weren't always directed toward his livelihood and his military career. As an eligible bachelor about the countryside (he did not marry until his mid-30s), he participated in the active social life in which a scion of Tidewater plantation upbringing was expected to indulge.

A Time of Decision

Casting a shadow over Meredith's social and vocational life as he reached his 30th birthday in 1821 was an awareness of the distressed economy of Tidewater Virginia and its implications for someone who was both ambitious and willing to take risks to achieve success, someone who, like Thomas Jefferson at age 30, had "founded no family fortune," a circumstance considered "late for colonials" and not better considered in 1821.[14] Meredith also had health concerns. He suffered from an unrecorded ailment, perhaps a recurring respiratory illness that was aggravated by living near the region's coastal marshes. If so, the sudatory atmosphere, whose "vapors" were widely believed to be responsible for many afflictions, would have been pernicious. (Thomas Jefferson had found cause for concern about Virginia's climate and its effect upon the health of the commonwealth's inhabitants, suggesting in his meteorological notes that "It will be for physicians to observe the coincidences of the diseases of each season, with the particular winds then prevalent, the quantities of heat and rain, &c.")[15] The weight of these disparate influences (and a desire to become wealthy) would finally spur Meredith to leave his ancestral home in the late summer of 1823: "He regrets leaving the place of his nativity ... but the climate of the Northern Neck is unfriendly to his constitution," wrote his friend John Hanard in a letter of introduction.[16] It was a move that proffered future success, but as well offered much opportunity for failure. For some time, his vision had been focused on the country that lay beyond the Appalachian Mountains, even beyond the Mississippi River.

Notes

1. value of her exports: *Dictionary of American History*, Vol. 7, 235.

2. "were military men": Garry Wills, *Inventing America*, 25. Information about Meredith Marmaduke's militia commissions is found in Joseph Fox, Westmoreland County Clerk document, August 14, 1823. Box 1, Folder 2, Sappington-Marmaduke Papers, MHS.

3. twice boarded the British ship-of-the-line: Myron E. Lyman and William W. Hankins, *1812 Chronological List*, 19.

4. Westmoreland County was invaded many times: Lyman and Hankins, *Encounters With the British*, map 7, 351. Papers, MHS.

5. a tender had chased an American ship into the Yeocomico River: Lyman and Hankins, *1812 Chronological List*, 19.

6. British later claimed this raid: Lyman and Hankins, Ibid., 25.

7. Vincent and his uncle, William Marmaduke: *Virginia Militia, War of 1812 Muster and Payrolls*, 1812–1815. Library of Virginia, Record Group 46, Box 1, folder 5, 118th Regiment. Vincent Marmaduke wrote Meredith in 1850, "You were the captain of the artillery company I was in." Vincent Marmaduke to M. M. Marmaduke, September 23, 1850. Box 4, Folder 7, Sappington-Marmaduke Papers, MHS.

8. "we returned to the ships carrying with us 135 refugee Negroes": Lyman and Hankins, *1812 Chronological List*, 28.

9. "to fail financially was to drop into obscurity": Page Smith, *The Shaping of America*, 779–80.

Years of Preparation

10. "Uncle V. Marmaduke's family": Vincent McClanahan to Meredith Marmaduke, September 22, 1823. Ibid.

11. he was appointed Commissioner of Revenue: Joseph Fox, Westmoreland County Clerk, document dated August 14, 1823. Box 1, Folder 2, Sappington-Marmaduke Papers, MHS.

12. Information about Meredith Marmaduke's tenure as deputy marshal for the Spotsylvania Superior Court of Chancery is found in John Hanard to Col. P. P. Barbour, February 5, 1823. Box 1, Folder 2, Sappington-Marmaduke Papers, MHS.

13. Joseph Fox, Westmoreland County Clerk, document August 14, 1823. Box 1, Folder 2, Sappington-Marmaduke Papers, MHS. Henry Hungerford's rank as a major in the 111th Militia Regiment during the War of 1812 is found in Hungerford Family File, Westmoreland County, Virginia, Historical Society Genealogy Repository. Henry Hungerford identifies himself as Meredith Marmaduke's uncle in Hungerford to Marmaduke, September 23, 1823. Folder 2, Marmaduke Papers C1021, SHSMO. The two were only three years apart in age, Marmaduke commissioned a lieutenant colonel in the 111th Militia Regiment.

14. "had founded no family fortune": Wills, *Inventing America*, 14.

15. Information about Meredith Marmaduke's tenure as deputy marshal for the Spotsylvania Superior Court of Chancery is found in John Hanard to Col. P. P. Barbour, February 5, 1823. Box 1, Folder 2, Sappington-Marmaduke Papers, MHS.

16. "He regrets leaving the place of his nativity": John Hanard letter of introduction, February 5, 1823. Box 1, Folder 2, Sappington-Marmaduke Papers, MHS. References to Meredith Marmaduke's health are also found in letters from Vincent Marmaduke and Vincent McClanahan, September 15 and 22, 1823, respectively, Ibid.

CHAPTER 3

THE MOVE WEST

Monday, September 22, 1823, Virginia

Dear Uncle,

Your letter came to hand on the 17th inst. My mother & self and all the family were extremely glad to hear that your health are much improving. We were all thankful to god that you escaped so great a danger at the cotton Mountains, and that your crew move on very prosperously, also your Waggon and horses hold out well. … You will write us as often as it is Convenient. I remain your most affectionate nephew, Vincent McClanahan.

p.s. You must excuse bad dictating and writing.[1]

Deciding for Missouri
The realization that he was not going to become wealthy as a county officeholder and the deputy marshal of a regional chancery court came to Meredith sometime around his 30th birthday, perhaps as early as 1819 when he purchased a tract of land in Missouri. He could not see a profitable future for himself as a plantation owner in Virginia; his family's estate had been inherited by his older brother, Vincent, and the traditional tobacco-ruled economy of the Tidewater region was in a downhill slide with little prospect for recovery in the near future. Clearly, he realized that his life required a change if he was to prosper.

It appears that by the winter of 1822–23 he had determined he would relocate to Missouri. This was not a spur-of-the-moment decision. There is every indication that he had considered the move for some time. An early indication of his interest in the state appears in a deed recorded in Richmond County, Virginia, June 13, 1819, for his purchase of 160 acres of land in the Missouri Territory "which is particularly described in a warrant by President James Monroe."[2] The seller was Samuel Piersol, who had inherited a military land warrant as the brother and sole heir of Private Jeremiah Piersol. Jeremiah had served in Captain Henry H. Van Dalsem's company of the 15th Infantry during the War of 1812. He enlisted for two years on June 18, 1812, and eventually arrived in the village of Sackett's Harbor, a remote location that became an important military outpost on Lake Ontario in northern New York. Lacking adequate sanitary facilities, the village was unprepared for the massive influx of soldiers and sailors in 1813, and as a result the area became a breeding ground for many infectious diseases, including typhus. Jeremiah Piersol was often on the Army's sick list at Sackett's Harbor, and he died there in January 1814 from an unspecified illness.[3]

At the beginning of the War of 1812, the U.S. Congress passed acts that allowed the government to award a cash bounty and 160 acres of land to men who enlisted in the army for five years or the duration of the war. Unlike earlier military bounty land warrants, those of the War of 1812 could not be transferred or assigned but could be inherited. By doing this, Congress hoped to eliminate the pervasive speculation that had occurred with warrants issued to Revolutionary War veterans. War of 1812 warrants were issued for 6 million acres of land in the western territories that eventually became the states of Indiana, Illinois, Arkansas, and Missouri, an area of fertile soils and rich forests. The land Meredith bought from Jeremiah Piersol's brother, Samuel, in 1819 was located in Chariton County (originally part of a larger Howard County), only 25 miles north of where he would eventually settle in Saline County. Meredith's ownership of the quarter-section is further mentioned in an 1824 letter asking a business associate to pay the annual property tax for him, because he was not in Missouri at the time and traveling in the Southwest.[4] This tract of land may be the reason for what apparently are erroneous statements in several biographical sketches of Meredith that allege he was in Missouri in 1819 when, in fact, there is ample evidence that he was still in Virginia. Two events place Meredith in Westmoreland County, Virginia, at the time. On the first day of January he bought a slave there, and then in June he registered — in adjoining Richmond County — the Missouri land he had purchased from Samuel Piersol, apparently sight unseen.

A lengthy journey to Missouri would not likely have been started in the middle of summer if he hoped to return to Virginia before winter made travel difficult and uncertain. At least six weeks' time was required for the trip out, another six to return; then there would be time spent exploring the country — otherwise, why go? Meredith still had obligations that required his presence in Virginia during this time: his duties as Westmoreland County tax collector and his work as a deputy marshal for the Spotsylvania Superior Court of Chancery. Neither responsibility could easily have been left unattended. Virginia planters often made exploratory expeditions before they moved their families and belongings to Tennessee and Kentucky in the most active years of that migration. It seems unlikely, however, that Meredith would have embarked on such an extended journey (more than 2,000 miles round-trip) to Missouri in 1819. What is known about his activities during the years 1819 to 1823 shows that he was in Virginia, and that he was primarily engaged in improving his financial situation and buying slaves that he would take to Missouri in 1823.

A Pile of Mountains

The last week of August 1823, Meredith (his 32nd birthday occurred August 28) left Westmoreland County astride a horse accompanied by five or six slaves riding in a wagon. Their destination was the frontier village of Franklin, Missouri, 150 miles beyond St. Louis on the Missouri River and a thousand miles distant from Virginia. The journey would take two months. Certainly in Meredith's mind as he led the way out of Virginia's Northern Neck were thoughts of the many mountains and streams to be crossed before reaching the Ohio River Valley and the hazards along the way. Once they emerged from the Allegheny Mountains, the road west would be much easier. Little is known about the journey. If Meredith kept a diary (something he did on a trip to the Territory of Nuevo Mexico in 1824), it has been lost, so to reconstruct his migration it is necessary to rely on letters and documents from his papers to discover his route of travel and who he took with him. Nephew Vincent McClanahan's September 22 letter that references "the cotton Mountains," and "your crew ... also your Waggon and horses" that held out "well" are important clues. Another piece of the story is revealed in a letter written to Meredith by his uncle, Henry Hungerford, on September 23, 1823, in which he says, "I wrote to you three weeks since and addressed to you at *Lexington, Kentucky*" [author's italics].[5] Meredith's brother, Vincent, also mentions Lexington in a letter. A third piece of information is contained in a letter Meredith's friend Dr. George R. Pitts penned to him on October 20, 1823, saying he is "pleased to hear that you had a fortunate travel as far as Frankford [Kentucky] and hope by this time you may have completed your journey."[6]

As he traveled, Meredith was writing to friends and relatives in Virginia, perhaps to assure them of his welfare, but also to inform them about the journey itself. He would try in the next few years to interest members of his family in joining him in Missouri. Pitts's letter was in response to one he had received from Meredith "by last mail." With the revelations in these letters, and the help of maps and archive resources — and some guesswork — it is possible to trace the route taken by Meredith and the slaves as they traveled from Virginia to Missouri.

There were three possible routes they could take to cross the Appalachian ranges. One was the Wilderness Road, a southern path through the Cumberland Gap into southeastern Kentucky. A northern route was the Cumberland Road (an extension of the National Road from Baltimore) beginning at Cumberland in western Maryland and going to Wheeling (now West Virginia) and Pittsburgh. At the time, Wheeling was a principal port of embarkation for immigrants going down the Ohio River. Both the Wilderness and Cumberland Roads were well known and heavily used, with plenty of facilities for travelers.

A third route across the mountains opened in 1790 from the James River in eastern Virginia to the Great Kanawha River valley in what is now West Virginia. This road is the one Meredith chose. Taking the most direct route from Westmoreland County, he and the slaves crossed the Rappahannock River to Port Royal, went south to Richmond and then west on the James River-Kanawha River road. The route carried them over the Blue Ridge Mountains to Lexington in the Shenandoah Valley, then into the Allegheny Mountains and on to Lewisburg. An early-day traveler on this section of the Kanawha River road, looking over the countryside from atop a ridge, described what he saw as "one continued pile of Mountains" bisected by valleys, each home to a creek or river that had to be forded, one 28 times before it was passed.[7] Virginians going to and returning from Kentucky and Ohio made the Kanawha River road a busy route in the early years of the 19th century. West Virginia historian Charles Ambler describes the traffic saying that "By 1808, cattle drivers from Ohio and Kentucky were passing over the Kanawha ... in search of eastern markets for such of their hogs, sheep, and cattle as survived the attacks of bears and wolves en-route. ... By 1826, the number of hogs passing this way annually was estimated at sixty thousand, while going to the West, at the same time, might have been seen immigrants, slave coffles [a group of slaves chained together], and wagons of all descriptions."[8] Tolls were collected on the road as early as 1809 — 25 cents for a wagon, team, and driver; 6¼ cents for a horse and rider. The toll for livestock was based on the damage done to the road with cattle being charged only one-quarter cent per head, while hogs and sheep required payment of 3 cents per head. By 1814, the main route west for travelers from southern and central Virginia was via Lewisburg (in what is now West Virginia), across the New River at Boyer's Ferry, through Vandalia (now Fayetteville, West Virginia), over Cotton Hill to the Great Falls of Kanawha and continuing along the south side of the Kanawha.[9] By 1821, the Kanawha River Road had been rebuilt westward from Lewisburg. This new road stayed north of the New River.

About 60 miles west of Lewisburg, Meredith and the slaves came to Gauley Mountain on the north side of the New River. On the south side was Cotton Hill Mountain, rising more than 2,000 feet above sea level — the "cotton Mountains" mentioned in Vincent McClanahan's letter. Traveling through here on his way to Kentucky in 1789, 31-year-old Joel Watkins observed that Gauley Mountain was "as high and Defiant of access" as any he had yet seen.[10] Some 34 years later, somewhere on the side of Gauley Mountain, Meredith and the slaves experienced an incident of "so great a danger" (in Vincent McClanahan's words) that he was compelled to write about the event soon afterward in a letter to his sister's family. Now lost, that letter's disclosures can only be surmised but the risk of serious injury or death was present at every creek and river in their path, and every mountain that had to be traversed. Fortunately, Meredith and the slaves survived their ordeal on the "cotton Mountains" unharmed and descended to the confluence of the Gauley and New Rivers that together form the Kanawha River. Not far downstream they passed Kanawah Falls, and a few miles further came to Montgomery's Ferry where they crossed the Kanawha to reach a road that carried them southwest through the mountains to Pike County, Kentucky, and on to Lexington.

In addition to being situated on the most direct route to Missouri, Lexington may have drawn Meredith there for a different reason. In a complicated financial transaction common among relatives and neighbors in the Tidewater region, James Hunter, a brother to John Hunter, Meredith's brother-in-law, owed his father's estate "12 Pounds, 2 Shillings, 3 Pence," for which he had signed a "Bill Penal" (an IOU) payable by September 19, 1811, now long overdue. In 1823, Meredith's brother, Vincent, owed James Hunter, now living in Kentucky, some money and was on the verge of being sued by Thomas Spence, administrator of the Hunter estate, to satisfy James's claim. Vincent was also in possession of property owned by James, and Spence was threatening to attach that as well.[11] It is a reasonable assumption that Meredith visited Lexington at the behest of his brother Vincent in an effort to clarify the issue with James Hunter's estate before a suit was filed in the Westmoreland Chancery Court. (Meredith did not stay long in Lexington — Henry Hungerford's September 23 letter sent there was forwarded to Missouri.) The next leg of the journey took Meredith and the slaves on a well-traveled road to Frankford and then to the Ohio River town of Louisville, whose 10,000 inhabitants at the time included 400 prostitutes.[12] At Portland, a short distance below the Falls of the Ohio, Meredith paid for ferry passage across the river to Jeffersonville, Indiana, and then followed the road that ran to Vincennes, Indiana, and on to St. Louis, a 300-mile passage.

Influential Friends

Among the personal effects that Meredith carried with him were two documents that he retained for the rest of his life. The first recounted the military and civil offices he had held in Westmoreland County. On August 14, 1823, less than two weeks before leaving Virginia, Meredith visited Joseph Fox, the county clerk, and acquired from him a record of the county and military offices he had held from 1811 to 1823. (Joseph Fox died four months later. Vincent Marmaduke reported his death, telling Meredith that county officials "said if you were here there would be little or no opposition" to his having the office.[13]) The second document Meredith carried west was a letter, dated February 2, 1823, written by John Hanard of the Fredericksburg, Virginia, Chancery Court. Addressed to Colonel P. P. Barbour, Hanard introduced Meredith as, "my friend ... who visits the city of Washington ... with a view of obtaining some appointment in the Western Country under the General Government." Hanard goes on to laud Meredith as a "gentleman [of] integrity and worth, he having for nearly six years past acted in the capacity of [Deputy] Marshal of the [Fredericksburg Chancery Court] in six counties of Virginia. ... I regret losing him as an officer. He regrets leaving the place of his nativity where he is esteemed & respected ... but the climate of the Northern Neck is unfriendly to his constitution. He has determined to emigrate. ... Should he, thro' your influence & that of others to whom he has letters, obtain an appointment, I feel assured that you nor they will ever have cause to regret it."[14]

The "others" whom Marmaduke may have seen in Washington are unknown, but he did visit Colonel Barbour there and in doing so opened the doors of some influential people in the capital city. At the time of Meredith's visit to Washington City, Philip Pendleton Barbour was the Speaker of the U.S. House of Representatives where he had been a member since 1814. He would eventually become an associate judge of the U.S. Supreme Court. Of equal interest to Meredith was the potential to also visit Philip's brother, James, who was the U.S. Senator from Virginia at the time and had been governor of Virginia during the War of 1812. As governor, James Barbour had approved Meredith's promotion to the rank of captain in the state's 111th Militia Regiment in 1813. Now, as Virginia's senator, Barbour would recognize Meredith both as a veteran officer of that war and as a fellow Virginian. (The Barbours could boast of tenure in Virginia since the earliest colonial days, as could the Marmadukes.) James Barbour went on to have a distinguished career as U.S. Secretary of War under President John Quincy Adams and later served as minister to Great Britain. Meredith's journey to the nation's capital in 1823 did not result in an appointment to a federal position in the West, but there is no doubt that he gained some important contacts (and most likely letters of introduction to persons of interest in Missouri) by the effort.

A third document of considerable value to Meredith caught up with him soon after he reached Missouri. In a letter written November 10, 1823, Vincent Marmaduke informed his brother that, "Shortly after you left this country there came a letter of recommendation to you from The President [James Monroe], which Mayor Walker received, and we had a conversation about it. I told him I thought he had better write on to Lescenton [Lexington] Kentucky to inform you there was such a recommendation for you and to send it on to St. Louis where you would be sure to get it least you had past Lexenton [sic] before it would get there and then you would not get it at all as I thought it might be of Great Service to you in that country."[15] Other letters Meredith took west, these of unknown content, had been forwarded to him in Westmoreland County by F. Bates in early August.[16] They were probably letters to be delivered to friends and relatives of the writers whom Meredith expected to see along the road to Missouri. Although regular mail service had been established in 1818 between Washington City and Wheeling on the Ohio River, and from there to the west, it was not uncommon for someone going west to be called upon to carry mail. Besides, delivering letters from friends might result in an offer to eat supper and spend the night.

The letters of introduction and other documents that Meredith carried to Missouri would serve as affirmation of his accomplishments in both civil and military offices, and of his personal character. Their testimony would be acknowledged by anyone to whom they were presented. There is little doubt that he used these papers to establish himself with people of influence in Missouri affairs, among others perhaps William Clark, superintendent of Indian Affairs for the West, whose office was in St. Louis and with whom Meredith would communicate in the future. He may also have used the letters to obtain lines of credit with merchants of St. Louis, as his interest in the Santa Fe trade would soon be disclosed.

The Slaves

The Virginia Marmadukes had owned slaves since arriving in the colony in the 1600s, and Meredith was no exception to the practice. His first known purchase of a slave occurred January 1, 1819, when he bought a "Negro boy, Tom," from William Stocke Jett, in Westmoreland County.[17] In November of 1822, Meredith acquired another slave, this one a black man named Perimus, bought from Washington Glascock for $88.50. Then in 1823, as the time neared for relocating to Missouri, he bought four more black slaves. In January 1823, Thomas L. James of Northumberland County sold Meredith a boy named Lewis for $175. In May, Meredith bought Daniel from Thomas Spence for $350. A girl, Lavina, was acquired in July for $500 from Robert W. McCarty of Richmond, Virginia, and 30 days later, on August 23, the eve of his departure from Virginia, Meredith paid William A. Spark of Westmoreland County $250 for a black man named Minny.[18] These transactions, particularly those that occurred in 1823, leave no doubt that Meredith intended to take slaves to Missouri.

Transporting slaves to Kentucky and Tennessee was a common practice of Virginia planters who crossed the Appalachian Mountains in the years following the American Revolution. David H. Fischer and James C. Kelly in their book, *Bound Away, Virginia and the Westward Movement,* cite the story of David Mead, a "Portable Planter," who moved his entire plantation from Virginia to Kentucky in 1795 in a "cavalcade" that included three wagons, 21 horses, and about 50 people "black and white."[19] After the War of 1812, thousands of these trans-Appalachian settlers picked up and moved west once again, many of them going to Missouri and taking their slaves with them. A

St. Louis newspaper in 1819 noted that new immigrants to Missouri from Kentucky and Tennessee were accompanied by "great numbers of slaves." The state's population more than tripled in a decade, going from 20,000 residents in 1810 to 66,000 in 1820. The slave population in Missouri increased during the same period from 3,000 to nearly 10,000. During these years, thousands of slaves were transported to the states in the Mississippi Delta region to work on newly established cotton plantations there. This great transport of slaves from east to west was prompted not only by the need for manual labor, but by a clause in the Northwest Ordinance, passed by Congress in 1787, that forbade slave ownership in the states of Ohio, Michigan, Indiana, and Illinois. Missouri achieved statehood in 1821, partially as the result of the Missouri Compromise, a controversial congressional act of 1820 that allowed slave ownership in the state while prohibiting it elsewhere in much of the territory that comprised the Louisiana Purchase. As a result, Tennessee and Kentucky planters who wanted to retain their slaves while taking advantage of Missouri's less expensive land flocked to the state.

Separation from family and friends in Virginia was something Meredith willingly accepted as a consequence of relocation to Missouri, but the slaves who went with him undoubtedly wept as they left behind mothers, fathers, siblings, cousins, and friends, with the knowledge that they would probably never see them again. Francis Fedric, a 14-year-old slave who was taken to Kentucky in 1818, later recalled the sadness of the occasion: "My master had determined to give up his plantation in Virginia and go to Kentucky. I shall never forget the heart-rending scenes which I witnessed before we started. Men and women down on their knees begging to be purchased to go with their wives or husbands, who worked for my master, children crying and imploring not to have their parents sent away from them; but all their beseeching and tears were of no avail. They were ruthlessly separated, most of them for ever. Still, after so many years, their wailings and lamentations and piercing cries sound in my ears …"[20] Meredith's slaves would go to a strange land to live among strangers, having no knowledge about their future home, nor any experience of life beyond the confines of the Virginia plantations that had succored them (however well or poorly) since birth.

Traveling alone with a "crew" of slaves who "moved on very prosperously," not rebelling or running away at some point on the thousand-mile journey, attests to a relationship between Meredith and his slaves that was based on a degree of trust. Masters often gained such trust by granting familial status to their slaves; a plantation had a white family and a black family, and the welfare of each was of concern. Meredith's uncle, Henry Hungerford, writing to him on September 23, 1823, mentions members of his black family by name, as if Meredith knew them personally. "Walker, Daniel & Henry was sick — which indisposition terminated in a bilious fever, of a very aggravated nature, & proved fatal to poor Henry, who died the Monday following," he wrote. "Docs. Wheelwright & Collins attended him. On the Thursday following Maria was taken with the same fever, & having lost Henry, determined to have both doctors again, & by great attention & skill, am pleased to say she is in a full way to recover. On Friday last Nancy was taken & is now ill & Walker on the next day. Both are now under a physician. Thus you will see out of seven blacks, five has been ill, one of which has died. Such a turn I never experienced before & I pray God to exempt me from it the balance of my life. My white family is well."21

Whatever his original intention for taking slaves to Missouri (whether to work on his Chariton County property or elsewhere) Meredith found a ready market for their labor when he arrived at Franklin in 1823. He viewed his slaves as property, having value both as labor for his needs and as assets that could be hired out, men and young boys put to work as field hands, women and girls as domestic help. Advertisements in newspapers offered slaves for hire. One slave owner in Howard County was willing to rent out a black woman "Healthy and Masculine," who he said could split a hundred fence rails a day. This demand for labor on the frontier increased the value of slaves brought to the Booneslick region. An appraisal of the estate of Thomas McMahan, who died in 1821 in Cooper County, across the Missouri River from Franklin, determined that "one Negro Man" and "one Negro Woman" were worth $500 and $400 respectively.22 Dr. John Sappington (of whom we shall hear more), then residing in Howard County, was buying slaves in Tennessee in May 1821, paying Shimmey Meritt of Williamson County $500 for a black girl named "Mourning." Soon after, he purchased "Bill," a black boy, from Will L. Brown, again paying $500.23 When Meredith arrived in Franklin he could have sold his slaves for almost double the price he had paid for them in Virginia. Instead, he advertised them for rent and thereby secured an income that helped to support him as he became established. Renting slaves provided an economic benefit for the owner and those who hired them, and it was a practice Meredith kept for many years. Johnson Wetmore of Franklin responded to Meredith's solicitation in 1830, writing "I have just been told by Genl. Smith that you have a good hand to hire for the balance of the present year. Will you please write by return of mail and say if we can have him for our steam mill purposes at a fair price. We wish him to take charge of a good ox team. If we get him the sooner we have him the better, and you may send him down as soon as convenient. The Genl. has been kind enough to say that he will speak to you on the subject of security for his hire, which I understand the advertisement mentions."24

Arrival in Missouri

Despite having 10,000 residents, making it a fair-sized city, St. Louis presented the appearance of a frontier town when Meredith arrived in October 1823. An early map depicts the city at that time as being some 20 blocks wide by half a dozen deep, strung out along the Mississippi River. A recent newcomer from the east recalled many of the town's buildings as log structures whose walls were upright poles, set in place stockade-fashion, although wealthier residents such as the fur-trading Chouteau brothers, Auguste and Pierre, occupied frame dwellings some of which were two and three stories tall.25 Traders, fur trappers, explorers, Indians, and a smattering of professional men — among them lawyers, doctors, and government agents — mingled on the streets and in the shops. French, Spanish, English, and a variety of Indian tongues spoke to the mixture of cultures that had gathered at this distant place. On the riverfront, a fleet of flatboats attested to commerce with Ohio ports and downriver at New Orleans, the import of which was not lost on Meredith. He remained in St. Louis several days to acquaint himself with the governmental agencies, the merchants, and the people who influenced the affairs and trade of the West before going on up the Missouri River to the small village of Franklin. There, the prospect of entering the Santa Fe trade soon became his major focus as he became acquainted with those who had made the trip that year and with others who were interested in going to Mexican territory in 1824.

Although he left the unsalutary climate of Virginia to breathe in the clean air of the West, improving his physical health was not Meredith's only reason for relocating to Missouri. He also sought an economic atmosphere more conducive to obtaining the wealth required to fulfill his Virginia legacy. While walking the muddy streets of Franklin during the winter of 1823–24, Meredith recognized an opportunity for financial gain from an investment in the Santa Fe trade. He also recognized the inherent risk in such a long-distance venture and sought to minimize it by renting his slaves to tradesmen, merchants, and farmers who needed manual labor, an asset in short supply on the Missouri frontier. In doing so, he became one of the earliest entrepreneurial traders to go down the Santa Fe Trail.

Notes

1. "Dear Uncle": Vincent McClanahan to Meredith Marmaduke, September 22,1823. Box 1, Folder 2, Sappington-Marmaduke Papers, MHS.

2. Marmaduke's 1819 purchase of 160 acres in Missouri is recorded in Richmond County, Virginia, Deed Book No. 21, 421.

3. Jeremiah Piersol's military records: NARA Record Group 94, Records of the Adjutant General's Office, 1780s–1917, Microfilm Publication M233 Register of Enlistments in the United States Army, compiled 1798–1914, 150–51; Record Group 49, Records of the Bureau of Land Management 1865–2006, Microfilm Publication M848, Index of Patentees for Military Bounty Land Warrants Issued under the Act of 1812 Located in Missouri, 152–153; M848, Military Bounty Land Warrants under the Act of 1812, Warrant # 20565.

4. Meredith's ownership of the quarter-section: Marmaduke to John Hardeman, October 13, 1824. Folder 5, Glen Hardeman Papers C3655, SHSMO.

5. "I wrote to you three weeks since": Henry Hungerford to Meredith Marmaduke, September 23, 1823. Folder 2, Marmaduke Papers C1021, SHSMO.

6. "pleased to hear that you had a fortunate travel": George R. Pitts to Meredith Marmaduke, October 20, 1823. Folder 2, Marmaduke Papers C1021, SHSMO.

7. "one continued pile of Mountains": Ellen Eslinger, *Running Mad for Kentucky*, 159.

8. "By 1808, cattle drivers from Ohio": Charles Henry Ambler, *A History of West Virginia*, 201.

9. "via Lewisburg, across the New River." J. T. Peters and H. D. Carden, *History of Fayette County, West Virginia*, chapter 8, np.

10. "as high and defiant of access": Eslinger, *Running Mad for Kentucky*, 161.

11. Court records relating to James Hunter's indebtedness are in: ADMX of John Hunter vs. James Hunter and Vincent Marmaduke, Library of Virginia Chancery Records Index No. 1825–002. On August 30, 1825, the plaintiff obtained a decree against Hunter and Marmaduke for the amount claimed plus interest from 1811 and a penalty.

12. "400 prostitutes": Samuel B. Judah, *A Journal of Travel from New York to Indiana in 1827*, 346.

13. "said if you were here there would be little or no opposition": Vincent Marmaduke to Meredith, January 22, 1824. Folder 2, Marmaduke Papers C1021, SHSMO.

14. The Hanard and Fox documents are dated February 2 and August 14, 1823, respectively. Box 1, Folder 2, Sappington-Marmaduke Papers, MHS.

15. "Shortly after you left this country": Vincent Marmaduke to Meredith Marmaduke, November 10, 1823. Ibid.

16. F. Bates to Marmaduke, August 1, 1823. Ibid.

17. Receipt for "Negro boy, Tom," January 1, 1819. Box 1, Folder 1, Sappington-Marmaduke Papers, MHS.

18. Receipts for Perimus, Lewis, Lavina and Minny are in Box 1, Folder 2, Sappington-Marmaduke Papers, MHS. The receipt for Daniel is in Folder 2, Marmaduke Papers C1021, SHSMO.

19. "Portable Planter": David H. Fischer and James C. Kelly, *Bound Away, Virginia and the Westward Movement*, 159.

20. "My master had determined to give up his plantation": Francis Fedric, *Slave Life in Virginia and Kentucky*, 14, 15.

21. "Walker, Daniel & Henry was sick": Henry Hungerford to Marmaduke, September 23, 1823. Folder 2, Marmaduke Papers C1021, SHSMO.

22. Thomas McMahan appraisal: December 22, 1821. Box 1, Folder 1, Sappington-Marmaduke Papers, MHS.

23. Dr. Sappington's purchase of slaves in Tennessee: May 1 and June 5, 1821. Box 2, Folder 1, Sappington-Marmaduke Papers, MHS.

24. "I have just been told by Genl. Smith": Johnson Wetmore to Meredith Marmaduke, September 5, 1830. Box 1, Folder 6, Sappington-Marmaduke Papers, MHS.

25. "I Well Remember: David Holmes Conrad's Recollections of St. Louis, 1819–1822," *MHR*, Vol. 90, No. 1 (October 1995) Part 1, 3 & 9; Vol. 90. No. 2 (January 1996), Part 2, 129.

CHAPTER 4

A STAR OF NO INCONSIDERABLE MAGNITUDE

Boone's Lick, Boon's Lick, Boonslick or Booneslick? In literature, letters, and documents, this region in central Missouri is spelled several different ways. The state's official highway map offers three versions, listing a Boonesboro, a Boonville, and a Boone County, all of which are named after the state's most famous frontiersman. The pioneers who settled the area in the early years of the 19th century certainly weren't concerned about proper orthography. Most just called it the Boonslick Country, or more succinctly "the Boonslick," and let it go at that. Modern-day biographers of Daniel Boone, however, have concluded that he always spelled his name with an "e" on the end, thus making all other forms local variations. Perhaps "Boonslick" rolled more easily off the tongue. (In this book, "Booneslick" refers to the region in Missouri, whereas "Boone's Lick" is used to identify the salt spring in Howard County.)

Meredith Marmaduke arrived in the Booneslick region in the fall of 1823 and made it his home for the rest of his life. Here he would marry, raise a family, establish successful commercial and agricultural enterprises, rise to power in Missouri politics, and gain the land and wealth that was unavailable to him in Virginia. Ultimately he would lose much of his prosperity and experience the discomfort of being in opposition to members of his family in the strife of civil war. At every turn in Meredith's life, the Booneslick country loomed large. It is appropriate, therefore, to examine the nature of the region and the character of the people who settled there.

Defined as early as 1819 as "both sides of the Missouri River from the mouth of the Osage River to the western Indian boundary,"[1] the Booneslick region, originally part of the St. Charles District of territorial Missouri, is today identified as 13 counties in the heart of the state, but three — Cooper, Howard, and Saline — form the historic "heart" of the Booneslick. Howard and Cooper Counties differ in a significant way from Saline. In Saline County, the great forests that clothed much of the nation east of Missouri in the 1800s, whose trees had nurtured pioneering Americans for more than two centuries, end their westward march along the Missouri River. There marks the beginning of transition from forest to treeless prairie that extends from Texas to Canada and westward to include the arid, high plains. On his first journey to Santa Fe in 1821, trader William Becknell noticed the transition soon after leaving the Missouri River. "Our company crossed the Missouri [from Howard to Saline County] near the Arrow Rock ferry ... and encamped six miles from the ferry. The next morning ... we proceeded on our journey over a beautiful rolling prairie country. ... the eye catches a distant view of the Missouri on the right and a growth of lofty timber adjoining it about two miles wide."[2]

The Arrow Rock mentioned by Becknell is a limestone bluff on the eastern edge of Saline County, where the Missouri River turns north to form a great bend 95 miles in length. Early European travelers discovered a trail at Arrow Rock that led them west, straight across the mouth of the bend, cutting in half the distance traveled before rejoining the river near present-day Lexington, in Lafayette County. This ancient track became part of the Santa Fe Trail, and the village of Arrow Rock that grew atop the bluff served the area's settlers, as well as countless travelers — explorers, traders, trappers, and military expeditions — going farther west.

The Booneslick nomenclature arises from early interest in the region by members of the Boone family. Daniel Boone, who settled in St. Charles County (ironically, not considered a part of the Booneslick region), is often mistakenly said to have discovered the salt spring (the "lick") to which his name is attached, and in Kentucky he had several times been involved with salt-making ventures. But credit for the identity of the Missouri saltworks (and thus, the identification of the region) must go to his sons, Nathan and Daniel Morgan Boone. In December 1804 Nathan, traveling in western Howard County, explored a salt spring that flowed in a shallow, wooded hollow a short distance north of the Missouri River. The Boone brothers were not the first to discover salt springs in central Missouri. Early Spanish and French explorers visited the saline springs and seeps in the Booneslick region, and a later 19th-century survey of active salt springs in Howard County lists 12 large enough to be mentioned, with many smaller sites known to exist.

Recognizing the potential of the site for making salt, the following year Nathan Boone and his older brother, Daniel Morgan, established a commercial salt-making operation whose product was rafted down the river to St. Louis. The Boone brothers' "Lick" eventually passed into the hands of others and salt continued to be made at the site for many years. Today the Boone's Lick State Historic Site interprets for visitors the role and importance of salt springs in the early development of the Booneslick region, and a mural in the state Capitol building in Jefferson City depicts Daniel Boone's sons making salt. Used to preserve meat, salt was a prized commodity and numerous saltworks — an important source of income for early settlers — operated in the Booneslick region to satisfy this need.

Saline County (the name speaks to the subject) had many saltworks, too. Early Missouri settler John Heath was making salt from springs along the Lamine River around 1808, and journalist Henry M. Brackenridge noted activity there in 1811 on his way up the Missouri River.

Edward Reavis started making salt in 1817 on the Lamine and Blackwater Rivers and was in business for 15 years. The largest salt spring in the county, appropriately named "Big Spring," was operated in the 1820s by John A. Jones.[3] An April 1827 issue of a St. Louis newspaper notes Jones' salt operation and provides an interesting glimpse into Meredith Marmaduke's presence in the Booneslick at that time. Reporting on a Congressional act to establish "post roads" in the state, the newspaper identified one route as going "from Fulton by Columbia, Rockport, Booneville, *Meredith Marmaduke's* [author's italics], and Jones' Salt Works. ..."⁴ Meredith had been in Missouri only 3½ years, and for a year of that time he was in Santa Fe, yet he was already well-enough established that his presence on the frontier was notable.

Early River Travelers

As the Booneslick is the heart of Missouri, so then is the Missouri River the artery that nurtured the Booneslick and by extension the passageway that led beyond the Mississippi River to the Far West. The first Europeans to see the Missouri River were the adventurous Frenchmen Jacques Marquette and Louis Joliet. A Jesuit priest, Father Marquette tells of the discovery of the mouth of the Missouri on a June day in 1673 while he and Joliet were descending the Mississippi River by canoe. Hearing the roar of the Missouri's thunderous current in full flood stage, Father Marquette feared they were approaching "a rapid into which we were about to run." Their canoe swept into the torrent, he later recalled having "seen nothing more dreadful. A mass of large and entire trees, branches and floating islands was issuing from the mouth of the river ... with such impetuosity that we could not without great danger risk passing through it. So great was the agitation that the water was very muddy, and could not get clear."⁵ The outpouring of the Missouri quickly carried Marquette and Joliet beyond the mouth and it was left for others to explore the great river they had discovered. During the next 40 years, various Europeans would tentatively go up the Missouri, trapping the feeder streams and creeks, trading with Indians, and searching for mineral wealth, but most failed to record their impressions.

The earliest-known description of the Missouri River, an account of the distance traveled each day and the features observed, appears in the journal of Etienne de Bourgmont, a French explorer who in 1714 went up the Missouri in a canoe to live for three years with his Indian wife and her people. His passage through the heart of the Booneslick country is shown on a map historians have associated with his journal. Drawn there is the course of a side stream at which he stopped, what he called the "Rivière de la Mine" — today's Lamine River — whose flow enters the Missouri in Cooper County.⁶ Bourgmont reported finding Indians mining lead on the small stream. Ninety years later Meriwether Lewis and William Clark, on their historic journey to the Pacific Ocean, spent the better part of a day exploring the Lamine River. Writing in his journal on June 8, 1804, Clark said the expedition "came to Mine river. ... which falls into the Missouri from the south." After hiking 12 miles up the Lamine he reported finding "rich salt springs," and recalled French reports that lead ore was present in the river's valley. The next day Clark and his companions passed "a cliff of rocks, called the Arrow Rock, near to which is a prairie called the Prairie of Arrows. ... At this cliff the Missouri is confined within a bed of two hundred yards; and about four miles to the south-east is a large lick and salt spring of great strength."⁷ The following winter, Nathan Boone would turn aside at Arrow Rock from his passage along the Missouri River to explore a nearby salt spring, known thereafter as Boone's Lick.

Further exploration of the lower Missouri basin was soon to come. In the summer of 1811, the many-talented lawyer, judge, and writer Henry Marie Brackenridge traveled through the Booneslick during a two-year exploration of the Louisiana Purchase country and thereafter wrote a series of essays describing the topography, mineral deposits, and plant and animal life he observed. Published in St. Louis the following winter, the essays were reprinted in periodicals throughout the country, stimulating so much interest that they were gathered into a book, *Views of Louisiana; Together With A Journal Of A Voyage Up The Missouri River, In 1811.* A keen observer of all things natural, Brackenridge's description of the countryside, together with the observations of Captain Clark recorded seven years earlier, provides a picture of the pre-settlement appearance of the Booneslick country that in some aspects is not much different from today. As he went up the Missouri, there unfolded before Brackenridge on both sides of the river the magnificent limestone bluffs and timbered hills — separated by miles-long, rich black-dirt fields — that extend for more than 200 miles. Paddling his canoe above Arrow Rock, he left behind the high bluffs and entered the rolling, tallgrass prairie landscape that extends for hundreds of miles to the Rocky Mountains. In the lower reaches of the Missouri, Brackenridge observed an abundance of cottonwood, pecan, and mulberry trees growing along the feeder creeks and rivers, while in the big river itself he came upon islands that were "covered with cedar trees." Beyond Arrow Rock, he found the woods and prairies "overrun with strawberry vines," whose fruit he sampled and deemed "excellent."[8] William Clark, sparser in description than Brackenridge, simply said the Booneslick was "good land, well watered, and supplied with timber." He was impressed by the heavy growth of cane thickets and "high nettles" in the river bottoms, while above Arrow Rock the prairie was "generally without any covering except grass," unlike prairies east of the Mississippi River.[9]

Brackenridge's *Views of Louisiana,* and Lewis and Clark's *Journals of the Expedition,* were both published in 1814. Their distribution east of the Mississippi River helped to invigorate an already restless population in the states of Virginia, Tennessee, and Kentucky who in the next few years would migrate to Missouri by the thousands, seeking new land on which to settle, land that Amos Stoddard, military commandant of Upper Louisiana, proclaimed "from its climate, population, soil, and productions … will in all human probability, soon become a star of no inconsiderable magnitude in the American Constellation."[10]

The Rise and Decline of Franklin

No settlement of any size existed on the Missouri River above St. Charles in 1811, no road reached much beyond the bounds of that town except a somewhat vague travel route known as "the trace" or the "Boonslick trace,"[11] yet at that early year people were planting crops and family roots in the Booneslick country. Those who made the difficult journey beyond St. Charles were land-hungry. The Cooper families are an example. Colonel Benjamin Cooper lived briefly in St. Charles before attempting to settle near the Boone brothers' salt spring in 1808. He was soon ordered back downriver by Territorial Governor William Clark, who was attempting to prevent encroachment in areas not yet ceded by Indians for settlement. In 1810, Benjamin and his family returned to the Booneslick country, accompanied this time by his brothers Sarshal and Braxton, and their families. Members of the Cooper clan, like most who came to the Booneslick country in the early years of the 19th century, were not deterred by the challenge of living on the frontier. Benjamin had served as a ranger in a Virginia militia company during the Revolutionary War before moving to Kentucky, where he fought

Indians with Daniel Boone. During the War of 1812, he joined a Missouri militia unit and again faced hostile Indians in conflicts along the Missouri River. His brothers were both attacked by Indians during the latter war. Braxton Cooper was shot by an Indian in September 1814 as he was cutting wood at his home in Cooper Bottom, and Sarshal — a captain in a Missouri militia company — died at his Booneslick home in 1815 after being shot by an Indian who poked his musket through a hole in the chinking between the logs of the cabin's wall. Sarshal's youngest child is said to have been seated on his lap at the time.

Indian attacks in the Booneslick country during the War of 1812 caused some dislocation, but the war's end in 1814 brought renewed interest in settlement. Howard County was formed out of St. Charles County in 1816 with a thousand families in the region, comprising an area much larger then than today, nearly one-quarter of the state. A small settlement known as Hannah Cole's Fort, on the south bank of the Missouri River where Boonville now stands, was named the first county seat. Then in 1817 Franklin, a landing in Cooper's Bottom north of the river, was designated as the new seat of county government. With the appointment of a court and county officers came protection for property rights and a sense of personal safety, generating a flood of settlers so great that Howard County's population grew to 9,000 within a year. Someone counted the number of wagons and carriages going from St. Charles to Franklin — on what came to be known as the Boonslick Road — in October 1818 and reported nearly 300 for the month. And despite cold weather, in the first three months of 1819 an average of 20 families were traveling the road each week. The rapid increase in population brought the need for division into smaller counties. Cooper County was organized out of Howard in 1818 with Boonville its seat. Charles Lucas and Asa Morgan platted the townsite the following year. Unfortunately, Lucas didn't live to see Boonville develop. Eight weeks after completing his survey he was killed in a pistol duel with Thomas Hart Benton, a lawyer transplanted from Tennessee who was destined to become one of Missouri's first two senators (and a close friend of Meredith Marmaduke). Another split occurred in 1820 when the western end of Cooper County was sectioned off and named Saline County. Old Jefferson, a few wooden shacks planted in the mud on a bank above the Missouri River, became its seat of governance. Of these three early Booneslick towns — Franklin, Boonville, and Old Jefferson — only Boonville, situated on a bluff, would exist a decade later. The land holding up the buildings at Franklin and Old Jefferson would be swallowed by the river.

From its rough beginning in 1817, Franklin took on a more proper look (at least on paper) in 1820 when its town site was surveyed and platted. The carefully drawn map of the village, viewable today in the State Historical Society of Missouri archives, projects the hopes of the town's organizers in a tidy arrangement of 98 lots, each 165 by132 feet, laid out in blocks of four on a grid of wide streets that follow the cardinal points of the compass. Among the first buyers of land in the town was Thomas Hardeman, an upriver planter who purchased three corner lots facing the courthouse square. Another lot purchaser was the old explorer and free trapper Ezekiel Williams, who first went up the Missouri River in 1807 looking for beaver in the foothills of the Rocky Mountains. Seven years later, worn down by the rigors of a trapper's life, Ezekiel married a Missouri widow and began to farm near where Benjamin Cooper had settled. He bought one lot on a side street in Franklin, only to see his investment eaten away by the river a few years later.[12] A United States Land Office to serve western Missouri counties opened in Franklin in February 1819. Housed in a rough log cabin by the river, its first agent, General Thomas Adams Smith, appointed by President James Monroe as a receiver of public monies, collected a half million dollars the first year and issued patents for nearly 15,000 acres. "First quality" land along the Missouri was selling for as much as $6 an acre, three times the minimum amount required to purchase federal land at the time.[13] Buyers of the land were mostly planters from Virginia, Kentucky, Tennessee, and North Carolina, who came to the Booneslick with money and slaves — as did Meredith Marmaduke.

That same year (1819), a portentous event occurred on May 28 when the first steamboat strong enough to survive a trip up the Missouri River arrived at Franklin. The *Independence,* built at Pittsburgh, took 13 days to reach there from St. Louis. Carrying passengers and "a cargo of flour, whisky, sugar, iron and castings,"[14] the steamboat's arrival was celebrated by the town's residents, who staged a banquet where they offered 31 "eloquent" toasts and made speeches about the good times to come. Leaving Franklin three days later, the *Independence* chugged another 45 miles upstream before giving up and returning to St. Louis. No better luck attended the United States Army, which sent six steamboats loaded with soldiers and supplies up the Missouri in 1819, five of them so feeble they might as well have stayed tied to the waterfront at St. Louis. Two failed to get as far as Fort Bellefontaine, six miles above the mouth of the Missouri. Another sank after striking a snag at the mouth of the Osage River. Two others called at Franklin in late summer then went on upstream, one halting when its boiler failed near the Kansas River, the other clawing its way to the vicinity of present-day Omaha before halting for the winter. The sixth steamboat on the Missouri that year was the *Western Engineer,* and it was the strangest craft ever seen on the river.[15] Major Stephen H. Long, an army engineer assigned to explore the Platte River, supervised the boat's construction in Pittsburgh. He specified a hull design that drew only 30 inches of water when fully loaded, in order to navigate the western streams, and he designed part of the superstructure of the *Western Engineer* to look like a gigantic serpent, hoping the apparition would frighten any Indians he might encounter. To enhance the illusion, waste steam from the boat's three boilers vented through the serpent's large head at the bow, as the stern-mounted paddle wheel churned the muddy water. Witnesses reported that visiting Indians at Franklin were suitably impressed upon seeing a giant snake carry the boat on its back as it steamed to the town's landing.

Passengers aboard the *Western Engineer* were impressed to find Franklin a thriving commercial center so far in the wilderness, reporting that the town contained "about one hundred and twenty log houses ... several framed dwellings ... and two of brick, thirteen shops ... of merchandise, four taverns, two smiths' shops, two large team-mills, two billiard rooms, a court-house, a log prison ... post office, and a printing press. ..."[16] Although the village never achieved the prominence its original developers had envisioned, when Meredith arrived with his slaves in October 1823 Franklin was a busy commercial center, second only to St. Louis in population with nearly 1,800 residents. The town continued to prosper until the Missouri River changed its course

A Star of No Inconsiderable Magnitude

in 1826. Floods in that and subsequent years ate away the very land on which the village sat, washing away the soil until there was nothing left to hold buildings in place. In 1828, old Franklin was abandoned, some residents and businesses going to nearby New Franklin, atop the northern bluff, others relocating to Fayette, 10 miles farther north and well away from the insatiable appetite of the Missouri River, or across the river to Boonville. Eventually the river gave back the land and today corn grows on the townsite, although the fields are sometimes inundated when the ever-hungry Missouri breaks through the levee that attempts to restrain it.

This, then, was the Missouri frontier when Meredith Marmaduke arrived in the fall of 1823. He found Franklin's dusty (often muddy) streets clogged with carriages, wagons, and horsemen, with newcomers arriving almost daily by stagecoach and steamboat — a fermentable mixture of tradesmen, merchants, farmers, trappers, lawyers, doctors, teachers, soldiers, and not a few charlatans, many actively engaged in buying, selling, trading, manufacturing, and outfitting for western exploration. Although Franklin's eminence as the westernmost commercial center for an expanding nation lasted little more than a decade, the Booneslick country's prominence as "a star of no inconsiderable magnitude" has survived to today. And although he chose Franklin as his destination when he left Virginia, it appears that Meredith was not impressed with the town, perhaps doubting its stability, for in the next few years he made no effort to settle there or buy land in the river bottoms, preferring instead the high, open ground of the tallgrass prairie beyond the bluff at Arrow Rock. He made his first purchase of land in Saline County in 1828; however, before he could establish himself there he needed to "engage in a project to make a fortune" and this required developing relationships with men already in the Booneslick country, many of whom were — or would soon become — active in the economic, political, and social development of Missouri.[17]

Notes

1. "both sides of the Missouri River from the mouth of the Osage River": Walter Schroeder. *Spread of Settlement in Howard County 1810–1859. MHR*, October 1968, 2.

2. "Our company crossed the Missouri": William Becknell, *Missouri Intelligencer,* April 22, 1823.

3. The largest salt spring in the county: *History of Saline County,* 164, 200.

4. "from Fulton by Columbia, Rockport": "Advertisements in the Pioneer Press, Post Roads in 1827," *MHR,* Vol. 28, No. 3 (April 1934), 219.

5. "a rapid into which we were about to run": Louis P. Kellogg, "The Mississippi Voyage of Joliet and Marquette," *Early Narratives of the Northwest,* 1634–1699, 249.

6. "Rivière de la Mine," Floyd C. Shoemaker, *Missouri Day by Day,* Vol. 1, 266; W. Raymond Wood, compiler, *An Atlas of Early Maps of the American Midwest,* Map, Plate 1. Notes in the margin of the Bourgmont journal refer to a map that relates to his 1714 journey. It is believed that this map was prepared c.1714 by French cartographer Guillaume Delisle from information contained in the journal.

7. "came to Mine river. ... which falls into the Missouri from the south": Nicholas Biddle, *The Journals of the Expedition Under The Command of Capts. Lewis and Clark,* Vol. 1, 7. Clark's description of Arrow Rock is on page 7. September 18, 1806, on their return from the West the explorers again camped "nearly opposite to the Mine River." Biddle, Vol. 2, 544.

8. "covered with cedar trees": Henry M. Brackenridge, *Views of Louisiana,* Vol. 1, 60–62.

9. "good land, well watered and supplied with timber": Biddle, Vol. 1, 6-7.

10. "from its climate, population, soil, and productions": Report of Captain Amos Stoddard, Commandant of Upper Louisiana, March 9, 1804. Folder 4, Amos Stoddard Papers, A1577. Duane Myer, *The Heritage of Missouri*, 107.

11. "travel route known as 'the trace' ": Donald H. Welsh, ed., "Travel by Stage on the Boonslick Road," *MHR*, Vol. 54, No. 4 (July 1960), 335.

12. Ezekiel Williams's purchase of a lot in Franklin is shown on an 1820 plat map found in Folder 12, Glen O. Hardeman Papers C3655, SHSMO.

13. "First quality" land along the Missouri was selling for as much as $6 an acre: R. Douglas Hurt, "Planters and Slavery in Little Dixie," *MHR*, Vol. 88, No. 4 (July 1994), 397.

14. "a cargo of flour, whisky, sugar, iron and castings": *Missouri Intelligencer*, May 28, 1819; Floyd C. Shoemaker, *Day by Day*, Vol. 1, 364.

15. The description of the steamboats arriving at Franklin in 1819 is in: McLarty, "The First Steamboats on the Missouri," *MHR*, Vol. 51, No. 4 (July 1957), 374.

16. "about one hundred and twenty log houses . . . several framed dwellings": "Old Franklin: A Frontier Town of the Twenties," *The Mississippi Valley Historical Review*, Vol. IX, No. 4 (March 1923), 269–70.

17. "engage in a project to make a fortune": Henry Hungerford to Meredith Marmaduke, May 3, 1824. Box 1, Folder 2, Sappington-Marmaduke Papers, MHS.

CHAPTER 5

PEOPLE OF HIGH STANDING

As a frontier settlement, Franklin in the 1820s attracted an assortment of characters, most arriving in the Booneslick country intending to establish themselves as solid citizens. Many came from Kentucky and Tennessee with family roots in Virginia and were considered to be "people of high standing," by Virginia measurement.[1] Unfortunately, there were others who arrived during this period in Missouri's development that were — undoubtedly — shady characters, the sort who accompanied every jump westward in hopes of finding easy money before moving on. Those who came with more serious notions — the farmers, shopkeepers, tradesmen, and professional men who saw advantage in settlement — needed to know who was legitimate among the newcomers and who was not if they were to feel secure in their dealings with them. Two such men, respectable Tennesseans who early on settled in Howard County, were Thomas and John Hardeman, father and son, prosperous and, most importantly, acquainted with many of the Booneslick residents who would be prominent in the future of the state. After his arrival at Franklin, Meredith Marmaduke needed to make the acquaintance of such men in order to establish his bona fides, his standing as someone who was trustworthy. It was not as easy as perhaps he had hoped. Writing to his brother, Vincent, soon after reaching Missouri in October 1823, Meredith alluded to some difficulties. "I think if I understand your writing," Vincent replied in November, "you do not find the people in that country as friendly as you expected. ..." The following January, Vincent again questioned his brother's satisfaction with Missouri, saying "I should like to know ... whether you do intend to settle in that country or not as I don't think you are as much pleased with it as you hoped."[2] Meredith's relationships with people of influence in the Booneslick country were something he had to resolve quickly. In doing this, he made use of some information about John Hardeman that had come his way the previous spring.

The Hardemans

Although no record survives of their meeting if ever one existed, Meredith introduced himself to Thomas and John Hardeman soon after reaching Franklin. Father and son owned river-bottom farms five miles west of town and operated a ferry carrying travelers over the Missouri River to and from the site known as Arrow Rock. Knowledge of John Hardeman's presence on the Missouri frontier came to Meredith earlier in 1823 through a letter printed in a Washington City [Washington, DC] newspaper that circulated in Virginia. Meredith probably did not previously know of Thomas Hardeman, although he would later refer to him as "my particular old friend,"[3] but there is little doubt that when he left Virginia Meredith was aware of John Hardeman's presence in Howard County. The Hardeman family was well established in the practice of frontier settlement and business. Born in 1750, Thomas Hardeman was a fifth-generation Virginian with a love for adventurous life. His first journey west of the Appalachian Mountains occurred in 1768 when he went as far as the Cumberland Valley in Tennessee with a party of hunters and trappers, before returning to Virginia. Ten years later, a family man, Thomas moved his wife and children to the back country of western North Carolina. Seven more years passed before he felt the urge to move on once again. This time, family and possessions went by flatboat down the Holston and Tennessee Rivers and up the Ohio and Cumberland Rivers to settle near present-day Nashville. Here the family, growing to eight sons and five daughters, carved out a life as planters, storekeepers, and brokers of produce and furs. They prospered in the wilderness and Thomas eventually acquired 7,000 acres of fine Tennessee land, a goodly portion of which he divided among his children as they matured. An interest in politics ran in the family. In North Carolina and Tennessee, Thomas held county and state offices, never losing an election, and several of his sons held local offices from time to time. Although his sons were all at one time or another involved in the family's ventures, it was his second son, John, to whom Thomas felt particularly close and they often partnered in various enterprises.

In 1816, still very much the frontiersman, Thomas Hardeman again heard the call of faraway places. Nicholas Perkins Hardeman, the family biographer, describes Thomas as one who "doused the fires, called the dogs, and gathered his possessions for another wandering."[4] This time, Thomas set out alone (his wife had died and the children were on their own) and relocated to Howard County, along the Missouri River.

Although Thomas's son John had studied law and was admitted to the Tennessee bar, the legal scene was not his strong suit nor, it seems, was storekeeping of any great interest. After trying both — practicing law and operating a general store in Franklin, Tennessee, for several years — John found horticulture a more intriguing enterprise and established a farm where he experimented with various cultivation methods and different types of plants. Tiring of his Tennessee interests in 1817, John followed his father to Missouri that year, buying from him 275 acres on which he established new agricultural enterprises, Fruitage Farm and Hardeman's Garden, where he planted and harvested fruit trees and vegetables and cultivated exotic plants grown from seeds and cuttings acquired from distant places. John also bought 2,000 acres of land in central Missouri for speculation and again tried his hand at storekeeping — in Franklin, Missouri — but sold out after a few years to concentrate on his beloved farm and garden, as well as the ferry business he ran with his father.

In Tennessee, Thomas Hardeman had been an Indian fighter, a planter, politician, storekeeper, and mill owner. In Missouri, Thomas maintained an interest in politics, standing for election as a delegate from Howard County to Missouri's 1820 Constitutional Convention (a precursor to statehood in 1821). It was the only election Thomas Hardeman ever lost. There is also speculation that in the early years of the Santa Fe trade he accompanied one of the caravans, and he probably invested in one or more of those ventures. By the fall of 1823, Thomas was 74 years old, still farming and operating the ferry with John.

Missouri Senator Thomas Hart Benton had known the Hardemans in Tennessee, and he described John Hardeman as a "gentleman of science ... greatly attached to the pursuits of agriculture."[5] In 1822, as a new senator of a new state, Benton traveled up the Missouri River to visit John Hardeman at Fruitage Farm and afterward — always promoting Missouri's interests — asked him to write a description of his agricultural practices. John's reply, a copy of which Benton sent to the Washington *National Intelligencer*, was seen in that newspaper in the spring of 1823 by Henry Lee, a scion of Virginia's Lee family of Stratford Hall plantation in Westmoreland County, not far from the Marmadukes' plantation. After learning about John Hardeman's Missouri farm, Lee wrote to him in April 1823 saying he wanted to buy "3 or 4000 acres," adding "I have a wife who has been politely bred and educated, and expect to carry with me about 40 slaves."[6] Henry Lee's interest in Missouri is also shown in a letter Meredith received in October 1823 from his friend in Virginia, Dr. George R. Pitts, who reported that "Maj. Lee & family are in Fredirickburg [sic] [Virginia] and calculate on remaining the winter. ... It is the Majs. desire to move to your country as soon as his affairs are settled."[7]

Henry Lee's affairs were troublesome. The son of "Light Horse Harry" Lee, and a half brother to Civil War General Robert E. Lee, Henry is known as "Black Horse Harry" for a scandal that erupted over a love affair in 1822 with his wife's younger sister, Elizabeth, who was his ward. Black Horse Harry also misappropriated funds from Elizabeth's inheritance trust, and tried to conceal the theft by marrying her to a shady suitor. Henry Lee's problems only grew worse when he was forced to sell the Lee family's ancestral home, Stratford Hall, in order to settle the charge of embezzlement of his ward's funds.

Henry Lee was four years older than Meredith Marmaduke; as neighbors in Westmoreland County, they had grown up knowing each other. Lee undoubtedly was aware of Meredith's interest in Missouri. It is reasonable to envision the two of them meeting at Henry Hungerford's tavern discussing John Hardeman's expansive description of farming in Missouri — in which he (tongue-in-cheek) tells of harvesting 1,200 pounds of cotton per acre, and digging radishes three feet long and turnips nearly a yard in circumference — and talking to each other about going west.[8] Expecting Lee to move to Missouri (perhaps to join him in some capacity), Meredith was disappointed to learn otherwise while he was in New Mexico late in 1824, writing to John Hardeman that he regretted "to learn Major Lee's determination, knowing as I do, his disposition. I fear the situation which he is about to assume will be his entire ruin."[9] Lee remained in the east, eventually regaining respectability after befriending the future president, Andrew Jackson. A political speech writer, biographer, and historian, Lee died in Paris in 1837.

John Hardeman was 15 years older than Meredith and was knowledgeable about frontier ways. When they met in Howard County, they quickly discovered many common interests. Both were experienced in legal affairs. John had studied law and was admitted to the Tennessee Bar in 1810, though he did not establish a practice; Meredith for six years had drafted and served legal documents for a Virginia chancery court and thereby gained enough knowledge to draw up his own contracts and other legal papers. John had operated a general store in Tennessee for several years; Meredith had leanings in that direction. John was a farmer; Meredith intended to have a plantation in Missouri. In many ways, Meredith Marmaduke's interests mirrored the life of John Hardeman, so it is not unusual to discover the two quickly becoming allied, relying upon each other for advice and assistance with business and personal matters that grew to encompass property, money, even family members. They trusted each other enough that they traded powers of attorney, Meredith doing so eight months after arriving at Franklin. On May 14, 1824, two days before he left Franklin to travel to Santa Fe, Meredith appointed John Hardeman the agent for his affairs while he was gone that summer. He restated his confidence in John in a letter written soon after his arrival at Santa Fe, when he determined that he would remain in New Mexico until the following spring.

William Becknell

John and Thomas Hardeman undoubtedly helped Meredith meet people who were influential in the Booneslick settlements. One person he sought out for information about New Mexico was 35-year-old William Becknell, who had already led two successful trading caravans to Santa Fe. Accompanied by five men, Becknell left Franklin on September 1, 1821, and headed for the Southwest. Their string of horses carried packs holding cloth goods and small personal and household items they hoped to sell upon reaching New Mexico. In some respects, William Becknell's 1821 probing expedition established a pattern of organization and conduct for the yearly caravans that prevailed throughout the life of the Santa Fe trade. A notice placed by Becknell in the June 25, 1821, issue of the *Missouri Intelligencer* spelled out the responsibilities of members of the proposed company, saying they were bound "by oath to submit to such orders and rules as the company when assembled shall think proper to enforce." Each man was to equip himself with "a horse, a good rifle, and as much ammunition as the company may think necessary for a two or 3 months trip. ... Every man will furnish his equal part of the fitting out of our trade, and receive an equal part of the product." Anticipating 30 men joining his company, Becknell believed that an investment of $10 from each would be sufficient to purchase "the quantity of merchandise to be traded on."[10] The benefits derived from sales were to be divided among the company members when they returned to Missouri. With the exception of operating as a stock company, sharing costs and profits, the basic mold for most future Santa Fe trading companies was established around these terms. Traders always traveled together for companionship and the protection a large group afforded against aggressive Indians, but most future Santa Fe traders would buy and transport merchandise at their own expense and profit — or suffer loss — as individual entrepreneurs or in partnership with one or two others.

His early expeditions to New Mexico earned William Becknell the sobriquet "Founder of the Santa Fe Trail." But he and those who accompanied him deserve credit for more than opening a profitable avenue of trade between St. Louis and Mexico. The silver and gold coins and bullion, the Spanish woolen blankets, the furs, and the livestock (horses and mules) they brought back sparked the beginning of a lively commerce with the Southwest that would enrich the Booneslick country and establish Missouri as the dominant state on the American frontier for many years. Not until the Union Pacific Railroad laid its track on the west bank of the Missouri River at Omaha in 1865 would Missouri's position be seriously challenged. Becknell's success in the Santa Fe trade also marked him as someone whose advice would be helpful to anyone contemplating going there.

Augustus Storrs

Another Franklin resident with whom Meredith soon became acquainted was Augustus Storrs. During the winter of 1823–24, Meredith worked as a clerk in the mercantile store that Storrs operated at Franklin. At one time the town's postmaster, later appointed clerk to the Missouri legislature, Storrs was well connected politically. Already a veteran of one trip to Santa Fe, Storrs would travel with Meredith in the 1824 caravan, taking a stock of goods to trade. After his return from the Southwest in the fall of 1824, Storrs was asked by Senator Thomas H. Benton to write a report about his Santa Fe experience. Storrs's lengthy letter answered 22 questions posed to him by Benton, who then presented the report to the U.S. Senate and sent a copy to the popular weekly newspaper, *Niles' Weekly Register*, knowing it would be read by many people who had more than a casual interest in the westward expansion of trade. In the conclusion of his report, Storrs recommended the "appointment of two agents to that country [Mexico] ... [in] considerations of our own interest and other benefits that would flow from it. The one [agent] to reside at Chihuahua, the seat of government of the internal provinces, with powers to negotiate concerning the duty. ... The other to reside at Santa Fe, with powers ... to form treaties of peace," with Indians of the southwest.[11] In the spring of 1825 Storrs's recommendations were accepted by Congress and the administration (with the helping hand of Thomas Benton), and within two months' time he was appointed by President John Quincy Adams to be the United States Consul at Santa Fe. Augustus Storrs eventually obtained Mexican citizenship and in 1831 moved to Chihuahua to engage in business as a trader. Having a friend at court in Santa Fe undoubtedly would be beneficial to Meredith in the next few years, although there is no evidence that he and Storrs collaborated in any way.

Samuel McClure

The circumstances of the first meeting between Meredith and Colonel Samuel McClure are unknown but in the spring of 1824 the two men came together in Franklin and formed a partnership to engage in that year's expedition to Santa Fe. They also established a friendship that, like so many of Meredith's future financial and political alliances, evolved into a combined business and social relationship that endured throughout their lives. The two also had much in common. Of Irish birth, McClure was a year older than Meredith and he, too, had been active in a Virginia militia company during the War of 1812. Samuel's family settled near Wheeling, in Ohio County, Virginia (now West Virginia), after migrating from Ireland around the turn of the 19th century. When the War of 1812 began, McClure enlisted in a local militia and by 1814 he was the captain of a cavalry company raised in Ohio County and attached to the Third Regiment of Virginia Cavalry. Later, McClure and his company were one of two

Ohio County units sent east to Norfolk, in the Tidewater region, to guard against raids by British naval and marine forces.[12] When the war ended, McClure returned to his home near Wheeling and lived there for a time with his wife and young daughter. The first evidence of his presence in Missouri is in January 1820 when a notice appeared in a St. Louis newspaper that a letter was being held for him in the post office in St. Louis. After his return from Santa Fe (in 1825), Samuel was reported in Mexico again during the summer of 1826 when he obtained a permit from the governor at Santa Fe to travel and trade in Sonora and Chihuahua.[13] McClure eventually settled in Saline County, Missouri, with his family and remained there until 1835 when he returned to Ohio County, Virginia, to live on a farm he called Cherry Hill. His affairs in Missouri were not complete when he left in 1835, so early the following year he asked Meredith for help in collecting money owed him. Some difficulties arose and in July 1836 he again wrote to his friend, this time to apologize for the problems Meredith had encountered, saying he was "truly sorry that my Friends has put you to so mutch [sic] trouble in collecting, both on your account & theirs. I was in hopes as the amt. was not large that they would of come forward & lifted their notes & not put themselves to the expense and you to the trouble of Bringing suits on them. However they must falt [sic] themselves as they had time & no undue advantage taken. I must confess that I feel sorry that you were compelled to resort to Legal Means but as you say it was useless to wait longer. When I look at my mode of doing business, often paying well for indulgence, additional trouble & little thanks ... I must say the plan is not a good one."[14]

The practice of calling upon one's friends for assistance in pursuing financial and legal matters was commonplace in the early years of the 19th century. The absence of a national currency, compounded by the fluctuating exchange rates of the various bank-issued currencies in circulation; a scarcity of courts in some places; the distance traveled and time spent in trying to stay abreast of one's financial dealings (especially when accounts were not paid); and debtors who often fled to less-organized regions of the country to avoid payment were problems faced by all who entered into contracts or transacted business during those years. Throughout his lifetime, Meredith was often asked to assist in collecting debts owed his friends and he often found himself asking others for the same courtesy. Over the years, Sam McClure and Meredith continued to correspond with each other and occasionally, when Meredith passed through Wheeling while going to and returning from Westmoreland County, were able to visit and reminisce about their Santa Fe adventure. Living with Sam (now a widower) at Cherry Hill in 1850 were his aged mother and aunt, his widowed daughter and her 12-year-old son, and a sister-in-law. He remained in Virginia until his death at age 77 in 1867.

Dr. John Sappington

Often crossing the Missouri River to Howard County from his home in Saline County, Dr. John Sappington was a frequent passenger on the Hardemans' ferry, and it is not far-fetched to imagine John Hardeman in 1823 suggesting to Meredith Marmaduke that he speak with the doctor about the potential for prospering in the Booneslick country. Meredith did meet Dr. Sappington sometime that winter, although exactly when is unknown, and it proved to be a fruitful convergence. No one among the many "people of high standing" Meredith met at Franklin during the winter of 1823–24 had more influence on his life than did John Sappington. Their close relationship during the next 32 years, until Sappington's death in 1856, could easily be considered that of father and son; indeed, Meredith found in John Sappington the father he had lost when an infant, the father he never knew. In coming years, Dr. Sappington would be Meredith's mentor and the two men would combine their talents to build a family-based commercial and political enterprise whose scope ultimately encompassed the state and in some respects reached from Michigan to the Gulf of Mexico.

Born in Maryland in 1776, John Sappington was 9 years old when his father, Dr. Mark Sappington, summoned by *his* brother John, also a physician, moved his family to the Cumberland River basin near Nashville in central Tennessee. There Mark Sappington prospered as a physician and merchant until his death in the early 1790s (his brother John died in New Orleans during the same period). As a youth, Mark's son John studied medicine under his father's tutelage, acquiring the knowledge and skills necessary to become a physician in early 19th-century America. In 1804, John married a Kentucky girl, Jane Breathitt, and the couple lived for several years at Franklin, Tennessee, south of Nashville, where John practiced medicine and became a respected member of the community.[15] In 1807, he and Jane moved to Kentucky to be near members of her politically oriented Breathitt family, but in two years returned to Tennessee where John resumed his medical practice and "initiated a period of personal economic success" by speculating in land and trading and transporting cotton and tobacco that he sold in New Orleans.[16] Franklin, Tennessee, was also the home of the prosperous Hardeman family and of Thomas Hart Benton, then a young lawyer practicing in Nashville and the surrounding area. A close friendship, with business interests, developed among Dr. Sappington, Thomas Benton, and members of the Hardeman family, all of whom were seeking to prosper in the nascent agricultural economy of central and western Tennessee.

In the winter of 1814, perhaps seeking formal recognition of his professional ability, John Sappington, now 38 years old, traveled to Philadelphia to study medicine at the University of Pennsylvania. Already possessing considerable experience as a practical, "hands-on" frontier doctor, he must have found academic study less than fruitful as he failed to complete the curriculum to receive a degree from that institution, leaving in the spring of 1815. His medical knowledge, however, was sufficient to enable him to continue to practice at Franklin, Tennessee, where he remained until 1817. That year, responding to an adventurous inclination and seeking opportunities for greater wealth by speculating in land, he moved his family — Jane and their seven children — to Missouri Territory. Prior to the move, Thomas Hart Benton — now living in St. Louis and sensing Missouri's economic potential, knowing that good men were needed to settle the frontier — offered Sappington inducements to relocate to Missouri where he believed "the foundations of a great fortune" could be laid in buying and selling land.[17] Dr. Sappington and his family reportedly made the trip from Tennessee "with their servants [slaves] in carriages," accompanied by a party of neighbors "including Jesse Lankford, a master builder in Sappington's employ."[18] When this entourage reached St. Louis, Benton assigned his personal slave to act as Sappington's guide, loaned him money to buy land, and gave the doctor letters of introduction to contacts in the city and territory who could help him find tracts worth purchasing for speculation. Among those contacts were famed explorer William Clark, now the superintendent for Indian affairs in the West, and General William Rector, surveyor general for federal lands in Illinois, Missouri, and Arkansas.

Dr. Sappington eventually moved his family to Howard County and settled near Glasgow, on the Missouri River, where he practiced medicine and studied the country. Two years later, he relocated to Saline County and established his home and medical practice at Jonesboro (present-day Napton) on the prairie seven miles beyond the village of Arrow Rock. He is described as "eminently a doctor who rode horseback and practiced medicine," traits that quickly attracted a large following in the Booneslick country.[19]

One of Sappington's medical tenets flew in the face of contemporary practice in an age when medical knowledge based upon provable science was scant and not far removed from sorcery. He did not believe that a patient could be bled to good health, an erroneous "cure" whose origin in medical lore predates the birth of Christ. Bleeding was widely trumpeted by Dr. Benjamin Rush from his position as professor of medical theory at the University of Pennsylvania in the early 1800s. Ridding someone of "bad humors" by bleeding was a prevalent medical practice during much of the 18th and 19th centuries (George Washington, for one, was bled until he died from shock caused by an insufficiency of blood). Sappington's experience had shown him the inefficacy of bleeding as a method of treatment and he refused to do it. As a result, undoubtedly many of his patients were relieved of their ailments instead of dying from inappropriate therapy.

Sappington's principal interest in advancing medical knowledge, however, was the development of a quinine pill to treat sufferers of what was popularly called the "ague" — malaria, a disease whose origin was unknown but whose deadly effects were widespread throughout much of the nation. He and other progressive physicians had long relied upon quinine in the form of ground-up "Peruvian bark" (stripped from the cinchona tree, a tropical plant) to provide relief to malarial patients. In 1823, a chemical derivative, quinine sulphate powder, became available in large quantities. Through experimentation over the next decade, the good doctor developed a process to manufacture the powder in the form of a tablet he named "Sappington's Anti-Fever Pills." National distribution of the pills followed and by the middle 1830s his company, Sappington and Sons, was an economic success.

His steadfast application of commonsense therapy (patients who were not bled or purged did better than those who were subjected to these treacherous practices), and his faith in the efficacy of quinine to relieve the debilitating fevers, headaches, and painful joints caused by malaria placed Dr. Sappington far ahead of the majority of his colleagues (some of whom voiced strong opposition to his beliefs) in the care of patients. Conversely, his efforts earned him great respect throughout the country by those who were beneficiaries of his kind of medicine.

John G. Miller

Many of the men Meredith met in Franklin and Howard County in the 1820s were political and commercial leaders who, in the years preceding the Civil War, transformed the state from a wilderness to an agricultural and commercial power, gateway to the expanding West. Among these was John G. Miller, a Virginian who arrived at Franklin in 1817 to manage the federal land office, and who made Howard County his home until near the end of his life, dying in St. Louis in 1846. When Missouri governor Frederick Bates died in 1825 (still in office), Miller sought to replace him and with support from Thomas Hart Benton won the office in a special election. A popular politician, he was unopposed in the 1828 election for the governorship, and later served six years as a representative in the U.S. Congress. As governor, Miller eased his friend Meredith Marmaduke into Saline County political offices, appointing him successively to the positions of surveyor, justice of the peace, and justice of the county court, all in the relatively short span of four years between 1827 and 1831. (There is no question but that Dr. Sappington also had a hand in advancing Meredith's political career.)

The two men remained close friends and firm political allies throughout their lives. Retired from Congress in 1842, in December of 1845 — nearing his 65th birthday — with his political antennae still active, Miller wrote a long letter to Meredith to express his concerns about the deliberations of members of a state constitutional convention: "From what little I have seen of the proceedings ... I very much fear it will aim to do too much. I consider our constitution as it now stands, in the general, a most safe and amiable one. I therefore hope the convention will ... touch upon it lightly."[20] John Miller, active in Missouri politics for many years, died three months later. Described as "neither combative by nature nor unduly partisan,"[21] Miller projected a style of political leadership emulated by Meredith Marmaduke.

Thomas Adams Smith

Another influential Franklin resident Meredith came to know soon after arriving in Missouri was retired Brigadier General Thomas Adams Smith, for whom Fort Smith, Arkansas, is named. As commander of the Ninth Military District, Smith supervised Major Stephen Long's surveys of the Arkansas River valley in 1817. Resigning his commission the following year he was appointed receiver of public monies at Franklin, Missouri, a post he held for 10 years. Smith had solid political connections in Washington, where he was a "fast friend" of Thomas Hart Benton. He even loaned Benton a set of pistols that he used in two duels with attorney Charles Lucas in 1817. During a legal hearing in St. Louis, Lucas said something that the always testy Benton interpreted as an affront to his honor and he challenged Lucas to a duel. The two met on Bloody Island in the Mississippi River on August 12 and fired at each other. Lucas was wounded in the neck, Benton in a leg. Lucas's wound prevented him from continuing the duel and Benton released his opponent from any further obligation. But peace eluded the combatants. Rumors spread that Benton had acted unfairly. In response, a second challenge was sent by Benton to Lucas, who accepted. The two met again September 27 and this time Benton's shot was true. Lucas fell mortally wounded and died within an hour.[22]

In 1828, after purchasing 5,000 acres of land in Saline County, Brigadier General Smith moved to a farm on Salt Fork Creek a few miles west of where Meredith had begun to acquire land. Smith named his farm "Experiment," ostensibly because he knew little about farming. He and Meredith were associated in numerous Saline County activities in coming years. In 1830, Smith acted as a go-between and provided a reference for mill owner Johnson Wetmore who wanted to hire one of Meredith's slaves: "The Genl. Has been kind enough to say that he will speak to you on the subject of security for his [the slave's] hire," wrote Wetmore, "which I understand the advertisement mentions."[23]

Meredith and General Smith appear together again in documents in 1835 when they were asked by the descendants of John Hardeman to oversee the disposition of slaves in the settlement of his estate.[24] General Thomas Smith died at his home in Saline County in 1844.

Other Early Booneslick Connections

Another influential Booneslick resident Meredith befriended in his endeavor to establish himself as a respectable citizen on the frontier was Captain Alphonso Wetmore. Since 1819 Franklin had been Wetmore's headquarters as paymaster for army regiments stationed at posts on the western frontier. An avid writer and historian, Wetmore authored a play, produced in a St. Louis theater in 1821, and wrote stories and articles for various periodicals. He also found time to collect information about the Santa Fe Trail and its commerce, and twice in the early years of the trade he was called upon to provide reports to Congress.

In the spring of 1824, Meredith asked Alphonso Wetmore, who was going to travel east, to assist him in the transfer of money from Virginia to Missouri. Part of the money Meredith subsequently sent in a letter to a "Mr. Powell" in New Orleans; he became uneasy when Powell didn't receive it as expected, and Meredith wrote to John Hardeman inquiring about the matter. That fall, Meredith, then at "Tous. N. Mexico" [Taos, New Mexico], wrote to Hardeman, trying to clarify for him the date the money was sent. Meredith said he was dismayed to learn that "Mr. Powell should not have recd. his money in time ... but think it probable that no accident has befallen it. You recollect that Capt. Wetmore was detained much longer to the east than expected. Shortly after his return I recd. the money of him & in the presence of Mr. Geo. Knox, enclosed it to Mr. Powell. Mr. Knox also waited on me and saw me deliver the letter to W. Samuels P.M. [postmaster] which was Mr. Powell's instructions to me. ... Now I do not think that I recd the money from Capt W. earlier than between the 1st & 10th May so that there could not have been time for the letter to have reached N. Orleans before he [Powell] wrote [to Hardeman]."[25]

Six months after leaving Virginia and arriving unknown on the Missouri frontier, Meredith Marmaduke already enjoyed the acquaintance, friendship, and trust of influential people in the region, men who were shaping the future of Missouri and of the nation as it expanded westward. His association with these "men of high standing," these "shakers and movers," was not short term; in most cases the relationships would continue until death, each man contributing to the welfare and success of the other as best he could. Meredith recognized the advantages to himself of such close affiliations, and the mutual trust they engendered, as the basis for his future business and political success. He practiced this *modus vivendi* for the rest of his life.

People of High Standing

Notes

1. "people of high standing": Vincent Marmaduke to Meredith Marmaduke, November 10, 1823. Sappington-Marmaduke Papers, Box 1, Folder 2, MHS.

2. "I should like to know … whether you do intend to settle in that country": Vincent Marmaduke to Meredith Marmaduke, January 22, 1824. Sappington-Marmaduke Papers, Box 1, Folder 2, MHS.

3. "my particular old friend": Meredith Marmaduke to John Hardeman, August 5, 1824. Sappington-Marmaduke Papers, Box 1, Folder 3, MHS.

4. "doused the fires, called the dogs and gathered his possessions for another wandering": Nicholas Hardeman, *Wilderness Calling*, 13.

5. "a gentleman of science … greatly attached to the pursuits of agriculture": *Missouri Intelligencer*, June 10, 1823, Reel 10950, Newspaper Archives, SHSMO.

6. "I have a wife who has been politely bred and educated": Henry Lee to John Hardeman, April 1, 1823. Glen O. Hardeman Papers, C3655, Folder 5. SHSMO manuscript collection.

7. "Maj. Lee & family are in Fredericksburg": George R. Pitts to Meredith Marmaduke, October 20, 1823. Marmaduke Papers, C1021, Folder 2. SHSMO manuscript collection.

8. Henry Hungerford's tavern in Washington Court House is mentioned in a letter from him to Meredith Marmaduke June 15, 1831, Sappington-Marmaduke Papers, Box 1, Folder 7, MHS. Hungerford had lost his wife two months previously, his children were living with their grandmother "and my youngest with a wet nurse … What to do for support … I know not. I have been obliged to abandon keeping tavern."

9. "to learn Major Lee's determination": Meredith Marmaduke to John Hardeman, October 15, 1824. Glen O. Hardeman Papers, C3655, Folder 5. SHSMO manuscript collection.

10. "by oath to submit to such orders and rules": *Missouri Intelligencer*, June 25, 1821, Reel 11512, Newspaper Archives, SHSMO.

11. "appointment of two agents to that country": *Niles' Weekly Register*, Vol. 27, January 15, 1825, 316. In addition to Augustus Storrs, another Missouri resident, Joshua Pilcher — fur trader, Indian agent, merchant in St. Louis, and owner at the time of the Missouri Fur Company, also a friend of Senator Benton — was appointed a U.S. Consul to Mexico. Pilcher's post was at Chihuahua, capital of the Mexican state immediately south of New Mexico; however, he was unable to accept the assignment because of illness. In 1838, President Martin Van Buren named Pilcher as superintendent of Indian affairs at St. Louis to succeed the venerable William Clark, a position he held until his death in 1843. Pilcher's tenure in the Indian bureau was threatened in 1840 and he turned to Meredith Marmaduke for help. Pilcher wrote a five-page letter in which he explained his duties and area of responsibility, giving reasons for maintaining his office at St. Louis. He mentions numerous attempts to transfer the office to Clay County, Missouri, and characterizes those who wanted to transfer the office as seeking to profit themselves from the purchase and disbursement of Indian treaty goods. Eight days after writing his first letter, Pilcher sent a second, brief, letter to Marmaduke, thanking him for his "attention to my report," and saying he thought he could defeat the attempt "in Congress." Beyond this, there is no evidence of a relationship between Pilcher and Meredith; however, both were members of the Freemasons of Missouri and it is likely that they were acquainted: Joshua Pilcher to Meredith Marmaduke, December 16 and 24, 1840. Sappington-Marmaduke Papers, Box 2, Folder 6, MHS.

12. Samuel McClure's service in the War of 1812 is found in Virgil A. Lewis, *The soldiery of West Virginia*, 167; Stuart Butler, *Guide to Virginia Militia Units in the War of 1812*, 155.

13. McClure's presence in New Mexico during August and September of 1826 is reported by David J. Weber, *The Taos Trappers*. University of Oklahoma Press, Norman, 119–20, fn.14.

14. "I am truly sorry that my Friends has put you to so mutch trouble in collecting": Samuel McClure to Meredith Marmaduke, July, n.d., 1836. Sappington-Marmaduke Papers, Box 2, Folder 2, MHS.

15. In 1804, John married a Kentucky girl, Jane Breathitt: Breathitt family members were important political leaders in Kentucky. Jane's brother, John, was elected to the Kentucky legislature in 1811 and later served as the state's lieutenant governor and governor. Another brother, James, also served in the state's

legislature during 1818–19, and James Breathitt Jr., a descendant of John, held state offices during the early decades of the 20th century.

16. "initiated a period of personal economic success": Lynn Morrow, "Dr. John Sappington, Southern Patriarch in the New West," *MHR*, Vol. 90, No. 1 (October 1995), 39–40. Missouri historian Lynn Morrow relates that "From the Revolutionary War to the Civil War, the [Sappington] family produced a dozen or more 'Dr. Sappingtons' from Chesapeake Bay to east Texas."

17. "the foundations of a great fortune" could be laid in buying and selling land. Ibid, 41.

18. "with their servants in carriages": Hall, Thomas B. Jr., and Thomas B. Hall III., *Dr. John Sappington of Saline County, Missouri 1776–1856*, 3.

19. "eminently a doctor who rode horseback and practiced medicine": Ibid, 4.

20. "From what little I have seen of the proceedings": John Miller to Meredith Marmaduke, December 11, 1845. Sappington-Marmaduke Papers, Box 3, Folder 6, MHS.

21. "neither combative by nature nor unduly partisan": Perry McCandless, John Miller 1781–1846, *Dictionary of Missouri Biography*, 547.

22. Benton-Lucas duel: Charles Lucas's second in both duels with Benton was Joshua Barton, an ancestor of the author and the brother of Missouri's first senator, David Barton (named to the office prior to Benton's appointment as a Missouri senator). In 1816, Joshua dueled with Thomas Hempstead, the brother of Missouri's first territorial representative. Benton served as Hempstead's second. No blood was let in this event; however, all parties gained "considerable notoriety." Partially as a result of these duels, bad blood existed between David Barton and Thomas H. Benton, already on opposite sides of the political fence, never reconciling their differences. At the time of the 1817 Benton-Lucas duels, Joshua Barton was the U.S. district attorney for St. Louis. He would himself die in a duel on Bloody Island in 1823.

23. "The Genl. Has been kind enough to say": Johnson Wetmore to Marmaduke, September 5, 1830. B1, F6, Sappington-Marmaduke Papers, MHS.

24. oversee the disposition of the slaves: Bond for $6,000 given by J. Locke Hardeman, Thomas Hardeman and Lucretia Hardeman to Thomas A. Smith and Meredith Marmaduke, March 11, 1835. Box 2, Folder 2, Sappington-Marmaduke Papers, MHS.

25. "Mr. Powell should not have recd. his money": Meredith Marmaduke's explanation of his actions with regard to Alphonso Wetmore and "Mr. Powell" in the spring of 1824 is in Marmaduke to John Hardeman, October 15, 1824. Glen O. Hardeman Papers, C3655, Folder 5. SHSMO.

CHAPTER 6
CONCEALED INTENTIONS

Going to Santa Fe was not something Meredith Marmaduke mentioned in letters he sent to friends and relatives in Virginia during the fall of 1823. Whatever his intentions were in that regard, he kept to himself. Instead he wrote about his health, which had been a concern when he left Virginia and was now considerably improved, and asked for news from home. And he tried to interest some of his Virginia correspondents in joining him in Missouri. Replies to his letters undoubtedly helped him cope with feelings of loneliness brought on by his family and friends being so distant, but they also sometimes brought disquieting information. Excerpts from some of those letters disclose the two-sided nature of such correspondence.

"Dear Brother ... your letter dated the 2 of October gave me great satisfaction to hear of your good health. ... Betsy [Vincent's wife] was delivered of a fine son on the 23 of September and had a pretty good time and the child kep [sic] well for three or four weeks and then was taken sick and lay for ten or twelve days as sick a poor thing as you ever saw. I thought there was no hopes of its being sav'd, but thanks be to god it has recovered in a great measure so that I think it is out of danger. ... I saw our sister yesterday and all the family and red [sic] your letter to her which gave her great satisfaction. ... I remain your affectionate brother until death, Vincent Marmaduke."[1]

"Dear Uncle ... all the family were extremely glad to hear that your health are much improving. ... My mother has been very ill since you left here. She was first taken with a breaking out on her face, arms & breast — afterward a violent pain in the head ensued which continued 10 or 12 Days. She was amediately [sic] bled, evacuated and blistered, but she at this time is nearly relieved from the pain, and mending so as she can go about. ... I expect we shall all go out with you when you come, in the fall of 1825. ... I remain your most affectionate nephew, Vincent McClanahan."[2]

"Dear Cousin ... agreeable to your request I shall give you a detail of what has transpired since you left Virginia. There has been a great many deaths, and among the rest Mrs. Graham['s] son, Lucy Frasier, Mr. Clifford, Mr. Murrah, Mrs. Belfield, Mrs. Horlslick, and cousin Richard Redmun, and I think more children. ... May you be happy in life, tranquil in death, and if we never meet on earth, I hope we will where distance can never separate congenial minds, or death disfavor the kiss of kindred or affection, and write in sweet Hosannas to the living God is the prayer of your affectionate cousin, Frances."[3]

Meredith wrote to Henry Hungerford on October 25 and if he mentioned going to

Santa Fe, the declaration made no impression on Hungerford. His six-page reply to Meredith, written four days after the start of the new year, is all about Westmoreland County politics:

"I would have wrote you before this, but for one cause or other — to reply to the serious subjects detailed in yours would consume all my paper. I will therefore only wish you a continuation of increase of health & much prosperity, and proceed to give you a little important information from this quarter. ... Your old friend, Mr. Fox [the county clerk], is no more & John Graham Esq., is elected his successor. Never did fortune frown on or thwart the view of anyone more than myself, on this occasion."[4] Hungerford was in Alexandria when Fox died and though he tried to rally support for his election to the office on his return to Westmoreland County, Hungerford's effort was unsuccessful.

Vincent Marmaduke also wrote in January (again, no mention of Santa Fe), telling Meredith about the clerk's death, and offering an interesting bit of additional information: "I expect you have heard about the death of Mr. Fox. He departed this life some time in the month of December and there was a number of candidates for the clerkship. I do not know how the votes was but John Grayham is the clerk. I had a conversation with Col. Middleton on the subject of the office and he said if you were here there would be little or no opposition as he should vote for you in preference to any other man."[5] Meredith's nascent political ambition, set aside when he left Virginia the previous summer, would lie dormant for the next several years while he concentrated on making money in the Santa Fe trade.

A Decision is Made

Meredith kept his intention to enter the Santa Fe trade a secret from his family and closest friends before leaving Virginia and said nothing in letters he wrote to them after arriving in Missouri, yet he apparently had that in mind all the time. Finally, in early December 1823 he brought the matter out of the shadows. Writing to an acquaintance in Virginia, he mentioned he would be leaving Missouri on an extended trip to Mexico. A few days later, writing to his brother, Vincent, he chose to not disclose this information. Did he believe that such news coming so soon after his exodus from Virginia would be upsetting to family members? Judging from the reactions of his brother and sister when they did hear about his proposed trip, this is likely.

"We recvd. your letter dated the 9 of December," Vincent Marmaduke replied in late January, "which gave us great satisfaction to hear of your good health and all yours along with you. ... I saw a letter the other day you rote [sic] to Mr. Norwood saying something about your going to take a rout over the rocky mountains for a considerable time which I would not advise you to do as you have just got good health. I think I should try to take better care of it than that as I know you can live without exposing your self in that way."[6]

When Meredith's eldest sister, Elizabeth (wife of John McClanahan), learned about her "Dear Brother" intending to go west — fearful that he might perish in the wilderness — she implored him to abandon his plan and return to Virginia. "I long to see you and I hope you will not neglect coming here at the time you mentioned, if I should survive until that time. Let me persuade you not to embark on that journey you mentioned to South America [Mexico] for I believe if you should that you will never more return. I am sincerely sorry that ever you had such a thought."[7] Elizabeth's pitiful plea, not mailed until the last week of May, arrived in Missouri too late for Meredith to read, as he was already on the long trail to Santa Fe.

Meredith's interest in Santa Fe may have been sparked by reports of the gains made by traders going there in 1821 and 1822. News of the William Becknell and Benjamin Cooper expeditions in those years circulated among newspapers in the east and would have been seen. Meredith also may have read Zebulon Pike's journal, *An Account of Expeditions to the Sources of the Mississippi and through the Western parts of Louisiana*, published in 1810, translated into several languages and widely distributed. Pike was a career soldier, a young lieutenant, when he was sent from St. Louis in the summer of 1806 with instructions from General James Wilkinson, governor of Louisiana Territory, to complete several assignments dealing with the Osage, Kansa, and Pawnee Indians. Wilkinson also tasked him with mapping the Arkansas River to the western border of the Louisiana Territory while recording his observations of the geography, mineral and other resources, and the people he might encounter. After exploring the Arkansas River, he was to then find the Red River and follow that waterway southeast, recording the same observations, before returning to St. Louis. In accomplishing these tasks, he would not only broaden knowledge of the newly acquired territory adjacent to Mexico, he would also help establish awareness of the United States' administration of a region whose boundaries were being disputed by Spanish authorities in Mexico.

Completing his assignment with the Pawnee in Nebraska, Pike made his way to the Arkansas River in today's central Kansas and followed it to its headwaters in the Rocky Mountains, discovering Pike's Peak on the way. At the Royal Gorge, Pike turned south into the San Juan Valley in territory claimed by Spain. Discovered there that winter by Spanish troops who had been alerted to their presence, Pike and his men were taken into custody and escorted to Santa Fe before being sent on to Chihuahua for interrogation by military authorities. Accused of being a spy, the Mexican authorities escorted Pike (and his soldiers) out of Mexico and released them at Natchitoches, Louisiana, in June 1807. Pike's account of his expeditions gave Americans their first good look at the land and the people of the Louisiana Purchase territory, and opened their eyes to the potential it held for exploitation and settlement. His maps and description of the land between Missouri and New Mexico, along with his depiction of the social, business, and political life in Mexico, were instrumental in the future establishment of the Santa Fe Trail, over which commercial traffic began to travel following Mexico's independence from Spain in 1821. Given his interest in Santa Fe and the possibility of trading there, it is unlikely that Meredith Marmaduke would have failed to acquire and read a copy of Pike's report on his travel to the Southwest.

Success and Failure of the Early Traders
Leeds Town, 3rd May 1824
Dear Colonel,
The want of capital in this country, and enterprise, will prevent me from engaging with you in your proposed project to make a fortune. I should like very much to be rich, but being deficient in the aforgoing [sic] requisites, together with a

dreadful apprehension of the Indians, tomahawks & scalping knives, induces me at once, to say, I cannot accept of your proposition.[8]

With little money and less taste for adventure, Henry Hungerford states plainly that no matter how difficult life is in Virginia, he is not interested in exposing his scalp to the heathens of the western plains, even if it means passing up an opportunity to "make a fortune." His response to Meredith's entreaty, written "about three weeks since," to join him on the upcoming trading expedition to Santa Fe points up the most significant problem faced by anyone setting out on the path to New Mexico — Indians whose land they had to cross. In 1792, Pedro Vial certainly had his trouble with Indians along what would become the Santa Fe Trail. One of the earliest travelers between Santa Fe and St. Louis, Vial, of French Creole origin, was commissioned by Governor Fernando de la Concha (administrator of New Mexico under the Spanish Crown) to travel between Santa Fe and St. Louis, and return with a report on the "daily distances; the rivers he finds [and] their flow ... the mountains and tablelands which present themselves to him ... the tribes he finds, their customs ... and whatever else he believes can be of use for new information and clearness."[9]

Riding horses, Vial and two young companions left Santa Fe on May 21, traveling east out of the Rocky Mountains into the Great Plains, their destination the Missouri River, which they were instructed to follow downstream to St. Louis once they found it. All went well until they reached the Arkansas River somewhere in Kansas on June 29, at which time they came upon a band of "Cances" Indians hunting buffalo. "We found them about four in the afternoon in their hunting camp on the [opposite] shore of the Napeste River," Vial wrote in his report. "As they approached us on the opposite side with river between us, we fired some shots into the air, to get them to see us. They immediately set out and came to stop us. ..." Although friendly at first, the Indians (of the Kansa tribe) soon changed their tactics, and "took possession of our horses, and of all our possessions and cut the clothes which we wore with knives ... leaving us totally naked. They were of a mind to kill us, whereupon some of them cried out ... to not kill us with guns or arrows because of the great risk that would be run of killing one another as they surrounded us; but that if they killed us it should be by hatchet blows or by spears."

In such a contentious situation, exactly how Vial was able to understand the Indians' intentions is unclear, and he may be forgiven for a bit of literary drama in describing their predicament, but a subsequent event shows how close he and his companions came to losing their lives. As the Indians continued to threaten them, one of Vial's companions had "a dagger thrust in the abdomen which would have proved fatal had he not shrunk away when the blow was delivered." A nearby Indian who tried to parry the dagger thrust was severely wounded with an injury to an arm. Although the three explorers were spared death, they found themselves held as captives, "naked in the [Arkansas River] camp until the fifteenth of August," when the Indians took them to their village on the Kansas River.[10] The ordeal of Vial and his companions did not end until French fur traders procured their release some weeks later. Outfitted with clothing and a canoe, Pedro Vial and his companions finally arrived at St. Louis in early October. They remained there until the following summer before setting out on the return journey, reaching Santa Fe in November 1793. Prior to Mexico's independence in 1821, Spanish authorities did not greet their French and American neighbors with a friendly handshake. For decades, Spanish authorities had tried to prevent "foreign" interests from getting a foothold in Mexico's northern states, believing that any such intrusion would eventually lead to settlement and the loss of territory. Their fears in this regard were heightened by the appearance in Santa Fe in 1739 by the Frenchmen Pierre and Paul Mallet, who came from St. Louis. The brothers ascended the Missouri River to the Platte River in Nebraska, turned south to the Arkansas, and on to a route that paralleled what would become the Santa Fe Trail. Although Spanish reports of the visit lauded the Mallets for their accomplishment in coming from St. Louis, "the bad policy of the Governor Mendoza in permitting the Mallet party ... to return after having spied out the land" was regarded as "most mischievous" by Spanish authorities. Upon their return to St. Louis, the Mallet brothers gave the French governor of Louisiana a detailed description of what they had seen in Santa Fe.[11]

Trade within Mexico prior to independence was controlled by merchants who obtained their goods from Europe, landing them at ports on the Gulf of Mexico and transporting them overland for great distances (more than 2,000 miles from Vera Cruz to Santa Fe) to reach the far-flung towns and villages. These merchants enjoyed a monopoly and priced their merchandise accordingly. Goods coming from the Mississippi Valley (800 miles away) were less expensive simply because they didn't have so far to travel. To allow American traders to do business in Santa Fe would disrupt the existing markets and put Mexican merchants out of business. As a result Mexico's northern border with the United States was closed to the importation of goods.

Despite the problems Mississippi Valley entrepreneurs faced in the early years of the 19th century, the potential for opening trade with Mexico created a westward pull they found difficult to ignore. In 1804, William Morrison, an enterprising merchant at Kaskaskia, Illinois, sent Jean Baptiste La Lande to Santa Fe with a pack of trade goods. La Lande went up the Missouri River to the Platte River in Nebraska, then followed the south fork of the Platte into Colorado. Along the Front Range, he turned south on the Indian trace that traversed Raton Pass, and entered New Mexico. Somehow satisfying the authorities at Santa Fe, La Lande sold Morrison's goods, settled down to stay, and kept his benefactor's earnings. Despite future attempts by Morrison, the loss was never recovered. Another early traveler to New Mexico, a hunter, trapper, and would-be trader, was James Purcell. In 1802, he departed St. Louis for the West and after several misadventures — in which he was robbed by Indians of his furs, then recovered them only to lose them in the Missouri River — found his way to Santa Fe in 1805. He, too, liked what he found there and made New Mexico his home.

Not everyone traveling to the Spanish province to trade in these years would be as lucky as La Lande and Purcell. The residents of the mountain village of Taos, north of Santa Fe, awoke one cold February morning in 1810 to find three hopeful American traders, their Mexican guide, and several slaves in the town plaza with goods they were eager to dispose of. St. Louis merchants James Patterson and Joseph McLanahan, and retired army officer Reuben Smith, quickly found themselves jailed at Santa Fe by Spanish authorities who thought them spies. Taken to Chihuahua, it would be two years before they were released in Louisiana. Not to be outdone, in 1812 another party of 10 Americans — known thereafter as the McKnight-Baird expedition — left St. Louis bound for Santa Fe, reportedly with $10,000 in trade goods. When they arrived they were promptly jailed and had their merchandise seized and sold to pay for room and board while they were in prison (one account claims at the rate of 18 cents per day). They were eventually taken to Chihuahua where they spent the next eight years as laborers working in mines. Only a decree by the king of Spain secured their release in 1820.

Becknell's Gamble

Scholars have speculated considerably as to whether William Becknell went west in 1821 to trade with Indians or if he, in fact, headed for Santa Fe in the hope that Mexico's recent independence opened the way for Americans to do business in the new country. The text of a notice placed by Becknell in the June 25 issue of the *Missouri Intelligencer* (at Franklin) leaves open either possibility, but an understanding of his situation at the time would seem to preclude any thought of trading with Indians. He had a great need for money, one that likely could not be satisfied by a protracted journey to the West. In the newspaper notice, he invites interested parties to join him in "a company of men destined to the westward for the purpose of trading for Horses and Mules, and catching Wild Animals of every description." Catching wild animals implies hunting and trapping. There is nothing in Becknell's known life prior to 1821 to indicate that he was a hunter or a trapper. In mentioning these activities, he may have tried to camouflage his real purpose for going west — which was to trade at Santa Fe — while attempting to delude potential competitors.

Since arriving in Missouri in 1810, Becknell had engaged in numerous commercial and trading activities and unfortunately had failed to prosper. In 1811, he worked for James and Jesse Morrison, brothers of William Morrison, the Kaskaskia, Illinois, merchant who had hired La Lande.[12] Among the extensive Morrison interests were outlying wholesale and retail stores (one in St. Charles, another at Cape Girardeau, Missouri), a fleet of cargo boats, and contracts to supply military posts in the Mississippi and Missouri valleys. Under the direction of William, James and Jesse partnered with the Boone brothers at their Howard County salt lick in 1805, providing them with kettles in which the brine was reduced and transport of the finished product to St. Louis. By the time Becknell joined the Morrison business operations along the Missouri River, that family had acquired the Boone brothers' interest in their Howard County salt lick. During the War of 1812, Becknell was a member of Daniel Morgan Boone's Ranger Company, building fortifications and standing guard along the Missouri and Mississippi Rivers. He was honorably discharged in 1815, none the richer for the experience, and promptly returned to work for the Morrisons, which included making salt at the Boone's Lick works. In 1818, he acquired a license to operate a ferry upriver from Franklin while managing the saltworks for the Morrisons. He soon acquired a partnership in the saltworks business.

Becknell also speculated in land with borrowed money, a practice that turned against him in 1819 when the land market collapsed and he was unable to pay notes on time. In 1821, in an effort to secure a steady income and salvage his investments, he sought election to Missouri's first legislature as the representative for Howard County, but lost his bid in a field of 38 other hopeful candidates. On May 29 that year, he was arrested for nonrepayment of money borrowed from a friend nearly a year earlier. Bonded out of custody, in serious financial difficulty, Becknell determined upon a trading expedition to Santa Fe in hopes that the venture would pay his debts and save his personal reputation.

By advertising that he intended to trade for horses and mules in the West, Becknell implied trading with Indians, or Mexicans, or both. If it was with Indians, he made no effort to do so after he left Franklin in late summer 1821, and he was not disappointed in their absence when he reached the Arkansas River in late September. "It is a … surprise to us," he wrote in a journal, "that we have seen no Indians, or fresh signs of them, although we have traversed their most frequented hunting grounds; but considering their furtive habits, and predatory disposition, *the absence of their company during our journey, will not be a matter of regret*," [italics added].[13] This admission is a strong indication that Becknell all along intended to trade with Mexicans, and it is unlikely that he would risk imprisonment in doing so. In truth, he really had no choice but to go to Santa Fe. There a fast trade could be conducted and he could then return to Missouri in time to avert a personal financial catastrophe.

Becknell led his company directly to Santa Fe (via the mountain route over Raton Pass) where the party was warmly received by authorities. The goods so laboriously hauled across the plains were traded at a profit and in December, Becknell and one other, "Mr. M'Laughlin," began the return trip to Missouri.[14] The others in the company remained in Santa Fe for the winter.

On his return trip, Becknell explored a new route to the Arkansas River. From Santa Fe he went east-northeast to the Cimarron River and followed it east until reaching a point where he turned north for the Arkansas. Between the two streams he crossed desolate, waterless plain, forging a trail that came to be known as the Cimarron Cutoff. The remainder of the trip was uneventful and he reached Franklin on January 20, 1822, having shortened the journey between Missouri and New Mexico from 75 to 48 days.

During his absence from Franklin, five lawsuits for indebtedness were filed against Becknell in Howard County Circuit Court, several earlier complaints were decided against him by the court, and his farm, slaves and "one hundred salt kettles" had been seized by the county sheriff for possible sale to satisfy creditors' claims.[15] Soon after his return to Franklin, several of the complaints against Becknell were dismissed at the request of the plaintiffs, and he was able to regain his homestead, indicating that he had resolved issues with some if not all of his creditors.

These actions are a good indication that Becknell's Santa Fe gamble had paid off, although how successful he really was on this first journey is unknown. Still, he and "M'Laughlin" are reported to have brought back mules and burros, woolen blankets, and so many Spanish coins that they decided to dump them on the street in Franklin to "show off" their good fortune. As for the other members of the company, a story is also told of a Franklin woman who loaned her brother $60 to buy his outfit and trade goods, and received $900 as her share of the profits from the 1821 expedition, a 1,500 percent return of her investment!

A Rush to Santa Fe

With silver dollars scattered on the sidewalk and ample piles of dung dumped on their street by Mexican mules and burros, it's no wonder the residents of Franklin were aroused to the potential of trade with Mexico following Becknell's return in January 1822. A vision of such riches drove four caravans to Santa Fe that year. Colonel Benjamin Cooper, with his nephews Braxton Jr. and Stephen, and 12 others, led the first company to leave Franklin that spring, their $4,000 to $5,000 worth of goods packed on horses and mules. They reached Taos without incident. A company led by William Becknell was not so lucky. Starting a week after Cooper, Becknell and 21 men rolled three wagons loaded with merchandise worth $3,000 onto the trail, thereby becoming the first of thousands of such vehicles that would make the trip to Santa Fe during the next 58 years. Becknell and his companions had more trouble with buffalo and Indians than they did with the creaking wagons. At the Arkansas River, a herd of bison stampeded their horses, scattering them into the night. While searching for the horses the next morning, two of Becknell's party were overtaken by Indians, "stripped, barbarously whipped, and robbed of their horses, guns and clothes," but otherwise unharmed.[16] They reached Santa Fe without further serious incident, taking the cutoff to the Cimarron River, back-tracking the route Becknell had used to return to Franklin earlier in the year.

Like so many early Booneslick hopefuls, John G. Heath had tried his hand at various enterprises before entering the Santa Fe trade in 1822. Not content as an attorney practicing in the St. Charles District, Heath went up the Missouri River in 1812 to see if he could find his fortune, settling for a while in the area of the Gasconade River and Loutre Island, reportedly hunting and trading with Indians. He later operated a saltworks at "Heath's Lick" along the Lamine River south of Arrow Rock. He also found time to serve a term in Missouri's Territorial House of Representatives, and on January 21, 1822, was granted a license to operate a ferry across the Gasconade River at the town of Gasconade. Apparently, Santa Fe held greater promise for wealth than did ferrykeeping, and not long after William Becknell's caravan left Franklin in 1822, a small company led by John Heath took to the trail with packhorses carrying their merchandise. They caught up with Becknell at the Arkansas River and the combined companies traveled together as far as San Miguel in New Mexico, where Heath and some members of his company stayed while Becknell and the others went on to Santa Fe. The last outfit to strike the trail in 1822 was that of James Baird (of the 1812 McKnight-Baird expedition who was imprisoned in Mexico for eight years) and William Chambers. Starting west in late fall they were caught in a blizzard at the Arkansas River and forced to encamp there for the winter, finally straggling into Santa Fe the following spring. After selling their goods, the Baird-Chambers company was dissolved at Taos in 1823.

Only one Franklin caravan went to Santa Fe in 1823, led by Benjamin Cooper and Joel Walker. The 30 men and about 60 packhorses, each reportedly carrying $200 in trade goods, had good luck until they reached the Little Arkansas River. There, Indians ran off all but eight of their horses. Unable to proceed, several of the men returned to Missouri, bought additional horses and then rejoined their comrades. Cooper-Walker and company joined the Baird-Chambers party on the Arkansas River (by now re-equipped with horses and mules obtained in New Mexico) and the two groups started for Santa Fe. On the dry plain between the Arkansas and Cimarron Rivers they ran out of water and it is reported that to survive some in the party drank blood from buffalo they killed. Such was the life of an early Santa Fe trader.

Despite these setbacks, the 1822 and 1823 trading seasons were successful. Benjamin Cooper's company, for example, returned to Missouri reportedly with "400 Jacks and Jennets and mules, a quantity of beaver and a considerable sum in species."[17] The actual profit from these ventures is difficult to divine. Most traders were reluctant to reveal such information, hoping to ward off potential competitors. And if they did say something it was likely to be misleading. The 1822 Becknell company is credited with making 2,000 percent profit; however, Becknell himself used general terms when he declared that "a very great advance is obtained on goods, and the trade is very profitable." He also said that money and mules were plentiful, and that the Mexicans were not hesitant to pay the price if an article suited their fancy[18].

Organizing the 1824 Caravan

Mr. Shaw's tavern, on the square in Franklin, was a busy site on the afternoon of April 1, 1824. Ten days earlier, a notice had appeared in the Franklin newspaper requesting "Those persons who intend to join the trading expedition to Santa Fe this spring" to meet at the tavern at 2 o'clock "to determine whether it will be expedient to pack or convey their goods in small wagons; and to make such other preliminary arrangements as the company may deem proper."[19] Robert W. Morris, a Franklin merchant, placed the announcement in the newspaper, implying in its lead sentence that considerable discussion about Santa Fe had already taken place on the streets of Franklin. Now, it wasn't a question of traders going to Santa Fe, but one of how they would travel. As Morris explained, the meeting had been called to create "unanimity with regard to the mode of conveyance and the course to be pursued," and to produce "uniformity of equipment, which is desirable so far as convenience will permit."

The meeting was well attended by prospective traders (the 1824 caravan was the largest yet to take to the trail) and hopeful local merchants who were interested in knowing who planned to make the journey. Stephen Cooper, Colonel Benjamin Cooper's nephew, who already had two Santa Fe trips under his belt, accompanying his uncle in 1822 and 1823, is sometimes credited with organizing the 1824 caravan. He was probably at the meeting that day, but it seems more likely that others — Morris, Meredith Marmaduke, Augustus Storrs, and probably John Hardeman, his brother Bailey and their father, Thomas, among them — had a larger hand in dealing with the assemblage. In his notice about the meeting, anticipating that many questions would arise there about one subject in particular, Robert Morris acknowledged what was probably the greatest concern of all who were considering making the trip to Santa Fe: "I understand that apprehensions of danger from the Indians cause many to hesitate about going. All the information which a strict enquiry has furnished me with, goes to shew [sic] that no fears need arise from this source. It has been rumored that there is an extensive combination of several Indian tribes against the whites. The naked truth is that a small band of Osages, being irritated by the frequent intrusions of the people of Arkansas on their best hunting ground, made an attack on one of these parties who were killing their buffaloe for the hides and tallow. ... This, however, I believe to be the fact — and no circumstances, no other outrages authorize the inference that any tribe whose parties we shall be liable to meet have a disposition to be at war with the Americans. It is perfectly unreasonable to suppose that they would willingly provoke a conflict, the consequences of which would involve them in certain and immediate ruin. ... It will, in my estimation, only be necessary to guard against their stealing, which judicious regulations will almost to a certainty prevent."[20]

Robert Morris, obviously, was a man given not only to organizing in the name of efficiency, but someone who also was out to make a pig's ear into a silk purse. How he answered doubters' questions at Shaw's tavern about his assessment of the disposition of the Indians is not known, but the consensus among the traders and others gathered there to determine how they would travel was that they should be prepared for the worst. A decision made that afternoon required each man joining the company to come equipped with a rifle, a pistol, four pounds of powder, eight pounds of lead, and enough provision to last 20 days.[21] The group also decided that the caravan would rendezvous at Vernon, Missouri, (a site unknown today) on May 5. The rendezvous did not occur, however, until the last week of May, and the locale was near Fort Osage in Jackson County.

A Partnership Forms

Around the time of the meeting at Shaw's Tavern, Samuel McClure and Meredith Marmaduke formed a partnership bearing their names for the purpose of trading in Santa Fe. The terms of the partnership can only be surmised, but the agreement probably bound each man to a specified amount of money invested and established that profits would be shared in proportion to the investment. However much that was, it would have been a considerable amount of money for the two men to raise (several thousand dollars), with payments going for goods to be traded, a wagon to transport them, horses and mules for hauling and riding, provisions for sustenance, the tariff that would have to be paid on the trade goods once they reached New Mexico, and a license to trade they would have to purchase from the Spanish governor. John Hardeman (and perhaps his father, also) may have been a financial backer for Meredith. This seems likely, given their close relationship in other matters, and in his book *Wilderness Calling*, Nicholas P. Hardeman, the family's biographer, refers to John as a "business associate" of Meredith in that year's Santa Fe trade.[22]

In Franklin on May 5, 1824, McClure and Meredith expanded the scope of their partnership. In an effort to gain a larger share of the trade in New Mexico, the pair initiated a contract that day with Washington Sydnor to establish him both as an individual trader and as an agent working on behalf of the firm of McClure & Marmaduke. The partners agreed to furnish Sydnor with $250 worth of "goods to be purchased in the Town of Franklin ... and to be selected by ... Sydnor." They also agreed to "convey from this place to New Mexico all the cloathing [sic] & provisions which may be necessary," or which Sydnor asked them to take, and to "... furnish him with provisions from this place onward in his journey, in such quantity and quality as is agreed upon by the Company generally, and that they will on this journey render the said Sydnor such assistance from time to time as may be in their power. ..." Sydnor had to provide transportation for himself and his trade goods. By this move McClure & Marmaduke acquired a third salesman, allowing them to trade in Santa Fe and at the same time in outlying villages where they hoped to get ahead of their competitors. The terms of the contract (in Meredith's handwriting), especially the details laid out with regard to his responsibilities, illustrates the depth of Meredith's thinking before leaving Franklin. It also appears that Sydnor's addition to the company was based upon his ability to speak Spanish, or at least some:

"… Washington Sydnor … agrees … that he will select, receive and convey the said two hundred and fifty dollars worth of goods from this place (Franklin Mo.) to New Mexico … and that he will travel with … McClure and Marmaduke from this place to that and that he will render to them all the assistance that may be required of him on this journey thro', or that it may be in his power in promoting and facilitating the movement of the said McClure & Marmaduke from this to that place. … Sydnor on his part further … agrees that he will continue and remain with them, from and after his arrival in the said Country of Mexico, until he shall have succeeded in selling to the best advantage the goods which he … shall have conveyed thither. And that during all the time which he may be thus bound to remain and continue with … McClure and Marmaduke, that he … will render unto … [them] all the assistance that he possibly can, in endeavoring to aid them in selling and disposing of their goods, in every way that he can, both *as interpreter of their Language, so far as he knows* and also as relates to the travelling [sic] and *moving about from place to place after their arrival there* [italics for emphasis added]."

Sydnor, on his part, agreed that as soon as he sold the last of his merchandise he would reimburse McClure and Marmaduke for the goods which they furnished him, and that he would next "divide equally in half the whole amount of profits which may have accrued upon the sale of the aforesaid goods, and that he will then, at the same time, pay over to … McClure and Marmaduke the one half of the aforesaid profits, retaining to himself the other remaining half of the profits owing upon the sale of the goods. …"[23] The success of this strategy, establishing Washington Sydnor as McClure and Marmaduke's agent, isn't known since nothing more is heard of Sydnor; however, the carefully drafted terms in the agreement illustrate Meredith's canniness in business matters and foretell the tactics he would use in coming years to manage his financial and political affairs.

Notes

1. "Dear Brother … your letter dated the 2 of October": Vincent Marmaduke to Meredith Marmaduke, November 10, 1823. Box 1, Folder 2, Sappington-Marmaduke Papers, MHS.

2. "Dear Uncle … all the family": Vincent McClanahan to Meredith Marmaduke, September 22, 1823. Box 12, Folder 2, Ibid.

3. "Dear Cousin … agreeable to your request": Francis Porter to Meredith Marmaduke, January 1824. Folder 2, Marmaduke Papers, C1021, SHSMO.

4. "I would have wrote you before this": Henry Hungerford to Meredith Marmaduke, January 4, 1824. Box 1, Folder 2, Sappington-Marmaduke Papers, MHS.

5. "I expect you have heard of the death of Mr. Fox": Vincent Marmaduke to Meredith Marmaduke, January 22, 1824. Marmaduke Papers, C1021, Folder 2. SHSMO. The "Col. Middleton" mentioned is

To Make a Fortune in Missouri

William Middleton, a county magistrate judge at the time of the election to fill Cox's office. He, too, had been a captain of artillery in Westmoreland County's 111th Regiment during the War of 1812, serving with Meredith Marmaduke at the unit's principle engagements. Col. Middleton is also mentioned in Henry Hungerford's letter of January 4 as one of several judges who declined to "go on the bench" when it came time to vote for Cox's successor, believing they could prevail in Hungerford's favor at a future date.

6. "We recvd. your letter dated the 9 of December": Vincent Marmaduke to Meredith Marmaduke, January 22, 1824. Folder 2, Ibid.

7. "I long to see you and I hope you will not neglect coming here at the time you mentioned": Written at end of letter, Vincent McClanahan to Meredith Marmaduke, May 16, 1824. Folder 3, Ibid.

8. "Leeds Town, 3rd May 1824, Dear Colonel": After losing his wife and business the previous winter, Hungerford relocated to Leeds, Virginia, in early April of 1824, where "I contemplate conducting a small business … and if possible to bring to a close all the unsettled business. The last, Col., was a fatal year to me." Henry Hungerford to Marmaduke, May 3, 1824. Box 1, Folder 2, Sappington-Marmaduke Papers, MHS.

9. "daily distances": Walter Williams & Floyd Shoemaker, et al, *Missouri, Mother of the West*, Vol. 1, 593. With both St. Louis and Santa Fe under Spanish flag in 1792, it is not surprising that de la Concha would attempt to establish a trade route between the two. Within a few years, however, control of "Luisiana" would shift to French, and eventually to U.S. ownership, and traders arriving at Santa Fe from St. Louis were arrested and their goods were seized.

10. Pedro's Vial's journal: Translated from the General Archives of the Indies, in Houck, Louis, ed., *Spanish Regime in Missouri*: Vol. 1, 357–58. Napeste River is a misspelling of Rio Napestle, so named by Spanish Explorer Uribarri in 1696 for the upper Arkansas.

11. "the bad policy of the Governor Mendoza": Floyd C. Shoemaker, Fur Trade and Western Exploration, *Missouri and Missourians*, Vol. 1, 359, 365.

12. "William Morrison, an enterprising merchant at Kaskaskia": The most complete account to date of William Morrison's activities in the Booneslick country is in: Lynn Morrow, "Boone's Lick in Western Expansion: James Mackay, the Boones, and the Morrisons," *Boone's Lick Heritage Quarterly*, Vol. 13, No. 3 (Fall 2014).

13. "the absence of their company": David A. White, comp., *News of the Plains and Rockies 1803–1865*, Vol. 2, 62.

14. "Mr. M'Laughlin": Ibid, 51.

15. "one hundred salt Kettles": Larry Beachum, *William Becknell, Father of the Santa Fe Trade*, 22.

16. "stripped, barbarously whipped, and robbed of their horses, guns and clothes": White, *News of the Plains and Rockies*, Vol. 2, 66. On his 1821 trip to Santa Fe, Becknell's party somehow escaped detection by Indians, his journal making mention only of friendly Caw (Kansa) Indians encountered in eastern Kansas on his return late in December. The other trading expedition to New Mexico that year, led by Thomas James and John McKnight, wasn't so lucky. Traveling by boat up the Arkansas and Cimarron Rivers, then by horse to the Canadian River, they passed through the heart of Comanche country and were forced to pay tribute several times, losing in this way some $2,000 worth of trade goods.

17. "400 Jacks and Jennets and mules, a quantity of beaver and a considerable sum in species": David J. Weber, *The Taos Trappers*, fn., 63, citing an article from the Franklin *Missouri Intelligencer* reprinted in the Jackson, Missouri, *Independent Patriot*, November 29, 1823.

18. Becknell company is credited with making 2,000 percent profit: F. F. Stevens, *Missouri and the Santa Fe Trade*, second article, 302.

19. "Those persons who intend to join the trading expedition": *Missouri Intelligencer*, March 20, 1824.

20. "I understand that apprehensions of danger from the Indians": Ibid.

21. "a rifle, a pistol, four pounds of powder, eight pounds of lead, and enough provision to last 20 days": R. L. Duffas, *The Santa Fe Trail*, 82. Josiah Gregg, who went to Santa Fe in 1831, wrote of his journey that "ordinary supplies for each man's consumption during the journey are about fifty pounds of flour, as

many more of bacon, ten of coffee and twenty of sugar. Beans, crackers, and trifles of that description, are comfortable appendages, but being looked upon as *dispensable expenses*, are seldom to be found ... on the road." Josiah Gregg, *Commerce of the Plains*, Vol. 1, 35.

22. a "business associate" of Meredith in that year's Santa Fe trade. Hardeman, *Wilderness Calling*, 102.

23. Contract between McClure & Marmaduke and Washington Sydnor: Memorandum of an agreement between Samuel McClure & M. M. Marmaduke, and Washington Sydnor, May 5, 1824. Box 1, Folder 2, Sappington-Marmaduke Papers, MHS.

CHAPTER 7

A LONG AND LONESOME TRAVEL

"Crossed the river at Hardeman's Ferry six miles above Franklin on Sunday the 16th day of May 1824 and encamped two miles from the ferry in a beautiful prairie. ... 1825 May 31st. This day left Santa Fe ... AMEN."[1]

Interposed between the day Meredith Marmaduke left Franklin for Santa Fe and the day he rode away from the dusty New Mexican village, tossing an "AMEN!" over his shoulder, are 380 eventful days, 865 miles of formidable and dangerous trail, and countless challenges and adventures. It's unfortunate that only 79 of those days are accounted for in the pages of the journal he wrote during that time. That he kept a journal was unusual; no other document of that nature has been associated with his life, and that raises a question about the journal's purpose. Was it written out of a desire to preserve memories of the experience, or did he have a more practical objective in mind? The latter suggestion has to be considered in view of the journal's ultimate destiny.

Nathaniel Patten, editor of the *Missouri Intelligencer*, published the earliest report on the Santa Fe Trail, an account of William Becknell's "Two Expeditions from Boone's Lick to Santa Fe" in the April 22, 1823, edition of the newspaper. Historians have generally concluded that Patten actually wrote the account from Becknell's recollections, as most thought Becknell's known writings "show that he could not have written the published journals unassisted."[2] The Becknell journal relates his 1821 and 1822 travels to Santa Fe and return to Franklin, and is a running commentary — general in nature — as opposed to a detailed reporting of the expedition's progress and the country through which they passed. In his introduction to Becknell's account, Patten demonstrates that he understood the importance of the Santa Fe trade in establishing American influence in the West, writing that it would "open a free intercourse, acquaint us with the soil, climate and peculiarities of the interior of that interesting country, and give a new, unexplored & profitable source of trade to Missouri." Unfortunately, Becknell's journal failed to provide much information that would advance the knowledge promised in Patten's declaration. Becknell was interested in getting his goods to market and had little interest in the "soil, climate and peculiarities" of the West. On the other hand, Meredith Marmaduke brought an educated, inquisitive mind to the question of advancing knowledge of the West, able to accurately communicate the intelligence he gained on the trail. Recognizing this capacity in Meredith, it is not unrealistic to envision Nathaniel Patten suggesting to him that such a work, the first descriptive account of the Santa Fe Trail, would be a valuable service to many, and that he, Patten, was prepared to publish the journal on Marmaduke's return from New Mexico. The idea would have appealed to Meredith, who was trying to establish himself on the Missouri frontier (with future political ambitions in mind) and probably saw the published chronicle as a way to advance that objective.

A Long and Lonesome Travel

Within a few days after his return to Franklin in early August of 1825, Meredith's lengthy journal was in Patten's hands. The tireless editor immediately set to work determining what parts of it he would publish, and then undertook the laborious task of composing the typeset words one letter at a time, a process that took days to complete. An abbreviated, extracted version of Meredith's journal appeared in the *Intelligencer* the first week of September. Patten knew that his work would be reprinted by other newspapers throughout the country, a practice common among periodicals of that time. What he and no one else foresaw was that the complete, unabridged journal would not be published for another 172 years, finally appearing in *Wagon Tracks*, the journal of the Santa Fe Trail Association. Where Meredith's work of "personal knowledge and correct information," a "Santa Fe Trail classic,"[3] languished all those years is unknown except for a mention by the early western historian Josiah Gregg who, writing in 1844 about the 1824 Santa Fe caravan, noted that "Colonel Marmaduke, the present governor of the state of Missouri ... has been pleased to place his diary of that eventful journey at my disposal."[4] If Gregg returned the journal to Meredith is an open question, since it was not found in Marmaduke's papers in Missouri. Eventually, the University of California's Bancroft Library in Berkeley acquired the journal, where it still resides today.

Meredith's chronicle differs significantly from what editor Patten presented in Becknell's commentary. From the first day on the trail, Meredith established a basic pattern of recording information that he retained for the entire journey. The days are named along with the date and the distance traveled, and usually a brief description of each night's campsite. The journal notes the availability of deer, buffalo, and other animals they hunted for food. Meredith briefly describes the topography of the land through which the caravan passed each day, noting timber (or the lack of trees) that could be used for firewood, as well as streams and springs and the quality of their waters. Road conditions received particular mention of difficulties encountered such as at river crossings. During the first 12 days on the trail, Meredith entered his observations without interposing personal reflections or anecdotes. His entry for Thursday, May 27, is typical: "Travelled say 15 miles and encamped on one of the western branches of the Big Blue, the prairie, rolling and hilly, and crossed several branches of the Big Blue, and in one instance had to dig the banks and let the waggons [sic] and Dearborns down by ropes — this day saw a few more Elk & some deer — observed the Prairie much more free of gopher mounds than in the lower parts of Missouri, saw but few birds. The Prairie thro' which we have travelled has been remarkable rich and firm, and the whole face of it in some places covered with most beautiful flowers."[5] All of this was information that would become valuable to future travelers on the trail, and it is obvious that Meredith had this in mind in keeping a daily journal.

A Long and Lonesome Travel

As the caravan moved west during subsequent weeks, interesting events happened, both to himself and others, and Meredith's narrative becomes more expansive. The first time he writes about himself is Friday, May 28, 12 days after leaving Franklin: "I this day sprang from my saddle in order to avoid being thrown by my horse who was frightened." Then on the 29th: "I this day shot a very large raccoon which I saw run up an oak tree." Reporting the events of Monday, June 7, he wrote: "This night we had a tremendous gust of wind & rain, and the horses broke by the guard in defiance of every exertion to stop them. ... I experienced a very unpleasant night being exposed to the whole storm on guard." On June 9, he "saw at least 5,000 Buffaloe, chiefly bulls." And the next day, "I believe I saw at least 10,000 buffaloe, as the Prairies were literally Covered for many miles with them." The number of buffalo seen on Friday, June 11, was estimated to be "at least 12 or 15,000. Our hunters killed 3." Camping in the neighborhood of so many buffalo that night proved to be unwise: "About 1 o'Clock in the morning a number of Buffaloe Crossed the river at the encampment and passed thro' it, which frightened off about 2/3 of the Horses belonging to the party." The camp turned out to recover the spooked horses, "many of which were during the [next] day found and brot into Camp — at night it was ascertained that between 25 & 30 were still absent. All the Horses belonging to the dearborn [wagon] in which I was interested ran off — 3 of them were found and brot back during the day. 2 mules remained unfound upon whose services we [Marmaduke and Sam McClure] had exclusively relied for the Conveyance of our baggage — which circumstance, was the Cause of considerable anxiety on our part. I rode out this evening in search of the lost animals."

Unsuccessful in finding the mules, on June 15, McClure and Meredith borrowed one mule "which added to the horses we had were able to haul our Dearborn on — we therefore determined to Continue on our rout with the Company who all seemed to manifest a very friendly disposition towards assisting those on, who had unfortunately lost their animals — the number of which was now ascertained to be about 25 — which caused many to walk who had made arrangements and Confidently expected to ride." The following day he and McClure "set out afresh after the loss of our horses for the Spanish Country — and we find ourselves pretty nearly on foot," with about five hundred miles to go, "a walk which is quite sufficient to discourage any man especially at this Season of the year."

Anecdotes such as this appear more frequently as the journal progresses, and they become more lengthy once the caravan reaches the Arkansas River (on June 10, 25 days after leaving Franklin), and later, on the nearly waterless march to and up the Cimarron River to the foothills of the Rocky Mountains (15 days, June 28 to July 12). On June 18, the company passed Pawnee Rock, a western Kansas bluff comprised of Dakota sandstone that rises above the prairie. Although Meredith didn't mention the site in his journal, either on this trip or during a later passage he carved his name into the stone alongside the names of many others who had passed the bluff. His signature was seen in 1857 by Saline County resident William Napton Jr., who later described the site when writing about his journey to Santa Fe that year.

"This bluff, facing the road on the right side, at a distance perhaps of a hundred yards, was of brown sandstone about fifty feet high, the bluff end extending down to the river bottom," Napton wrote. "I found many names cut in the soft stone, among them that of Colonel M. M. Marmaduke. . . and James H. Lucas, a prominent and wealthy citizen of St. Louis."[6]

Few of Meredith's fellow travelers in 1824 are identified in the journal by name, and the number of times names are mentioned is meager. The first companions he names appear in the entry for May 24, after eight days on the trail, when the caravan had gathered at the rendezvous camp near Fort Osage in western Missouri. Meredith recorded the election of three officers to guide the expedition, and noted the number of men, vehicles, and animals in the caravan: "A. Legrand was elected Captain — Paul Anderson Lieut., and [unreadable] Simpson, Ensign.[7] We this evening ascertained the whole strength of our company to be 81 persons and 2 servants; we also had 2 road waggons, 20 dearborns, 2 carts and one small piece of cannon about 3 lbs. ... we have with us about 200 horses and mules."[8] The next trader named is Frances Samuels who, on June 3, "was caught in a noose of a rope confined to a Horse, around his feet and dragged a considerable distance in that way the horse going at full speed and miraculously escaped without injury." No one else is mentioned by name until June 22 when Meredith recorded that "Paul Anderson sent out a Spanish indian [sic] to bring meat into camp, and Carelessly he lost his mule." Brief mentions of Paul Anderson appear several more times in the journal, but other than these few people Meredith mentions no one else by name until the caravan came to the "Ranche ... of a Mr. Juan Pino. ... This man is wealthy having 1,60,000 [sic] head of sheep and many cattle, horses & mules — we encamped near his house where we had fine spring water." This visit occurred July 22 about 30 miles east of the small village of San Miguel del Bado (St. Michael of the Ford), one of the oldest towns in New Mexico, which the caravan reached three days later.

Arrival at Santa Fe

The morning of July 28, after camping overnight at the tiny village of St. James, three miles west of San Miguel, Meredith was anxious to get on with the business of trading his merchandise. Reaching Santa Fe that day, he took time in the evening to write a long passage in his journal describing his arrival and his first impressions of the town and its Catholic inhabitants:

"I this morning left Camp early, in pursuit of a man who was employed yesterday to pack 2 Trunks of goods for us to St.a Fe and who had gone on a head with them — and travelled about 37 miles, and arrived at Santa Fe about Dusk, did not overtake the Packer, but found all safe. Santa Fe is quite a Populous place, but is built entirely of Mud houses, there being not a brick or wood house in the whole City. Its population may be estimated at about [no figure given] souls. Some parts of the City are tolerably regularly built, other parts very irregular. The inhabitants appear to be friendly — and some of them are very wealthy, whilst by far the greater part of them are the most wretched, poor miserable Creatures that I have ever seen, Yet they appear to me to be quite happy & contented in their miserable Priest-ridden situation. This City is well supplied with fine water. Provisions very scarce and many, very many beggars walking the streets. I put up with an old hospitable gentleman of the name of Deago Montoyo, who appears to have quite an agreeable family — left the Dearbourn behind with the waggon party to follow on — found the road to this place exceedingly bad for waggons."

Meredith's view of Santa Fe's "priest-ridden" populace exposes an attitude toward Catholicism that was widely held among Americans following two periods of Protestant revivalism during the 18th and early 19th centuries, times of "significant religious development,"[9] as some historians termed it. Often called the First and Second Great Awakenings, these movements de-emphasized the traditional church structure and ceremony, and changed the role of clergy, in favor of an evangelical-revivalist doctrine, espoused by itinerant preachers, that found particular interest on the frontier where a majority of the population identified most often with Baptist, Presbyterian, or Methodist faiths. At the time of the American Revolution and for a period of years thereafter, the Catholic Church was not strongly represented in the nation.

On Thursday, July 29, Meredith explored Santa Fe. Unable to "converse with the Natives," he "ate a few fine apricots which are tolerably plenty here." The wagon train finally reached the village on Friday, "all safe, except our dearbourn had been again upset, and a little injured. ... after a long and lonesome travel." The next day was spent arranging the taxes with the collector, "who appears to me to be an astonishingly obliging man. ... The duty imposed by law on all traders appears to be 25 pct, which is considered exceedingly high and unreasonable and was the Cause of Considerable discontent among the Americans — who however succeeded in arranging their taxes very satisfactorily with the Collector." Unstated but implied is the tax collector's willingness to negotiate the rate, if there was an advantage to him in the bargain.

Although the traders reached a satisfactory agreement with Santa Fe's authorities, they believed that an illegal tax had been imposed when they first entered New Mexico. In an effort to have this earlier tax overturned, Meredith wrote to James "Santiago" S. Wilcocks, the American consul at Mexico City, on behalf of all the traders, and laid their complaint before him, hoping for a favorable reply. Wilcocks did little to assuage their feelings: "Gentlemen, I received ... your favor of the 13th December, in which you complain of an imposition which you seemed to think had been practiced on you by the Alcalde [mayor] of the village of San Miguel, and have to say in reply, that if you only paid the twenty-five percent duty you speak of, on your goods, you got them into the country at a cheaper rate through that place than you could have done at any of the seaports."[10] Elsewhere, he wrote, they would have paid 28 percent. Meredith's journal says nothing about paying a tariff at San Miguel, leaving open the possibility that the village's Alcalde did extort something from the traders as they passed through.

McClure and Marmaduke began trading in earnest the first day of August, finding it "difficult to do to an advantage, owing to the Scarcity of money and the abundance of goods — for which we brot on for this market." The next day, in a classic takeover move designed to control prices and gain market share, they bought out one of their competitors. Francis Samuels, who had been dragged behind his horse in the unfortunate incident some weeks earlier, and who evidently was easily discouraged, sold his stock of goods to them for $703.73. The total amount of money the partners invested in their venture isn't known, but in the purchase of trade goods alone they probably spent several thousand dollars.[11]

Sanguine Expectations

Meredith's initial appraisal of the New Mexico market (that it was unable to quickly absorb all the merchandise now in Santa Fe) appears in a letter to John Hardeman written only five days after he had arrived there. In assessing the potential for a profitable venture, he speculated that "many of the company whose sanguine expectations ran pretty high in a pecuniary point of view," would be disappointed. "Yet I do not despair of making this quite a profitable trip to us." He also was uncomplimentary of his fellow traders, saying that many of them had "greatly mismanaged their affairs in this country in a monied point of view."[12] His assessment proved to be correct. Two months later, the firm of McClure & Marmaduke still had a significant quantity of merchandise on hand.

Writing again to John Hardeman in October, Meredith disclosed that he and McClure intended to remain in Santa Fe for the winter, selling their merchandise there and in surrounding villages until "we shall have succeeding in effecting a sale of the most saleable goods and reduced our stock considerably say $2000 — then with the balance of the goods to go to the lower country and exchange them for mules."[13] They had already tried the market in "the lower Country" (Paso del Norte, today's Juarez, Mexico) in September and October, and found it wanting. Marmaduke sent merchandise that he valued at $696.62 to Mexico on September 21, possibly on consignment with Glen Owen, a fellow trader and a brother-in-law to John Hardeman, who left Santa Fe about that date en route to Paso del Norte.[14] In his October letter, Meredith told Hardeman that "Capt. Owen left this, I think, about 6 weeks since, for the lower country. He had not then vended many goods." During this time McClure and Marmaduke remained in New Mexico, reluctant to risk much of their investment in an unknown marketplace on the Rio Grande River more than 400 miles away. Their concern was valid. Unbeknownst to them, someone already at Paso del Norte that fall had taken stock of the trading situation there and wasn't impressed. Described by the editor of the *Missouri Intelligencer* as "a man of intelligence and veracity, and not being himself engaged in the trade," the observer wrote to the newspaper on September 21, as Captain Owen was leaving Santa Fe, saying that "Cash is scarce here, or, rather, it is in the hands of a few, who are able to live without parting with it. This trade is done, as all will inform you."[15]

Sales were as slow in Paso del Norte as they were in Santa Fe; all of McClure and Marmaduke's goods sent south were returned unsold on October 10. For 10 months after the journal entries ended on August 2, Meredith's activities are mostly unknown except for what little information is contained in his letters to John Hardeman, and in a letter McClure wrote in December 1827 indicating that the two traveled to El Paso sometime during the winter of 1824–25: "Yours by Mr. [unreadable name] I recd. and note its contents. as to the report therein stated respecting Doc.r Jn. Heath [Doctor John Heath] is no more than what was current & in the mouth of almost every Mexican & Spaniard in New Mexico [unreadable word] when yourself and I was in St. Afe [Santa Fe] and then at the Paso [Paso del Norte]. The same was in circulation the same that you mention that is to say Doc.r Jno Heath wrote to a Spanish gentleman (or a Priest) in the Paso or its neighborhood stating that he considered it to be his duty to apprise the Mexicans of the character and discription [sic] of men who composed the company that went through in that country *that spring* [emphasis added] and for him and his friends to be on their guard against them."¹⁶ Referring to "that spring," McClure places this event in 1825. The letter containing Heath's attempt to discredit his fellow traders was seen by a number of them who were at "the Paso" at the time, and McClure mentions several of them in his letter to Meredith.

Sometime during the winter of 1824–25, the partners visited a Navajo settlement and it must have been an interesting experience. Writing to Meredith more than 20 years later, McClure asked if he ever reflected back "on our old travels, do you recollect of the agreeable night & the following day we spent returning from the Navajoes Nation?" One wonders if the "agreeable night" was spent in the company of an Indian maiden. It was not unusual for traders and trappers to enjoy the company of native women when the opportunity to do so presented itself.¹⁷

Vice and Virtue

Living among the people of Santa Fe during the winter and spring of 1824–25 did not alter Meredith's initial judgment of New Mexicans as "the greater part of them ... wretched, poor miserable Creatures." The final entry in his journal, written May 31, 1825, the day he left Santa Fe to return to Missouri, is a lengthy discourse on "the subject of Manners, Customs, &c. &c. of the Country & people." His observations reflect both a winter's worth of thinking about the subject, and an almost total lack of knowledge about the history and traditions of the culture he attempted to describe. Of particular concern to him was the "blind zeal of the people, all professing the Catholic religion. ... The homage and adoration which they pay to their priests ... is much greater than they themselves pay to their God as all their worship ... consists in the most unmeaning Ceremony that can possibly be Conceived." Still, he said, they "appear to live more happily under their religious yoke than any other [religious] profession I have ever known. ..."

A tinge of righteousness creeps into Meredith's assessment of the average New Mexican's morality. He was "reluctantly compelled" to say that they were "a people so entirely destitute of Correct principles in the general ... for I scarcely know a single vice that is not indulged to a very great excess except that of intoxication. ..." And sobriety, he felt, was due more to a "scarcity of Ardent spirits and the very high price which it commands," than any desire to not imbibe. "Thieving, lieing ... whoring — gambling &c. in a word every vice reigns among this people to the greatest extent that this poor miserable situation will possibly permit." Nor did modesty ... have the most of Meredith's condemnation: "their ideas of de[cency] indiscriminately and freely Converse imperfect notion, as the men and wom[en] acts that can possibly be conceived, without together on the most gross and vul[gar] ...." Meredith granted the New Mexicans "one the least embarrassment or ...ality to Strangers." Despite their "scarcity of human solitary virtue, and th[os]e who "would more willingly divide their morsel with the diet" he felt there Spanish, prejudiced against Catholicism, carrying a Virginian's stranger ... tion of civility, Meredith found himself isolated from the positive cultural Un[?] Mexican society and was drawn to recording the negative behavior of some of Santa Fe's less fortunate citizens. He closed his journal on a sour note, writing, "There are among these people few men of information, and I believe no women at all of education. Perhaps in the general their priests are the best informed men among them, and I do verily believe ... them to be the most abandoned scoundrels that disgrace human nature. Amen. MMM."

Trouble on the Trail Home

Meredith and 16 other homeward-bound traders came together as a traveling company the evening of May 31, 1825, at a location he termed the "ranch called the Alimo," 10 miles east of Santa Fe. The next day the group crossed Glorieta Pass in the Sangre de Cristo Mountains, pushing ahead of them a herd of more than 600 mules and horses, animals taken in trade during the previous winter. A few days later they were overtaken by a party of Mexicans coming from Santa Fe, who were also going to the United States and would travel with the Americans for the next two months. Among the Mexicans was Don Manuel Simon de Escudero, a wealthy attorney and land owner of Chihuahua City in Mexico, a man with proven diplomatic skills, who had come to Santa Fe with the aim of buying goods from the American traders there and taking them back to interior Mexico to be sold. Instead, he found himself being sent east by Bartolome Baca, the governor of New Mexico, on a mission to "treat with the president or government of the United States."[18] Indians from north of the Mexico border, Comanches, Kiowas, and Pawnees, raiding into New Mexico and plundering its residents, were a concern to Baca and he was anxious to obtain American help in suppressing those incursions, as well as securing the safety of the trade coming from Missouri. Escudero's arrival at Santa Fe was timely and the attorney was soon caught up in the (unsanctioned by the Mexican government) diplomatic venture proposed by Baca. Escudero departed Santa Fe in early June with 22 other Mexican citizens, "among them Romualdo Garcia from Sonora, Ramon Garcia from Chihuahua, and their servants" (who later would return to Santa Fe), and Escudero's nephew, Pedro Escudero.[19] With the addition of the Mexicans, the combined company on its way to Missouri now numbered 40 persons. Soon thereafter they were joined by a party of 35 men from Tennessee, bringing the total strength of the group to 75.[20] During the two-month-long journey, Manuel Escudero, the two Garcias, Meredith, and Sam McClure, all "gentlemen" with similar interests, undoubtedly became friends. Contacts between them continued after the arrival at Franklin in August and it may have been Meredith who introduced Escudero to John Hardeman. In any event, Hardeman was entrusted with a "bar of silver" brought on Mexico by Escudero, to hold until he asked for its return at a later date.[21] In pursuit of his way to the U.S. capital at Washington, Manuel Escudero eventually made the Mexican consul in residence there that, he was cordially, but firmly, told by Mexico, he had no portfolio for treating with the representative of the governor of New from Washington, Escudero went to Philadelphia and government. Turned away eventually take to Santa Fe. merchandise he would

Very Rudely Treated

On July 13, the caravan in which Meredith and Sam McClure were the Arkansas River in high water in southern Kansas and went into camp, a quiet journey so far without a serious incident. The following day they moved a few miles and halted in the morning near a creek that emptied into the Little Arkansas River. Here, some of the group left the camp to hunt buffalo. An account of what happened next, written by an unknown member of the returning company, appeared under the headline "Mexican Adventures," in the August 5, 1825, issue of the *Missouri Intelligencer*:

"About two hours after their [the hunting party] absence, the rest of the company who remained about the camp were aroused by the calling out of some of the men that 'Indians were among the horses.' At this instant the greater part of the company ran with their arms among the horses and Indians, (for by this time they were pretty well mixed together) and endeavored to check both horses and Indians, one of the company only being mounted. At this crises the Indians appeared to manifest no hostile intentions, continually crying out 'Was ashes,' 'Was ashes,' and others endeavoring to frighten off the horses by their halloing and riding among them, which they succeeded in doing, so that it is supposed about two thirds of the animals were driven off by them, in despite of every exertion to prevent them. Immediately some 6 or 7 men mounted some horses, and others mules, and went in pursuit. After proceeding a few miles, it was discovered that the animals were divided into four parties — the men then separated, a part pursuing one drove and the rest another; both succeeded in taking each a drove, one of which amounting to 63 horses and mules, arrived safe in camp; the other was retaken by the Indians and driven to their camp, which was not more than four or five miles from ours. In the mean time these Indians had fallen in with the party who went out hunting, and forcibly took them all to their camp, at the same time robbing and taking from them every thing they wanted, and other wise very rudely treating them. On the return of the party who pursued the horses the Indians had taken off it was ascertained that there were between two and three hundred warriors in camp, many of whom appeared disposed to provoke some difference, so that they might find a pretence [sic] for taking all our property, or perhaps murdering the whole party. In this, however, they failed, as the whole company manifested a determination not to involve themselves in any difficulty whatever, choosing to submit to the most violent outrages, rather than resent them, as it was but too evident that resistance would have been madness, there being in their own and our camp between 6 and 700 warriors, and about 12 or 15 effective men in ours. During the whole of this evening and the next day until evening, there were continually many of them in our camp, constantly endeavoring to steal from us or take by force such articles as they wanted. During the evening of the 14th, & morning of the 15th, when the whole cavalcade of the Osages moved to our camp, they did return some 50 or 60 of our animals which they had driven off, chiefly those that were of the least value; retaining the best, to the number of about 130. There was with these Indians a man who spoke their language fluently, as also the French language, so that our company had no difficulty in conversing freely with them. They were told that their conduct would be represented to the proper officers of our government, and that a just recompense would be demanded of them. ... One of the Company."[22]

After harassing the camp for two days, the Indians rode away with their plunder and the traders resumed their journey, arriving without further trouble at Fort Osage the evening of July 27. George Sibley, chief factor of the trading post built in 1808 to serve the Osage Indians, recorded the event in his diary: "This evening Col. Marmaduke arrived at my House with Mr. James Moore, direct from S[an]ta Fe, which place they left about the 1st of June. They came with a large Party, who brought a great number of Mules, Asses, &c. They were met by a Large Band of Osage Indians at the Arkansas, not far from the Mouth of the Little Arkansas ... by whom they were robbed of about 120 head of Animals, & some other property, and were otherwise ill treated."[23]

A Demand for Compensation

Having lost property to the raiders, Meredith and Sam McClure wasted no time in seeking its return when they reached Franklin in early August. Two weeks later, Manuel Escudero left Franklin for St. Louis, carrying a letter from Meredith to General William Clark, who was then serving as superintendent of Indian affairs west of the Mississippi River. The letter included a list of the livestock and other items stolen by the Osage Indians. The firm of McClure & Marmaduke had lost three horses valued at $90, 12 unbroken mules "between 3 and 4 years old" valued at $600, and two Spanish blankets, a butcher knife and two "ropes-largo" worth $8. In addition, Meredith said his personal loss was a "Dark colored mule between 4 & 5 years old," that he valued at $50, and noted that McClure lost "one excellent Pack saddle, made of Leather and Iron, of the value of 5.00." Meredith also listed the loss of a Spanish blanket, hat, and overcoat belonging to John Lucas, a Mexican "Servant" he had hired to help manage the horses and mules while on the trail from Santa Fe.[24] Escudero delivered the letter to Clark on August 30, at the same time seeking indemnification for his losses in the robbery. Clark responded to Meredith's letter the following day, saying that he would send Alexander McNair, the agent for the Osage Indians, the list of stolen property along with the demand for its return. Identification of the horses and mules was possible by looking for the brand marks on each animal, which Meredith provided in his letter.[25] McNair and his sub-agent, Paul Choteau, found some of the livestock within 15 days; they were retaken and held under guard to prevent their theft again. By late November, seven mules belonging to McClure & Marmaduke had been retrieved and returned to the partners at Franklin. Three horses and the mule owned by Meredith were not recovered. William Clark wrote to Meredith the following spring to advise him that the Indians had agreed to pay for those animals and that $333 was being withheld from annuity money due the Osage Nation, "& as soon as the appropriation is made ... all the other claim allowed will be paid. I shall insert in the papers the names of all claimants entitled to receive indemnity for their losses."[26]

Clark's reference to "all claimants," along with a newspaper notice in the July 13, 1826, issue of the *Missouri Intelligencer* (a year after the robbery occurred), make it clear that other traders who lost property in the 1825 assault near the Little Arkansas River were pursuing their claims at the same time. The *Intelligencer* article listed 13 people to be paid from the Indians' annuity: "Henry Gratiot, Charles Downy, George Doughlass [sic], Joseph Bezet, Benjamin Briggs, Ewing Young, L. [S.] McClure & M. M. Marmaduke, Reys Baskes [Vasquez], James Pursely, Baily Hardeman, William (Negro), William Renick." The money could be obtained at Clark's office in St. Louis, either in person or by a representative. Meredith asked the mercantile firm of Smith & Knox for help and in September he received $275 to cover his and McClure's claims, as well as that of Reys Vasquez who had given McClure authority to accept the money in his behalf.[27] A longer list (23 additional names in a separate group) of men eligible for compensation because of losses to Indians of various tribes appeared in the July 20, 1826, issue of the St. Louis *Missouri Republican*. Among these were frontiersmen Nathan Boone, Ramon Garcia, Auguste Chouteau, Thomas Patterson, and Baptiste Boone. It seems that William Clark was able to clear a backlog of claims at one time.

The lack of correspondence reaching Virginia during Meredith's prolonged stay in New Mexico during 1824 and 1825 was worrisome for his family and friends. His brother, Vincent, wrote to John Hardeman asking if he would inquire about Meredith, his letter crossing paths with one from Meredith penned the day he returned to Franklin. In response, Vincent related his wife's death the previous April "after a long and tedious spell of consumption," and told Meredith that his friend "Captn. Hungerford has been at the point of death for a long time but has recovered."[28] He also answered Meredith's inquiry about the price of "common size" mules in Virginia saying "it seems to be the opinion … that they are worth about $50 but money is very scarce." Despite his loss to the Osage Indians, Meredith had animals to sell and he was scouting the country for the best price, even if it meant driving the stock to the East Coast. At the same time, he and Sam McClure were buying livestock. Three weeks after their return from Santa Fe they purchased six mules, three horses, and three "Jack Asses" from Romualdo Garcia, paying him $320 for the 12 animals.[29] The mules, alone, were worth the price; never one to pass up a bargain, Meredith knew he could sell the animals profitably in the Booneslick region.

Notes

1. "Crossed the river at Hardeman's Ferry": Harry C. Myers, "Meredith Miles Marmaduke's Journal of a Tour to New Mexico," *Wagon Tracks: Santa Fe Trail Association Quarterly*, Vol. 12, No. 1 (November 1997), 9, 14, 15. All subsequent quotations from the journal are from Myers' article.

2. "show that he could not have written the published journals unassisted.": David A. White, compiler. *News of the Plains and Rockies 1803–1865*, Vol. 2. 49.

3. "personal knowledge and correct information": *Missouri Advertiser*, September 2, 1825. "Santa Fe Trail classic": Myers, 8.

4. "Colonel Marmaduke, the present governor": Josiah Gregg, *Scenes and Incidents of the Western Prairies*, 24. Interestingly, James L. Collins, who returned from Santa Fe with Marmaduke in 1828, wrote him in 1854 asking to use Meredith's "notes" in preparing an account of "the Santa Fe trades, and traders." Unlike Gregg, there is no evidence that Meredith loaned his journal to Collins, who never published. J. L. Collins to Meredith Marmaduke, May 13, 1854. Folder 19, Marmaduke Papers C1021, SHSMO.

5. "Travelled say 15 miles and encamped": Myers, 9.

6. "This bluff, facing the road on the right side": William B. Napton Jr., *Over the Santa Fe Trail*, 26. The son of noted Missouri attorney and jurist William B. Napton Sr., the younger Napton was 18 years old when he went to Santa Fe as a young man in 1857 with a wagon train commanded by "Jim Crow" Chiles of Jackson County, Missouri. Born in 1839, Napton Jr. was raised in Saline County where his family was well acquainted with "Colonel Marmaduke."

7. "A. Legrand was elected Captain": Alexander Le Grand was educated in law but left that profession and devoted himself for nine years to trading and trapping in the West. He first went to Santa Fe in 1823. His

To Make a Fortune in Missouri

last reported appearance was at Houston, Texas, in 1839. Thrapp, *Encyclopedia of Frontier Biography*, Vol. 2, 840. Paul Anderson, with his brother William, was a member of the Baird company that made a late start to Santa Fe in 1822 and spent the winter camped on the Arkansas River. He also was among a group of merchants that included Sam McClure who received permits to trade in Sonora and Chihuahua in 1826. Anderson requested Mexican citizenship in 1830 and went to California that year. Weber, *The Taos Trappers*, 59, 121. Absalom Simpson was elected ensign (lowest officer rank in the military, elected by his peers, an important assignment above regular troops). *Missouri Intelligencer*, June 5, 1824.

8. Josiah Gregg said that a portion of the company used pack mules to transport their goods. Gregg, *Scenes and Incidents of the Western Prairies*, 24; Marmaduke, on leaving the Cimarron River in northeastern New Mexico July 7, noted in his journal that "The packers this day left us for Tous, at noon."

9. "significant religious development": *Religion in 18th Century America*, National Endowment for the Humanities; edsitement.gov/curriculum-unit/religion-18th-century-america. For more on the role of the Catholic Church in the settlement and life of early New Mexico, see George D. Torok, *From the Pass to the Pueblos*, 24–28.

10. "Gentlemen, I received ... your favor": "Important to New-Mexican Traders," *Missouri Intelligencer*, August 26, 1825.

11. "difficult to do to an advantage": Marmaduke to John Hardeman, August 5, 1824. Box 1, Folder 3, Sappington-Marmaduke Papers, MHS.

12. "Yet I do not despair": Ibid.

13. "we shall have succeeding in effecting a sale": Marmaduke to John Hardeman, October 13, 1824. Folder 5, Glen O. Hardeman Papers C3655, SHSMO.

14. Merchandise that Meredith valued at $696.62: Memorandum of goods in pack taken down the river Sept. 21st, 1864. Folder 3, Marmaduke Papers C1021, SHSMO manuscript collection. Marmaduke recorded a two-page list of the trade goods, describing the items, cost for each and sale price, and the total retail value. A notation on the list shows the goods were returned October 10 with no indication anything was sold.

15. "a man of intelligence and veracity": "Trade to New Mexico," *Missouri Intelligencer*, June 4, 1824. American traders going to Paso del Norte traveled along the "Royal Highway," a trail from central Mexico to the pueblos in New Mexico that Spanish explorers and traders had used since 1598. The 404-mile section of the trail from Santa Fe to El Paso, Texas, is designated today as El Camino Real de Tierra Adentro National Historic Trail, supervised by the U.S. National Park Service and the Bureau of Land Management. An interpretive facility, the El Camino Real International Heritage Center, a New Mexico State Monument, rises today at the northern end of the 90-mile-long Jornada del Muerto, the Dead Man's Journey, the most dangerous section of the trail. Travelers here faced the possibility of death by dehydration, exhaustion, and searing desert heat during summer.

16. McClure to Marmaduke, December 24, 1827. MHS/S&M Box 1, Folder 3.

17. "on our old travels, do you recollect": McClure to Meredith Marmaduke, February 28, 1847. Box 4, Folder 2, Sappington-Marmaduke Papers, MHS. It is doubtful the Indian settlement visited by McClure and Marmaduke was part of the Navajo Nation. More likely it was a Pueblo Indian village, the nearest being Nambe Pueblo, 20 miles north of Santa Fe, a day's ride as indicated in McClure's letter. The Navajo were nomadic raiders in the 1820s, preying on more settled native tribes such as the Puebloans of New Mexico. In 1824, the Mexican government sent troops through the Navajo territory in an attempt to subdue them. The Puebloan people often served with Provincial troops to protect villages from raiders such as the Navajo, Apache, and Comanche, and to protect caravans on the Santa Fe Trail. For more, see: David J. Weber, *The Mexican Frontier, 1821–1846*.

18. "treat with the president or government of the United States:" David J. Weber, "Señor Escudero Goes to Washington," *Western Historical Quarterly*, Vol. 43, No. 4 (Winter 2012), 420. After stopping at St. Louis, Escudero eventually reached the nation's capital where he was received by Mexico's minister plenipotentiary, who explained that his mission was not sanctioned by Mexico's central government and therefore it would be improper for him to meet with American officials. Returning to St. Louis, Escudero began preparing for his return to Mexico as a trader.

A Long and Lonesome Travel

19. "among them Romualdo Garcia from Sonora:" Ibid, 425.

20. The company on its way to Missouri now numbered 40 persons: Ibid, fn. 30, 425, 426. In giving the number of people in the caravan — the American traders, the Mexicans, and the company of 35 from Tennessee — Weber cites: " 'From the Internal Provinces,' published in the *Washington Gazette*, 16 September 1825, reprinted from an article that appeared in a St. Louis newspaper, 12 September 1825." Examination of a microfilm copy of the September 12, 1825, issue of the *Missouri Republican* newspaper, published in St. Louis, held in the State Historical Society of Missouri archives, was unsuccessful in locating the cited article. The poor condition of the microfilm image made a large portion of the newspaper unreadable. Little is known about the Tennessee traders mentioned by Weber; however, an article in the March 16, 1826, issue of the *Missouri Republican* mentions a caravan of traders who "left Jackson [Tennessee] April 1, 1825, en route to Santa Fe."

21. "bar of silver": Manuel Escudero to John Hardeman, September 4, 1825. Folder 16, Glen O. Hardeman Papers C3655, SHSMO. Writing from St. Louis, Escudero asked Hardeman to "send by the bearer, my nephew Don Pedro Escudero, the bar of silver left in your charge."

22. "About two hours after their absence": "Mexican Adventures," *Missouri Intelligencer*, August 5, 1825. This account, obviously firsthand, calls into question the fate of the "thirty-five men from Tennessee," cited by Weber. If there were only "12 or 15 effective men" at the camp when the Indians plundered it, then the Tennessee contingent must have already split off and taken a different trail back to the settlements. It is also unlikely that the Indians would have behaved as they did if the Tennesseans had been on hand, bringing the number of "effective men" to near 50.

23. "This evening Col. Marmaduke arrived at my House": Kate L. Gregg, ed., *The Road to Santa Fe*, 54–55. Sibley had recently been appointed a member of a federal commission charged with surveying the Santa Fe Trail, a project that had been initiated by Missouri Senator Thomas H. Benton. Sibley left Fort Osage the morning after Meredith's visit to take up those duties.

24. "between 3 and 4 years old" valued at $600: Statement of property taken from Samuel McClure and M.M. Marmaduke the 14th day of July 1825. Box 1, Folder 3, Sappington-Marmaduke Papers, MHS.

25. Clark responded to Meredith the following day: William Clark to Meredith Marmaduke, August 31, 1825. Box 1, Folder 3, Sappington-Marmaduke Papers, MHS. On September 10 August P. Choteau was paid $113.25 for "guarding horses stolen from white people,"; Israel St. Cyr received $10 on November 7, and Baptiste Jacko was paid $20 on November 20, for "delivering stolen horses to the settlements." Accounts of Alexander McNair, 1824–1826, *U.S. Superintendency of Indian Affairs, St. Louis, Records, 1807–1855*, Vol. 25. C2969, SHSMO.

26. "& as soon as the appropriation is made": William Clark to Meredith Marmaduke, June 5, 1826. Box 2, Folder 3, Sappington-Marmaduke Papers, MHS.

27. Meredith asked the mercantile firm of Smith & Knox for help: Receipt, Messrs. Smith & Knox, September 25, 1826. Folder 27, Thomas A. Smith Papers C1029, SHSMO.

28. "after a long and tedious spell of consumption": Vincent Marmaduke to Meredith Marmaduke, September 12, 1825. Box 1, Folder 3, Sappington-Marmaduke Papers, MHS.

29. Three weeks after their return from Santa Fe they purchased six mules, three horses and three "Jack Asses" from Romualdo Garcia: Purchase receipt, August 26, 1825, Ibid.

CHAPTER 8

TROUBLE ON THE RETURN

The firm of McClure & Marmaduke was active in the Santa Fe trade in 1826, although Meredith remained in Missouri that year while McClure carried the company's merchandise to New Mexico and beyond. He joined the caravan leaving Franklin the last week in May and arrived at Santa Fe on August 16. In line with Meredith's desire to control as much of the trade as possible, the partners filled at least two wagons with goods. After reaching Santa Fe, McClure reported that his "teams was quite sufficient for their loads."[1] On the trail a few days behind the main body of traders, Manuel Escudero, with "six or seven new and substantial built waggons ... heavily laden with merchandise," passed through Franklin on June 2.[2] He left in his wake unpaid accounts for advances on the trade goods he was hauling, including $3,000 loaned him by a Philadelphia merchant and an unknown amount of money loaned him by Meredith. McClure anxiously watched for the Mexican lawyer-emissary-trader's arrival at Santa Fe; he had promised Meredith he would use his "best Endeavors" to collect his partner's money. Unfortunately Escudero — his star as an unofficial ambassador tarnished in his ill-considered journey to Washington — faced political conditions in New Mexico that were not in his favor. His welcome by a new governor at Santa Fe was frosty. Nevertheless, he managed to dispose of his goods before returning to his home in Chihuahua. Meredith is presumed to have recovered the money owed him.

The role of McClure & Marmaduke in the 1826–27 Santa Fe trade is unclear, but one aspect of the partnership is known to have continued during this time, giving rise to the possibility that McClure went to Santa Fe that year as the company's sole agent. Writing to Meredith on Christmas Eve 1827, McClure discussed their jointly owned livestock, recently brought from New Mexico, that he was keeping at his farm in Howard County. He was "in hopes we will get through with the most of our mares in Spring[.] wet and muddy times is worse on them than a steady cold. I brot home some of our poorest mares[,] they keep poor as well as our Jenny. Nothing thrives but my Belley Jenny Stud[,] he is as fatt as cream." McClure, himself, was not in good health and this may have contributed to his decision to withdraw from the trade after 1827. "I have had a pretty tuff time of it ... had many Backsetts. ... Still but weak and standing but badly."[3] The rigors of the Santa Fe Trail had taken their toll on Meredith's partner.

Although no account books are known to exist that could provide an insight into the success of their four-year-long partnership, it is likely that both of them did well financially. The mules and horses they obtained in Mexico found a ready market in

Missouri, and Mexican coins jingled their way east as part of their baggage. Meredith was interested in loaning that money when terms were favorable. In January of 1826, in Saline County and unable to cross the ice-bound Missouri River, he wrote to "Col. McClure" in Franklin telling him that he had drawn a draft on McClure "in favor of Mr. Smith for $300. He is in need of $150 more [and] will examine three rolls of the Santa Fe money, and if he will consent to receive it, let him have of it. ... Please arrange this, in such way as to serve us both. I expect to cross the river the first moment that the ice will allow me."4

New Partners in 1828
As McClure & Marmaduke was dissolving, Meredith formed a new company for "trading to the Mexican Country" in the fall of 1827. Known as M. M. Marmaduke & Co., the partnership included Meredith, Thomas McMahan, and Erasmus Darwin (E. D.) Sappington. Their agreement called for McMahan to "put into the common stock" 500 hats, "2 hundred and fifty of which shall be ... first quality waterproof Rosum hats $3.50 each ... one hundred and fifty waterproof Rosum knapped [sic] with Raccoon fur at $3.00, and the remaining one hundred to be glue stiffened at $2.75 ... with good fashionable ... trimming for them all." Meredith and Sappington together agreed to provide merchandise, Dearborn wagons and teams "to an amount not varying very far from 16 or 18 hundred dollars."5 The partners shared expenses equally for the venture, and each could add to their share of the common stock at any time with the profit to be divided proportionally. In early December, Meredith contracted with Alexander McCausland, a Franklin merchant, to purchase trade goods for the coming year. He would "take of [McCausland] 12 or 15 hundred dollars worth of goods, at an advance of 20 percent on the Philadelphia or N. York cost, exclusive of carriage or any other charges," terms Meredith had earlier proposed.6 The selection of merchandise was left up to the Franklin storekeeper, who was also soliciting other traders going to Santa Fe. Meredith's letter, delivered to McCausland by E. D. Sappington, specified that the goods "most suitable and saleable in that market are the kind I shall want." There was a caveat, however. "I must impose upon you ... that immediately on the arrival of your goods [you] send an express directly," Meredith requested, "notifying me of that fact so that I may have an equal oppy. [opportunity] with others of making my selections, for I do consider that there is considerable advantage in this." His experience in the trade had shown Meredith that shoddy merchandise was difficult to sell to the Mexicans. He also instructed McCausland to include in his selection of goods "pretty many" black silk veils, which were in high demand by the ladies of Santa Fe. Meredith also purchased a small stock of goods from D. Kyle & Co., another Franklin merchant, paying him 20 percent over his cost.

The *Missouri Intelligencer & Boon's Lick Advertiser* (now being published in Fayette) noted in its May 2, 1828, issue that Franklin was the "busy, bustling and commercial scene, in buying, selling and packing goods, practising [sic] mules, &c. &c." The editor exuberantly predicted that the amount of goods going west this year "will not, perhaps, fall much short of $100,000." Last-minute preparations occupied the members of Marmaduke & Co. in mid-May. On the 12th, Meredith hired blacksmith Benjamin Huston to make alterations to a Dearborn wagon, and paid him for horse and mule shoes, and 50 feet of chain. The following day, the partners met in Franklin and signed a new agreement that specified "the amount each man has put in trade." Thomas McMahan's merchandise cost him $1,578, Meredith's outlay for goods was $1,469, and 19-year-old E. D. Sappington's trading stock cost him $855.[7] At Blue Springs in Jackson County, Missouri, on May 17 the partners joined 37 other wagons, containing "about $41,000" worth of merchandise, that had gathered for the trip to New Mexico.[8] By the middle of July, the caravan was in Santa Fe, having passed through Indian country and the arid Cimarron cutoff without serious incident.

A Fast Trade

Meredith did not want to prolong his stay in Santa Fe in 1828. He intended a quick sale of his goods and a fast return to Missouri, after trading for as many mules and horses as possible. Several months earlier, when considering the possibility of breeding mules to sell, he had asked George Sibley for his thoughts about how well jennets (donkey mares that could be bred to male horses, thus producing mules) adjusted to living in Missouri. Meredith wanted to know if they could survive in the state's winter climate. If so, he believed the jennet offspring would find a ready market in the Booneslick country and beyond. Sibley related his experience with jennets he had brought from Mexico in 1826; however, his observations were not encouraging enough for Meredith to trade heavily for them at Santa Fe in 1828.[9] Instead, he looked to mules and male Mexican donkeys (the latter often referred to as "jacks" or "jackasses") as his major interest, although he did trade for some horses. Mules would sell readily in Missouri on his return, providing a quick source of cash. Mare horses, on the other hand, could be bred to the Mexican donkeys and would produce mule colts as offspring. Their strength, stamina, and willingness to work made mules highly desired by teamsters and farmers, and Meredith recognized their potential as a source of income.

Within a few days after arriving at Santa Fe, Meredith and his partners began to prepare for their return home. They had sold most of their merchandise, probably at wholesale prices, and a second caravan from Missouri — arriving the first week of August — found the market "a bad prospect," thanks to "those that sold out … [and] got but 20 per cent on cost."[10] In a stable yard on July 22, Meredith began the task of identifying the mules belonging to Marmaduke & Co. by branding the letter "S" on the right jaw of each animal and recording a brief description of each in a notebook that doubled as an accounting ledger. Later entries show the partners had acquired at least 62 mules, 16 horses, and two jacks by the time they left Santa Fe. (The horses and donkeys are not listed in the notebook as branded, although they probably were.)

Meredith also recorded the branding and description of 20 animals belonging to "Harris & Scott," presumed to be Nathan Harris and William Scott, two traders who had accompanied the wagon train from Missouri to Santa Fe, and who returned with the partners and others in August.[11] A reconciliation of income and expenses for Marmaduke & Co., along with accounting entries for Harris & Scott, was entered in the notebook by Meredith in late July. Once again, as he did in 1824, Meredith attempted to gain more control over the price of goods being sold at Santa Fe by buying out a competitor. He made a pact with Harris and Scott on the journey west when the neophyte traders realized it would be to their advantage to throw in with

Meredith, acknowledging his experience and his ability to deal with the Mexican authorities, principally the import tax assessor. Marmaduke & Co. managed all aspects of Harris & Scott's trade, including paying the $318 import tax on their goods and advancing the pair money for miscellaneous expenses. The combined sales by the two companies totaled $8,075 (rounded to the nearest dollar), including $2,712 in cash with the balance in animals taken in trade. Harris & Scott's portion of the total sales amounted to $2,198, of which $740 was in cash. The animals taken in trade were divided accordingly with Harris & Scott's share valued at $1,458. To determine this, Meredith priced mules at $25 each; mares, other horses, and jennets at $12 apiece; and jacks at $100 each. After reimbursing Marmaduke & Co. for their portion of the import tax and other expenses, Harris & Scott received 36 horses, 20 mules, one jack, and their share of the cash. Their animals would be worth considerably more when driven to Missouri.

That account reconciled, Meredith next turned his attention to the expenses incurred so far by his company. The import tax paid on goods they brought into New Mexico amounted to $659. Miscellaneous expenses (saddles, tack, and other gear) totaled $75. Adding in the $3,902 expended for trade goods (listed earlier) brought their total cash outlay to $4,636. Their share of the total sales amounted to $5,877 of which $1,972 was the partners' portion of the cash, with the balance in animals taken in trade. On August 2, Meredith recorded the specie the company had on hand: "In roll $1,200, in leather bag 500, in striped & Check domestic bag 200, in blue Sock 32," with $40 stashed in the other blue sock. To break even, their portion of the livestock would have to be worth $2,764. Using the scale Meredith devised for settling the Harris & Scott account, the animals belonging to Marmaduke & Co., as listed in the notebook, were worth $3,905 at Santa Fe, giving them with the specie an initial profit of $1,241. Now all they had to do was get their livestock home without any loss. If they were successful, the profit side of the ledger would benefit significantly.

Trouble on the Return

"About 70 or 80 of our fellow-citizens, we learn, have arrived from a trading expedition to the Province of New Mexico. We understand they have realized a handsome profit on their outfit. We regret to learn that Capt. Daniel Munro [Monroe], one of our oldest and most respectable citizens, was killed by the Pawnee Indians, on his return home — and also a son of Capt. Samuel C. M'Nees, of Franklin."

This brief notice in the September 12, 1828, issue of the *Missouri Intelligencer & Boon's Lick Advertiser* related only half the story of the traders' encounter with Indians on the journey home. No accurate figures exist to tell the number of men in the homeward-bound caravan that came together on the east side of Glorieta Pass in mid-August of 1828, but most accounts place it somewhere between 70 and 80, enough, one would think, to dissuade any marauding Indians from wanting to bother them. Unfortunately, for Meredith and the others in this caravan, fate determined otherwise. The large number of animals they pushed along the trail — more than 1,000, perhaps as many as 1,200 — was too tempting. And, too, when Indians were on the prowl there always existed the possibility of stirring up a hornet's nest of trouble.

Some of the other men accompanying Meredith and his partners as they traveled east were James L. Collins, Milton Sublette, Jesse Turley, Nathan Harris, William Scott, "Long Jim" and "Big Jim" Barnes, and 13 others whose names Meredith later recalled as being with the company.[12] Several days after leaving the rendezvous site, Daniel Monroe and young Robert McNees — who had been sent ahead of the long, dusty line of men, wagons, and animals to search for water — laid down to rest at a shady spot alongside a creek in northeastern New Mexico. When the caravan caught up with them later that day McNees was dead and Monroe was dying, both having been shot by Indians thought to be Comanches through whose territory the train was passing. The two men were placed in a wagon and carried on until Monroe died, at which time both were buried at a site near the Cimarron River. At about this same time, a small band of Indians approached the train, perhaps Comanches but more likely Pawnees who had nothing to do with the deaths of McNees and Monroe. Without warning, members of the caravan attacked the natives, acting either out of fear or in retaliation, and a number of the Indians were killed. Some, however, escaped to relate the incident to others in the band. The unprovoked attack only served to antagonize the Indians, who likely already had in mind raiding the caravan and driving off some of the livestock.

Because he was not an aggressive person, it is difficult to imagine Meredith participating in the initial attack; however, one chronicler of the Santa Fe trade claims he was involved. William Waldo, a "Santa Fe trader, merchant, and farmer," steamboat captain, and at one time an unsuccessful nominee for governor of California, related that Meredith, in company with Milton Sublette and five others "had a deathly conflict with one hundred and fifty Comanches, west of the Arkansas River" in 1828.[13] The number of Indians cited is wrong, as is perhaps the tribe to which they belonged, but the number of traders involved in the attack corresponds with what is known, and the location — "west of the Arkansas" — places the site on the Cimarron. Taken together, these establish Waldo's account as happening prior to a subsequent raid in which the caravan's livestock was stolen. If his somewhat embellished portrayal is true, Waldo's knowledge of the event may have come directly from Meredith himself. Both men were active in speculative ventures on the upper Osage River in Missouri during the late 1830s and early '40s, Waldo as a merchant at Harmony Mission and Meredith as a buyer of land along the Osage River in St. Clair County. The two men would have known each other.

After burying McNees and Monroe, the caravan continued north, crossing the Arkansas River on August 28 where they went into camp. That night, after slipping among the animal herd, Pawnee Indians ran off "about 600 head of stock chiefly mules, the balance horses, jacks and Jennies, which had been either bot [sic] or taken in payment of merchandize" [sic].[14] The number of animals lost by Meredith and his partners in the raid is difficult to determine with accuracy — the figures appearing in records and subsequent correspondence are different and irreconcilable — but a good estimate is that they were robbed of at least 65 mules and five horses, although the number could be higher.[15]

30 Years of Frustration

If Meredith expected to recover his stolen livestock from the Pawnee as easily and quickly as he had in 1825, he was mistaken. That claim had been readily acknowledged to Superintendent of Indian Affairs William Clark by the Osage Indians, who then returned some of the animals to Meredith and agreed to pay for his unrecovered livestock from the tribe's annuity funds. This time, the response was different. Meredith again looked to William Clark for help but the Pawnee were not cooperative, aware of the potential loss of their annuity money if they admitted the theft. The number of animals involved was much greater than the loss suffered three years earlier, and they had been dispersed already among the Pawnee or traded to other Plains Indians. Finding the animals claimed by an individual would have been difficult. Hearing that some of his mules might be with the Osage Indians, Meredith wrote their agent to ask his help in locating them — and thereby risked invalidating his claim for indemnification. The procedure for resolving Indian depredation claims had been established by Congress in 1796 in a revision to the Trade and Intercourse Act that was intended to prevent hostilities on the American frontier. A section of the new law created an indemnity process by which non-Indians and Indians could be compensated for a loss resulting from an action between the two parties. A claim for a depredation committed by an Indian would be considered by the government: (1) if the accused was a member of a tribe "in amity" with the government; (2) if the offense occurred when the accused Indian had gone beyond the boundary line of Indian country (established by treaty); (3) if the victim provided proof of his loss; and (4) if he did not pursue the claim on his own (which Meredith did in writing the agent for the Osage tribe).[16]

The 1796 law developed administrative procedures to handle such claims. First, the agent receiving the claim was to ask the nation of the accused Indian for satisfaction (most claims were for the loss of property). If a claim was not resolved at this level, the agent was required to wait a reasonable amount of time (initially 18 months, later reduced to 12) before sending the claim and documents proving it to the president. (Indian depredation claims were handled by the War Department until 1849, at which time the Bureau of Indian Affairs transferred to the Department of Interior.) If the claim was approved, the president could order indemnification with money deducted from annuity funds belonging to the offending tribe. The indemnity system was not the only recourse a non-Indian had to resolve a claim; he could appeal to Congress, although there was little interest there in considering such matters except that evinced by a congressman for a client. In November 1828, Meredith wrote to Missouri congressman Edward Bates on behalf of the larger group of traders who had been robbed, seeking his help in getting a claim submitted to the U.S. House of Representatives. Bates wrote he was "sorry to hear of your loss in the Santa Fe road," and said he had "by resolution," set the House Military Committee at work to find a solution to the problem of Indian depredation along the trail. He advocated the establishment of a fort "at or near where the road crosses the Arkansas, and have half the garrison mounted to convoy the caravans, & to pursue & promptly punish any aggression on the part of the Indians." Otherwise, he offered Meredith no help in the way of recovery or compensation for the traders' loss.[17] Failing there, in May of 1829 Meredith appealed to Secretary of War John H. Eaton, who administered the Bureau of Indian Affairs, for his help. Eaton undoubtedly expressed sympathy for the traders' problem but offered little beyond that. Meredith's claim languished until a change to the Trade and Intercourse Act in 1834 offered new hope.

Under the new law, the federal treasury became the "last resort" in the process of satisfying depredation claims. Now, if an Indian nation refused to acknowledge liability, or if its treaty funds were insufficient to pay a claim, the government would assume that responsibility. Learning this, in 1835 Meredith, with suggestions from fellow trader James L. Collins, drafted a new memorial to Congress in behalf of himself, E. D. Sappington, Thomas McMahan, Collins, William Scott, Philip Thompson, "and others of the State of Missouri," to present their claims for indemnification.[18] A major problem encountered at this time and in coming years in trying to move the petition through Congress was that institution's continual lack of interest in paying such claims, and its ability to avoid acting despite an individual politician's interest in helping his constituency. Historian Larry Skogen's study for his seminal work, *Indian Depredation Claims, 1796–1920*, led him to conclude that "Congress's penchant for not paying claims except when the government possessed a direct liability remained the guiding principle in the Capitol during the first half of the nineteenth century."[19] Another issue Meredith faced was proving which Indians were responsible for the robbery — were they Pawnee, Osage, or Comanche? To resolve this, Collins obtained affidavits in 1850 from Mexican citizens "Jose Maguel Lujan, and our old servant Concious Archuleta." In a letter to Meredith, Collins explained how he located the two men after 22 years had passed:

"I have had more troble [sic] to find Lujan than I expected. I knew that such a man had some years ago stated to me the facts contained in his affidavit but I had forgot the name and I could get no clue to it, only by inquiring for a man that was once a prisoner with Pawnee Indians, and this every person seemed to have forgot. After many inquiries, and two trips to San Maguil and Las Vegas, I accidentally found our old servant Concious Archuleta. From him I [obtained] the name and residence of the prisoner and finally found him and gave him fifteen dollars to come to Santa Fe where his deposition could be taken without its appearing in my own hand writing. The two affidavits taken together will make the proof strong against the Pawnees, and I think with what you can collect at home, the robbery can be clearly made out against those Indians. At any rate I turn the matter over to you and those interested at home. If it should be necessary to address proof as to each individual loss I will attend that in due time. My loss however I think was about 130 head, perhaps a few more or less. The sooner the claim is presented the better. The papers should, at any rate, be filed this session of Congress."[20]

To further strengthen the petition, traders William Scott and Philip Thompson were deposed in Saline County and their statements, with those of Lujan and Archuleta, Meredith sent to Missouri Representative John S. Phelps in Washington. His response pointed out problems and offered some advice:

"There is not the slightest probability of accomplishing anything at this session of Congress as all the people's business is in arrears. ... I think it advisable not to present your petition at this session. ... The depositions taken [in Saline County] are not so particular and specific as I think is advisable. The deponents in each instance swear that 'he believes the number of animals above stated to be just and true to the best of his knowledge & belief.' Nowhere in the deposition does he state that claimants owned the number of animals stated in the account and that he lost them by the acts of the Indians on 28th August. This is an oversight ... let the deponents subscribe the affidavits, and probably it would be best to prove the value of the animals at the time of the loss."[21]

Work on perfecting the petition continued with James Collins taking a more active role in the traders' struggle to be indemnified. During the second session of the 32nd Congress, meeting from December 6, 1852, to March 3, 1853, he was in Washington, trying to get Meredith's petition referred to the Senate Committee on Indian Affairs. Conversations with members of Congress led him to believe the claim would receive a favorable recommendation; however, he reported that the process would be slow "owing to the great amount of business before that committee." Collins also suggested they hire someone to lobby for their cause, telling Meredith that an influential agent could probably do more than a member of Congress.[22] What he didn't anticipate was opposition later that year by William K. Sebastian of Arkansas, Chairman of the Senate Committee on Indian Affairs, who halted any further action in that chamber. An effort to get a similar bill introduced in the House Committee on Indian Affairs in 1853 also stalled, Missouri Representative John G. Miller telling Meredith that unless the Senate acted on the measure he saw no future for the claim in his chamber. In 1854, Collins, having determined to act as agent for himself and the other claimants, continued to press the petition on Congress, this time seeking the support of Alfred Greenwood, Chairman of the House Committee on Indian Affairs, who took it under advisement. Nothing more happened in the House until December 1857, when the petition was revived by newly elected Missouri Representative Samuel Woodson, a member of the Committee on Indian Affairs. Four months later, on April 17, House Resolution 505 was reported out of that committee as "a Bill for the Relief of M. M. Marmaduke and others." The bill authorized the Secretary of the Interior (now administering Indian affairs) to determine the number and value of the "horses, mules, and asses forcibly taken and driven off from M. M. Marmaduke, E. D. Sappington, Thomas McMahan, Jesse B. Turley, Philip W. Thomson, James L. Collins, William Scott, and James Wood." The bill cited the Pawnee Indians as being responsible for the theft. Meredith and the others were to be paid "out of any moneys in the Treasury not otherwise appropriated." Unfortunately, the 30-year-long struggle for indemnification would, in the end, prove fruitless for the traders. The House bill was never considered by the Senate.[23] In 1859, concern about the possibility of fraudulent depredation claims led Congress to repeal the provision of the 1834 law that guaranteed payment from the treasury. This, with the growing unrest of the looming Civil War, doomed to failure any further effort by Meredith and the other traders to obtain compensation for their loss some 30 years earlier.

The year 1828 is the last for which evidence exists showing Meredith Marmaduke's active participation in the Santa Fe trade. That he intended to continue commerce there in 1829, expanding beyond Santa Fe, and that he still was intrigued with the potential of breeding jennets with horses is evident in the existence of a draft contract that he wrote on July 22, 1828, only a few days after arriving in New Mexico. If completed, the compact would have been with someone from the state of Sonora, Mexico, and it would have obligated Meredith to "send on with the Company that may leave Missouri for Santa Fe in the spring of ... 1829 an amount of goods corresponding as nearly as can be procured to a list" that was to be furnished by the other party. Meredith proposed to purchase $2,400 worth of merchandise at Franklin prices to which he would add a 75 percent commission, the whole to be paid upon delivery of the goods in Santa Fe by Meredith or his agent. Payment was to be in the form of "two hundred, large, fine, likely young Jennetts, between the ages of 2 and 10 years, and four likely young Jennett Jacks, and also twelve, broke, gentle likely young mules, all in good order and condition." Meredith protected himself by disclaiming any liability in the event the merchandise was damaged in an accident on the trail. He also called for an examination of the livestock by "two persons ... mutually chosen" to assure that the animals met the terms of the agreement. He would receive the livestock at any point between Santa Fe and the Red River (in New Mexico) that was agreeable to the other party in the contract.[24]

Meredith evidently had someone in mind when he drew up the document because it was to be signed the same day it was drafted. Why it was never executed is an open question. The other party may have become discouraged at seeing the Santa Fe market overwhelmed with goods that summer, or he may not have found the terms of the contract agreeable. That aside, the document's existence today provides a window into Meredith's thoughts at the time about his future as a trader, and demonstrates his evolution from salesman on the streets of Santa Fe in 1824 to sophisticated buyer, shipper, and wholesale merchant in 1828. His decision not to travel to Santa Fe to trade after his return home in 1828 is understandable from a business perspective. He was discouraged, of course, by the financial loss he sustained as a result of the Pawnee raid and theft of his stock. But that came after three years (1824–25, 1826, and 1827) in which he apparently enjoyed satisfactory profits. He also understood the dynamics of the Mexican market, probably better than anyone else who was trading there at the time, so why give it up? The answer is seen in his desire to switch from retail to wholesale marketing, and the lack of a contract of that nature for 1829. Other factors that may have influenced his decision include the increasing competition and the resulting decline in the rate of profit he could expect; the amount of time — five to six months — required to make a round-trip journey between Missouri and Santa Fe (time that could be more profitably spent in Missouri); and the routine hazards encountered along the trail — dangerous river crossings, exposure to violent weather, and the continual threat of thievery by raiding Indians. In 1829, he took a different direction in his quest to make a fortune, one that held the promise of profit without having to leave the Booneslick country.[25]

Notes

1. "teams was quite sufficient for their loads": Samuel McClure to Meredith Marmaduke, August 22, 1826. Box 1, Folder 3 Sappington-Marmaduke Papers, MHS. At Santa Fe, McClure was also trying to settle financial matters that dated back to 1824–25.

2. "six or seven new and substantial built waggons": *Missouri Intelligencer*, June 9, 1826.

3. "in hopes we will get through with the most of our mares": McClure to Marmaduke, December 24, 1827. Box 1, Folder 3, Sappington-Marmaduke Papers, MHS. McClure apparently had few fond memories of his time among the Mexicans. Writing to Meredith in 1846, in the middle of the Mexican-American War, he

To Make a Fortune in Missouri

exposed his feelings, saying he thought "certainly you would be one of the first to turn out & silence those dastardly Spaniards & have some satisfaction of those that hated us so indifferently when among them": McClure to Marmaduke, September 10, 1846. Box 4, Folder 1, Sappington-Marmaduke Papers, MHS.

4. "in favor of Mr. Smith for $300": Meredith Marmaduke to Col. McClure, January 26, 1826. Box 1, Folder 3, Sappington-Marmaduke Papers, MHS.

5. A new company for "trading to the Mexican Country": Details of the two contracts between Marmaduke, McMahan, and Sappington are contained in a memoranda dated October 30, 1827, and one dated May 13, 1828, both in: Folder 16, John Sappington Papers C1027, SHSMO.

6. "take of [McCausland] 12 or 15 hundred dollars worth of goods": Three letters regarding the purchase of goods are: McCausland to Marmaduke, December 11, 1827; Marmaduke to McCausland, December 14, 1827; and McCausland to Marmaduke, December 24, 1827, all in Folder 16, John Sappington Papers C1027, SHSMO.

7. "the amount each man has put in trade." Memorandum of an Agreement, May 13, 1828, Folder 16, John Sappington Papers C1027, SHSMO.

8. "about $41,000" worth of merchandise: *Missouri Intelligencer*, May 30, 1828. A second wagon train, reportedly carrying more than $100,000 in goods, left Missouri at the end of May. Led by Alphonso Wetmore, it didn't reach Santa Fe until early August. For more about this train see Wetmore's diary in Archer B. Hulbert, *Southwest on the Turquoise Trail*, pp. 182–195.

9. Sibley related his experience with jennets he had brought from Mexico: Sibley to Marmaduke, November 20, 1827. Folder 4, Marmaduke Papers C1021, SHSMO.

10. "a bad prospect": Hardeman, *Wilderness Calling*, 113.

11. "Harris & Scott": Notebook ledger, July 22 - August 2, 1828, Vol. 2. John Sappington Papers C1027, SHSMO. The notebook contains lists of the animals branded for each company; a page titled "memo of mares branded;" an expense page for each partner; a page titled "account of expenses;" another that shows expenses incurred in behalf of Harris & Scott; several pages that reconcile the income, expense and distribution of money and animals; and two pages that list animals belonging to Harris and Scott, the Marmaduke company, and James L. Collins. It is obvious that Meredith's financial calculations were done over a period of several days and that several false starts were made, with some pages being scribbled through.

12. Some of the other men accompanying Meredith: Document titled "Persons recollected in Company at time robbery was committed," dated August 28, 1828. Box 1, Folder 4, Sappington-Marmaduke Papers, MHS.

13. "Santa Fe trader, merchant, and farmer": William Waldo, "Recollections of a Septuagenarian," *Glimpses of the Past*, Missouri Historical Society, Vol. V, No's. 4–6, (April–June 1938) (1880), 60, 65. The original title given the manuscript by William Waldo was "Biographical Sketches of Various Explorers, Fur-Traders, Trappers and Hunters." William was one of six Waldo brothers from Pennsylvania seeking their fortunes in Missouri and the west during this period. The most prosperous was David, a physician, Santa Fe trader, land speculator and banker, who wielded considerable political influence in Jackson County, where he settled. At his death in 1878, he was described as "one of the oldest, wealthiest and most respected men in Jackson County." Many parallel comparisons can be drawn in the lives of David Waldo and Meredith Marmaduke, including their affiliation with the St. Louis lodge of Free Masons.

14. "about 600 head of stock chiefly mules, the balance horses, jacks and Jennies": Memorial to Congress, February 27, 1835. Box 2, Folder 2, Sappington-Marmaduke Papers, MHS.

15. The number of animals lost by Meredith and his partners: Affidavit, January 20, 1851. Box 5, Folder 1, Sappington-Marmaduke Papers, MHS. William L. Scott and Philip W. Thompson, both members of the 1828 caravan, attested by affidavit in Saline County that the animals lost by M. M. Marmaduke & Co. were 65 mules and 5 horses. A discrepancy occurs in the number of animals owned when comparing the count Meredith did near the end of his stay in Santa Fe, when he listed 80, with the later distribution among the three partners of the livestock they managed to get to Franklin, when they had 25 animals. If the affidavit is accepted as correct, then M. M. Marmaduke & Co. left Santa Fe with 95 animals instead of the 80 previously noted. For more see: Memo of valuation of stock, September 23, 1828. Folder 17, John Sappington Papers C1027, SHSMO.

Trouble on the Return

16. A claim for a depredation committed by an Indian would be considered by the government: "An Act to Regulate Trade and Intercourse with the Indian Tribes, and to Preserve Peace on the Frontiers, May 19, 1796." *United States Statutes at Large*.

17. "sorry to hear of your loss in the Santa Fe road": Edward Bates to Meredith Marmaduke, February 2, 1929. Box 1, Folder 5, Sappington-Marmaduke Papers, MHS. Bates's letter also discussed Meredith's concern about the "graduation of the price of lands, ascending to their real quality factual value." Anything affecting Missouri's public lands was of interest to Meredith, who eyed the cheap, unsettled acres for their potential in creating his future prairie plantation.

18. Memorial to Congress in behalf of himself: Memorial, February 27, 1835; and James L. Collins to Marmaduke, n.d. Box 2, Folder 2, Sappington-Marmaduke Papers, MHS.

19. "Congress's penchant for not paying claims": Larry C. Skogen, *Indian Depredation Claims, 1796–1920*, 31.

20. "Jose Maguel Lujan, and our old servant Concious Archuleta": James L. Collins to Marmaduke, November 28, 1850. Box 4, Folder 7, Sappington-Marmaduke Papers, MHS.

21. "There is not the slightest probability of accomplishing anything": John S. Phelps to Marmaduke, February 13, 1851. Box 5, Folder 1, Sappington-Marmaduke Papers, MHS.

22. "owing to the great amount of business before that committee": James L. Collins to Marmaduke, date missing. Box 1, Folder 4, Sappington-Marmaduke Papers, MHS. A span of time during which Collins's letter was written (December 6, 1851, to March 3, 1852, the dates of the second session of the 32nd Congress) can be determined by the following extract from a paragraph in his letter: "Kossuth, foreign intervention, and the compromise measures of last session of Congress has consumed the first part of this session. ..." Louis Kossuth was a revolutionary Hungarian politician who spoke to a Joint Meeting of the U.S. Congress in December 1851 and was entertained in the White House by President Millard Fillmore in January 1852. At first welcomed in America as a "hero," subsequent radical comments made Kossuth a political liability and by July he was in London. Most likely, Collins's letter was written late in the session. The news that Senator Sebastian opposed their claim reached Marmaduke in a letter from Representative Miller written March 29, 1854. Box 5, Folder 4, Sappington-Marmaduke Papers, MHS.

23. "a Bill for the Relief of M. M. Marmaduke and others": Bills and Resolutions, House of Representatives, 35th Congress, 1st Session, H.R. 505 (Report No. 293), April 17, 1858. Library of Congress.

24. "send on with the Company that may leave Missouri": Memo of a Contract made and entered into this 22nd day of July 1828. Folder 17, John Sappington Papers C1027, SHSMO.

25. In 1829, he took a different direction: Although historian W. B. Napton Jr. claimed that Marmaduke made four trips to Santa Fe, no evidence has been found to support this. Napton, *Over the Santa Fe Trail in 1857*, 107. However, there is a strong belief among scholars that in coming years he consigned goods to other traders and remained active in the market in this way.

CHAPTER 9

A PARTNER FOR HYMOON'S ALTAR

During the winter of 1823–24, as he contemplated going to Santa Fe, Meredith was also looking for a wife. At 32 years old, a bachelor on the verge of a journey fraught with danger during which he would be gone for many months, he held marriage high in his mind. He had left a sweetheart in Virginia, probably because she was not interested in marrying someone whose plans included moving to the "wild West." Meredith was somewhere between Lexington, Kentucky, and Missouri the previous summer when his brother wrote to tell him "Sarah Hunter has not been in our neighborhood since *you left her* [emphasis added]. She is at Mr. Jenkinses as I am told."[1] Vincent again made a point of telling Meredith about Sarah's welfare in a letter written in early November, saying "Couzen Nancy Jenkins has a fine sone since you left us. Sally [Sarah] Hunter has been with her ever since *she left you* [emphasis added] and has been sick as I have heard."[2] And in October of 1824, Vincent McClanahan wrote to Meredith (at the time in Santa Fe) telling him that Sarah Hunter was soon to be married to Thomas Omohundro.[3]

Any romantic interest between Sarah and Meredith faded when he left Virginia, but he didn't give up the idea of marriage. In early December of 1823, he wrote to Frances Porter, a cousin in Westmoreland County, asking if she knew of anyone who might be interested in marriage. Her response told him of several recent marriages in her neighborhood, and then answered his query about prospective brides. "From your letter you rote [sic] to us," she replied, "I am apt to suppose that providence has not as yet directed you to the little girl you thought might be in reserve for you in your wild country. As you requested me to inform you who wish to marry, I believe there are many among us that would have no objection to stand before hymoons alter [sic] [Hymen, or Hymenaios, the god of marriage, from Greek mythology] provided they would meet with persons that would suit."[4] Evidently Meredith didn't "suit," since no young ladies' names were put forth for his consideration.

Another letter inquiring about potential brides went in the mail at Franklin the first week of December addressed to Richard Payne at Westmoreland Courthouse. Payne responded early in the new year telling his "Dear Friend" that there were "no important marriages that I recolect [sic] of worth mentioning. The young ladies you mention are all single as yet & recvd. of me your respects with smiling faces."[5] Smiling faces, yes, but again no particular young lady declared her interest in joining Meredith in Missouri.

That the women Meredith had so far seen in Missouri failed to come up to his expectations is apparent in a letter written early in 1824 by his cousin Samson Porter, in Virginia, whom Meredith had earlier written entreating him to come west and join him. At the time, Samson was himself searching for a wife, telling Meredith that he had "been at three weddings this year and hoped to be at more than a half dozen, but I am none the better for it, I only look on." As for joining Meredith in Missouri and finding a wife there, Samson, whose spelling left much to be desired, ventured "but when I reflect on your contry & what sort of ruf French girls you have to make choice of I feel sorry for you, & you for yourself, particularly when you think of Westmoreland and the adjoining counties where Beauty with all its variety of good qualities resides, I hope their is one apiece for us yet, tho the bucks are thining of them very fast. I have a pretty good notion of one, and she will have to say yes or no this year, depend upon it. Let this suffice on this score respecting your contry and the probability of geting their. My notion has well nigh vanished, tho last fall I had a great desire. ... If I was to leave this part of the country I should be so much lamented, it might cause the death of many, so I must stay till I can get my conjugal affairs fixed."[6]

Meredith's search in Virginia for a mail-order bride failed to produce the hoped-for result, but fortunately someone new came into his life. Prior to going to Santa Fe in 1824, he met Lavinia Sappington, the second-born of Dr. John Sappington's seven daughters. The date of their meeting isn't known, although it is believed to have been May 16, 1824, when Meredith — then on his way to Santa Fe — camped a few miles beyond the Arrow Rock landing and called upon the doctor at his home to obtain quinine powder. The beauty of dark-haired 16-year-old Lavinia, seen in her father's home that night, was not lost on Meredith. While no likeness of her at that age exists, a portrait painted eight years later by Missouri artist George Caleb Bingham shows a woman of slender build with piercing dark eyes, high cheek bones, and a straight, firm mouth — unsmiling yet pleasant in appearance, her black hair parted in the middle above a high forehead. A newspaper editor who visited Bingham at his Columbia, Missouri, studio in 1835, after viewing "a collection of well finished portraits" (among which may have been those of Lavinia and her parents), commented that "the pencil of our artist, might be permitted occasionally, a stroke or two more of flattery, with advantage. In some instances too faithfully a copy of features is unfavorable in effect."[7] Despite Bingham giving Lavinia a stiff, almost chiseled appearance (a result of his style of composition during that period of his development as an artist), her beauty is apparent in the painting.

Courtship Delayed

Upon leaving the Sappington home the evening before he started for Santa Fe, Meredith had to set aside his feelings about Lavinia. Any thoughts of courtship and marriage would await his return from the West, and if he wrote to her during his 14-month absence from Missouri, the letters are lost. When he did return, however, he wasted no time in knocking on Dr. Sappington's door with his heart in his hand, asking if he could court Lavinia. Southern tradition required a father to assure that his daughters were well provided-for in their marriages, and prospective sons-in-law were carefully examined to determine their moral values and probable economic prospects.

A Partner for Hymoon's Altar

Meredith must have speedily met with Dr. Sappington's expectations for he and Lavinia married on January 4, 1826, barely five months after his return from New Mexico. Unfortunately, the drama of their courtship can only be surmised since no letters or family anecdotes survive to tell the story. Courtship and marriage customs among American families during the early 19th century were different than today. If a man received permission to court a family's daughter, and if she consented to be courted, he could then begin to visit her, usually in the confines of her home. Community social gatherings such as picnics and camp meetings focused on church and school, where a couple could meet away from home, would have to await the establishment of those institutions — there were no public schools in Saline County in 1825, and the only church in Arrow Rock Township at the time had nine members who would gather occasionally in someone's home for worship. There was no such thing as a "date" in the modern sense that allowed prospective lovers to be together unchaperoned for a lengthy period of time. Such strict oversight, however, was no guarantee that a couple would abstain from romantic activities, even sexual activities, for where there is a will, a way will be found. Consequently, engagements were usually short-lived in the belief that it was better to consummate the marriage than to prolong a courtship that may result in a child conceived out of wedlock. In colonial and post-Revolutionary America, long engagements were not practical in localities where an itinerant preacher was expected to perform the ceremony; the engaged couple had to be ready to take their vows when the preacher came by.

With nothing to tell us about Meredith and Lavinia's courtship, questions arise that need answering. Were they in love, or did one or both marry with the belief that — over time — a deeper affection would develop between them and that their children would be the adhesive holding their marriage together? Certainly Meredith was smitten by the youthful Lavinia, but nothing tells us he was a romantic suitor. Evidence of his personality during these years can be deduced from his actions, and letters that have survived, and these show him to be pragmatic in his approach to life. He had left his home and family in Virginia in order to carve out a future for himself in the West. A wife and children figured into that future, and now, at age 34 in September 1825, nearly twice Lavinia's age, he knew it was time for him to marry and start his family. She, at 18, was still able to look around for a suitable husband, perhaps one nearer her age; however, not many more years could pass before she would be considered a candidate for spinsterhood. There is every reason to believe that Lavinia was looking for a husband and the security that the right man could provide. If love accompanied, so much the better.

Lavinia was popular with the young men of the Booneslick region. Suitors undoubtedly called upon the family with a view toward courting the daughter of the wealthy and influential Dr. Sappington. In fact, one young man thought he had already won Lavinia's affection. During Meredith's absence in New Mexico, John Hardeman's 20-year-old nephew, Seth, a college student at Franklin, Tennessee, visited his uncle in Howard County during the summer of 1825 and while there fell in love with Lavinia Sappington. She responded by flirting with him. Their brief romance, with promises implied if not formally made, became a concern for Lavinia after her marriage and she must have said something to Meredith about it. Wanting to avoid any difficulty with the Hardeman family, he wrote to Seth and informed him of the marriage. Responding to Meredith's letter, the somewhat naive Seth (not a good speller) could not hide his disappointment at being jilted.

"Dear Sir, I recd your letter of the 11th June last. ... On seeing [sic] its contents I was mutch astonished to hear of the manner in which the marrage of Miss L. was conducted. altho I knew she was vary anxious to marry I did not think she would have maried so, soon & so secretly after promising she never would marry any but me as no one. I did not consider her under obligation to wait for me, nor did I promise her to return though I was to have written which I did & from that I understand she did not wait the arrival of my letters. To be short her conduct has proven her to be a different kind of girl from what I had taken her to be & I assure you I think myself extremely fortunate in getting off as well as I have done."[8] After reproving Lavinia for her "conduct," and believing Meredith blameless in the matter, Seth related news about the tobacco and cotton harvests in Tennessee and a duel fought in Nashville — the amicable tone indicating his desire to retain his friendship with Meredith. Four years later, Seth Hardeman drowned while attempting to swim the Mississippi River.

A Grand Affair

Doctor Sappington's "commodious" two-story log house at Pilot Hickory, his plantation on the Saline County prairie, was the site of Meredith and Lavinia's wedding. Peyton Nowlin, a "gospel minister" of the Baptist faith described in later years as a "sedate, formal old gentleman, dry as to manners and sermons, but with a kind heart," performed the ceremony. He had been marrying couples in Saline County since 1821. Guests at the wedding included Sam McClure, a "Miss Collins, of Howard County, and members of the family of Mr. Nowlin." Some of Dr. Sappington's nearby neighbors, perhaps the McMahans and Brownlees, residents of the neighborhood known as the "Sappington Settlement," were probably also at the wedding, and maybe some of the Hardeman family crossed the river to be there. But few came from any distance, a lack of accommodations limiting attendance to those who lived no more than a buggy ride away, and the size of Dr. Sappington's house — although "commodious" — further restricted the number of guests.[9]

The event was an important time in Dr. Sappington's home. Much like today, there would have been weeks of preparation beforehand. Guests had to be invited, attendants chosen, and the bride's wedding dress ordered — probably coming from a merchant in St. Louis or perhaps Philadelphia. While it was not uncommon at frontier weddings for the bride and groom to be dressed in "home-spun apparel — buckskin, jeans, cotton and linsey,"[10] Lavinia and Meredith undoubtedly enjoyed a better quality of dress, their higher economic and social status permitting (even requiring) an appropriate costume. One can only speculate about happenings at the wedding itself, but reflecting the couples' Southern roots, traditions transplanted from Virginia and Tennessee would have ruled the day. The vows spoken, the party would begin. Frontier families, starved for entertainment, made the most of every opportunity that came along. Tables would be laid with a feast of cured and fresh meats, hot and cold dishes, and soups prepared with vegetables retrieved from a cold cellar, fresh breads, cakes, and pastries — all prepared and served by Sappington plantation slaves. An abundant supply of wine, brandy, and whiskey (some ordered from Philadelphia) served to toast the bride and groom, stimulate appetites, and invigorate all who partook. Later, those who had brought a musical instrument — a violin, generally — would be called upon to play familiar English or Celtic reels and jigs, perhaps even a minuet, and dancing might last until dawn. Eventually the festivities would end, guests would leave, and the exhausted newlywed couple could gracefully begin married life.

After the wedding Lavinia and Meredith lived in Dr. Sappington's home, staying there until their own house, being built less than a mile away, was completed. Marmaduke hired Samuel Reid of Cooper County in June 1826 to "chive and nail on all the laths ... plaster the said house ... with 2 coats ... and white wash the same." Reid also agreed to erect a "chimney of Rock (the shaft to be of brick) with 2 fire places, the one above and the other below stairs, and fit in grates for burning coal ... and pencil point and lay the Hearths of the same." For this work, Reid received "two Horses estimated at Sixty dollars."[11] Meredith was obliged to furnish the timber for the laths, and the rock, brick and mortar, and fireplace grates. The acreage where the house was being built had been patented by Dr. Sappington some years previously, the title transferring to Meredith and Lavinia on February 1, 1828. The deed conveying the property noted the existence of a "bank of stove coal" on the land and specified that Dr. Sappington and Meredith "shall have free and full and uninterrupted privilege of getting, taking and using the coal."[12] An additional 80 acres, adjoining the original tract on the northeast corner, was also purchased by Meredith at the same time. Coal on this property was also to be shared. The bank of "stone coal" (a difficult-to-ignite hard coal that burned best on a raised grate) lying exposed between Dr. Sappington's home and his son-in-law's property, was mined by slaves and provided a handy and inexpensive source of fuel for Meredith and Lavinia in their house on the nearly treeless prairie. Burning coal was not without its problems, however. Writing to Meredith in the winter of 1840–41, Lavinia said her father was "complaining ... of a cough. He thinks it probable that it is from the stove coal dust. He has had the grate broken out of his room and is burning wood. I expect I shall take a bad cough too, to get clear of the hateful coal."[13] Meredith and Lavinia lived in their first house for 18 years before replacing it with a larger home, which stood for 135 years.

The Family Increases

In a span of 20 years following their marriage Lavinia gave birth to 10 children — three daughters and seven sons — nine of them living beyond infancy. In this she mirrored her mother's family: Jane Breathitt Sappington had nine children, in gender opposite of Lavinia's — two sons, and seven daughters, one of whom died at age 13. Lavinia was 19 at the birth of her first child, aged 38 when the last was born in 1846. With no certain way to prevent pregnancy other than practicing periodic abstinence, the "total fertility rate" among white American women in the first four decades of the 1800s ranged between six and seven births per woman (compared to 2.13 births per woman in the year 2000).[14] In 1838, condoms and diaphragms made of vulcanized rubber became available in the United States; however, in 1873 a federal act made advertising and distributing such materials illegal — declaring them "Obscene Literature and Articles of Immoral Use." Sixty-five years would pass before the restrictions were lifted by a federal court.

Meredith and Lavinia's first child, Jane, was born March 30, 1827, some 15 months after their marriage. Another daughter, Sarah Porter, followed in 1829. Their first son, Vincent, was born in 1831. He was followed by John Sappington Marmaduke in 1833, Meredith Miles Jr. in 1835, and a third daughter, Lavinia, in 1838. In the next three years and nine months, mother Lavinia gave birth to three sons — Darwin in 1840, Layton (who died in infancy) in 1841, and Henry Hungerford Marmaduke in 1842. A seventh son, Leslie was born in 1846.

Lavinia was fortunate that all her children except one lived to adulthood (eight of her mother's nine children lived to adulthood). Infant mortality rates in America during the first half of the 19th century are unknown since no records exist from which data can be obtained; however, an inference for that period can be drawn from demographic data for the decade 1850–60, which shows infant deaths per 1,000 births of white children were 216, while infant black children died at the rate of 340 per 1,000 births. Supporting this is a 1991 study suggesting that 23 percent of children born in 1850 died before reaching age 1, and 30 percent died by age 5.[15] Cholera, typhoid fever, scarlet fever, smallpox, measles, malaria, and a host of other illnesses, infections, and accidents caused the death, on average, of a third of a family's children during the period 1800 to 1850. The good fortune of Lavinia and her mother in raising all but two of their 19 children to adulthood can be attributed to having a doctor in the family, especially one who was advanced in his practice and able to protect his children and grandchildren.

Dr. Sappington surely attended the births of his own children and cared for them as they grew up. He also delivered at least the first two of Lavinia's children; however, in 1831 she may have turned to her father's partner for the birth of her third and subsequent children. Lavinia was impressed upon meeting Dr. George Penn, lately of Virginia, in 1830. He had joined her father's practice late that year at a time when, Lavinia recounted in a letter to her brother William, "There has been a great Deal of sickness in this country this fall. Father has been riding very constantly until within 2 months past. He has a partner in his practice [who] appears to be a very Dear & agreeable man, Father thinks will do well." A note written on the side of Lavinia's letter told that Dr. Penn was living in her father's house.[16]

In 1835, another physician joined the Sappington practice. Dr. William Price arrived in Saline County that year to begin a partnership with Dr. Sappington and in September married his 15-year-old daughter, Mary Ellen. The increasing population of the Booneslick region brought about the need for competent medical care in Saline, Cooper, and Howard Counties. Nowhere is this more evident than during the early 1830s when a series of cholera outbreaks struck Saline County. Dr. Sappington and his partners treated 59 cases in the vicinity of Arrow Rock during the period 1832 to 1835. The treatment prescribed, "large and repeated doses of laudanum (opium)," accompanied by drinking "repeated draughts of strong, hot toddy; essence of peppermint; camphor, and red-pepper tea" must have worked, writes historian Michael Dickey, for only six deaths occurred.[17] Meredith, Lavinia, and their children — five in number by June of 1835 (Meredith Jr. was born that month) — escaped exposure to the deadly disease.

A Booneslick Holiday

Lavinia's role as a wife early in her marriage is partially illustrated in a letter written in January 1831 to her brother, William Breathitt Sappington, who was attending Cumberland Presbyterian College in Princeton, Kentucky, at the time. After explaining why she hadn't previously written, "knowing Father had frequently to [do so] on business," and writing about the weather, "We have had an exceptionally hard winter … The ground has not been clear of snow for 5 or 6 weeks … I believe they have been driving loaded waggons across the Missouri for weeks,"[18] she told William about his family's activities during the recent holiday season:

"We have had a very merry Christmas. The Miss Sappingtons have had beaus in profusion. Mr. Shackelford of our family gave a splendid Ball Christmas Eve.[19] Jane, Louisa, Susan, Mary Ellen, and Darwin, attended. They went up Friday and returned Sunday evening attended by a host of gallants, too numerous to mention," (however, in a side note she names 'young Mr. Shackelford, Doct. Penn, who now lives with your father, Jackson [Claiborne Fox] of Franklin, Thos. Conway, Mr. Wetmore, brother of the Capt. of Franklin') "and on Monday evening they had a party at father's house. I believe they danced and played cards all night. Would you believe me when I tell you that Father not only played cards, but actually danced several sets, and was amongst the merriest of the company? The young ladies and gentlemen all went up to Jonesborough the next morning, got through the day there; came here in the evening, had a card party, which lasted till about 12 o'clock. The principal part of the company went to Father's, and Judge Tuckers [Nathaniel Beverly Tucker] the next day which was Wednesday. They were all invited to dine at Judge Tuckers, but the day was so exceedingly bad, that man nor beast dared venture out. So it was a disappointment, however Thursday was a better day, and Judge Tucker gave notice that the party would be expected that day, and accordingly went, dined, suped, and danced till day. By this time there were some sore feet, and heavy eyes, but would not flag. They noded [sic] all day Friday until evening; commenced dancing at Father's and danced till about midnight. Next morning which was New Year's morning, Jane recollected was her birthday, so they must try it again, and danced till Sunday dawned upon them, and so they were compelled to break up & go home, and sleep a little before Monday. And now what do you think of such a Christmas for Saline?"

A note of wistfulness is detected in Lavinia's pleasing narrative of the holiday season. The 23-year-old mother of two, six months pregnant, watched from the sideline while the younger, unattached merrymakers went off to the parties that began Christmas Eve and carried through until the new year was two days old. Seeing her sisters, "the Miss Sappingtons," flirting with "the host of gallants" must have evoked memories of when she was not married and was free to dance, dine, and play cards until dawn. Only on Monday, two days after Christmas, did she attend a party — at her father's home. Even there she was an observer, noting his uncharacteristic behavior — playing cards, dancing — as he got caught up in the festive mood of the season, but evidently not dancing with her. The roving party reached Lavinia and Meredith's home Tuesday evening for card playing that ended at midnight, definitely a more subdued activity than the revelry that characterized the weeklong celebration. As a wife and mother, Lavinia had to deal with social constraints and responsibilities that limited her activities during the holiday season. Lavinia's letter does not mention Meredith's presence at these festivities, though he surely was at his home on Tuesday evening. He is mentioned only briefly (and then by title) at the end of the letter when Lavinia tells her brother that "Col. Marmaduke proposes to start to the East in a week to be gone 3 or 4 months." Although married couples in the early 19th century were more willing than their parents to demonstrate affection for each other and for their children, there remained a reluctance to express such feelings too openly, thus it was "Col. Marmaduke" instead of Meredith. However Lavinia and Meredith addressed each other in their home, outside of there — and in correspondence among family members and others — the intimacy conveyed by the use of first names remained a private matter. Throughout their lives, they were always addressed as "Col." and "Mrs." Marmaduke.

Marmaduke Family Life

Early in their marriage Lavinia and Meredith developed a pattern of family life organized around the agricultural, business, and political interests he pursued as he sought to establish and secure the family fortune. While overseeing his Saline County farmlands, the foundation of his wealth, the business and political activities in which Meredith engaged were widespread and often required him to be away from home for extended periods of time. For example, he made a second journey to Santa Fe to trade in 1828, a two-month-long trip to New Orleans in 1830, and traveled east for "3 or 4 months" in 1831, a journey undertaken despite the pending birth of his third child. As a partner in a store at Jonesboro at the time, Meredith went to Pittsburgh and Philadelphia that year to arrange the purchase and shipment of merchandise for the store. That business concluded, he then went on to Virginia to visit his family there, the first time in eight years he had seen his brother and sisters. While he was away on this extended trip, Lavinia gave birth to their first son, Vincent. In later years, business interests would require him to go east again, and also travel extensively in Missouri, Arkansas, and Louisiana. At one time, Meredith contemplated going to Texas to investigate the potential there for speculating in land.

These journeys could take weeks or months to complete. Travel by horse or stagecoach was over poor roads, often in inclement weather. The 65-mile stagecoach ride between Arrow Rock and Jefferson City, for example, took a day and a half with a stop in Boonville. "Could you not leave Jefferson Saturday morning in the stage and get here Sunday 12 o'clock?" Lavinia pleaded in a letter to Meredith in 1841.[20] Travel to St. Louis from the Saline County home when the Missouri River was closed by ice or low water meant a three-day stage ride from Franklin via the Boone's Lick Road. Going beyond Missouri required steamboat passage on the Mississippi and Ohio Rivers to Wheeling or Pittsburgh, or south on the Mississippi to Natchez or New Orleans. Depending on the water stage of the Ohio, and the number of stops made along the way, this portion of the journey could take two or three weeks. Fortunately for those making the trip, steamboats were more comfortable than stagecoaches. Deck passengers — business owners, politicians, lawyers, and merchants like Meredith — would gather during the day with "feet on railing ... smoking good cigars," and talk their way up the river. Their nights were spent at card tables, where the conversations continued as the miles slipped away beneath them.

When Meredith was away on an extended trip, Lavinia had to deal with a variety of business and farm matters that were normally his responsibility. Men who owed Meredith money often called at the house wanting to pay their debts. Not always aware of the details of the loan, Lavinia had to make decisions that she hoped were correct. "Mr. McMahan (merchant) was here yesterday to settle his account," she wrote Meredith. "You left no instructions with me about it and I did get Father to settle it. The amount was for 60$. Mr. Ramine was here some weeks ago to pay some money. I did not know anything about it and was afraid to do anything with it. He said he could pay the whole in the spring. No person has called for the money you left with me. I believe I have forgotten who you said it was for."[21]

Another area that fell to Lavinia's care when Meredith was gone was oversight of their farm and slaves. She accepted these duties in her role as the mistress of a Southern-style plantation, passing along information in her letters that she hoped would keep him aware of what was happening at home: "Mr. Hunt finished hauling your wheat to the mill yesterday. The new wheat was very good and measured 350 bushels. The old wheat was very indifferent. Mr. Wever said he would scale [number unreadable] pounds in the bushel howy [however]. Mr. Hunt was not willing to and said he would let you settle with him when you get home." Writing again two weeks later, she updated Meredith on the progress of the wheat harvest, and other farm matters: "Mr. Hunt is engaged in getting out your wheat but has not delivered any yet. The road is so bad that they cannot haul. I believe your stock is doing well. You have been gone a long time for our pork has been fattened, killed and I am now engaged in smoking it." The health of the farm's slaves was also a matter of concern for Lavinia, who reported to Meredith that, "Minnie's leg I mentioned some time ago being sore, is getting better and I believe will mend nicely. I believe it has been 6 weeks since he has been able to do anything. With that exception, the Negroes have been healthy."[22]

Lavinia never failed to report on their children in her letters to Meredith. Her letters reveal both her love for them, and occasional frustration at being their lone caretaker. "The children are all very well. Meredith was very sick one day an [sic] 2 nights. He vomited a great deal one night. I think it was occasioned by eating a quantity of frozen apples. He has got entirely well. Little Darwin and Lavinia are as fat as they can be ..." Another letter written five days later brought more news about the children. "Little Lavinia says she will help Papa a heap of times when he comes from Jefferson. It is needless to say for you know Darwin is the smartest and finest looking boy in the world. He has become very much spoiled being so sick so much this winter but I will make him a good boy before you come home. He won't sleep in the cradle nor any way but with me and it makes it very tiresome to me these long nights."[23]

Always immersed in domestic affairs — managing her home, caring for their children — when Meredith was at home Lavinia found her duties expanded to include serving as a hostess for a continual stream of guests. Business and politics brought many visitors to the Marmaduke home. One of the most prominent regular visitors was Senator Thomas Hart Benton, an "intimate personal friend" of Meredith's (and of Dr. Sappington) who, while there, "received adherents and friends."[24] Meredith evidently encouraged Benton's use of his home as a base for meeting with constituents and political supporters.

Unfortunately, letters Meredith wrote to Lavinia have not been found so it's difficult to determine the intrinsic nature of his communication with her. Certainly, he spoke of personal and business matters, but did he demonstrate affection? Was he at all romantic? Did he encourage her when she was stressed? He did share his concern when problems arose in the family. In a letter to her brother, William, Lavinia remarked that their 21-year-old brother, Darwin, "falls in love with every pretty girl he sees," and that this had caused him "to make so many mistakes in his accounts that Col. Marmaduke has advised him to quit them altogether till he gets ready to marry." Meredith and Darwin were partners in a store at Jonesboro, at the time.[25]

Prospering financially, marrying, fathering children, and establishing a home and a plantation were foundation stones that Meredith Marmaduke carried west in 1823. In quick order, he set all of these firmly in Saline County soil, building a base for future wealth and political influence that would surpass anything he might have obtained in his native Virginia. His timely entry into the Santa Fe trade during its earliest years rewarded him with money and valuable animals, assets he enlarged upon in coming years. And though the eastern terminus of the Santa Fe Trail moved beyond Franklin, jumping first to Fort Osage by 1830 and then on to Independence, Meredith was able to further his involvement in that market by consigning goods to other traders, a practice he continued as late as 1838.[26] The trip to "Hymoon's Altar" ended Meredith's anxiety about his posterity and, as he must have known it would, gave him access to people and resources that otherwise might never have come his way. By 1831, he was positioned to become a trusted associate in his father-in-law's business interests. For Lavinia, the change from carefree young maiden to the wife of an ambitious older husband, the mother of five (in the decade following her marriage), and the mistress of a nascent plantation that over time would encompass some 8,000 acres, brought challenges that she sometimes struggled to manage. These dual duties, mother and mistress, governed her life as Meredith's business and political influence expanded.

Notes

[1]. "Sarah Hunter has not been in our neighborhood": Vincent Marmaduke to Meredith Marmaduke, September 15, 1823. Box 1, Folder 2, Sappington-Marmaduke Papers, MHS.

[2]. "Couzen Nancy Jenkins has a fine sone": Vincent Marmaduke to Meredith Marmaduke, November 10, 1823. Box 1, Folder 2, Sappington-Marmaduke Papers, MHS.

[3]. Sarah Hunter's marriage to Thomas Omohundro.: Vincent McClanahan to Meredith Marmaduke, October 11, 1824. Folder 3, Marmaduke Papers C1021, SHSMO.

[4]. "I am apt to suppose that providence has not as yet directed you": Francis Porter to Meredith Marmaduke, January 1824. Folder 2, Ibid.

[5]. "No important marriages that I recolect": Richard Payne to Meredith Marmaduke, February 28, 1824. Ibid.

[6]. "been at three weddings this year": Samson Porter to Meredith Marmaduke, February 3, 1824. Ibid.

[7]. "a collection of well finished portraits": John F. McDermott, George Caleb Bingham, Portraitist, 21.

[8]. "Dear Sir, I recd your letter of the 11th June last": Seth Hardeman to Meredith Marmaduke, October 21, 1826. Box 1, Folder 3, Sappington-Marmaduke Papers, MHS.

A Partner for Hymoon's Altar

9. "sedate, formal old gentleman, dry as to manners and sermons": *History of Saline County 1881*, 174, 180.

10. "home-spun apparel — buckskin, jeans, cotton and linsey,": Ibid., 181

11. "chive and nail on all the laths": Meredith Marmaduke and Samuel Reid contract, June 8, 1826. Box 1, Folder 3, Sappington-Marmaduke Papers, MHS.

12. "shall have free and full and uninterrupted privilege of getting, taking and using the coal": Saline County Deed Book A, 1821–1835, page 110. Microfilm Reel C6227, Missouri State Archives, Jefferson City.

13. "complaining … of a cough": Lavinia to Meredith Marmaduke, January 7, 1841. Box 3, Folder 1, Sappington-Marmaduke Papers, MHS.

14. "total fertility rate": Michael Haines, "Fertility and Mortality in the United States," EH.Net Encyclopedia, edited by Robert Whaples, March 19, 2008 (electronic document). Haines' data for the period 1800–1850 is drawn largely from studies based upon genealogies, parish registers, biographical data, and other local records.

15. Supporting this is a 1991 study: Samuel H. Preston and Michael R. Haines, *Fatal Years: Child Mortality in Late Nineteenth-Century America*. National Bureau of Economic Research, Princeton University Press 1991, 49–87. Massachusetts in 1842 became the first state to record births, deaths, and marriages. Not until 1933 were all states recording this information.

16. "There has been a great Deal of sickness in this country this fall": Lavinia Marmaduke to William B. Sappington, January 8, 1831. Box 1, Folder 6, Sappington-Marmaduke Papers, MHS. Dr. Penn is reported living on a farm in Saline County in 1828. Michael Dickey, *Arrow Rock: Crossroads of the Missouri Frontier*, 75. However Lavinia's letter, stating that he was living in her father's home in late 1830, indicates that he may have arrived in the area later.

17. "large and repeated doses of laudanum (opium)": Dickey, 165.

18. "We have had an exceptionally hard winter": Lavinia Marmaduke to William B. Sappington, January 8, 1831. Box 1, Folder 6, Sappington-Marmaduke Papers, MHS. A 22-year-old Saline County resident at the time later described the winter of 1830–31 as "the cold winter," with unusually low temperatures and "a great snowstorm, phenomenal as to magnitude." Snow began to fall on Christmas Day and didn't stop until the first of January, becoming four feet deep. An unending wind blew from the north for six weeks, then at noon on the 13th of February there was a total eclipse of the sun, followed by a gradual thaw. William B. Napton, *Past and Present of Saline County, Missouri*, 98.

19. "Mr. Shackleford of our family": Kinship has not been established. Thomas Shackleford, born Virginia 1790 or 1796, moved first to Kentucky, then to Williamson County (Franklin), Tennessee, where he married Eliza C. Pulliam in 1817. He arrived in Saline County about 1825. An acquaintance of Dr. Sappington in Tennessee, Shackleford empowered him in 1820 to act in his behalf in the purchase of Saline County land. *History of Howard and Cooper Counties*, 470–71; Thomas Shackleford to John Sappington, March 25, 1820. Folder 10, Sappington Papers C1027, SHSMO.

20. "Could you not leave Jefferson Saturday morning": Lavinia Marmaduke to Meredith Marmaduke, January 12, 1841. Box 3, Folder 1, Sappington-Marmaduke Papers, MHS.

21. "Mr. McMahan (merchant) was here yesterday to settle his account": Lavinia to Meredith, January 12, 1841. Box 3, Folder 1, Sappington-Marmaduke Papers, MHS.

22. "Mr. Hunt finished hauling your wheat to the mill yesterday": Lavinia's remarks about wheat are in letters written to Meredith, January 7 and 25, 1841. Box 3, Folder 1, Ibid.

23. "The children are all very well": Lavinia's remarks about her children are in letters written to Meredith, January 7, 12, and 25, 1841. Box 3, Folder 1, Ibid.

24. "intimate personal friend" of Meredith's, who made himself at home and while there "received adherents and friends": *1881 History of Saline County, Missouri*, 472.

25. "falls in love with every pretty girl he sees": Lavinia Marmaduke to William B. Sappington, January 8, 1831. Box 1, Folder 7, Ibid.

26. consigning goods to other traders as late as 1838: A letter from Marmaduke's brother-in-law, Claiborne Fox Jackson, reveals Meredith's continued involvement at this late date: "I was told a few days ago that this man Williams living near Boons Lick who is owing you for goods taken to Santa Fe, went to the South last fall or winter with mules and sold them on credit." C. F. Jackson to Meredith Marmaduke, May 7, 1839. Box 2, Folder 4, Ibid.

CHAPTER 10
ALL IN THE FAMILY

Lavinia Sappington proved to be the woman Meredith needed in his life. For 38 years, until his death, she fulfilled his desire for a companion, someone with whom he enjoyed an intimate relationship; who gave him children for his posterity; and who served as hostess and governess of their Booneslick home. Marriage to Lavinia, however, gave Meredith more than companionship and children; it propelled him into a significant position in his father-in-law's thriving business organization. Missouri historian Lynn Morrow relates that by the early 1820s John Sappington was heavily involved in "an extensive regional trade in agriculture, money lending, and medical services."[1] While overseers directed activities on his farms, managed his slaves, and operated a cotton gin and a saltworks, Dr. Sappington traveled the Booneslick country tending to his medical practice and trading the products of his plantation, selling potatoes, wheat, salt, beef, and pork, often extending credit and loaning money. As this trade expanded, he found it necessary to hire attorneys to collect money owed him by merchants, farmers, and others with whom he did business. Approaching age 50 and seeking to moderate his participation in these activities, Dr. Sappington began to involve family members in his business affairs and solicited physicians as partners in his medical practice. He wanted to devote time to farming and land speculation, and was perfecting a pill form of quinine that he hoped to market nationally.

John Sappington also began to marry off his daughters, Eliza in 1821 and Lavinia in 1826. That all of them married while comparatively young may have been intentional. As a doctor, he was aware of the strain that multiple births place on a woman's health, and also knew that the older a woman is when she has children the greater the risk to her health. A more pleasant outcome might be possible for his daughters if they bore their children when young, and ended child-bearing still healthy and able to enjoy life. On the other hand, it was not unusual on the frontier, where men greatly outnumbered the available supply of potential wives, for women to marry in their teenage years. Of Dr. Sappington's six daughters who lived beyond adolescence, Eliza and Mary Ellen were both 15 years old when he consented to their marriages, Susan was 16, and Louisa, Jane, and Lavinia were 18. A woman's role in American society at this period revolved around the children she produced and the home she kept. Educational opportunities were limited, particularly in rural areas, and women who worked outside the home were usually unskilled, doing menial labor at jobs that lacked prestige. Coming from the South, where tradition dictated that a woman's role was governed by family, social, and environmental conventions that limited her choices, John Sappington sought to ensure his daughters' futures by selecting the right husbands for them, and then giving his sons-in-law positions in his businesses. As he had with his daughters, he also determined to assure his sons' success by involving them in the family businesses, keeping the family's wealth intact. In 1828, William went off to college in Kentucky with the hope that he would eventually oversee all of Dr. Sappington's expanding commercial interests. In 1829, Darwin, who had no desire to further his education beyond what he learned from home tutoring, received financial backing to open a mercantile store at the nearby village of Jonesboro.

A Scoundrel's Scandal

The prospering world of Dr. Sappington was rocked in early June 1830 when attorney Nathaniel Beverley Tucker appeared before the Saline County Circuit Court, meeting in chancery session, and filed a lawsuit against Sappington's daughter Eliza, her brother Darwin, and Meredith Marmaduke. Acting as "next friend" on behalf of Mary Ann Mills Parsons, Tucker revealed that Eliza's husband, Alonzo Pearson, was in fact Augustine Parsons, the husband of Mary Ann Parsons whom he had deserted nine years earlier at Cahawba, Alabama, when she was pregnant. Mrs. Parsons had been searching for her missing husband ever since and now claimed that he was both a bigamist — having married her at Milledgeville, Georgia, in 1820 — and a thief who had absconded with "about the sum of $7,000" from her estate, now believed to be "in the hands of" Meredith, Eliza, and Darwin. The suit asked that Pearson/Parsons be "required to answer the allegations," and that the other defendants disclose "what money, property or credits" they may possess that belonged to Pearson, and that these assets be seized and used for Mrs. Parsons's benefit. She also sued for alimony to support herself and her son.[2]

Alonzo Pearson arrived under his assumed name in Saline County in 1821 and reportedly taught school there for a brief period. Looking to better his position in the community (and his personal wealth), he soon began courting Eliza Sappington and they were married in a ceremony at her father's home in September of that year. In line with John Sappington's desire to have a manager oversee his business interests, his new son-in-law eventually took on that responsibility. Then, in the spring of 1829, Pearson and his brother-in-law, 20-year-old Darwin Sappington, became partners in a general merchandise store they opened at Jonesboro, calling their company "Pearson and Sappington."[3] Each partner contributed $1,000 to establish the company. Pearson later added $3,000 to his "portion of stock, to be put in trade."[4] If he had not already done so, Darwin — with his father's backing — undoubtedly increased his contribution to the partnership in an equal amount at the same time.

St. Louis wholesale houses provided some of the merchandise purchased by Pearson and Sappington in 1829; however, early the following year Alonzo Pearson went to Philadelphia to acquire the store's stock of goods. In a letter written that spring to William Sappington in Kentucky, Meredith reported that "Mr. Pearson has not yet ret. from the east, expect him in 2 or 3 weeks with 8, 10 or 12,000$ worth of goods. I expect to go to Orleans in May next."[5] Meredith was in New Orleans when he received a letter from Darwin informing him of the Pearson bigamy scandal.

Dear Col. Marmaduke,

    It is with pain that I have to let you no what has happened since you left here. My Dear Col believing it to be my duty to let you no it. Mr. Pearson has ... been marryed [sic] to another woman before he ever saw my sister he married her in Georgia, left her & repoart [sic] says he has taken a large sum of money from her she has one child.

    Dreadful my God. He stood his tryal [sic] committed to jail or give bail for his appearance at [court] he has given bail. ... Beleaving [sic] that you will see publications to that affect and nowing not how to account for it I consider it my duty to mention it. His tryal will [commence] the first Monday in July next. I am attending to the business hear. I have cloased [sic] the door at Arrow Rock until you come hoam. ... Sister Eliza is as well as could be expected. ... Pearson looks more like a dead man than like a living one. Your [sincere] friend, E. D. Sappington.[6]

Even before Tucker filed the lawsuit, Alonzo Pearson became aware that his presence in Missouri and his marriage to Eliza Sappington had been discovered. He also had received word of the impending lawsuit and had fled to escape the likelihood of being arrested on a charge of bigamy. In court, attorney Tucker noted that Pearson "has of late found that he was detected, and has, a second time, absconded after having made provision for the unfortunate woman, whom he had beguiled into a pretended marriage, equal to the amount of the dowry received from her father." Learning of his son-in-law's duplicity, Dr. Sappington quickly moved to repossess the dowry and took steps to forestall any action by either Mrs. Parsons or Alonzo Pearson that might negatively affect the Sappington assets. Pearson's culpability was further shown several months later in November when Meredith (sitting as one of the judges of the county court, an administrative body) witnessed an affidavit in which Darwin stated that the previous summer when he confronted Pearson with an accusation of bigamy, "[he] acknowledged himself to be the husband of a Lady in the State of Georgia. ... that his true name was Augustine Parsons, and that his wife now living was born Mary Ann Mills." Darwin said that Pearson "denied no part of this charge, and distinctly stated many particulars. ..."[7]

    The defendants' responses to Mrs. Parsons's lawsuit were presented in circuit court that fall. Meredith was dropped from the complaint when it became known that he had no property or money that belonged to Pearson. Darwin and Eliza, however, remained as defendants, he because of the Pearson and Sappington partnership and the possibility of money owed Pearson from that operation. In his response, Darwin said the value of the partnership was "unsettled, and that he is ready to have the same settled under the direction of this Court." In fact, the store and its goods were mortgaged to Dr. Sappington and eastern merchants, leaving little to be derived from any attachment of assets. Eliza told the court that she possessed nothing more than a "few articles of domestic & personal comfort" left with her by Pearson when he fled from Missouri. Not seeing any chance for recovery of Mrs. Parsons's lost $7,000 from either Meredith or the Sappington family, in 1832 "next friend" Beverley Tucker filed a second lawsuit on her behalf in Saline County, this time against "Augustine Parsons, alias Alonzo Pearson." Meredith was called to testify at a hearing in that complaint (because of a conversation he had with Pearson regarding the amount of money the latter had that belonged to Mrs. Parsons), and later filed an affidavit to clarify his testimony when it became apparent that mistakes were made in recording what he had said.[8]

In addition to recovering Eliza's dowry, Dr. Sappington sought to shield her and the children from the embarrassment of the bigamous marriage. He prevailed upon his longtime Howard County friend, now Missouri's governor, John Miller to shepherd a bill through the state's General Assembly to grant Eliza a dissolution of her marriage from Alonzo Pearson. Missouri statutes at the time empowered the legislature to do this. (Eliza's case was one of the last to occur this way; new legislation gave circuit courts the responsibility, although the General Assembly still had to be petitioned for permission to file the case at court.) The bill, introduced in the state House of Representatives by William Becknell, presented "the petition of Eliza Whitsett Sappington, praying the Legislature to pass an act divorcing her from the bonds of matrimony contracted by her with Alonzo Pearson." Becknell's bill called for making the marriage "absolutely and utterly void from the beginning."[9] It passed the House but hit a rough spot in the state Senate. Governor Miller was still lining up votes when the bill was prematurely considered in the upper chamber, and Meredith was soon called upon to help resolve a legal snag that had developed. In his office at Jefferson City the day after Christmas, the governor wrote a private letter to Meredith telling him the bill was voted on "contrary to my wish, and was lost by one vote, which was the vote of the President of the Senate." There was hope, however; a motion for reconsideration "succeeded & the bill is now on the table. It will I hope remain there until we can hear from you. The objection used against it was that [Eliza's] name was not subscribed to the petition, consequently no evidence that she desired any thing of this body. Mr. Bates [Senator Edward Bates] is the principle opposed, however ... he says if she would forward her signature to the petition, attested by yourself, he would support it. ... I should have written to Doctor Sappington, but for the delicacy of the matter."[10]

When he received Governor Miller's letter, Meredith, acting on impulse, hastily wrote to Edward Bates and chastised him for failing to support the bill. Bates' carefully crafted reply, although lengthy, is reproduced here — both for the view it gives about the reasons for his opposition to Eliza's petition, and for the insight it provides into the legal mind of the man who eventually would become President Abraham Lincoln's Attorney General throughout most of the Civil War.

To Col. M. M. Marmaduke

Sir, Your letter of the 30th ultimo has just reached me, & I will not pretend to conceal my entire surprise at the passionate tone & accusatory style in which you have thought proper to address me.

You do not ask me for an explanation, & I certainly should not trouble you with one, but for the belief on my part, that you have been misled in erroneous information of the course I took in regard to the bill in question, & of my reasons for that course, and but for my desire not to suffer the harmony which has subsisted between us from the time of our first acquaintance, to be marred by a passionate misconception on your part, or a hasty resentment on mine.

You assume it as a truth, that my opposition to the bill to declare null etc. the marriage of Miss Sappington to Mr. Pearson was founded upon the belief that 'Doct. Sappington was base enough to endeavor to practise [sic] an imposition upon the legislature, etc.' and then ask with emphatic earnestness 'What circumstance could justify me in believing any such thing?' This assumption & this emphatic interrogatory are alike unjust to Dr. S. & to me. I never did believe <u>any such thing</u>. I have known Dr. S. for several years, and & have always entertained & still entertain a high respect for his character & esteem for his person. And I really did suppose that a reputation for tolerable intelligence would have screened any member of the Assembly from the supposition that the lack of Mrs. Pearson's sign manual formed the basis of his opposition to the bill. I considered her fully & fairly a petitioner before the Senate, & yet, entertaining the opinions & professing the principles which I do, I should have been unworthy of a seat here, if I had suffered the bill to pass without my opposition. I opposed the bill because, in my opinion, it is dangerous in its principle & injurious in its effect upon society; and, as far as regards the unfortunate lady & the no less unfortunate children concerned, it is an <u>absolute nullity</u> — It is dangerous & injurious because it assumes & declares, without any legal proof, that Pearson is guilty of the enormous crime of Bigamy — It is an assumption of judicial powers by the legislature, & that too in a case in which no lawyer can believe legislation of any practical utility.

It is a nullity as regards the marriage, because if Pearson was married in Georgia, & that wife is alive, the marriage here must have been absolutely void, without an usurping declaration to that effect, by the Gen. Assembly — And if he <u>was not</u> married in Georgia, his marriage here was good & valid in law in spite of such legislative adjudication. As to the property — The marriage <u>in fact</u>, if void in law, could give Pearson no right to claim it; and if valid in law, the act just passed cannot take it from him. And as to the children — the idea that an act of Assembly was necessary to legitimate them, could only spring from an entire ignorance of the statute law, as it has stood for many years. Every man who will choose to examine the statute book must know that the issue of all marriages deemed null in law or dissolved by divorce, shall nevertheless be legitimate.

And now Sir, I have given you an explanation of my conduct & views upon this subject, not as called for by you, but due as I conceive necessary & to those relations which have always heretofore existed between us. After perusing it, I wish to believe you will not consider your conduct to Dr. S. altogether prudent & judicious, & as for Pearson take for granted that all who opposed the bill necessarily believed him a scoundrel. And as to me personally — I am sure that I hazard nothing in leaving it to your good judgment to determine whether your address to me was characterized by that candor & courtesy (to say nothing of delicacy) which, considering the official responsibility under which I acted & the years of friendly intercourse between us, I had a right to expect at the hands of Col. Marmaduke.

Respectfully Sir, Your obt. svt. E. Bates.[11]

When the General Assembly reconvened in January 1831, Eliza Pearson's amended petition was favorably received and her marriage to Alonzo was dissolved. Dr. Sappington moved his daughter and grandchildren into his home as they sought to distance themselves from the scandal. He also assured their financial well-being by retaining Alonzo Pearson's investment in the Sappington family businesses, and in coming years a share of the profits from those enterprises went toward the welfare of Eliza Pearson's children. Interestingly, writers of local history in years since the dissolution of the marriage have often depicted Eliza as the widow of Alonzo Pearson, an indication that the Sappington family was largely successful in obliterating the bigamy from the collective memory of the community.

Nathaniel Beverley Tucker

The nature of the relationship that existed between Nathaniel Beverley Tucker (he preferred "Beverley" as his name) and Meredith Marmaduke at the time of Mrs. Parsons's lawsuit calls for examination. Was there something more than a lawyer's advocacy in Tucker's naming of Meredith as a defendant, especially since he had no potential liability and was speedily dismissed from the suit? Although the two were neighbors (from 1829 until 1833) in Arrow Rock township, where they developed plantations and owned slaves and had similar conservative political leanings (although Meredith was a Jackson Democrat and Tucker a Whig), letters written to Meredith at this time by a friend point to the possibility of a less-than-congenial relationship.

Dr. George R. Pitts moved from Virginia to Missouri's St. Charles County in 1828 to practice medicine. Whether or not he knew Beverley Tucker previously, he complained about him to Meredith, whom he had known in Virginia and with whom he had frequently communicated before moving to Missouri. All three men were Tidewater-born; Meredith and Pitts were from Westmoreland County while Tucker grew up south of there near the mouth of the Appomattox River, his father an attorney in nearby Richmond. Older than Meredith by seven years, Tucker matriculated from William & Mary College to practice law, then served in the War of 1812. Meredith and Tucker may have run afoul of each other either during the war, or afterward when both were serving the legal needs of Virginia. In 1815, Missouri beckoned and Tucker settled in the Florissant Valley north of St. Louis, not far from the Missouri River and the nearby village of St. Charles. Short of funds to rent an office, he had a large, hollow sycamore tree on his land cut off 10 feet above the ground, "put on a roof, inserted a door and a window, moved in his desk and law books," and began to practice law.[12] In 1818, Territorial Governor William Clark appointed Tucker to the position of circuit judge for the Northern District of Missouri, a vast area that took in St. Louis and St. Charles Counties, and extended west to include the then-undivided Howard County. Responsible for civil and criminal court, and as general administrator for the evolving counties in north Missouri, Tucker held that influential position for 10 years before moving to Saline County where he practiced law and established his home, Ardmore Plantation, southwest of Arrow Rock.

Shortly before he left Florissant in late 1829, Tucker was the subject of a long letter Dr. Pitts wrote to Meredith, in which he responded to Meredith's earlier revelation that "Judge Tucker" might be moving to Saline County. Pitts expressed a considerable degree of enmity between him and Tucker (among other things, he disliked Tucker's sponsorship of another, competing, physician in St. Charles County). The tone of that letter implies that Meredith may have shared Pitts's concerns about Tucker's reputability:

> I received a few days past your last & very friendly letter, & I wish I could in return give you something interesting. The information in relation to Judge Tucker is what might have been expected. For some time past, I was aware that he could not with either safety or propriety remain in this neighborhood. For here, he is extremely unpopular & but for his pecuniary influence would scarcely be noticed. Even this is on the wane & it is supposed by some (who ought to know his circumstances) that he is as much in debt as he is worth.
>
> As it is possible he may be a neighbor of yours permit me to offer you this advice — watch him closely for his plans are deeply laid & perhaps few men are as well qualified to practise [sic] with success the art of deception as himself. Cautious, cunning & calculating like an old fox, for he cannot be caught but will forever find a hole to crawl out of. If you will notice his Whigsiognamy [Whig political philosophy] particularly, you will find portrayed in bold relief the cunning of Yankey [sic] & the slyness of the Jew. Unsuspecting myself, I was deceived by him. He is aware however that I now know him & this accounts for his silence to you in regard to me & my affairs. In a sly & sneaking way, he attempted to destroy me professionally in this neighborhood. By the merest accident, I made the discovery & immediately wrote to him on the subject. He did not give a reply, for he could not, aware that I had it in my power to establish on him acts of the grossest & most bare-faced meanness & duplicity. From that time (six months ago) he has studiously avoided my presence & I here declare to you my determination, if an opportunity ever offers, to make a strong Negro man of mine give him an old Virga. [Virginia] lashing, that is if I recollect forty save one, on his bare back.
>
> With so many acts of turpitude, it is astonishing how high he stands out of his own neighborhood! I have scrupulously avoided saying any thing against him, for one's character is of a substance too brittle to be handled roughly & when once broke, is not easily, or readily mended; & of course you must consider this as a matter exclusively & entirely between you & me.
>
> It was with sorrow I heard he was to marry a daughter of Genl. Smyth, a blooming girl, I hear, of 15. My God! What is his taste & what can be his calculations? ... George R. Pitts.[13]

Following his dismissal from Mrs. Parsons's lawsuit in the fall of 1830, Meredith passed that news along to Dr. Pitts, who responded with another scathing denunciation of Judge Tucker:

> Permit me to congratulate you on your fortunate escape from the difficulties by which you were surrounded. ... I was disappointed in not hearing from my quandam friend the Judge; for contemptible as he is, I must acknowledge, that I feel a curiosity to know, what is likely to be the ultimatum of his truly singular

& extraordinary career. The unfortunate condition of your sister in law, affords a melancholy instance of the constant necessity of circumspection, vigilance & caution in our intercourse with strangers — many of whom with a prepossessing & polished exterior, prove "wolves in sheeps clothing"; and here permit me a second time, to guard you against the machinations & deeply laid stratagems of Judge Tucker. This springs ... from the honest sincerity of my heart; for the more I reflect upon his character, the more forcibly am I satisfied of his villiany [sic] & turpitude. In <u>minor</u> things, he surpasses in cunning, either Aaron Burr, or H. Clay. ....[14]

In coming years, as late as 1840, Dr. Pitts continued his excoriation of Beverley Tucker in letters to Meredith, even though Tucker abruptly left the Booneslick country in 1833 to return to Virginia. Missing in this long-running diatribe are Meredith Marmaduke's letters to Dr. Pitts, but the fact that the verbal attacks continued for so long gives rise to the possibility that Meredith, either tacitly or openly, encouraged Pitts in his condemnatory behavior. For what purpose is not clear, but Pitts's accusations certainly would have caused Meredith to view Tucker's actions in Saline County with a degree of suspicion about his motivations.

From Trader to Merchant

Four mercantile companies doing business in Saline County during the nine-year period 1827 to 1836 bore some combination of the names Marmaduke, Sappington, and Pearson. They were: Pearson and Sappington; Marmaduke and Sappington; Marmaduke and Company; and E. D. Sappington and Company. The details of the interrelatedness of these companies are entangled in a knot of account-book entries, receipts, and correspondence that is almost impossible to unravel nearly 200 years later, without having knowledge of the deliberations that accompanied the creation of the separate entities. But some conclusions can be drawn from the information that is available. Meredith figured prominently in the first three companies, and may have had a role in the latter as well.

The firm of Pearson and Sappington was a general merchandise store that opened for business at Jonesboro in early 1829. Dr. Sappington paired his 20-year-old son Darwin with the older and more experienced Alonzo Pearson, who was charged with overseeing his young partner's development as a merchant. The firm operated only until the fall of 1830, when the partnership was dissolved following the disclosure of Pearson's bigamous marriage to Dr. Sappington's daughter.[15] At that time, the Jonesboro store was taken over by the first iteration of a company known as "Marmaduke and Sappington" that had been set up January 1, 1830, by Meredith and Dr. Sappington to operate a store at Arrow Rock.[16] Author John Beauchamp Jones (alias Luke Shortfield), who was himself a merchant in Arrow Rock for a brief time in the 1830s, described in his book, *The Western Merchant*, a typical western store that may well have been modeled on the Marmaduke and Sappington store: "The framework was of hewed logs, laid lengthwise and with the chinks between filled with clay and lime. The structure itself consisted of two rooms, each about twenty feet square — one to be used for a sales room, and the other for storing goods. Door and window in the sales room were equipped with locks and bolts — the building appeared little different from the scattering of log cabin homes in the surrounding territory. Interior walls were whitewashed, except in the sales room, which was shelved on all four sides. A counter of boards thirty inches wide and twelve feet long extended from the window to the partition wall between the two rooms."[17]

Dr. Sappington was a partner in Marmaduke and Sappington until late November 1831. On the 19th of that month, payments in the amount of $1,520 were sent to the Philadelphia firm of Siter & Price to be distributed by them to other local firms that held outstanding Marmaduke and Sappington invoices. This disbursement closed out the books on Dr. Sappington and Meredith's company, and they may have closed the Arrow Rock store at this time. Darwin Sappington then replaced his father in a partnership that continued to operate under the Marmaduke and Sappington name. Paired again with an older, more experienced tutor, Darwin developed a warm relationship with Meredith. Years later, in a letter to Meredith, Darwin recalled their working together, saying that letters from friends, "particularly those from one I have spent so many pleasant hours with in my youthful days," afforded him much pleasure.[18] In late 1831, the Marmaduke and Sappington Company store in Jonesboro was selling general merchandise and also keeping a stock of iron for purchase by blacksmiths, who needed the material for wagons going to Santa Fe. Part of their iron supply came from "the new Maramec Iron Company on the Meramec River in then Crawford County."[19] The store also served as a supplier for local Santa Fe traders who lacked favorable connections with eastern wholesale houses. Trade goods intended for Santa Fe were purchased in Philadelphia by Darwin in 1834 for someone identified as "Williams."[20] Later failing to pay for the merchandise after completing his trade at Santa Fe, Williams left Meredith and Darwin holding his unpaid note for several years. Then in 1839, Meredith received information that "this man Williams living near Boons Lick who is owing you for goods taken to Santa Fe, went to the South last fall or winter with mules and sold them on credit. These mules … were absolutely bot by Williams on his own account, and paid for with his own money. … Although the trade was conducted with great secrecy … there is much reason to believe that … they were in fact his property."[21] Whether Meredith and Darwin eventually collected from Williams is unknown, but their willingness to advance Williams his Santa Fe goods, and his reluctance to settle the account, underscores the tenuous nature of frontier mercantilism.

Meredith's standing among the Santa Fe traders is shown in a letter he received from James L. Collins in the summer of 1830. At Matamoros, Mexico, after trading in Santa Fe that year, Collins asked Meredith for help in reducing the tax Mexico charged on goods brought into that country. He compared the cost of importing goods via the Gulf of Mexico and the port of Matamoros, then overland to El Paso and Santa Fe, versus that of goods brought overland from Franklin to Santa Fe. Wanting to preserve Missouri's predominance in the trade, he concluded that if the U.S. Congress could be induced to press Mexico for a reduction of the tariff, "the odds must be greatly in favor of the Missourians. The object of this letter is that you would use your influence with our Members of Congress to this end."[22]

The firm of Marmaduke and Sappington remained in operation until the summer of 1836, although Meredith appears to have turned over his share of the business to Darwin some months earlier. The decision to close the store was prompted in large part by Dr. Sappington's decision to market his proprietary medicine, Sappington's Anti-Fever Pills, beyond the Booneslick country. To do this, in 1835 he established Sappington and Sons, a national sales organization that would be managed in the future by his sons and sons-in-law. The prospect of making a fortune peddling quinine pills to millions of people who were at risk for malaria evidently was more appealing to Meredith and Darwin than was selling groceries and general merchandise at the Jonesboro store. Another factor influencing their decision was the westward shift in the departure point for the Santa Fe Trail to Independence, Missouri, by this time.

The partnership known as M. M. Marmaduke & Co. was originally established in 1827, with Meredith, Darwin Sappington, and Thomas McMahan as the original proprietors, to trade in New Mexico in 1828 (by 1829 McMahan was no longer a partner). Its operation as a business is not seen again until 1832, when it reappears as Marmaduke and Company (with Darwin Sappington and Meredith as partners) in early summer at a site in Saline County called St. Helena. On May 17, 1832, Marmaduke and Company received a shipment of 20 boxes, barrels, and crates of general merchandise — cloth goods, dishes, hats, shawls, scarves, cloaks, muslin, ribbon, gloves, measuring cans, milk strainers, funnels, scoops, shovels, and other hardware items, as well as spoons, forks, buttons, shoes and shoe tacks, and five barrels of whiskey. Journal entries for this company list retail sales to individuals (and some to "Marmaduke and Sappington") until March 30, 1833, at which time entries for Marmaduke and Company cease. The firm's brief life in the 1830s is an indication that it was set up by Meredith and Darwin to compete with a store that was drawing business away from their store at Jonesboro. Five days after Marmaduke and Company went out of business, the journal reopens under the name "Marmaduke and Sappington."[23]

A fourth Sappington mercantile business operated conterminous with the others in the 1830s. E. D. Sappington and Company was Darwin's separate entity. Record books show it to be in business from January 1, 1830, until July 1, 1835. How it differed from the other mercantile companies operating at the same time is not clear. The daybooks, expense journals, and ledgers that have survived for all of these companies record instances of merchandise and money being transferred between the various entities, showing the interrelatedness of the Sappingtons and Meredith Marmaduke, thus supporting Dr. Sappington's desire to keep it all within the family.

The Traveling Merchant

As a storekeeper and long-distance trader, Meredith rode the steamboats east for three years, from 1831 to 1833, to buy merchandise from suppliers in Pittsburgh, and then traveled by wagon or stage hundreds of miles to make further purchases in Philadelphia. Although such travel involved a great deal of risk (steamboats were notorious for exploding or sinking after striking unseen objects, while overland travel had its share of accidents), this direct contact let him select the best-quality goods and enabled him to negotiate liberal credit terms, usually with payments extending out six months or more. He also arranged for insurance, packing, and shipment by steamboat to St. Louis, where the merchandise was transferred to one of the packets operating on the Missouri River.

Travel to the eastern cities was a common practice in the 1830s for many western merchants who would bypass suppliers in cities such as St. Louis and Louisville, in favor of better prices and terms in seaboard cities. By 1817, more than 15,000 wagons were arriving at Pittsburgh annually, loaded with merchandise valued at $16 million for shipment to the west. In his monograph, *The Pioneer Merchant in Mid-America*, historian Lewis Atherton depicts Philadelphia by 1828 as holding "first place among the seaboard cities in supplying Mid-America, with Baltimore also having a large share in the trade. In the same period St. Louis was the leading wholesale center in Mid-America. ... St. Louis could scarcely compare with Philadelphia and Baltimore, however, in the sense of being a real wholesale center, although her progress in that field was rapid during the next thirty years."[24] Following a safe and successful trip east, Meredith expected to make a much higher profit on goods bought there than what he would realize from merchandise bought in St. Louis.

After being under Meredith's tutelage for nearly three years, Darwin was sent east in 1834 to buy the company's supplies. At his hotel in Philadelphia in late January he received a letter from Meredith with some last-minute advice, its paternal tone reflecting a teacher following up with his student, now out of school.

Dear Darwin,

Although you have just started, a few ideas have suggested themselves to me, that had not before you left me.

Had you not better buy about 10 gallons of good Madiera [sic] wine, and about 10 more of Tenerife (or 15)?

As you will have a considerable amount of money in cash to lay out, and as that will be done in houses which we do not consider our regular houses, should money be considered very scarce in Philadelphia, you can possibly meet with some houses on the eve of failing and be able to purchase many things on your own terms. And indeed, in all the houses where you will buy for cash, you can Jew them down to almost your own terms. This is a practice that I do not in the general approve of, but if times are in Phil. as I expect you will find them, I have no doubt but what it will be a very common thing with those merchants who may buy with money.

If when you hand Rockhill, Hook's money, you are able to learn enough to satisfy you that they cannot purchase more goods there this spring, I would advise a small increase in our purchases. But should you not obtain any information on this subject, you will act as you had originally intended.

Should they succeed well below they may possibly put on a large lot of goods, time enough to be in our way, and it is important not to make too confident calculations on their movements in any respect.

Take just care and do not suffer any of our notes to be cashed at bank if they should pronounce them counterfeit, as we can return the most of them to the persons of whom we got them.

Do the best you can, and take time. Yrs very truly, M. M. Marmaduke.[25]

To Make a Fortune in Missouri

Thirteen days after posting his first letter to Darwin, Meredith wrote again with more suggestions, urging him to speed shipping of the new merchandise, which was badly needed at the store, and expressing concern about their finances. Instructions were given about what to do at St. Louis on the return passage, and Darwin was warned about a potential new competitor at Jonesboro.

Dear Darwin,

This will meet you in Pittsburgh. I think you will do well to purchase about 1000 spun cot. if it can possibly be sold at $2 a bundle. It is now in great demand here.

We have a considerable quantity of window glass now on hand. If you do not buy your wool hats in Phil., buy them in Pittsbg. Get 6 or 8 Doz. of them.

I have collected about 300$ since you left us, all of small debts. The weather has been bad, so that not much has been done. Our sales are about $20 per day. We shall be extremely scarce of goods before you return.

Tell old Beelen not to keep the goods in Pittsbg. one hour after they arrive.

I have no doubt but that young Tom Davis will take a store to this place in the Spring. He starts to Phil. on next Sunday.

We have a large amount of money to raise here shortly, to wit:

for Hall (he wants his)	$200.00
Genl. Smith (do)	600.00
How. (do, about)	300.00
Cecil (I don't know as to him)	300.00
Von Phul & McGill	500.00
For N. Orleans	500.00
& then for freight, say	300.00
	$2,700.00

All of which will be wanted on or before the 15 or 20 of April next. Can it be done? I fear not. I have now about $500 on hand. Hall wants his money on 15 Inst. Genl. Smith about the 20 Inst. So that you find every nerve will have to be strained here to meet engagements, if I am not even driven to borrow.

Do not get behind your goods, but come on with or a little ahead of them. You ought to be in St. Louis 2, 3 or 4 days, selecting castings & such other articles there as you may not buy in Phil. or Pittsbg. Take time in your purchases. Yrs. Very Truly, M. M. Marmaduke. p.s. Buy about 1 dozen Collin's axes in St. Louis or Pittsbg., if you have not bot them in Phil. p.s. All well. MMM.[26]

Darwin never received the second letter. Addressed to him "Care of Anthony Beelen, esq." in Pittsburgh, when it arrived he was already on his way home. The unopened letter eventually was returned to Jonesboro, after being postmarked April 2 at Pittsburgh.

New Orleans was another destination favored by western merchants in the 1830s, having an advantage over the eastern cities in the grocery field for domestic staples such as sugar and rice, and as the import center for coffee and tea coming from foreign ports. These goods found inexpensive transport into the nation's heartland on steamboats working the Mississippi, Ohio, and Missouri Rivers. The untimely death of his friend and former business associate John Hardeman, at New Orleans in September 1829, brought Meredith to that city eight months later, though the trip had other purposes as well. En route, at St. Louis he delivered a consignment of 79 barrels of salt to the commission house of "Mssrs. Gay & Estes."[27]

At New Orleans, Meredith purchased sugar and coffee for the Marmaduke and Sappington store at Arrow Rock, and the Pearson and Sappington store at Jonesboro. But he also was there to look into the circumstances surrounding a claim that had been filed against Hardeman's estate. John Hardeman was in New Orleans on his way home, after a successful trading venture to Santa Fe and El Paso, when he was bitten by a mosquito and contracted yellow fever, dying after a few days' illness. A claim against his estate in the amount of $1,643, for four visits by Dr. Jonas E. Kerr, four days "boarding to the innkeeper Knight," and interment in a city cemetery, was disputed by John's father, Thomas. Most of the money was claimed by the doctor, who Thomas accused of cheating "widows and orphans," and said he had "abundant reason to believe" that Dr. Kerr had killed his son for money. Thomas believed the total expense should not exceed $100.[28] Meredith and his neighbor, General Thomas A. Smith, another staunch friend of the Hardeman family, evidently thought likewise. Before Meredith embarked on his trip south, Smith had received legal advice from New Orleans that "about $1,000 would accrue to Hardeman's family if some friend would administer the estate in that city."[29] There is reason to believe that Meredith — who would soon be named the trustee for the benefit of John Hardeman's minor children, Leona and Glenn — arrived at New Orleans intent on investigating the greedy doctor's outrageous charge for his brief labor. In his family biography *Wilderness Calling*, Nicholas Perkins Hardeman, the best authority for the family's story, did not disclose the outcome of the New Orleans claim, the record of which has not been found.[30]

Word of Meredith's departure from the mercantile business, following the dissolution of the Marmaduke and Sappington company, reached John Locke Hardeman, John's eldest son, early in 1836 in a letter from Meredith. Responding from Madison County, Mississippi, Locke said it was news to him "that you have ceased to be a merchant," and mentioned a new interest on Meredith's horizon: "You still speak of Texas. It is doubtless a fine country, good soil and all that, but of doubtful health. Several of my relatives have visited that country. ..."[31] Texas was in Meredith's mind all right, but he had other interests in sight, and for the next five years he would assist Dr. Sappington in developing the nascent anti-fever pill business, while expanding his farm operations and enhancing his influence as a Democrat in Missouri's dominant political party.

Notes

1. "an extensive regional trade in agriculture, money lending, and medical services." Lynn Morrow, "Dr. John Sappington: Southern Patriarch in the New West." *MHR*, Vol. 90, No. 1 (October 1995), 43.

2. "about the sum of $7,000" from her estate. Saline County Circuit Court Case Files, 1841, Box 3, Folder 155, microfilm reel 29916, Missouri State Archives.

3. calling their company "Pearson and Sappington." Alonzo Pearson to James Keyte, May 16, 1829. Box 1, Folder 5, Sappington-Marmaduke Papers, MHS.

To Make a Fortune in Missouri

4. Pearson later added $3,000 to his "portion of stock, to be put in trade." Account book dated January 1, 1830–November 19, 1831, entry January 12, 1830. Folder 23, Marmaduke Papers C1021, SHSMO.

5. "Mr. Pearson has not yet ret. from the east": Marmaduke to William Sappington, March 23, 1830. Folder 18, Ibid.

6. "It is with pain that I have to let you no what has happened": E. D. Sappington to Marmaduke, June 18, 1830. Box 1, Folder 6, Sappington-Marmaduke Papers, MHS.

7. "has of late found that he was detected": Saline County Circuit Court Case Files, 1841, Box 3, Folder 155, microfilm reel 29916, Missouri State Archives.

8. The defendants' responses to Mrs. Parsons's lawsuit: Ibid.

9. "the petition of Eliza Whitsett Sappington": *House Journal of the First Session of the Sixth General Assembly of the State of Missouri, November 15, 1830*. Printed in Fayette, 1831.

10. "contrary to my wish, and was lost by one vote, which was the vote of the President of the Senate": John Miller to Marmaduke, December 26, 1830. Box 1, Folder 6, Sappington-Marmaduke Papers, MHS.

11. "Sir, Your letter of the 30th ultimo has just reached me": Edward Bates to Marmaduke, January 4, 1831. Box 1, Folder 7, Sappington-Marmaduke Papers, MHS. Edward Bates and Marmaduke corresponded occasionally over the years about political matters of interest to both men. Bates, described as the "ablest and most eloquent member" (Doris K. Goodwin, *Team of Rivals: The Political Genius of Abraham Lincoln*, 65) of Missouri's early legislature, was Missouri's first attorney general, later serving terms in the state's House and Senate, and in the U.S. House of Representatives before running for president against Abraham Lincoln, who brought him into his cabinet immediately after the election of 1860.

12. "put on a roof, inserted a door and a window, moved in his desk and law books," and began to practice law. Walter B. Stevens, *Centennial History of Missouri*, Vol. 1, 14.

13. "I received a few days past your last & very friendly letter": George R. Pitts to Marmaduke, October 18, 1829. Box 1, Folder 5, Sappington-Marmaduke Papers, MHS. Dr. George Pitts was an acquaintance of Marmaduke's in Virginia who moved his family to St. Charles County in Missouri in 1828 and established himself there as a physician, although he claimed to dislike the practice of medicine. Twenty-five letters Pitts wrote to Marmaduke (1823–1847) were retained by Marmaduke in his personal papers. Their contents depict Pitts as a quarrelsome complainer who had a problem controlling his consumption of alcohol ("Have been drunk but once since you left here."). But he was also an astute observer of state and national political affairs, and it is apparent that Marmaduke valued the information he received from Pitts, although he maintained an "arms-length" friendship with the fractious doctor. Pitts settled on a farm in Dardenne Township in St. Charles County and was arrested there in 1842 for selling liquor without a "dram shop license."

14. "Permit me to congratulate you on your fortunate escape from the difficulties by which you were surrounded": George R. Pitts to Marmaduke, October 11, 1830. Box 1, Folder 6, Ibid.

15. The firm of Pearson and Sappington: Petition for writ requiring Pearson and Sappington to account for monies collected after dissolving firm, November 5, 1831. Box 1, Folder 7, Sappington-Marmaduke Papers, MHS.

16. first iteration of a company known as "Marmaduke and Sappington": Account book titled "Kept by Meredith M. Marmaduke and Dr. Sappington when they ran a store at Jonesboro." Folder 23, Marmaduke Papers, SHSMO. There is some question as to whether the Arrow Rock store was operated in partnership with Dr. Sappington, or with Darwin Sappington. Either way, the businesses were all in the family.

17. "The framework was of hewed logs": Lewis Atherton, *The Pioneer Merchant in Mid-America*, 39; (John B. Jones, aka. Luke Shortfield, *The Western Merchant*, Philadelphia: Grigg, Eliot & Co., 1849.)

18. "particular those from one I have spent so many pleasant hours with in my youthful days": E. D. Sappington to Marmaduke, December 8, 1840. Box 2, Folder 6, Sappington-Marmaduke Papers, MHS.

19. new Maramec Iron Company: Lynn Morrow to author, March 29, 2015. Morrow cites documents in Clair Mann Collection C3556, SHSMO.

20. Trade goods for someone identified as "Williams": Memorandum for E. D. Sappington, Box 6, Folder

All in the Family

8. Sappington-Marmaduke Papers, MHS.

21. "this man Williams living near Boons Lick who is owing you for goods taken to Santa Fe": C. F. Jackson to Marmaduke May 7, 1839. Box 2, Folder 4, Sappington-Marmaduke papers, MHS. Trade goods for Williams had been obtained in Philadelphia by Darwin Sappington, who went there to purchase merchandise for Marmaduke and Company, and the firm of Marmaduke and Sappington, in 1834 and 1835. Marmaduke to E. D. Sappington, January 21, 1834. Box 2, Folder 1, Ibid; Marmaduke to E. D. Sappington, February 2, 1834. Folder 7, Marmaduke Papers C1021, SHSMO. Williams is specifically mentioned in: Memorandum for E. D. Sappington [undated]. Box 6, Folder 8, Sappington-Marmaduke Papers, MHS.

22. "the odds must be greatly in favor of the Missourians": James L. Collins to Marmaduke, July 25, 1830. Box 1, Folder 6, Ibid.

23. The partnership known as Marmaduke and Company: Marmaduke and Company daybooks, Vols. 1–3. Sappington-Marmaduke Papers, MHS. Vol. 1 entries record the sale of merchandise to individuals, and to Marmaduke and Sappington. Vol. 2, is titled "Invoice of Merchandise for Marmaduke and Company, Muddy, Saline County, Missouri, the 17th day of May, 1832." In Vol. 3, the first section of the journal is a duplicate entry of Vol. 1 during the period May 29, 1832, through March 30, 1833. On April 4, 1833, the journal changes and the entries are for Marmaduke and Sappington, at Jonesboro, continuing through to June, 1836.

24. "first place among the seaboard cities in supplying Mid-America": Atherton, *The Pioneer Merchant in Mid-America*, 47.

25. "Although you have just started, a few ideas have suggested themselves to me": Marmaduke to Darwin Sappington, January 21, 1834. Box 2, Folder 1, Sappington-Marmaduke Papers, MHS The wines suggested by Marmaduke were probably for consumption in the Marmaduke and Sappington households. Madeira (from Portugal) and Tenerife (produced in the Canary Islands) were the principal wines consumed in America from colonial days until the mid-1820s when Dr. Daniel Norborne Norton produced the "Norton" cultivar, which ultimately enabled the development of quality American wines. To that time, American attempts to produce good wine had been unsuccessful, particularly in Virginia. In 1834 Marmaduke, evidently wanting to develop a vineyard in Missouri, asked his brother in Virginia to send him grape seed: Vincent Marmaduke to Marmaduke, July 23, 1834, Ibid. For more on the role played by the Norton grape in Missouri's wine industry see: Todd Kliman, "The Ignoble Grape: The Rise, Fall, and Rise Again of the Outsider Norton," *MHR*, Vol. 109, No. 2 (January 2015). "Hook's Money": Hook must have been another store. Atherton, *The Pioneer Merchant in Mid-America*, 57, depicts E. D. Sappington and Company as "frequently filling orders for other merchants." Counterfeit "notes" (money) were a problem for merchants everywhere, exacerbated by individual banks printing their own currency which in many cases was easy to duplicate.

26. "This will meet you in Pittsburgh": Marmaduke to Darwin Sappington, February 3, 1834. Folder 7, Marmaduke Papers C1021, SHSMO. "Old Beelen" refers to the firm owned by A. W. Beelen in Pittsburgh, from whom they purchased pots, pans, kettles, plates, jars and hardware items: Invoice, April 21, 1831. Ibid.

27. "Mssrs. Gay & Estes": Note, Salt left in St. Louis for sale, June 4, 1830. Folder 6, Ibid. Sixty-nine of the barrels belonged to Pearson and Sappington, while the remaining 10 were consigned to Darwin Sappington.

28. "boarding to the innkeeper Knight": Thomas Hardeman to Marmaduke, October 20, 1831. Box 1, Folder 7, Sappington-Marmaduke Papers, MHS.

29. "about $1,000 would accrue to Hardeman's family if some friend would administer the estate in that city": Hardeman, *Wilderness Calling*, 115. This biography of the Hardeman family does not report on the success or failure of John Hardeman's estate to contest Dr. Kerr's claim. Whatever happened after Meredith looked into the matter is buried in the past.

30. trustee for the benefit of John Hardeman's minor children: Marmaduke to John Locke Hardeman, July 6, 1834. Affadavit transferring trusteeship of John Hardeman's minor children to John Locke Hardeman, January 31, 1835. Folder 23, Glenn O. Hardeman Papers C3655, SHSMO.

31. "that you have ceased to be a merchant": J. Locke Hardeman to Marmaduke, March 19, 1836. Box 2, Folder 2, Sappington-Marmaduke Papers, MHS.

CHAPTER 11

TASTING THE POLITICAL BONE

For nearly a quarter of a century after Missouri's admission into the Union, the state's often turbulent political scene was characterized by four distinct features: a tendency by some of the state's most prominent politicians to settle their disputes with guns; the evolution of political parties where there had been none; the presence of a powerful political machine controlled by men who operated from the heart of the Booneslick country; and money and banking as the major political issue in the state.

Missouri historian Floyd C. Shoemaker took note that when Missouri joined the Union in 1821 there was only one national political party of any significance, the Democratic-Republican Party, and it lacked a following in the state. When it came to politics, Shoemaker wrote, Missourians identified with individuals whose political philosophies approximated their own. The bitter adversarial relationship between Thomas Hart Benton and David Barton, Missouri's first U.S. senators, illustrates this and the effect such political partisanship had on the state's early development. Although their political careers began at the same time on a friendly note, the two soon espoused differing views of federal policies that affected Missourians. Senator Benton disliked a national bank, preferring a state bank whose paper currency was supported by gold and silver specie (known as "hard" money), a policy he believed to be beneficial to farmers and tradesmen by protecting their money from the depreciation that often accompanied "soft" money (paper currency not backed by specie). Barton, on the other hand, favored a national treasury and believed that requiring banks to back their currency with specie would work a hardship on merchants and manufacturers who needed a ready supply of "soft" money to conduct business. Benton favored slavery; Barton saw the practice as "the secret poison stealing its way to our vitals."[1] Barton wanted internal improvements — roads and canals — paid for by the national government; Benton thought otherwise. Benton fought against import duties; Barton sought to enhance farmers and merchants by the imposition of tariffs that would keep foreign goods out of the marketplace. These differing views of important national policies tugged Missourians both ways in the state's early years and the controversy contributed to the eventual acceptance of national parties as active political entities.

Not surprisingly, the two senators also differed in their support of presidential candidates in the 1824 and 1828 campaigns. In 1824, both men initially favored Henry Clay, but when no candidate received a majority of electoral votes the election went to the U.S. House of Representatives for resolution. Benton then favored Andrew

Jackson, and Barton supported John Quincy Adams, who won. In 1828, Barton headed the Adams faction in Missouri and called for a convention of "Friends of the Administration" to meet in March at Jefferson City. Benton rallied the Jackson men of the state who scheduled their convention early in January, also at Jefferson City. (One has to believe that both Dr. Sappington and Meredith Marmaduke, friends of Benton and supporters of Jackson, attended this meeting.) Both groups adopted resolutions favoring their presidential choice and nominated electoral candidates. These actions, however, did not result in the establishment of organized political parties in Missouri. That would not occur until 1831 when the presidential contest was between Andrew Jackson (having won the office in 1828) and Henry Clay. That year saw the rise of two distinct groups in the state — the National Republicans (who would become known as Whigs) headed by David Barton, who favored Clay, and Jackson's adherents, who were known as Democrats. By 1830, the Democrats were well organized and controlled the state's political scene from their stronghold in the Booneslick counties. The Whig Party, however, was on the ascendency, and some of its strongest supporters also lived in the counties along the Missouri River.

Rough-and-Tumble Politics

Aspiring politicians in Missouri's early years often resorted to violence in the form of dueling with pistols to uphold personal honor when they thought they had been insulted. Operating under a set of rules called the Code Duello, the practice of fighting a duel to "gain satisfaction" arrived with members of the Southern ruling class who migrated to Missouri in its territorial days. Two such political aspirants who fought one of the territory's earliest duels were Joshua Barton and Thomas Hempstead. Barton, who would become Missouri's first secretary of state and later a U.S. district attorney, was the brother of David Barton, one of Missouri's first United States senators elected in 1821. Thomas Hempstead was the brother of Edward Hempstead, the territory's first representative to Congress. Their duel, fought in 1816 over a perceived insult, ended without bloodshed, yet it set a pattern of behavior for Joshua Barton that would eventually lead to his death. Barton's second in the Hempstead duel was his law partner, Edward Bates, a future Missouri attorney general and United States attorney general (and future friend of Meredith Marmaduke), while Thomas Hart Benton (elected Missouri's other senator in 1821) served as Hempstead's second.

In 1817, Joshua Barton was again involved in a duel, this time as the second for St. Louis attorney Charles Lucas, who twice fought Thomas Benton over a dispute that arose when Lucas questioned Benton's right to vote in an election that summer. Benton "then applied abusive and ungentlemanly language to Lucas, and Lucas then challenged him."[2] In their first encounter, Lucas and Benton faced each other with drawn pistols, fired, and inflicted minor injuries. Later, responding to a rumor that he had acted unfairly at their first face-off, Benton issued a second challenge, and this time Lucas, with Joshua Barton again acting as his second, fell dead when hit by a bullet from Benton's pistol. Thomas H. Benton, who served Missouri for 30 years as a senator, was notorious for his interest in dueling. An adviser or second in several duels, he created a set of rules that were used by others who engaged in the practice. As an editor of the St. Louis *Enquirer*, Benton wrote a defense of duels in 1818, and as a lawyer he defended duelists in court. Near the end of his life, however, Benton expressed his regret for having killed Charles Lucas, "referring to himself as usual in the third person, he told of 'the pang which went through his heart' when he saw young Lucas fall. ..."3

Political violence erupted again for Joshua Barton in 1823 when he anonymously authored an article, with evidence supplied by his brother David, that appeared in a St. Louis newspaper accusing William C. Rector, surveyor-general for Illinois, Missouri, and Arkansas, of corruption and nepotism. Rector's brother, Thomas, upon discovering Joshua's authorship challenged him to a duel. They met on a sandbar in the Mississippi River where Barton was mortally wounded, living only a few minutes after he was shot by Rector. Interestingly, Thomas Rector died two years later in a knife fight on the St. Louis waterfront.

In 1822, the Missouri General Assembly passed legislation barring duels in the state, but that didn't stop the practice. In 1824, Abiel Leonard, an attorney in Howard County, and an acquaintance of Meredith Marmaduke, engaged in a duel with Major Taylor Berry who later died of pneumonia after being shot in the lungs by Leonard, who was uninjured. Convicted by a Howard County jury of challenging Berry to a duel, Leonard was fined $150 and disbarred. He later was reinstated as an attorney and eventually became a Missouri Supreme Court Justice. The practice of dueling to settle ruffled political feathers did not die out in Missouri until 1857, when Benjamin Gratz Brown, a future United States senator, challenged Thomas C. Reynolds, a United States district attorney and future lieutenant governor, to a second attempt to settle a bitter dispute that had gone on for several years. Reynold's poor eyesight had forced the first engagement to end without a shot being fired. He did better the second time, wounding Brown in the leg while escaping unscathed.

Meredith witnessed an incident at a Democratic Party meeting in Fayette in 1838 that almost became lethal. At an outdoor barbecue, James H. Birch, a Whig and editor of Fayette's newspaper, the *Western Monitor* (later, a member of Missouri's Supreme Court), and Claiborne Fox Jackson (Meredith's brother-in-law and a future Missouri governor) threatened each other with drawn knives. Birch's son, James H. Jr., related the incident some years later:

> "After the barbecue was over and the drinking was in order nearly 500 men were gathered around one of the long tables to hear toasts and speeches. At one of the tables was seated Colonel Benton, to the left of ... Jackson. At the other end Governor Boggs, who had come within one vote of beating Colonel Benton in the Democratic caucus for reelection as senator, was seated to the right of Judge ... Birch.
>
> "Birch and Jackson were in the flower of their youthful manhood, fired with ambition, and rivals for political honors. The toasts were to be read at one end and then repeated at the other. The first toast was read by Major Jackson and reread by Colonel Birch, and was to the President of the United Sates and was received and drunk with due solemnity.
>
> "The second toast was read by Colonel Birch and reread by Major Jackson, and was in honor of the governor of the state of Missouri. This was received and

responded to by those at the table and those surrounding it, for Governor Boggs was very popular with the people.

"All drank to it with enthusiastic expression, except one, and that one was Thomas H. Benton.

"He sat with folded arms, the vary incarnation of a despot, and refused even to raise his glass to his lips. This did not escape the eye of one who had waited and prayed for just such an opportunity.

"The next toast came from Major Jackson's end and was sent to Colonel Birch. But before it reached him he mounted a chair and in a voice which covered the entire audience, he shouted: 'Major Jackson, that toast will not be read at this end of the table until Colonel Benton apologizes for not having drunk to the toast of the governor.'

"Had a Nihilist exploded a bomb the consternation could not have been more complete. Gathering himself together, Major Jackson shouted back: 'What did you say, Colonel Birch?' And the answer came back more defiant than before.

"After a moment's consultation with Colonel Benton, Major Jackson mounted the table, drew his bowie knife and started down the table. It was an insult to his chief which could only be atoned for by the blood of the one who had cast it. Colonel Birch expected nothing less from Major Jackson, and mounted the table and drawing his bowie knife, started down the table to meet him. The men on either side of the table took in the situation and they were both taken from the table by their friends and disarmed."[4]

Not generally given to violent behavior, Meredith's depiction in a pair of paintings by the artist George Caleb Bingham brought him to the edge of challenging Bingham to a duel in 1853. The two paintings depict Missouri's lively antebellum political scene. In *The County Election*, completed in 1852, Bingham has a portly, white-haired Meredith standing on the porch of a building in Arrow Rock administering the oath to a voter while Darwin Sappington is tipping his hat to the next voter in line. Seated behind Meredith, Darwin's brother William is sharpening a quill pen to have it ready when needed. The artist himself sits at the edge of the porch sketching in a small notebook.[5] Elsewhere in the scene, free whiskey is being offered electors, some of whom are obviously drunk, before they approach the porch to cast their ballots. Bingham, a dedicated Whig, and Darwin Sappington, a Democrat, had bitterly competed in 1846 as candidates for state representative from Saline County. Bingham was initially declared the winner by three votes, only to be unseated later by Sappington. Two years later, the two would fight over the legislative seat again, the 1848 outcome different with Bingham clearly defeating his rival.

In his second political painting, *Stump Speaking*, finished in 1853, Bingham depicts Darwin Sappington "orating" to a crowd of skeptical listeners, while seated nearby "conspicuously on the platform is the orotund personage of M. M. Marmaduke [whom Bingham] disliked ... almost as bitterly as Sappington for political reasons." Meredith was so unhappy with his uncomplimentary portrayal in this painting — heavy sideburns and eyebrows frame a scowling face on a head that rests atop a bloated body — that he threatened to sue the artist for libel and even suggested the two should duel. Fortunately, friends convinced Meredith that "his broad belly was an easy target for Bingham who was both nimble and younger." Clearly, Bingham, who was making a statement in these two paintings, was not happy with what he considered to be a corrupt political cartel operating in Saline County.[6]

Early Political Days

Meredith's unheralded entry into Missouri's lively political scene in the late 1820s occurred as the volatile behavior that sometimes characterized the state's early days was becoming less acceptable. Growing up in post-Revolutionary Virginia where political activism was embodied in the lives of native sons such as George Washington, Thomas Jefferson, Patrick Henry, and James Madison, among others, Meredith had felt the presence of these men and their accomplishments. At his family's plantation in the Northern Neck, near the seat of national government in Washington City, he could almost rub elbows with such eminent men. So it is not surprising that in Missouri he would emulate the planter-become-politician tradition of his native state. The experience he gained during six years as tax collector and a justice of the peace in Virginia's Westmoreland County worked to his advantage as he sought to establish himself on Missouri's evolving political landscape. His ascent as a Missouri politician began in January 1827 as Saline County's official surveyor, then as justice of the peace for Arrow Rock Township in 1829, and finally as a judge of the county court in 1831. Appointment to these desirable local offices placing him in the public eye came over the signature of Governor John Miller, Dr. Sappington's longtime friend and political associate.

Flexing his political muscle in favor of family members and business associates was a common practice for Dr. Sappington. In 1838, he wrote Charles M. Cravens, then serving as Pettis County representative, asking him to withdraw from the upcoming election for senator from Missouri's 23rd district, in favor of Dr. George Penn, a Sappington and Marmaduke associate who had been the Saline County representative in 1834. Describing Dr. Penn as "a candidate that will ransack every hole and corner of the district" for votes, Sappington reminded Cravens of "past favors" then assured him he had been a "faithful representative for us and we have no doubt you will still be so. ... Let me therefore intreat [sic] you as an old personal and political friend ... to abandon all pretentions [sic] as Senator, and join with us heartily in the support of Doct. Penn."[7] Penn won the 1838 election and served as senator for one term.

With his father-in-law's guiding hand showing the way, Meredith took his place in the Booneslick-based political machine known as the "Central Clique," which was allied with Thomas Benton and the Democratic Party. Prominent among members of the Central Clique were Dr. Sappington, Dr. George Penn, Claiborne F. Jackson, Thomas Reynolds, Sterling Price, John J. Lowry, John Miller, and Thomas H. Harvey. As early as 1828, "aware of your influence in Saline County," John R. Grisham asked Meredith to establish a county committee to select a candidate for the U.S. Senate from among three supporters of presidential candidate Andrew Jackson, all of whom were "anti-administration men," vying for the office.[8] In February that same year, the Fayette *Missouri Intelligencer* announced that the site of Marmaduke (apparently Meredith's home) was designated a new post office in Saline County, an action that demonstrated

Meredith's growing political clout. A later issue of the newspaper published a notice received from Peyton Nowlin, postmaster of Marmaduke, advising Abraham Smith, Esq., that he had mail waiting for him "which if not taken out before the 1st day of October next" would be forwarded to the General Post Office as dead letters.[9]

During these formative years, Meredith stayed abreast of affairs in Jefferson City, corresponding with Charles Cravens, Saline County's representative in 1833, when news of the General Assembly's action on a bill to establish a state bank was not received at home in a timely manner, and with Dr. Penn when he was a senator, who regularly wrote Meredith about the status of bills being considered by the General Assembly.

Meredith also built relationships on a broader scale, communicating with officials in the nation's capital on matters pertaining to the Booneslick area, querying Thomas Benton about the possible removal of the federal land office from Franklin, and writing to Duff Green, a prominent member of President Andrew Jackson's "kitchen cabinet," about patronage in the government printing office, calling it "a press so prostituted" that it is "dangerous to the liberties of the people."[10] Meredith's brother-in-law, Claiborne Fox Jackson, also acted as a conduit for national and state political information that he knew was of interest to Meredith, telling him in 1837 that he (Jackson) is "no prophet but think it requires but little discrimination to observe that the seed of discord is about taking root in Va. & New York, which is ultimately to grow into a National Bank."[11] (Jackson married three of Dr. Sappington's daughters, the first two dying early in their marriages. His third wife was Eliza Sappington, after her nullification from marriage to Alonzo Pearson.)

Throughout his life, Meredith received political information gathered from locales across the nation and passed along to him by correspondents. Letters arrived at his home almost weekly from people in the East, Midwest, and South with news and opinions about politicians and political matters in their areas. These tidbits of information were usually penned — almost as afterthoughts — in the closing paragraphs of letters dealing with more important matters.

The preponderance of this type of communication in his correspondence leaves no doubt that Meredith cultivated his friends and business associates to do this, in effect creating a network that kept him apprised of public sentiment and political activities throughout Missouri and much of the rest of the nation east of the Great Plains. During the 1830–1839 decade, such information provided him with critical insight into state and national issues. Meredith was perceived as someone who had considerable political influence in Washington City. Such was his reputation that the residents of the growing town of Blackwater, in northwest Cooper County, sent him a petition in 1838 seeking a post office, saying the town "will take it as a particular favor if you will use your influence … you are better acquainted as how the business ought to be done. …"[12]

Meredith's roles as a county office holder, merchant, and supplier to the Santa Fe trade, business associate of his influential father-in-law, and a prospering farmer as well, enabled him to develop relationships with men who were influential in their communities, and who would eventually support his ascendency to Missouri's second-highest governing office.

Canvassing for a Candidate

Despite not having held a political office higher than Saline County judge, an administrative position, by 1839 Meredith was widely viewed by members of the Democratic Party as a viable candidate for lieutenant governor in the 1840 general election. An early hint of this interest came Meredith's way in January when his friend and associate Dr. George Penn, writing from his state Senate office in Jefferson City, planted a small seed that would grow in coming months. *"Nothing is yet done with regard to the selection of candidates for the office of Governor and Lieutenant Gov.* [Emphasis added] Judge Reynolds [Thomas Reynolds of the second judicial circuit] was here several days. … Judge Erickson [James Earickson of Howard County] is still here. … They are both willing to become candidates. If either should be taken up by the members of the Legislature I think it will be Judge Reynolds. Dr. Cannon [Franklin Cannon, Missouri lieutenant governor 1836–40] is supported in his claims by the south. The Dr. is a very firm and discreet man and would conduct the affairs of the state judiciously if elected Governor. Yet you know that I am opposed to rotation in office and long ago made this an objection to the running of Dr. Canon provided we could make some other judicious selection. Let me hear from you frequently."[13]

Eleven days later another of Meredith's friends, Thomas H. Harvey (who replaced Dr. Penn as Saline County representative in 1838 and then was elected to a state Senate seat in 1840), informed Meredith that there was "but little doubt but the democratic members [of the Senate] will recommend a convention to be held this fall for nomination of a Governor, etc."[14] While neither writer was so bold as to suggest to Meredith at this time that he come out as a candidate for state office, that undoubtedly was what they were working toward. The sooner he got his name before Democratic Party members at the county level, the better his chance of being nominated at the Democrats' convention later that year to campaign for the office of lieutenant governor.

A Timely Appointment

A fortunate, though unexpected, opportunity to enhance his recognition among Missourians came Meredith's way in early February 1839. That month, the state's General Assembly approved establishment of the University of Missouri at Columbia, and Meredith was asked to become one of the school's curators. The need for the institution had been tossed about by members of the legislature for some time; action stalled, however, because — although most preferred a site somewhere in central Missouri — no consensus could be reached among Central Clique politicians about the campus's specific location. The driving force behind the effort to create the first state university west of the Mississippi River was James S. Rollins, a freshman Missouri legislator in 1839. Rollins had studied law with Howard County attorney Abiel Leonard, completing his legal education at Transylvania University in Lexington, Kentucky. In coming years, he would rise in Missouri's political realm to become a state representative, senator, state Supreme Court judge, and U.S. Congressman in 1860. His great political ambition, never realized although he tried three times, was to be elected governor of Missouri.

To settle the contentious issue of where to locate the university, Rollins secured passage of a bill designating Boone, Callaway, Cole, Cooper, Howard, and Saline

Counties as potential sites. Bids were sought with a promise to award the school to the county that offered the most money and/or land. Three counties — Boone, Howard, and Cole — responded to the appeal, with Boone's bid of $117,000 winning over its rivals. The location issue resolved, Rollins next persuaded fellow legislator Henry S. Geyer of St. Louis to sponsor a bill to place control of the university in a 15-member board of curators to be appointed by the legislature, and fund the school with proceeds from the sale of public lands — a provision that failed to meet expectations and left the school underfunded for the next quarter century.

Soon thereafter, Meredith and General Thomas A. Smith, reputed to be the wealthiest man in Saline County, received appointments to the board of curators. (Notable men of Howard and Cooper Counties were also named to the board.) These appointments are evidence that James Rollins had trolled among the prominent men of the Booneslick country seeking financial help to bring the university to Boone County. Meredith's seat on the board of curators was most likely the result of a deal struck between Rollins and Dr. Sappington. When it became apparent that Saline County was not seriously pursuing acquisition of the university, Rollins looked to Dr. Sappington (among other Booneslick residents) for money, and the doctor, an advocate of public education who recognized the need for such a facility, extracted a *quid pro quo* for his generosity, the result being Meredith's seat on the influential board. (General Smith's financial support produced the same result.) Coming early in 1839, when he was being touted as a candidate for the lieutenant governor's office, notices of Meredith's appointment appearing in newspapers across the state gave him some welcome name recognition among Missouri's voters.

Aware of James Rollins's political acumen, Meredith maintained a connection with him in coming years. Although members of different parties (Rollins has been described by an acquaintance as "a Whig ... as long as there was any Whiggy left to stand by"), the two sometimes worked together to gain acceptance of their agendas.[15] And in 1857, a split among Missouri's Democrats enabled Meredith to publicly support Rollins in a special election to fill the office of governor, vacated when the sitting governor resigned to take a seat in the U.S. Senate. Unfortunately for Rollins, who ran on the American Party ticket, the Democratic Party's nominee won the race. At this stage in his life, and in the life of Missouri's fractious Democrats, Meredith figured that he had nothing to lose by endorsing Rollins, and it was an opportunity to return a favor granted nearly two decades earlier.

Avoiding Dissension

The decision to choose Meredith as their party's candidate for lieutenant governor was mostly a foregone conclusion when Missouri's Democrats met in convention at Jefferson City in October 1839, thanks to a grassroots effort at the county level by his supporters. Urged the previous spring to seek the nomination, Meredith let it be known that he was interested. An early decision gave his friends time to canvass fellow Democrats and secure support for him at county meetings where convention delegates were chosen and instructed how to vote. Dissension at the convention over candidates was something party leaders wanted to avoid, fearing a split among Democrats would give the opposition enough votes to swing the election, particularly for legislative seats, in their favor. As early as 1838, Dr. Sappington voiced concern about having more than one candidate for an office. Writing to Charles M. Cravens, representative to the state legislature from Pettis County, he warned "You are aware how vitally important it is that we should carry the next ... elections ... and you also know what violent efforts will be made by the opposition to defeat us. Their motto is divide and conker [conquer]. ..."[16]

Divisiveness within party ranks became a concern in Saline County a few years later. Following a contentious meeting of Democrats at Marshall, held to draw up a resolution calling for a convention to rewrite the state's constitution, George Penn worried that the county's Democrats "take a firm and decided stand" in opposition to the views of the Whig Party, which favored district conventions where they would have a greater voice in drafting the new document. Some attendees at the Marshall meeting were leaning toward regional rather than a state convention and Penn believed that "A division may take place among the Democrats of this county unless their [the Whig Party] designs are fully exposed."[17]

Support for Meredith's candidacy spread across the state in 1839. In Shelby County, a cousin, James Bragg Marmaduke, and Dr. John W. Long were named delegates to the upcoming convention and instructed to support Meredith in his bid for the nomination. James, a merchant, was prominent among the party's leaders in northeast Missouri and could be counted on to promote Meredith's candidacy in adjoining counties. At home, fully aware of his interest and influenced by George Penn, Dr. Sappington and others, Saline County's Democrats met in early August and named Meredith as a delegate to the convention, and their choice for lieutenant governor. With no serious opponent to Meredith's nomination arising, the convention delegates in Jefferson City unified around him as their man for the lieutenant governor's race, and selected Judge Thomas Reynolds, an experienced politician, to run for the governor's chair. Missouri's Democrats left the capital city in late October convinced that with this combination they would defeat whomever the Whigs put forth and maintain their majority in the state legislature.

The 1840 Whig convention, "the largest and most elaborately prepared ... of the contests in Missouri" took place during June at Rocheport, "in a stand of sugar trees" on a hill east of the town where for three days and nights large crowds were exhorted to action by James H. Birch, Abiel Leonard, James Rollins, and the artist, George Caleb Bingham.[18] Many of the attendees came from St. Louis on steamboats provided for that purpose by their Whig owners. When the hurrahs ended, John B. Clark was the party's candidate for the governor's office. A Howard County lawyer and colonel of militia during the Black Hawk War of 1832, Clark had recently commanded Missouri's militia during the state's conflict with Mormon settlers in the counties north and east of Kansas City. Tasked with forcing the unpopular religious group out of the state, his success in that effort gave him name recognition; otherwise, he was not known by the state's voters. His previous political experience consisted of 10 years' service as clerk of the Howard County court. Joseph Bogy, a lead mine owner from Ste. Genevieve County who had served in the Missouri Territorial legislature, and was later a state senator, was the Whig candidate for lieutenant governor. Bogy was Ste. Genevieve County treasurer at the time, a post he held until his death in 1842.

An Experienced Democrat

What Meredith Marmaduke lacked in the way of public office experience beyond the level of a county official, Thomas Reynolds possessed in abundance. Age 33 when he arrived in Missouri in 1829, Reynolds came from Illinois bearing a brilliant record as an attorney, clerk of the House of Representatives, attorney general, chief justice of the Supreme Court, and state representative and Speaker of the House, accomplishing this considerable service in the brief span of 10 years. Although popular among Illinois voters, he faced a name-recognition problem that was difficult to overcome. There was another young attorney in the state, John Reynolds (no relation), equally as respected and popular, whose political star was rapidly ascending, moving as quickly as was Thomas Reynolds's. John Reynolds served on the Illinois Supreme Court for six years, three of which were during Thomas Reynolds's tenure as chief justice; John also served in the Illinois House of Representatives for a term while Thomas was in that body. Was it possible for two "brightly burning tapers of the sky"[19] with the same last name to be illuminating Illinois's politics at the same time? Probably not, and therein lies the reason for Thomas Reynolds's removal to Missouri. Losing his bid for reelection to the Illinois legislature in 1828, he saw his political future in jeopardy. (With good reason: In the 1830s, John Reynolds was elected to a term as Illinois's governor and then served the state for two terms in the U.S. House of Representatives. To round out his political career, John next served two terms as a state representative.)

Having lost traction in Illinois, judging his prospects for political stardom were better elsewhere, Thomas Reynolds looked no farther than the Booneslick country to see his future. Packing his law books and household goods, he, his wife Eliza Ann, and their only child, a 4-year-old son, moved to Howard County in 1829, where he established a legal practice in Fayette and briefly edited the *Boonslick Democrat* newspaper. Politics were his love, and he soon found an outlet for his passion with the Democrats and the Central Clique. These affiliations led to his election in 1832 as Howard County's representative to the General Assembly, where he was quickly chosen to be Speaker of the House. Five years later, he became judge of Missouri's Second Judicial Circuit, a position he held until the spring of 1840 when he resigned to campaign for election as the state's governor.

Thomas Reynolds' practical knowledge about influencing voters and preventing chicanery by the opposition, gained from his years canvassing for public offices in Illinois, weighed heavily in the success of his and Meredith's campaign of 1840. Early that year, he directed his running mate's activities, giving Meredith advice and instructions:

"I have conversed with a great many of our friends, and they all concur in the opinion that you should visit the lower south between this and the election, and May and June would be a good time.

"The lower south is somewhat cooled by having no candidate near. Bagy [Bogy] lives in the south and will be in the southern counties, and local feeling will have an influence unless you mix with them and thereby show them respect. I cannot be mistaken in this view.

"I intend taking the lower south in my tour, but cannot say at what time I will be there.

"I trust you will arrange your business so as to make the trip in due time. Pass through Cole, Crawford, Washington, thence down through the Mississippi counties, passing last through Jefferson, Franklin & thence home.

"By all means see that the Democratic paper at Boonville supplies the adjoining counties with printed tickets in due time to be in every township on the morning of the election. Let the tickets be large enough to embrace the local candidates, but the name of the general candidates printed light in counties where the contest is between Feds & Democrats. See that Rives, Pettis, Benton & Van Buren [counties] are supplied. Get the aid of Shields of Boonville. I will attend to the north side. This must not be neglected. The tickets should be headed "The Democratic Ticket." This will cause a most happy effect by preventing imposition [fraud] and deviousness. Yours truely, Th. Reynolds."[20]

Missouri's political parties at this time printed "tickets" (slips of paper that identified their candidates) and placed them in the hands of faithful and persuasive members who handed them out at the polling houses (state law required one polling "house" in each township) on Election Day. When a voter entered the polling house, he either stated the candidates he supported or, it was hoped, he handed his ticket to an election judge who then recorded his votes in a book that had been issued by the county clerk. State law also required that the officer attending the election "cry, in an audible voice, the vote of each elector as given in," thus assuring that observers knew how each voter performed, as well as allowing party henchmen to count votes for their candidates.[21] Thomas Reynolds's concern about devious tactics, and his specific instructions about the printing that appeared on the Democratic Party tickets was borne out a month after the 1840 general election (held the first Monday in August) when the St. Louis *Argus* newspaper reported the use of a fraudulent ticket in some counties (Taney, Polk, Macon, Chariton, Livingston, Carroll, and Daviess are mentioned) during the recent election. Titled "The Union Democratic Ticket," the sham ticket listed John B. Clark (a Whig) for governor and Meredith for lieutenant governor, along with two Democratic candidates for Congress. The Union Democratic ticket was a ruse to mislead Democrats into voting for John Clark. The success of fraudulent tickets depended upon the illiteracy and/or the gullibility of the voter, the persuasiveness used by those distributing the tickets, and the inclination of voters to use the tickets inside the polling houses. The practice was so disruptive that Missouri's General Assembly passed an act in 1841 banning fraudulent tickets, imposing a stiff fine and jail time for violators.

Marmaduke's Manifesto

Not all campaign tactics used in 1840 were devised by Thomas Reynolds. Meredith realized that — not having previously held any high political office — he lacked recognition by voters in some areas of the state. To address this, he composed an article for publication knowing that an important statement by him would be reprinted by the partisan, Democrat-aligned newspapers, and perhaps as well by some whose loyalty lay with the Whig Party. The June 13, 1840, issue of the *Jeffersonian*

Republican (published at Jefferson City) printed a lengthy manifesto he addressed "To The People of Missouri," Meredith's "frank exposition of the political opinions which I hold," 2,400 words in length, filled three columns in the newspaper.[22] The document demonstrates a shrewd assessment of the interests and temperament of Missouri's voters, and showcases Meredith's ability as a communicator. Favoring commercial interests and the expansion of trade, he supported a program of internal improvements, particularly those that affected navigation on Missouri's rivers, if such improvements could be done without the state having to borrow money. He favored spending public money to place "within the reach of the most indigent and helpless youths ... a useful and beneficial education." Having presented his thoughts on these two issues, both driven by Missouri's increasing population and the resulting demand for better access to goods and services, Meredith quickly moved to the national issues that were gripping the state's populace.

Expressing his belief "that a large majority of the people of this State, will ... be governed more by the opinion held by aspirants to office in relation to the affairs of the general government, than those in relation to State policy," he believed he should express his opinions on those subjects "freely and candidly, notwithstanding" he was only seeking a state office, and consequently could have little influence on the affairs of the national government. Foremost among the national issues he saw affecting Missourians was the potential to secure patents for federal lands. He favored granting preemptions to actual settlers on the public lands and graduating the price of public lands, political ploys that his friend Thomas H. Benton had long used and that Meredith knew were popular with large and small landholders, farmers, and tradesmen. He spoke to the interests of merchants and business owners by stating his opposition to the national government "assuming in any way or manner whatever, the debts due by the States," believing that such a policy would place a burden upon the federal treasury that could only be relieved by heavy tariffs on goods produced or sold. And he was particularly firm in his opposition to the establishment of a national bank. He believed such a bank to be unconstitutional and attacked the recently closed national bank, accusing it of having manipulated the value of its paper currency over the past two decades to the detriment of the national economy "until finally the people of the United States willed its dissolution for its many sins and transgressions," a move by the Congress in March 1839.

Having come out in opposition to a national bank, Meredith next tackled two additional monetary issues that were of concern to Missourians — the establishment of "an Independent Treasury of the national government," which he believed should occur (a position supported by Whigs in the state), and the desirability of a having a state bank whose paper money was supported by gold and silver specie. This latter declaration placed him solidly in the "hard" money camp and gained the support of the Central Clique and its followers. At the same time, he knew that such a stand did not sit well with the "soft" element of the party (mainly in St. Louis), but correctly guessed that losing their votes in the fall would not be fatal to his campaign (he lost St Louis county by 700 votes). The remainder of his manifesto, more than half the document, he devoted to a detailed explanation of his reasons for advocating "hard" money and a national treasury.

The influence of the manifesto upon voters is difficult to determine, there being no mechanism either before or after the election for measuring their interest in his candidacy other than the results of the election, itself. Political speeches given from courthouse steps and under shade trees in county seat towns were the usual practice of candidates seeking office, the downside being that such addresses reached only a small segment of the citizenry. Additionally, the time and resources required to travel to attend such gatherings taxed any politician's strength. Having an office seeker's political credo in hand where it could be re-read and examined at will, especially a document as clear about his views as was Meredith's manifesto, generated a great conversation among both Democrats and Whigs in the weeks leading up to the general election in August.

An Inebriated Candidate

Not all was going well for the campaign in Missouri's northeastern counties. Thomas Reynolds had campaigned in Shelby County in May and shortly thereafter Meredith's cousin, James Marmaduke, urged him to "come and see us for several reasons. In the first place the opposition here is trying to move all the power of earth & heaven to defeat us. They resort to all kind of lies and trickery. ... Your attendance here with a speech will greatly help our Democratic candidates for the legislature. ... Another reason why we want you is this, though it is in confidence. Viz, yesterday, after Judge Reynolds arrived, having rode more than 25 or 30 miles without eating anything, he took with his new acquaintants three or four drinks of Brandy. His stomach being empty it totally disqualified him for a speech. It was an unfortunate circumstance. The Whigs make it out worse than it was. We have no doubt that your presence would repair the breach."[23] For several days James delayed mailing his letter so that he could listen to a speech by John Clark, the Whig candidate for governor, who was following Thomas Reynolds around the circuit of counties. "Gen. Clarke [sic] appeared here according to promise, he sung the old song of Extravagant expenditures of the government, & etc. We expect the Whig lawyers here at our circuit court. The Whig missionary Mr. U. Wright is also expected, and we want somebody to answer him."[24]

In late June, problems arose in the counties along the Missouri River above Saline County. A correspondent in Lexington wrote to advise Meredith that the Democrats of Lafayette County were split in their choice of candidates. Unless they could come together and settle the issue, the writer believed the party would be beaten in the county "not for the want of strength, but for the want of harmony in amongst our party."[25] Better news came that same week from Springfield when a correspondent there reported to Meredith that he could "expect the south western section of the state to be at their best, & do their duty on the first Monday of August next. The boys here, upon the governor & lieutenant governor election, are firm & united."[26]

That summer, while Meredith was addressing the big picture — the statewide campaign — the real work was taking place across Missouri at the township level. On the shoulders of ardent party members fell the burden of canvassing voters in an effort to find weaknesses and strengths. The canvass often required identifying individual voters and finding ways to turn them out on Election Day. Writing to Meredith five days before the August 3rd election, Thomas H. Harvey describes what he was doing to assure that Saline County voters would carry the banner favorably for Meredith and the Democrats. Harvey's description of his activities is a classic example of how the political process worked at the lowest level and shows the importance of personal contact with voters in their neighborhoods and homes.

Dear Col.,

I understand that Genl. Clark [is to be] at Old Jefferson [an early Saline County seat of government, on the river west of Glasgow] on Saturday, consequently I shall not be able to see you at the meeting on Saturday & probably not between this & the election. Will you not be at Old Jefferson? You will send up the tickets for the north side of the county ... those for Salt Pond (a south-county township) you will have to arrange for. Send them under seal.

I left here Monday morning early, & have returned ... late this evening, leave again in the morning before day for Salt Pond, return the following day, & the next for Old Jefferson.

On Saturday I was in the Grand Pass neighborhood when I met most of the people at their houses and at a shooting for beef. I find parties stand in the township, Whigs 26, it is possible 1 may not vote, Democrats 47 — one who may not vote. If he does it is doubtful how he will vote. The above is correct. We have as much right to claim Greenville as the Whigs.

I have boxed pretty well through Miami & Jefferson townships this week. I do not see how we can get less than liberal majority. I suppose tomorrow I shall learn something more about Salt Pond.

I will not be sanguine but if you can keep parties straight in Arrow Rock we have nothing to fear. You must see Kirby T. at the election, also Mr. Connor, & Harrold from the county seat. O. B. Pearson had better take Bill Fizer in tow on Sunday evening. There is a man by the name of Beazely who left Miami township lately in consequence of a difficulty with Dr. Smith. I understand he is about Jonesboro, probably at Dr. Penn's place. He is a good Democrat. He had better be attended to. I think it probable I shall be at High Hill on Monday, but keep this to your self. ... I send you a list of names who I think may probably attempt to vote, & I doubt not but there are many others that will try it. Would it not be best for the Democrats at Jonesboro to make a few questions of right to vote on the part of Democrats as possible. Yours. Thomas H. Harvey.[27]

We Are Gone, Hook and Line

Missouri law in 1840 required each county clerk to reveal the results of the general election within eight days after the close of the polling houses, by announcing them at the courthouse door. (Although general Election Day was the first Monday in August, the polls could be kept open for three days.) The clerk then had two days to forward the results to the Secretary of State who had up to 60 days to complete the certification process, thus pushing the official verification of the election results into October. Although the vote tally was not complete on August 4, Reynolds and Meredith had won their contests, Reynolds with 7,413 votes more than were cast for John Clark and Meredith with 7,508 votes more than his opponent. (Nearly 59,000 Missourians voted in the election.) The final count showed Meredith losing to Bogy in Clay, Cooper,

Callaway, Lafayette, Monroe, Ralls, Shelby, and St. Charles Counties.

Not all went well for the Democratic Party, however. Three days after the election, Claiborne Fox Jackson agonized over the loss of seats in the state legislature, telling Meredith, "We have the miserable news of our defeat in Lafayette. ... I have heard nothing but defeat after defeat from all quarters. Unless the counties to hear from shall come up much better ... we are gone hook and line, so far at least as the Legislature is concerned. Our majority in the House Rep. the last session was twenty one. So far as heard from, we have lost two in Cooper, one in Saline, two in Lafayette, one in Shelby, and one in Audrain, and have gained one in Ray." Jackson attributed the losses to an active Whig campaign. "Look at the meetings they have had," he continued. "Look at the stump orators in every county and township throughout the state. Look at the flood of documents with which the state has been inundated by them. ... You cannot go into one single house in this [Howard] county without finding it literally crammed with "Stockholders," "Old Soldiers," "Log Cabin Heroes," and all such paper," (printed materials distributed by the Whig Party).[28] The outcome of the election was not as bad as Jackson portrayed. Democrats retained a majority in the legislature sufficient to carry their position on most issues. Jackson's assessment of the reasons for the loss of legislative seats failed to identify the growing dissension among members of his own party. An increasing number of Missouri Democrats were unhappy over the unyielding power held by Senator Benton and the Central Clique, and their policy favoring hard currency. In fact, the senator's support in the state was beginning to slip after nearly 20 years in office. These and other issues that would arise during Meredith's term as lieutenant governor would become problematic for him, forcing him to reconsider his thoughts about seeking higher political office.

Notes

1. "the secret poison stealing its way to our vitals": Shoemaker, *Missouri and Missourians*, Vol. 1, 427.

2. "then applied abusive and ungentlemanly language to Lucas, and Lucas then challenged him": William R. Jackson, *Missouri Democracy: A History of the Party and its Representative Members, Past and Present*, Vol. 1, 98.

3. "referring to himself as usual in the third person, he told of 'the pang which went through his heart' when he saw young Lucas fall": Ibid., 91.

4. "After the barbecue was over and the drinking was in order": "The Birch-Jackson Encounter of 1838. Extracts from a letter written by James H. Birch in *The Kansas City Star*, reprinted in the *Smithville Star* September 20, 1906." MHR Vol 28, No. 3 (April 1934), 250.

5. Historian William H. Goetzmann uses the term "pompous" to describe Marmaduke's appearance in the painting. He attributes the identification of the figures in the paintings to Dr. Oscar F. Potter, a resident of Arrow Rock at the time the paintings were made. William H. Goetzmann and William N. Goetzmann, *The West of the Imagination*, 77.

6. "conspicuously on the platform is the orotund personage of M. M. Marmaduke": Lew Larkin, *Bingham, Fighting Artist*, 102–105. Larkin relates that Bingham also placed himself in this painting as a "shrewd, clear-headed opponent who is busy taking notes and who will, when his turn comes, make sophisms fly like cobwebs before the housekeeper's broom." Ibid. It is unclear whether, in using the word "orotund" to describe Marmaduke, Larkin intends it to be understood as "pompous," or was referring to his physical appearance.

7. "a candidate that will ransack every hole and corner of the district": John Sappington to Cravens, March

To Make a Fortune in Missouri

7, 1838. Folder 28, John Sappington Papers C1027, SHSMO.

8. "aware of your influence in Saline County": John R. Grisham to Marmaduke, April 4, 1828. Folder 4, Marmaduke Papers C1021, SHSMO.

9. "which if not taken out before the 1st day of October next": *Missouri Intelligencer*, July 10, 1829. Reel 10950, Newspaper Archives, SHSMO.

10. "A press so prostituted" that it is "dangerous to the liberties of the people": Duff Green to Marmaduke, April 31, 1830. Box 1, Folder 6, Sappington-Marmaduke Papers, MHS.

11. "no prophet but think it requires but little discrimination": Jackson to Marmaduke, September 22, 1837. Box 2, Folder 3, Sappington-Marmaduke Papers, MHS.

12. "will take it as a particular favor if you will use your influence": Isaac Parsons to Marmaduke, January 27, 1838. Ibid.

13. "*Nothing is yet done with regard to the selection of candidates*": Penn to Marmaduke, January 20, 1839. Box 2, Folder 4, Sappington-Marmaduke Papers, MHS. "Judge" Erickson is James Earickson of Howard County. Appointed state treasurer in January 1833, he held that office until his death May 26, 1839. Davis, and Durrie, 623. Earickson family members began settling in Chariton and Howard Counties in 1819, and were cofounders of Glasgow in 1836.

14. "but little doubt but the democratic members": Harvey to Marmaduke, January 31, 1839. Box 2, Folder 4, Sappington-Marmaduke Papers, MHS.

15. "a Whig … as long as there was any Whiggey left to stand by": Daniel Grissom, "Personal Recollections of Distinguished Missourians: James S. Rollins," *MHR*, Vol. 18, No. 4 (July 1924), 546. Meredith's announcement of support for Rollins appeared in the Jefferson City *Inquirer*, July 25, 1857. The American Party, also called the "Know-Nothing" Party, existed briefly in national politics following a breakup of the Whigs in the 1850s. It was supplanted by the rise of the Republican Party.

16. "You are aware how vitally important it is that we should carry the next … elections": John Sappington to Cravens, March 7, 1838. Folder 28, John Sappington Papers, C1027, SHSMO.

17. "A division may take place among the Democrats of this county": Penn to Marmaduke, September 27, 1843. Box 3, Folder 3, Sappington-Marmaduke Papers, MHS. Some (Democrat) speakers at the Marshall meeting opposed a state convention, urging instead adoption of a resolution calling for district meetings. Penn reported having a "long debate between Major [Thomas] Harvey and myself" over this issue.

18. "the largest and most elaborately prepared … of the contests in Missouri": William F. Switzler, et al., *Illustrated History of Missouri, from 1541 to 1877*, 256.

19. "brightly burning tapers of the sky": With apology to William Shakespeare, *Titus Andronicus*, iv, ii.

20. "I have conversed with a great many of our friends": Reynolds to Marmaduke, March 9, 1840. Box 2, Folder 5, Sappington-Marmaduke Papers, MHS.

21. "cry, in an audible voice, the vote of each elector as given in": *Revised Statutes of the State of Missouri*, 2nd ed., vol. 1, 1840, 237–241.

22. "To The People of Missouri." Meredith's "frank exposition of the political opinions which I hold": Jefferson City *Jeffersonian Republican*, June 13, 1840. All subsequent quotations regarding this document are from the same source. Discussion about political affairs often appeared in newspapers, frequently written by their editors; however, Marmaduke's letter is unusual in that it was dedicated entirely to his political beliefs and opinions and did not attempt to promote his personality as a candidate or his personal accomplishments. His appeal to the state's voters offered them an unequivocal statement of how he intended to act if he was elected lieutenant governor.

23. "come and see us for several reasons.": James B. Marmaduke to M. M. Marmaduke, May 9, 1840. Box 2, Folder 5, Sappington-Marmaduke Papers, MHS.

24. "Gen. Clarke [sic] appeared here according to promise": James B. Marmaduke to M. M. Marmaduke, May 9, 1840. Ibid. The "Whig missionary, U. Wright" is Uriel Wright, a doctor practicing in Fayette, Howard County. A member of the 1861 Missouri State Convention to determine whether the state

supported the Union or the Confederacy, Wright voted against secession, helping ensure Missouri's allegiance to the Union.

25. "not for the want of strength, but for the want of harmony in amongst our party": John Harrison to Marmaduke, June 23, 1840. Box 2, Folder 5, Sappington-Marmaduke Papers. MHS. Harrison was a wealthy merchant at Glasgow.

26. "expect the south western section of the state to be at their best": Joel Hardin to Marmaduke, June 20, 1840. Ibid.

27. "I understand that Genl. Clark [is to be] at Old Jefferson on Saturday": Harvey to Marmaduke, July 29, 1840. Folder 12, Marmaduke Papers C1021, SHSMO.

28. "We have the miserable news of our defeat in Lafayette": Jackson to Marmaduke, August 7, 1840. Box 2, Folder 6, Sappington-Marmaduke Papers, MHS.

CHAPTER 12

THE BONE TURNS BITTER

In his inaugural address to Missouri's 11th General Assembly on November 22, 1840, Meredith sought to reassure the legislators that as the newly elected lieutenant governor he was prepared to be chairman of the state Senate — his most important responsibility. Speaking in the Senate chamber of the new state Capitol building (replacing a building destroyed by fire two years earlier), he acknowledged his inexperience as a lawmaker, telling his colleagues this was the first time he had "ever been even a member of a legislative body."[1] This admitted, he assured his audience that he knew his duties, and he promised to provide "rigid enforcement of the rules of the house" and promote harmony in its deliberations. Within a month, he proved himself up to the challenge, resolving a contentious issue by casting a deciding vote in favor of a law making it possible for litigants to sue Missouri corporation owners. A St. Louis newspaper, the *Argus*, commended him for his vote, saying "The firmness of Col. Marmaduke … evidenced by his casting vote introducing this new, but important principle into our corporation system, does him infinite honor."[2] Fair and resolute action won Meredith the confidence of his fellow legislators, his rule over the Senate, in general, successful though not always free of discord.

Three events occurred during his term in office that can be said to have significantly affected his political career. The first of these surfaced soon after his election victory when he traveled to Jefferson City to prepare for the upcoming legislative session. The regular session of the Missouri General Assembly convened biennially, usually for four months at a time, beginning in November and ending in February. When it was in session, Meredith was unable to leave the capital city in order to visit his family. His months of absence during the fall and winter of 1840–41 took its toll on Lavinia. Depression enveloped her at home in Saline County, where she felt sidelined and unable to participate in his life. To alleviate her melancholic feelings, she vowed to write him weekly and expected him to do the same. But letters were not enough to dispel her gloom. Those she wrote in January 1841, after he had been gone for several months, shed light on her emotional state at the time. Although she tells Meredith about the activities of friends and family, her letters express a profound sense of loneliness and her frustration over her husband's failure to come home, even for a day or two. She wanted his presence and advice when the children were ill, and when deciding about such things as their schooling and the selection of their clothing. She envied his access to social activities in the capital city while she was unable to escape the demands of children and domestic duties for even a little while. Hoped-for trips to Jefferson City to be with Meredith for a few days fell through, the victim of adverse weather, ill health, or her inability to have companionship for the two-day journey on a stagecoach or steamboat (it was thought improper for a lady to travel alone). At night in his lodging at Jefferson City, reading Lavinia's letters must had caused Meredith considerable uneasiness; the strain his political ambition was putting on his family a continual worry. In response to Lavinia's gloominess, he reassured her of his love and promised to return home as soon as possible. Despite his assurances, Lavinia's frank depiction of her home as "Mt. Remote" as she opens one of her January letters speaks volumes about her state of mind.

Mt. Remote, Jan. 7th, 1841. My Dear Husband, Your letter found me where I have been almost all the winter (in cellar) and the only cheering reflection I had was that it would be only little more than a week before you would get home. Then receiving your letter saying it was uncertain when the Legislature would adjourn was another damper to my spirits. Surely you will not stay until March. If I was sure of it, I believe that I would take little Darwin and Vincent and go down on the stage and remain until you get ready to come home. You cannot imagine how lonesome I am. The children is not much company for they are a great care and trouble having it all to myself. The time passes heavily and slowly and not so with you. You are surrounded with company and new seenes [sic] every day. My circuit is to the meat house and back again. ... Meredith was very sick one day and 2 nights. He vomited a great deal one night. ... I shall write a letter next week. I hope then to know certainty when you will get home. ... Adieu my Dear Husband until next week. Lavinia Marmaduke.

January 12, 1841. My Dear Husband, I received your affectionate letter yesterday informing me that you expected to get home by the middle of February and that will be one long month from this day. Mr. [John Locke] Hardeman was here a few days ago. He said he thought from what he could see when he was down there it would be the first of March before the legislature would adjourn. If that be the case, you must come home. ... Could you not get off without censure? You do not know how badly I want to see you.

If you were far away where I knew I could not see you, I would not think so much about it. When you left home, I was sure that you would get home Christmas. When I thought there was no probability of you coming home, then I determined to go down to see you alone. Myself and all of the children have had the worst of colds, but in all getting better. ...

Why do you not send up the *Jefferson Enquirer*? I would rather read that paper now than any other, to see something about your movements in the Legislature. Mr. Hardeman told me there was a great deal of quarreling and no good feeling there particularly in the lower house. It has given me a great deal of uneasiness to know you would not dispute, and I do my Dear Husband keep out of difficulties for my sake. Think too of our dear little children. ...

... Write to me and let me know what time you wish our little girls to leave for school. I shall have a great deal of sewing to do for them. I hope to get Aunt Mary Sappington to assist me. Please let me know who you expect to board them with. You must write at least once a week and I will do the same. I know you will not read this long say nothing letter but once, but you know I always fill my letter with something if I have time. Yours truly and affectionately, Lavinia Marmaduke.

January 25, 1841. My Dear Husband, In my last letter I promised to write you every week. It is a pleasure to me to write to you but a greater pleasure to receive a letter from you. I read your letters over and over again. If we cannot see each other we can converse by letters. I know you do not let any one see my letters, so that I can say what I please. I was very sorry to hear that you were so unwell. I hope by this time that you are entirely well. I expect that it was some cold that you have taken.

Did you ever feel such a night as last Saturday night was a week ago? I thought when I got in bed I would freeze and did not get warm till mid-night. I had fire kept in the room all night and had a pitcher with about a pint of water in it on the mantlepiece. In the morning it was shivered to pieces. … I have no doubt but that night will long be remembered. …

Mr. [Claiborne] Jackson told me yesterday that it was usual for the Lieut. Governor to leave Jefferson before the Legislature adjourns and I hope My Dear Husband that you will avail yourself of that privilege and by doing so you might get home 2 weeks from this time. The nearer the time approaches for you to return the more impatient I am to see you, not withstanding I wish you to discharge your duties faithfully.[3]

Likely contributing to Lavinia's depression in early 1841 was the "morning sickness" that often afflicts a woman in the early stages of pregnancy. On August 1 that year, she gave birth to a son, Layton Price, who died in infancy and is buried in the Sappington Family Cemetery, located near the site of the Marmaduke home in Saline County.

When the General Assembly again met in November 1842 (this session lasting through the following February), Lavinia seemed more comfortable with Meredith being gone from home for weeks or months at a time. Domestic and family news fill the pages of her letters at this time, the depression she experienced two years earlier not apparent. Still, she hoped he would be able to come home at some time during the session. Two days before New Year's (he had spent another Christmas in Jefferson City while she and the children waited at home) she wrote to say "I know you are getting very anxious to hear from me. I have delayed writing to you until I could hear from Mr. Eddins." Lavinia's brother-in-law, Layton Eddins of Glasgow, and his wife, Susan, were supposed to escort her to Jefferson City where she would join Meredith, but the trip was called off when Susan became ill and could not be left alone. "Can't you possibly come home and see us if only for one day," Lavinia pleaded. "Do jump in the stage and come up. If I could go to see you as easily as you could come to see me, I would see you before next Thursday."[4]

Following the close of the 1842–43 legislative session, Meredith returned home to look after his family, his farm, and his business interests. A highlight of home life in 1843 was the arrival from Virginia of his 22-year-old namesake nephew, the son of Vincent Marmaduke, who styled himself M. M. Marmaduke Jr. (not to be confused with M. M. Marmaduke Jr., Meredith's son). After spending several months in Missouri, Meredith's nephew returned to the East Coast intending to relocate to Saline County later that year. But when he reached "ole West. [Westmoreland County] they was unwilling for me to leave them again, I determine to stay here as long as my father lives."5

A Refuge in Death

The bone-chilling cold and gray days that descend on Missouri in February spread their gloominess over a land and people longing for sunshine and warmth. Perhaps it was just such a dreary atmosphere that triggered Governor Thomas Reynolds's act of suicide the morning of February 9, 1844, about 39 months into his term. At 9 o'clock, in his office in the south wing of the governor's residence, Reynolds placed the muzzle of a rifle to his forehead and pulled the trigger. Passers-by on the street heard the gunshot and entered the building to find the governor "weltering in blood with the top of his head blown entirely off." In a letter found on a nearby table, addressed to his "most intimate friend, Col. William G. Minor," Reynolds blamed "the slanders and abuse of my enemies, which has rendered my life a burden to me," for his action.6

Colonel Minor, described as having "the warmest personal and political attachment" with Reynolds, later acknowledged the political difficulties his friend had encountered, saying that as governor he was "rancorously and mercilessly assailed" by Whig opponents. But Minor offered a different explanation for the governor's suicide: "In the winter of 1842–43 his health became very much impaired, so much so, indeed, that for a great portion of the session he was confined to his bed, and almost the entire session to his room. His health improved during the succeeding summer, but his disease returned about the beginning of the last winter, and continued to grow worse until within a few weeks before his death, when his health and appearance manifestly improved. His friends began to entertain the hope of his speedy recovery, but this hope was bitterly disappointed."7 Medical knowledge of the time would not have identified the cause of Reynolds' distress; however, the few symptoms described by Colonel Minor indicate the likelihood of a chronic illness, perhaps cancer or serious heart disease.

Rumors and stories about Governor Reynolds' suicide were plentiful in the weeks after the event. Meredith's friend, Dr. George Pitts, wrote that he believed "from what I have seen from the papers of the time [the suicide] was brought about by an accumulation of probably, both private and political afflictions."8 Joel Hardin, an ardent Democrat living in Springfield, Missouri, where he was the registrar in the public land office, attributed the suicide to "the slanderous tongues, and sins, of the foul mouthed Federal Party, now aspiring by all possible means to bring themselves into power."9 At home in Fayette, Governor Reynolds's wife, Eliza Ann, wasn't spared the indignity of condemnation by her neighbors. Layton Eddins related that "Public sentiment is much against Mrs. Reynolds, believing that she was one of the prominent causes of his death."10

The day Thomas Reynolds died Meredith became Missouri's eighth governor, aware that his term would expire in 11 months. Addressing the legislature, he reminded the lawmakers there were border disputes with Iowa and Arkansas that needed to be resolved and that a constitutional convention had to be called to rewrite that document, a move authorized by voters the previous year. He recommended improvements to the Osage and North Grand Rivers, advocated draining the rich swamplands of southeast Missouri (a program that required their release by the federal government), and called for enumerating the state militia in order to receive a full complement of muskets from the federal armory. His agenda also included building a special hospital for the mentally ill and using money from the sale of public lands to fund the state's seminary and public school accounts. His address to the legislature done, Meredith went home for a week before returning to the capital city. Lavinia and the children planned to join him there in April for a brief visit, traveling on the steamboat *Wapello* (a packet of the Missouri River trade), accompanied by Layton Eddins.

Issues at home kept Meredith on the road between Jefferson City and Saline County more than he intended in late summer of 1844. In August, Lavinia suffered an unknown illness that sent her to her bed, and Meredith returned to see to her care. Less than a week after his return to Jefferson City by stage coach in early September, their daughter, Jane, tasked by her father with reporting on the family's welfare, wrote to say that her mother was "improving slowly. … We have been very lonesome since you left us, and I have accused Ma of having the blues, but she will not admit it. I think, however, at your return it will disappear, 'be what it may.' "[11] Meredith returned home at least once more that fall; however, Thanksgiving found him in the capital city, Lavinia writing to say that she expected him home for Christmas.

A Candidate at the Wrong Time

In January 1844, the Democrats of St. Louis County were seeking to identify a candidate they could support for the office of governor in the August general election. To find a suitable nominee, they formed a committee and sent letters to six persons thought to be interested in the office, seeking answers to five questions. Two recipients of the questionnaire, Ratliff Boon of Louisiana, Missouri, and John P. Campbell of Springfield, replied to say they were not interested. Ratliff declared he was "insensible of having authorised [sic] the use of my name as an *aspirant* to any office." Campbell was in Texas and not expected to return to Missouri until the summer. The remaining four potential candidates, James Earickson of Glasgow, Austin King from Richmond, P. Williams of Paris, and Meredith, all promptly responded, indicating they were interested. The committee's questions concerned: redistricting the state to equalize representation in the legislature; bringing Missouri into compliance with recent changes to federal law that mandated one Congressional representative per district; the candidate's acceptance of the "principles [and] doctrine" of the national Democratic Party that had been adopted at its convention four years earlier; and the election of judges by popular vote rather than appointment by the governor for life, the existing procedure. A final question dealt with the thorny issue of money and banking. Did the candidate favor the "currency bills," considered but not adopted during the most recent legislative session? If they had passed, those acts would have penalized any person, corporation, or bank found guilty of accepting or circulating currency not supported by gold or silver.

Meredith responded at once, saying he favored amending the constitution to equalize representation by population and favored redistricting the state with one representative to Congress per district, but saw a problem with an existing federal act that he believed was inconsistent with the mandated change. He also said he supported the national Democratic Party's 1840 platform. His response to the "currency bills" question revealed a slight change from thoughts expressed in his manifesto three years earlier, showing his evolution as a politician who recognized the need to be less than absolute when answering a tough question. Now he placed himself on both sides of the issue, three years' experience dealing with the reality of political compromise helping him to see the necessity of appeasing the "soft" element in St. Louis while holding the support of the "hards." Wrapping his reply in populist rhetoric, he said that he had originally thought the provisions contained in the "currency bills" were unnecessary when similar legislation had been proposed a few years earlier, but that he now believed that had one of the earlier bills become a law "it would have saved the people of this state one or two millions of dollars, which they instead lost in worthless depreciated paper."[12]

A month after he responded to the first interrogatory from the St. Louis Democrats, Meredith received a second letter from the committee, this time wanting his response to a single question:

> Sir, Your name has been mentioned among our political friends as a candidate for the office of governor of this State; we have also, through the public press been favored with an exposition of your opinions on State and National policy. But there yet remains a material point on which the undersigned, as delegates from this county to the State Democratic Convention, to be held at Jefferson City, next month, are desirous of hearing from you. Are you willing to submit your pretensions to the office of governor to the decision of that convention, to abide thereby, and to support its nominees?
>
> We therefore respectfully solicit, at your earliest convenience, an answer to this question. We should wish it addressed to us at this place and a duplicate sent to the Editor of the *Inquirer* at Jefferson City. We remain, your most ob. servts, Samson Watson, William L. Sublette, Nicholas Tiernan.[13]

It was a loaded question, designed to place Meredith in an uncomfortable position in the event St. Louis' dissident Democrats were able to place a gubernatorial candidate of their persuasion on the party ticket. By agreeing to support the convention's nominee, no matter whom, Meredith might find himself supporting a soft-money candidate. On the other hand, he could not refuse to support the party's nominee. Faced with this dilemma, and believing that he was the convention's choice, Meredith replied that he had no problem accepting the decisions of the convention with regard to its nominees.

A Fading Star

Whether he realized it or not, as the obligatory welcoming speech opened Missouri's Democratic Party convention the first day of April 1844, Meredith's political career was dying. It had begun to unravel four years previously with the publication of his manifesto in which he aligned himself with the "hard" monetary policies of Thomas Benton and the Central Clique. Meredith's support for hard money helped him win the election in 1840, but it also lost him the support of the "soft" element of the Democratic Party in St. Louis, which wanted an increase in circulation and banking facilities. Now, four years later, those party members, even more unhappy with the Bank of the State of Missouri (chartered in 1837, headquartered in St. Louis, it became the only legal bank in the state) hoped to capture the agenda at the 1844 convention and nominate their own slate of candidates. The Whig party, meanwhile, was gaining influence across the state, claiming a bigger percentage of the votes cast in presidential elections each term after 1824. During the summer of 1839, Whig conventions took place in 34 Missouri counties prior to the party's state convention later that year. The following year, 43 percent of Missouri voters favored the Whig candidate for president. Whig candidates were also winning local elections, particularly in commercial areas such as St. Louis and counties along the Missouri and Mississippi Rivers. Marion, Ralls, Pike, Monroe, Audrain, Boone, Saline, and Lafayette Counties led the move toward the Whig party. The possibility of "soft" Democrats and Whigs in these counties combining votes in 1844 for a gubernatorial candidate of their persuasion was a worrisome problem for leaders of the Democratic Party, and Meredith's loss to his Whig opponent in St. Louis and a number of river counties in the 1840 lieutenant governor's race was another concern.

The soft-money Democrats' discontent with the practices of the state bank was born in the economic "panic" that struck the nation in the early days of 1837. Triggered by speculative lending practices in the west and south, along with falling land prices, a decline in the price farmers received for their cotton and other crops, and the failure of banks in New York and elsewhere, the financial crisis lasted until 1843. Missouri weathered the early years of the downturn, its economy stronger than many of its neighbor states due in part to the new state bank, which had exchanged most of the notes it held for hard money — gold and silver coins. As the "natural" trade center for the states bordering the upper Mississippi River, St. Louis's businessmen dealt in banknotes from Illinois and Iowa, as well as Wisconsin and Missouri, accepting them in exchange for goods and services. Many if not most of these notes were issued by banks that did not have specie to support their value, and therefore were subject to heavy discounting. (Arkansas notes, for example, were discounted as much as 50 percent in St. Louis in 1842.) They could not be exchanged at the state bank after 1837. In 1839, many St. Louis businesses withdrew money deposited in the state bank and placed it with other corporate entities, insurance companies in particular, who, acting as de facto banks, provided exchange services at par or at moderate discount rates. Historian Floyd C. Shoemaker relates that as a result, when the full effect of the national depression reached Missouri in 1842, St. Louis was particularly hard hit, its citizens "reaping the bitter fruit of the policy of making suspended paper the standard of value and receivable in all transactions at par."[14]

During 1842–43, specie became scarce in Missouri, and the state bank refused to expand its circulation or take any unusual risks. This policy, while good for the bank, had a further deleterious effect on the struggling St. Louis merchants and tradesmen who, as a consequence, had access to only small amounts of money to transact business.

In his analysis of the St. Louis situation during the years 1837 to 1843, Shoemaker says that the soft-money policy of the commercial interests resulted in "lax and even illegal banking methods."[15] Finally, in 1843 hard-money Democrats forced through a legislative bill to end such practices, prohibiting any business or financial institution from dealing in the currency of suspended banks. The strategy proved successful, and by 1844 the state's economy was recovering. In the struggle to control Missouri's financial structure, the advocates of hard money had won the round, but the fight was not over.

A Candidacy in Jeopardy

Feeling empowered going into the convention in April 1844, the soft-money Democrats of St. Louis and elsewhere across the state were prepared to challenge the "hards" for control of the proceedings with the hope they could nominate a gubernatorial candidate of their choosing. By means of parliamentary tactics, the Central Clique outmaneuvered the dissidents and retained their hold over the meeting, yet the leaders could not overcome a feeling that nominating Meredith as their candidate for governor would jeopardize their chances of retaining control of state government. Although he was the preferred candidate of Senator Benton and the Central Clique, most party members believed he would not attract enough of the dissident Democrats in the general election to assure his victory over a Whig opponent. On what was certainly a bitter day in his life, Meredith acceded to a request for his withdrawal from the contest in favor of John C. Edwards, a former Missouri secretary of state and U.S. congressman, whose "moderate and conciliatory views" would, the Central Clique hoped, find support among the dissident element of the party.[16] This did not happen. Dissatisfied with Edwards's nomination, the "softs" developed a ticket of their own under the banner of the Liberal Democratic Party and named a former Democrat-turned-Whig, Charles H. Allen, as their candidate for governor. Allen ran as a Whig, although that party did not present a ticket in Missouri that year. In the general election, Edwards handily defeated Allen, replacing Meredith as governor the following November.

When the 1844 Democratic convention ended, Meredith's career as a politician — so promising just four years earlier — had been swept aside and left awash on the muddy banks of political reality. His only serious attempt to reenter Missouri politics occurred in 1848 when he made an unsuccessful bid for the party's nomination for governor. His support prior to the state convention was viewed by George Penn as being weak. "The course so far taken by you and your friends is not likely to make you strong on the first ballot in the convention," Penn advised. "They have not been stimulated to that activity which would secure a large number of delegates committed to your support."[17] Lending credence to Penn's assessment are comments by many of Meredith's correspondents during these months, men who had been delegates at the last convention, wishing him success but saying they were not attending the convention this year.

In January 1848, Meredith won the endorsement of the St. Louis Democrats, but not by much. He learned about their support after "one of the hardest battles that ever came off ... last night. We succeeded in putting the faction down once more and instructed our delegates both to the State and District Convention to vote [for you]."

Meredith also learned that 10,000 circulars would be distributed around the state, announcing the decision to support his nomination.[18]

Claiborne Fox Jackson was also interested in becoming Missouri's governor in 1848. The relationship between Jackson and Meredith had been cordial over the years, but Jackson's political ambitions evidently trumped any deference he might have given to his brother-in-law. Jackson's friend, Sterling Price, said that Meredith was the first choice of St. Louis Democrats and Jackson their second choice. In Howard County (Jackson's home), the Democrats' annual meeting to appoint delegates to the convention saw delegates vote down a resolution complimenting Senator Benton and approve one supporting Jackson, who had earlier broken with the senator.[19] Another brother-in-law, Layton Eddins, told Meredith that "Mr. Jackson and his friends are dead against you," at the Howard County meeting.[20] When the 1848 Democratic Party convention ended, neither Jackson nor Meredith received the nomination, that going to Austin King who easily won the general election over his Whig opponent, James S. Rollins.

Meredith's ascension to the governor's office in 1844 may have come as the result of a tragedy, but the fact remains that he was at the shoulder of the state's highest executive as a result of his determination to succeed and his willingness to subject himself and his family to the demands of an active professional and public life. In coming years, friends would suggest that he consider running for Congress, or for the state legislature, but these, too, seemed always to be out of reach. In 1845, lacking a visible future as a politician, he wasted no time in returning to his initial objective in life — that of making a fortune for himself and his family.

Notes

1. "ever been even a member of a legislative body": St. Louis *Argus*, November 26, 1840. Reel 41226, Newspaper Archives, State Historical Society of Missouri.

2. "The firmness of Col. Marmaduke": St. Louis *Argus*, December 25, 1840. Ibid.

3. "Mt. Remote, Jan. 7th, 1841. My Dear Husband": Lavinia's letters to Marmaduke, January 7, 12, and 25, 1841, are found in Box 3, Folder 1, Sappington-Marmaduke Papers, MHS. Marmaduke's absences from home during his term of office included a several-months-long trip to the East Coast in the summer of 1842, visiting his family in Virginia. En route, he stopped at Pittsburgh where he was invited to "a public dinner" by "your Democratic friends" in the city in recognition of his "able adherence to Democratic principles." Forty-six Pittsburgh citizens, among them merchants with whom he had previously done business, signed a letter welcoming him to the city. Unfortunately, he was unable to attend the event as he had to leave that evening "for the Federal city." While in Pittsburgh, he purchased glass and a "carriage sofa" from his friend, the hardware goods merchant Anthony Beelen. Jno. Dunlap to Marmaduke, May 13, 1842. Box 3, Folder 2, Marmaduke and Sappington Papers, MHS. Anthony Beelen to Marmaduke, August 1, 1842. Ibid. *Jeffersonian Republican*, June 4, 1842. Reel 16359, Newspaper Archives, SHSMO.

4. "Can't you possibly come home and see us if only for one day": Lavinia to Marmaduke, December 29, 1842. Box 3, Folder 3, Sappington-Marmaduke Papers, MHS.

5. "ole West. they was unwilling for me to leave them again, I determine to stay here as long as my father lives." M. M. Marmaduke Jr. to Marmaduke, October 26, 1843. Ibid.

6. "weltering in blood with the top of his head blown entirely off": The description of the scene of Governor Reynolds's death is in William R. Jackson, *Missouri Democracy: A History of the Party and its Representative Members, Past and Present.* Vol. 1, fn. 38, 63.

7. "rancorously and mercilessly assailed": Governor Thomas Reynolds, *Jefferson Inquirer*, February 29,

To Make a Fortune in Missouri

1844. Reel 16349, Newspaper Archives, SHSMO. Colonel William Garrett Minor, born in Virginia, was a resident of Cole County, member of the Missouri General Assembly in 1842, the state's adjutant general in 1848, and secretary of the Missouri Senate when he died in 1851. A rather gory description of the suicide scene (one suspects the details were enhanced over the years) was published in the May 11, 1893, issue of the *Jefferson City Daily Tribune*, reprinting the story originally published in the *Boonville Advertiser*.

8. "from what I have seen from the papers of the time": Pitts to Marmaduke, March 25, 1844. Box 3, Folder 4, Sappington-Marmaduke Papers, MHS.

9. "the slanderous tongues, and sins, of the foul mouthed Federal Party": Hardin to Marmaduke, February 17, 1844. Ibid.

10. "Public sentiment is much against Mrs. Reynolds, believing that she was one of the prominent causes of his death": Eddins to W. B. Sappington, March 17, 1844. Folder 45, John Sappington Papers C1027, SHSMO.

11. "improving slowly. ... We have been very lonesome since you left us": Jane B. Marmaduke to Marmaduke, September 10, 1844. Box 3, Folder 5, Sappington-Marmaduke Papers, MHS.

12. "it would have saved the people of this state one or two millions of dollars": The text of the letters sent by the St. Louis Democratic committee to the six potential candidates for lieutenant governor and their replies were published in the *Jeffersonian Republican*, March 7, 1844. Reel 16349, Newspaper Archives, State Historical Society of Missouri.

13. "Sir, Your name has been mentioned among our political friends": Letter, Watson, Sublette, and Tiernan to Marmaduke, March 1, 1844. Box 3, Folder 4, Sappington-Marmaduke Papers, MHS.

14. "reaping the bitter fruit of the policy of making suspended paper the standard of value": Shoemaker, *Missouri and Missourians*, Vol. 1, 483; (*Jefferson Inquirer*, September 1, 1842).

15. "lax and even illegal banking methods": Shoemaker, *Missouri and Missourians*, Vol. 1, 480.

16. "moderate and conciliatory views": Christensen, et al., *Dictionary of Missouri Biography*, 275. Edwards's "views" may have been no more than wishful thinking on the part of the hard-money delegates. His political career relied upon Thomas Benton and the Central Clique for support, and he favored their banking policies. As a member of the Missouri legislature, a district judge in Cole County, and a justice on the Missouri Supreme Court for two years, he may have occasionally won the admiration of those opposing the "rule of the fathers," as the Central Clique was often characterized. In the 1844 election, Edwards received 5,621 more votes than Allen, out of 68,335 votes cast. Serving one term as governor, he afterward moved to California where he was elected mayor of Stockton in 1851.

17. "The course so far taken by you and your friends is not likely to make you strong": George Penn to Marmaduke, October 19, 1847. Box 4, Folder 2, Sappington-Marmaduke Papers, MHS.

18. "One of the hardest battles that ever came off ... was last night": Thomas Gray to Marmaduke, January 9 and 11, 1848. Box 4, Folder 4, Sappington-Marmaduke Papers, MHS.

19. Jackson's friend, Sterling Price, thought that Meredith was the first choice: John J. Lowry to Marmaduke, December 25, 1847. Folder 17, Marmaduke Papers C1021, SHSMO. Lowry had "just received" a letter from Price with information about the political posture of St. Louis's Democrats. Lowry also reported Benton's downfall among Howard County Democrats.

20. "Mr. Jackson and his friends are dead against you": L. S. Eddins to Marmaduke, May 28, 1848. Box 4, Folder 5, Sappington-Marmaduke Papers, MHS.

CHAPTER 13

IF LIFE AND HEALTH LAST

Sylvester Hall was a dedicated man. His willingness to continue peddling Dr. Sappington's Anti-Fever Pills after what he endured while traversing the White River Valley in southeast Arkansas is worthy of commendation. Many men finding themselves faced with Hall's misfortune would have given up and gone home. His problems began soon after he left the more-settled delta lands lying between the White River and the Mississippi River. He was headed southwest, intending to go to the remote village of Arkansas Post, situated near the confluence of the White and Arkansas Rivers. Even today the wilderness through which he traveled is nearly impassable, much of it heavily timbered wetlands that are contained in the Dale Bumpers White River National Wildlife Refuge. Writing to Meredith Marmaduke on a spring day in 1839, Hall penned a vivid description of what had happened to him while riding through the pestilence-ridden swampland along the White River.

> April 17th 1839, Arkansas Monroe County
> Col. M. M. Marmaduke
> Dear Sir,
>
> It is my misfortune this day to be afoot in consequence of the Buffalo gnats. I left Mr. Stevenson [his supervisor] nine days ago at Batesville. I started from there to go into Phillips [county] Arkansas and [unreadable] with medicine. After I had finished depositing [medicine] in Phillips I started for Arkansas [Post] and in going across a low swampy country for some six or eight miles in Monroe County the gnats killed the horse in spight [sic] of all I and others could do for him. After I got to a house we worked with him from two o'clock until nine at night and die he did and left me afoot 85 miles from Little Rock with only twenty dollars, so I have the pleasure of walking to Little Rock, if it be anywhere we can buy another. The cause of me having no more money is this. Where I have been there has never been any medicine deposited until this year. It is the big bay horse that Mr. Stevenson started with that is dead. I have walked thirty miles to day and carried the saddlebags, the saddle and blanket. I was obliged to leave when the horse died. I tried to buy one and get them to [wait for payment] until I could go to the Post of Arkansas which lay about fifty miles on but they asked me from one hundred to one hundred and thirty dollars for poneys [sic]. I did not suppose it was your wish for me to buy a poney at them prices. I had only one hundred &

eleven boxes of medicine when the horse died and that I left with Col. A. J. Evans of this county. We have been detained by high water, bad collections, money scarce. I have not for myself collected more than $800. I suppose I have taken notes to the amount of $15 or 16 hundred dollars and sold some three or four hundred boxes at a dollar per box and about 60 boxes for cash. So my misfortunes are not don [sic] with yet. I remain yours etc., Sylvester Hall.[1]

Sylvester Hall's experience, although unique in its circumstances, typifies the perils faced by traveling salesmen in rural Midwest America during the 1830s and '40s. Theirs was not a job for the fainthearted, and the agents sent into the field by the firm of Sappington and Sons to sell the company's medicine were no exception. Fortunately, they had a superior product to sell, quinine in a pill form — the only medicine of the time that could truly benefit the sufferers of malaria, then generally known as the "ague."

The Missouri Chills

Malaria is a scourge of mankind dating back thousands of years, a deadly disease, evidence of which has been found in ancient African, Egyptian, Roman, and Chinese civilizations. Its source, parasitic protozoans of the genus *Plasmodium* transmitted among humans by many species of female *Anopheles* mosquitoes, was not identified until 1898. From Roman times the illness was believed to be caused by "bad air" (thus the term *mal aria* from medieval Italian) emanating from swamps and marshlands. Unrecorded among the writings of Aztec and Mayan civilizations, the disease is believed to have traveled to America in the blood of European explorers, and slaves from West Africa. Some historians believe that Christopher Columbus and his crew were infected when they arrived in 1493, on his second voyage.

English colonists also carried the parasites in their blood; Jamestown's settlers are recorded as suffering bouts of the ague in the mid-1600s. Ever mobile, the deadly sickness moved westward across the nation, following the Tennessee and Ohio Rivers to the Mississippi and beyond, progressing in step with settlers who unknowingly carried the genesis of the disease in their blood. In 1768, an officer at Fort Kaskaskia in southern Illinois recorded that during September of that year, "there was not one Commissioned officer, non Commissioned or Private man But one Sergt. 1 Corpl. and about nine men but was seized [with fever] … We have now sent to the Grave three Officers, twenty five men Twelve Women and fifteen Children."[2]

In 1807, an epidemic of malaria struck the Ohio River Valley, leaving hundreds in its wake complaining of "bilious, intermittent, and remittent fevers." St. Louis, at the confluence of the Missouri and Mississippi Rivers, was a locus for malarial fever. A doctor there in 1809 said the incidence of ague was so prevalent that he could identify residents of nearby Illinois by the paleness of their faces. By the time Meredith reached Missouri in 1823, malaria was so widespread that it affected nearly every section of the state and was commonly known as the "Missouri Chills." All up and down the Mississippi River Valley, from New Orleans to Wisconsin, there was "a whole lot of shakin' goin' on" — the ague at home among the population living in the river's basin and the lowlands of the interior.

Yarbs, Roots, and Minerals

The practice of medicine in the early 1800s was characterized by the application of therapy that often had little or no effect on the illness a patient was suffering. Malaria was no exception to this. Common medicines used by doctors and home folk to relieve symptoms and hopefully provide cures were of two basic types: botanic medicines — concoctions made from roots, herbs, and plants — and metallic medicines — compounds containing minerals such as mercury, antimony, sodium, and potassium. Such medicaments were widely used whether they were efficacious or not. Worse yet, many doctors resorted to bleeding and purging patients as a way to improve their health, in truth adding to their misery and often hastening their demise. Even worse was the possibility that the "doctor" who prescribed treatment was not a trained physician. Frontier society was raw enough that almost anyone who wanted to adopt the title "Doctor," no matter his previous occupation or experience, could hang out his shingle and begin treating patients. One such, Doctor T. J. Luster of Springfield, Illinois, practiced "yarb and root" medicine in the early 1800s, claiming he could cure "Sciatic, weak lungs, fits, inward weakness and nervous affections; liver complaints, fever and ague, pleurisy, asthma, coughs, colds, dyspepsia, rheumatism, cancers, rickets, fever sores, piles, worms and tape worms, and many other diseases that affect the human system."[3] Doctor Luster was one of many who found the practice of medicine an easy calling.

In the larger towns, some physicians operated a retail drug store with their practice, stocking it with patent medicines and selling remedies they concocted using bulk components purchased at Philadelphia and New York. Dr. Bernard G. Farrar, who began practicing medicine in St. Louis in 1809, had several drug stores during his lifetime, one in partnership with Joseph Charless, a prominent city journalist. In addition to a supply of nostrums and drugs, Farrar and Charless sold "a variety of spices, paints and stationary."[4] Fifteen years later, in rural Saline County, John Sappington's work as a doctor, a compounder of medicines, and an operator of mercantile stores, was in line with the customs of the time. He, however, also experimented with a little-understood, yellowish, bitter powder — quinine sulphate — that held promise as a remedy for the ague.

Quinine sulphate is a chemical compound derived from the bark of trees of the genus *Cinchona*, originally grown only in South America. Its efficacy in treating the fever, chills, and concurrent shaking caused by malaria was observed 400 years ago when Jesuit priests watched Peruvian Indians with those symptoms ingest powdered bark from cinchona trees to relieve their illness. Brought to Europe in 1632, cinchona bark began selling in North America by the 1700s. Finely ground and mixed with liquid, the pulverized bark brought relief to those who were able to obtain it. In 1820, French scientists succeeded in extracting quinine sulphate from cinchona bark. The resulting powder became more widely distributed and was the focus of Dr. Sappington's experiments in the 1820s to find the proper dosage and frequency of use, and to develop a form of the medicine that delivered a measured amount each time it was ingested. He succeeded with a pill containing quinine whose bitter taste was disguised in a mixture of licorice, myrrh (a fragrant gum resin), and oil of sassafras. He now had an inexpensive and easily distributed form of a miracle medicine that would bring relief to thousands of sufferers. It needed to be exploited, both for the benefit of mankind — and for the wealth it would generate for the doctor and his family.

The Firm

Meredith Marmaduke entered the pill business in 1835 when Dr. Sappington formed a company known as Sappington and Sons to sell the new quinine medicine. "The Firm," as the company was known to its principal members, numbered the doctor and his sons William and Darwin, and the doctor's four sons-in-law, Meredith, Claiborne Jackson, Layton Eddins, and Dr. William Price. Dr. Sappington designated the states that encompassed the major watersheds of the upper and lower Midwest — the Ohio River Valley, the Mississippi River Valley, and the Arkansas-White River-Red River Valleys — as the primary area for the sale of his medicine.[5] Divvying up the business, he assigned a sales region to each of the firm's members. Field agents were hired to visit communities where the incidence of fever and the population were both great enough to warrant placing the medicine with retail outlets, perhaps a store owner or a druggist, often just someone who was considered reliable. Cash, as payment for the medicine, was obtained where possible; however, thousands of boxes of pills were left on consignment — secured by certificates (personal notes). Where the medicine was consigned, agents later returned to collect the money (or the unsold pills).

In the assignment of territories it appears that Meredith initially drew Arkansas, Louisiana, and the Mexican territory of Texas as his primary sales region, adding Mississippi at a later time. At times, Claiborne Jackson and Dr. Price managed Arkansas and Texas, although Jackson's interest in the pill business was mostly devoted to serving as the company's banker, exchanging currency and looking for investments that would return a profit. Dr. Price also bought the raw quinine and oversaw manufacturing, packaging, and distribution of medicine to the company's field agents. States east of the Mississippi River — Kentucky, Tennessee, Alabama, Georgia, Wisconsin, Illinois, Indiana, Ohio, and Michigan — were assigned to Darwin and William Sappington, and their brother-in-law, Layton Eddins.[6] Dr. Sappington retained Missouri where he could easily handle sales and distribution by mail. Other, more distant, Sappington family members were sometimes given sales routes. A nephew, James Burke, took 18,000 boxes of pills to Virginia and the Carolinas in 1835; another nephew at one time had a route in several Tennessee counties. Dr. Sappington also employed William J. Eddins, brother of Layton, as a field agent. Events in the lives of the principal members of the company occasionally caused territories to change hands for short periods. During his years as lieutenant governor and governor, Meredith's territory was managed by others. Dr. Sappington's sons handled sales in Mississippi, while Dr. Price and Claiborne Jackson added Louisiana to their territory, which at the time included Arkansas and Texas.

In 1843, Dr. Sappington dissolved Sappington and Sons and established four smaller, autonomous companies, ceding to them his financial interest. Darwin and William Sappington received one company, another was given to Meredith, a third went to Claiborne Jackson and Dr. William Price, and the fourth was a trust funded by the other companies, managed by Dr. C. M. Bradford for the benefit of Dr. Sappington's grandchildren by his daughter's marriage to Alonzo Pearson. In this reorganization, Dr.

Price retained the manufacturing operation from which the others obtained the pills they would sell.

An accurate accounting of the management of the original and subsequent companies is difficult to obtain, given that there was considerable overlap of duties and shifting of personnel throughout the years the pill business was active. Company members and field agents often assisted in the distribution of the pills and the collection of money in another's territory. Economic necessity, distant lines of communication, and the demanding life of a traveling salesman required that operation of the companies be flexible enough to accommodate unforeseen circumstances. There also had to be a great deal of trust between the proprietors and their field agents in the collection and exchange of money.

A Journey to Louisiana

In early January 1838, Meredith left Missouri and traveled by horse through Arkansas and Louisiana to meet with field agents who were attempting to collect money for pills that had been left on consignment the previous spring. Reports of poor sales, despite a plenitude of malaria in the population, had reached Saline County, and he was anxious to discover the cause. He also was Dr. Sappington's agent in an effort to collect a large amount of money from Joseph H. Boone, on whom the doctor held a note. At Alexandria, Louisiana, in mid-February, Meredith reported his progress in a letter to the doctor, entrusted to a company agent returning to Missouri. His experiences on the road, related in the letter, offer a glimpse into the difficulties encountered and the dangers faced by traveling salesmen in the semi-settled interior regions of the south. The letter depicts the extensive involvement Meredith had in Dr. Sappington's business affairs at this time, and shows a close relationship between the two in matters relating to their families and farms. Meredith also reveals a heretofore hidden sense of humor in his self-deprecatory comment about trading for a horse "that will barely carry me." (Short in stature, Meredith weighed considerably more than 200 pounds, a burden that could only be borne any distance on the back of a large, strong animal.)

> Dear Doctor,
> An oppy [opportunity] now offers to write you by Mr. Carson [William Carson, a field agent] who will leave this place in 1 or 2 days for Mo., and altho I had not yesterday intended to have written you before I saw Boon [Joseph H. Boone], yet I feel unwilling to let slip so good and safe an oppy [opportunity].
> I arrived at this place a few minutes since, all well. Our horses and mule are now in as good order as they were the day we left home, and if it were possible to get food for them, I have no doubt on my mind, but we could take them back home again (if the horse thieves did not take them from us). ... I feel confident if I take the mule to Texas that he will be stolen from me. This belief has very nearly determined me to endeavor to trade him off and get a horse that will barely carry me, believing that there would be less possibility of having that stolen. I have not yet finally determined what I will do, but a good offer will very soon determine me.
> On the subject of your land in Howard County ... after much trouble, and

assuming on my part, for you, considerable responsibility, I have succeeded in perfecting your title to the land. At any rate, I have done all that man could do with [the seller of the property].

I think but few indeed under all the circumstances would have succeeded as well as I have done. He [property seller] is ignorant & obstinate, and has been offered several times $1,000 for his right to that land. ... I am at a loss to know whether I had not better send your title papers [by this letter] for believe me, I have yet to go thru numberless thieves, robbers & cut throats before we meet, if ever we do. ...

Since my arrival I have rec.d some information on the subject of the sale of my medicine which induces me to believe that it has sold some better on this side of Red River, than on the north side. From all that I can learn, I think it possible that about one fourth part of the amount deposited by Mr. Tussey [Jonathan Tussey, a field agent] has sold, but this is still uncertain. My collections have not been good, but so far every agent made by Mr. Tussey I consider responsible and solvent men, so that I do not expect to lose one dollar. I have sold about 800 boxes and think it probable I shall succeed in selling some more. ...

From all that I can hear and learn about the medicine, I cannot resist the impression that there will sell in La. next year $15 or 20,000 for there is never any want of sickness in this country.

I have some difficulty on my mind about going into Texas. We have so much medicine on hand that we cannot put it all in La. & Ark., and from all that I can learn, expenses will be so high that it will take all the money that I can collect to defray them. Add to this the fact that if we get into that country and cannot at any price get grain for our horses, we shall certainly lose them all which will compel us to part with them at a mere trifle and buy others that will answer our purpose at a very high price. These considerations have their weight with me, but as I approach the Sabine [river] and receive further information I can then act with more propriety and judgment on the subject.

Home, and about home matters. Have you yet got a <u>good</u> teacher for our children? I feel great anxiety about those poor little creatures. Do get them in school if possible.

What about my stock? When did you and Tom [one of Dr. Sappington's slaves] see all or any of them? How do they look & have any died? I wish I knew the answers to all of the above inquiries.[7]

Meredith closed his letter complaining that he had "scarcely slept an hour last night watching a small creek that detained us all day in order to get across dry," highlighting yet another hazard in the life of a pill peddler on the road in Louisiana.

A Man of Little Honesty

Four days after writing to Dr. Sappington, Meredith surprised Joseph Boone when he tethered his horse at the debtor's cotton plantation near Marksville, a county seat village only a day's ride from Alexandria, in Avoyelles Parish. Boone, undoubtedly citing a lack of cash, declined to pay the $10,000 claim, but did agree to satisfy the indebtedness in 12 months, perhaps counting on the sale of the next cotton crop to bail him out of his trouble. With no way to force payment at this time, and realizing that he had to return to Missouri with something more than a verbal agreement, Meredith penned, on-the-spot, a terse, one-sentence-long promissory note that Boone signed. In doing so, he agreed to deposit the full amount of the debt to Dr. Sappington's credit with the mercantile firm of Burke, Watt & Co., in New Orleans, on February 16, 1839. As an incentive, perhaps hoping to ensure payment on time, Meredith included a clause in the note calling for 10 percent interest to accrue from the original date if the note was not paid when due.

A year later, Darwin Sappington, in New Orleans at the time, was refused payment when he presented the note at the mercantile house. Boone had not left any money there. During the next three years, Meredith, still acting as Dr. Sappington's agent, sued Boone in Avoyelles Parish and won a judgment in the doctor's favor. He was unable to collect, however, because when it became apparent to Boone that he was about to lose the suit, he abandoned his plantation and fled to the Republic of Texas (then an independent sovereign country), effectively getting beyond the jurisdiction of any United States court. A Louisiana attorney enlisted by Meredith to recover the debt from assets Boone had in that state informed him in 1842 that Boone's "creditors have had the land and plantation seized and sold, first having their mortgages recorded in this Parish. The whole plantation was sold for about $8,000. ... with little honesty left with this man, it is extremely doubtful whether a creditor in the United States can realize anything from him. The laws of [Texas] hold out but little encouragement and seem only calculated to encourage crime."[8]

Three more years passed before Meredith located Boone again and attempted to settle the debt, now his alone to collect after it had been assigned to him by Dr. Sappington in the 1843 reorganization. In February 1845, the United States Congress authorized the annexation of the Republic of Texas, adding it as the 28th state at the end of that year. Encouraged by this, anticipating he could now pursue his claim in a Texas court, Meredith wrote attorney Mathias Bingham "to engage your services in the case I have against the estate of Joseph H. Boon [sic], who died last year in Fort Bend County, which I understand is not very far from your residence." Meredith had learned the previous summer of Boone's whereabouts and that he had died, and understood that he "left at his death about fifty negroes [sic] together with much other property." Bingham was told "If you can make any arrangement so as to secure the debt, I am willing to compensate you liberally for it." The debt was now larger, "amounting to upward of $16,000," because of the interest clause Meredith had wisely included in the original note.[9]

Whether Meredith recovered anything from Joseph Boone's estate is an open question. He may have, or he might have decided at some point that it was futile to continue trying to collect a debt mired in a Texas court, and made no further attempt. The amount of money involved is considerable, even by today's standards, so it is difficult to see him abandoning the cause. However, although he was generally meticulous in the management of his financial affairs, no mention of Boone's debt appears in Meredith's papers, nor is it listed in an appraisal of his estate performed at the time of his death.[10]

Mr. Tymony Takes a Large Dram

Young Francis Tymony was looking for a job in January 1840. Born in Pennsylvania of immigrant Irish parents, the 25-year-old was living in Boonville, Missouri, when he wrote to Meredith to ask if Dr. Sappington had decided to hire him "as distributing agent of his medicine." His letter proved to be a fortuitous omen for Meredith, and for The Firm. Once on the payroll, Tymony became one of Meredith's most valued field agents, serving him for the next 15 years. Their harmonious relationship and the degree of respect Francis Tymony felt toward Meredith was such that he named his second son Francis Marmaduke Tymony. (Born in Saline County in 1850, this son died in Randolph County, Missouri, in 1929.) The elder Tymony proved to be a man "of industry and honesty of purpose," as he described himself.[11] Tracking his adventures as a peddler of Dr. Sappington's Anti-Fever Pills presents a vivid and colorful picture of the business itself, and of the lives of the men who conducted it.

By March of 1840, Tymony was on the road for Sappington and Sons, accompanied by James Heathman, an experienced field agent who supervised the new salesman as he learned the trade. The two, traveling with their boxes of medicine stowed in a horse-drawn wagon, left Boonville under less than favorable circumstances, Heathman later reporting to Meredith that "our runaway frolick at the outset [causing] our harness to become so mangled and broke that we were compelled to buy a new set." They charged this $18 expense to Dr. Sappington. A couple of days later, Heathman wrote Meredith from Fulton, Missouri, saying that in spite of their unpromising start they were getting on well and in fine spirits, although, he added, "I am a little fearful of Mr. Tymony. I tell you, he takes a large dram."[12]

Evidently, Francis Tymony's proclivity to satisfy his thirst with a "large dram" did not interfere with his work because he sold pills for The Firm the next year, continuing until the fall of 1841, when his employment ended because of the approaching cold weather. That October, he went east "over the mountains" to spend the winter with his family in Pennsylvania. Writing to Meredith before he left on the steamboat *Thames*, which he boarded after it returned to Boonville from upriver, young Tymony profusely thanked him "for the many tokens of your kindness and confidence I have received since our aquaintance [sic] and if there are any thing wanting on my part to prove my self worthy of it, I assure you it was the fault of the head and not of the heart. To be thought worthy of a good and true friend will still be my greatest ambition to aspire to. ... It may be that I will return to Missouri in the Spring ... [if so] it would give me pleasure to be employed by your company next season providing I could wish to travel, but as I ask you to communicate with me, we can talk of this here after."[13] Tymony returned to work for Sappington and Sons the following spring, and by 1844 he was a seasoned field agent, handling Meredith's medicine business in Mississippi and Louisiana.

That business had suffered during Meredith's tenure as lieutenant governor. Political duties and farm operations took much of his time and he was unable to closely supervise his agents. Consequently, they didn't perform as they should have, and despite an occasional tour through the two states by other members of the company, sales had gone down and collections, where the pills were left on consignment, were seriously in arrears.[14] As a result, by 1843 Meredith faced the possibility of losing a considerable

If Life and Health Last

amount of money. In January 1844, to bring the business back under his control, he sent Francis Tymony to Mississippi. A trusted agent, Tymony had demonstrated an ability to supervise sub-agents and resolve issues to Meredith's satisfaction. Arriving in Mississippi early in January, Tymony wrote Meredith from Hillsboro in Scott County. His letter (reproduced below with misspellings) describes some of the problems caused by Meredith's previous agents, many of whom are named, and shows the latitude given Tymony to resolve them. His colorful description of the people he meets and the country through which he travels make enjoyable reading as it provides insight into Mississippi life at that time.

Dear Col.,

I am here and I will try to relate as briefly as possible how I have got here. The boat I took at St. Louis was delaid taking in freight on the way and did not arive at Vicksburg until the 4th instant. I called on Dr. Emanuel and found instead of three or four hundred dollars in your debt but $79, there being three hundred & 21 boxes on hand. The reason of this is plain. Several bankrupts in Hinds Co. brought your medicine to him and sold it for a trifle. This medicine he placed out as medicine on hand when the receipt was presented.

I had found, and he did not deny, he had purchased as stated above but said he retained your medicine and sold theirs. Had the last two agents renewed the receipts it would have prevented this.

I called on Mr. Woodman, who refused to pay any but the principal of his note because it was not presented when due, said the agent never called on him until last spring. After calling several times in his store during the day and conversing pleasantly and familiarly with him, he at last made me an offer to pay interest from 1842 when I would return. This, I think, would be the best way to settle it. It is a dangerous experiment to trust the uncertainty of the law in this swindling state.

I left Mr. Haney's route, all except the county of Newton, with Dr. Emanuel where I have no doubt they will be safe until called for. I have his receipt for them.

I took the cars to Jackson next day, staid one night, and during the day on Saturday I found 43 boxes medicine sold for which I was paid, and sold 20 boxes to another drugist at 40 ct. per box cash. Called on Mr. Lewis who lives there, stated to him my business. He stated the business in his hands were transacted in other counties and he could not give me the information I required until my return. I asked the name of the counties that I might inquire from the dockets, but he said he did not recollect the counties. He states there are some real estate bank paper in his hand to the amount of $700 or $800 which is at your disposal. I can not tell wat it is worth.

I found no stage between this place and Jackson on account of high water and bad roads, but after some difficulty I obtained a horse from the mail contractors and left on Sunday morning. Crossed Pearl river, which is 60 feet above low water mark and has to be ferried one mile and a half and as dangerous as it can be, and rode here with the mail carrier, 52 miles that day.

Here I found Mr. Lack had sold the horse and saddle and had neather mony or horse. A number of pine hill boys were in town yesterday. I set out among them to suit myself in a horse. There were all gloriously drunk and such a rowdy set of cretures you never have seen, and on this account I did not succeed.

This morning I borrowed a horse and rode ten miles to the country and back to see a Mr. Beale, one of the hard cases on which I hold a receipt for 75 boxes, dated 1838. I took his note, returned and sold the same in a horse trade for fifty five dollars to one of the Piney boys, and a part of the debt of Mr. Lack of 20 dollars making in all $75 — for which I have got a most ancient horse. Will work that mony here or indeed else where so that I get a horse for paper which I thought yesterday completely worthless.

I sold fifty boxes of medicine to a store keeper here on his note, so that I think I have this day done a good days work.

I think it looks favorable for good sales of your medicine. Last year throughout the state has been very sickly. And I must tell you frankly that I think your business has been wretchedly neglected.

Mr. Parsons passed two five dollar bills on a fraudulent bank in Alabama over to Mr. Lack and one to the stage office. Mr. Lack having the mony in his hands says he will retain that amount. The stage contractor says he will take a detachment on the debts due you for his. I told him to go ahead that I will not pay it, nor he cannot make me do it. This I fear is but the beginning of my troubles on Parsons route.

Mr. Lack is not a solvent man but I will try to buy a saddle on his credit, but it will be but a very sorry one as there are no new saddles for sale in this shabby Piney town. I will leave here tomorrow, God willing, very glad to get away.

It has rained almost every day here since the beginning of November and still it rains like falling out of buckets and has every day since I came into the state. If you would see the general prospect of the country almost deluged with water. The roads abound with quick sand holes and I'll assure you my undertaking is not to be envied and the people a mongrel indian negro and white Poulition little carried from the brute. I can do [only] what any other can do placed in the same circumstances. The streams are all covering their swamps and bottoms and by those alone I apprehend difficulty. I don't mind rain or mud. I will go from here to Newton Co. ... The Legislature is now in session in Jackson passing laws to repudiate old debts. Jackson is crowded with black legs and cut throats. I have up to this time collected $145 besides the horse trade.

I shall now conclude my lengthy but hasty writen letter wishing you more peace of mind than your humble agent. Give my respects to your family to Dr. Sappington & family while I remain, With sincere respect, Yours Truly, F. Tymony.[15]

His work collecting Meredith's delinquent accounts in Mississippi and Louisiana concluded in the summer of 1844, and Francis Tymony went to Michigan to help Layton Eddins recover similar accounts there. Relaxing at his lodging on a Sunday in October, writing to Meredith, Tymony whimsically reflected on his life as a company agent. "I have been in my regular round of business, so familiar grown that I almost wonder wether I was not expressly made to be a collector. And if there is any life more lonsome, more lostsome, more divested of all the social and domestic enjoyment of this world, I pity the poor agent who has to endure it. Known everywhere, seldom welcome anywhere, a terror to delinquent Agents and swindling lawyers, I onward 'plod my weary way.'"16

Despite his somewhat rueful outlook, Tymony was proud of his work. Collections in Michigan so far were "upwards of five thousand dollars, this beats my southern collection, but had I half the sales of medicine there and have retraced the ground, I would have beaten this. I have myself collected three thousand and the other two the remainder." He was going to Ohio next, stopping in Detroit to get Michigan money exchanged "as it will not do to take it out of the state."

In the spring of 1845, Francis Tymony was in Memphis, his first stop on a tour through the south. This season he had an additional product to sell, a book written by Dr. Sappington. Titled *Theory and Treatment of Fevers*, the small volume offered readers self-help information and revealed the doctor's formula for making his anti-fever pills. Selling the book proved to be difficult; in fact, it was a burden for the field agents, a distraction from the more lucrative work of peddling pills and collecting money. Tymony understood *his* priorities, telling Meredith that he "found your books [shipped to Memphis], got waggons to convey them to Holy Springs [Holly Springs, Mississippi, 30 miles southeast of Memphis] where we sent all but about 70 which we left in Hernando, Desoto Co. *I then went in pursuit of money* [emphasis added], found all the medicine I left in Memphis sold, dimned [unknown word, perhaps meaning 'talked him out of'] the fellow out of fifty dollars, took his note — payable in exchange — for $45 more and now I am by candle light preparing the papers to leave in the morning. So much in the first days history of this adventure."17

Fire, flood, and his recent marriage figured heavily in Tymony's life at this time. At Vicksburg in mid-April he reported that he was well "thank God after the narrow escape for life by the burning of the Central House [hotel] of Memphis." Heavy rains had plagued his journey through northern Mississippi. One downpour "ran every brook and stream over its banks, and if I had the blues it was then. Consider the feelings of a new married man a thousand miles from home in a shabby cabin in the pine hills of Miss., with the expectation of overflowing streams for a thousand miles before him. ... All I fear is delay, times are not now as they have been in the days of single blessedness." Distributing the books became a significant problem. "You can scarcely believe the difficulty I have to forward the books safe to different points, the greatest care must be taken, to avoid mistakes, delays, etc. ... We will sell the books we can and leave the rest. I wish to God this long journey was over me and then farewell high waters and big swamps."18

A High-Handed Game

Francis Tymony's effort to rejuvenate Meredith's business in Mississippi and Louisiana evidently left many old accounts uncollected when he returned to Missouri in the fall of 1845. Seeing the potential for the loss of thousands of dollars, Meredith was reluctant to cease trying to get the money owed him, but realized that a different tactic was needed. That November he took into his confidence George T. Bicknell, and together they launched the firm of Marmaduke and Bicknell to manufacture Dr. Sappington's Anti-Fever Pills and sell them in Mississippi and Louisiana. Meredith was to furnish "fifty pounds of quinine, with the other ingredients" and make the pills at cost, and pay for the horse, wagon, and other gear needed to transport Bicknell and the medicine in the South. Bicknell, for his part, agreed to sell the pills himself where possible, and to establish distributors (as opposed to local agents) where he thought that was the best course. He also agreed to recover unsold copies of Dr. Sappington's book and find new outlets for their sale. Most important from Meredith's viewpoint, all of the IOU notes he was holding were given to Bicknell to collect. Anticipating difficulties, Meredith agreed to pay lawyers' fees in the event delinquent agents were sued. At the end of each year, any profit (after Meredith recovered his investment plus 10 percent interest, and Bicknell's living expenses and all bills were paid) was to be divided equally between the two partners.[19]

George Bicknell appeared to be an ideal manager for Meredith's pill business, exhibiting the persona of today's corporate director of marketing. Letters he wrote to Meredith in the years 1846–48 show him to be educated with a working knowledge of such diverse topics as marketing, advertising, printing, accounting, banking, and chemistry. He also was familiar with Philadelphia and Cincinnati business houses and the products they sold. Another, more shaded side of his character is detected in his correspondence. Among other traits revealed is an enigmatic personality, a puzzling mix of opposing qualities and often proposing strategies that, at times, Meredith no doubt found uncomfortable.[20]

In the first five months of 1846, George Bicknell endeavored to learn about Meredith's pill business. At Vicksburg, Mississippi, on February 3, having traveled the state's northern counties where he "dragged like a wounded snake my slow length along over hills and through mud," he advised Meredith about the present state of his pill business in that state. His detailed report concluded that the medicine could continue to be sold but not "to the extent that it has been [because] other preparations have got the public fast by the coat button."[21] He took aim at Dr. Sappington's book saying that with knowledge of the pills' composition available to the public, the "belief in their thaumaturgic [miracle] power in the minds of some will be dissipated." Local manufacture of counterfeit Sappington Anti-Fever Pills was a significant issue in the larger towns where druggists compounded their own versions. To combat this, Bicknell wanted to establish wholesale agents at Memphis, Vicksburg, Natchez, and New Orleans, "not that Sappington's Pills might be sold, but to prevent their sale," he wrote to Meredith. "This is paradoxical but if I do not convince you of the truth of my views, it will be because I have not paper enough. ... My plan is to supply one house in each of the places with a large quantity of medicine at the very lowest price, have cards printed and posted upon every other tree in Miss. & Louisiana stating that they are wholesale agents & that they have the genuine Sappington's pills. ... that no druggist is permitted to retail the medicine. The effect will be: First the wholesale agents will make no more medicine, other druggists will not find much sale for what they may make and will stop making. In the country, they will not buy anything to any extent 'till they get sick; when there is much sickness the country agents will first be drained, then they will buy in the large towns and from men who have the genuine article." He wanted 75 pounds of quinine to be made into pills, anticipating this amount could be distributed in the coming months.[22]

If Life and Health Last

Not satisfied with peddling only anti-fever pills, Bicknell sought to expand the line of medicinal products he could sell. He proposed to Meredith that they make "6 or ten thousand boxes of Gottlieb Feuchtwhanger's German Cathartic Pills." He described them as "expressly designed to cure all those diseases that originate in the derangement of that important viscus, the liver. A pill that will cure the fat-meat eating children of the sunny south of all the ills that flesh is heir to, except fevers." He told Meredith that "Dr. Price, Dr. Bicknell (that's myself) or most any other Doctor can invent a good purgative pill. ... If a good pill be made, slowly & surely it would win its way to renown. Only 25cts per Box." A bit later he suggested that it would be better if the pills could be sold under Dr. Sappington's name because "they would not require so much humbugging."[23]

At Philadelphia, Mississippi, in mid-May, on his way back to Missouri after a tour through Louisiana with a stop at New Orleans, Bicknell thought "it proper" — since the object of their business venture was to make money — "to make a few suggestions relative to the next Campaign. They are the offspring of much reflection and an accurate knowledge of matters and things as they now exist in this state. ...The price of [the pills] is now fixed at 75 [cents] per box, a commission of 33⅓ percent per sales made by subagents must be deducted, yielding therefore only 50cts a Box to the travelling [sic] agent. In order therefore that the most money may be made from these pills their composition must be a trifle cheaper."[24]

Bicknell displayed his knowledge of chemistry when he told Meredith: "After the crystals of the Sulphate of Quinine have been deposited a residuum will be found containing sulphate of quinine cinchonine and a resin. This residuum is called 'the precipitate Extract of Bark,' Sulphate of Quinine impure &c. It is much cheaper than quinine and in double doses is said to be as effectual. It can be procured in Philadelphia put up in jars. Enough of this ought to be procured to render Sappington's Pills cheap enough in their original cost to allow the sub agents 33⅓ percent for all sales. This suggestion deserves your consideration. I cannot state in this letter the reasons that have induced me to come to this conclusion."[25]

Bicknell's rash proposal to use impure quinine disregarded Dr. Sappington's years of research and experimentation to arrive at the proper formula and failed to take into account the effect an inferior product would have on the favorable reputation the pills had with the public. He also failed to understand that his scheme was something to which Meredith could never consent, for to do so would be to conspire against the interests of his father-in-law and other members of the Sappington family.

Another of Bicknell's suggestions took a sideswipe at another existing business practice. "No pills sold in this country are put up in so bungling a manner as Dr. John Sappington's, and with so little precaution against counterfeiters," he declared. To correct this, he recommended putting the pills into boxes made of wood, with Dr. Sappington's signature burned into the cover, along with a paper label "pasted on each side so [the box] could not be opened without tearing the label."

Other recommendations show knowledge of advanced marketing philosophy and techniques. "Pills like every thing else go out of fashion," he wrote to Meredith. "I look upon John Sappington's Cathartic Pills as the very thing to bring the Anti-Fever Pills [back] in fashion. Much, very much, depends upon the placard. If you simply say, 'Dr.

John Sappington's Cathartic Pills for sale here,'" that "humble and brief announcement" would not be read despite being printed on handbills two feet square with colored engravings. "A large handbill must be printed with a large engraving of wood, Hercules destroying the Hydra, or something equally emblematic and more original. ... If you do not keep up with the efforts of others, sales will be small."[26]

Bicknell's argument for the posters was favorably received. At St. Louis early in January 1847, preparing for his spring tour of the South, he sent copies of a newly printed "show card" to Meredith, and to Dr. Price, who had formulated a cathartic pill that Marmaduke and Bicknell would sell under his name. Before leaving St. Louis on the steamboat *Julia*, Bicknell packed boxes of medicine for later shipment to Natchez and New Orleans, leaving them with a forwarding agent.[27]

In northern Mississippi a few weeks later, he was not encouraged by what he found. "This country has been remarkably healthy the past year," he told Meredith, and reported that sales of the anti-fever pills amounted to only "between 3 and 4000 boxes," about one-third of what had been left on deposit.[28] Then in April, at Natchez, he wrote to say that the income "will be mighty small," Meredith's debtors had no money that he could collect and the previous year's sales were not as large as anticipated. Hoping to jump-start the business, Bicknell now proposed that they venture into new territory. "It has of late occurred to me that if the coming season in Mississippi be comparatively healthy (which may God in his good providence forbid) the area stock had better be taken to Texas or elsewhere. ... The attention of Patent medicine venders has of late been directed" to that state. He again argued for the anti-fever pills to be put into wooden boxes and gave Meredith specific instructions about their labeling and selling price. He also suggested that another pill, "Keucklehan's or some other person's Vermifuge [an anthelmintic to treat intestinal worms, developed by Dr. Augustus Kueckelhan of Boonville]," be added to their inventory to be sold along with Dr. Price's cathartic pills. More placards were needed, "400 large show cards. Hercules & etc., 130 printed on the same kind of paper as used heretofore & 250 on common printing paper to be pasted up. A paste can be made of gum tragacanth and carried in a tin bucket, that will be better and as cheap as tacks." The show card should make no reference to Dr. Sappington's book, but should "speak of the millions [of] boxes that have been sold, their popularity, their efficacy." His enthusiasm for this new venture lifted Bicknell's spirits. "Having put my foot into it, I feel like jumping all over in. The medicine can be sold, I am very confident, if the right methods be taken. The management that was politic 10 years ago will not succeed now." He was off for New Orleans and wanted Meredith to write to him there and "inform me about what you think of my suggestions about ... Texas."[29] A month later, in St. Tammany Parish, Louisiana, Bicknell reckoned that he would start next year's campaign with 8,000 boxes of unsold pills, "and unless Mississippi is extremely unhealthy they will not be needed in this country." He urged Meredith to decide about expanding into Texas. If the answer was yes, then Meredith should order "directly from Philadelphia ... 7000 labels and 7000 signatures of Dr. Sappington to be printed ... with the price of Sappington's pill at $1.00 per box. 350 lithographed show cards, 25,000 thin papers (to be pasted)." He felt strongly that Dr. Sappington's book had hurt the sale of the anti-fever pills, and he wanted nothing said about it on the new posters: "It is to be hoped that none of the books are in Texas." Bicknell's concern about Texas was predicated on his belief that if they were to sell pills there the following year (1848), the materials for their manufacture and promotion must be purchased now. He also wanted 2,000 more boxes of anti-fever pills, 10,000 boxes of Dr. Price's cathartic pills, and "3,000 packages of Keuklehan's Vermifuge," enough to "make a good wagon load."[30] From Louisiana, Bicknell traveled to Mississippi and at the end of July reported collecting $767.37 of old debt and $1,151.85 from the sale of pills. The money was paper currency issued by banks in "Mobile, Charleston, & Tennessee. If you wish Gold or Silver or Missouri paper, immediately ... write to me at St. Louis giving me instructions." He hoped to be in Memphis by late August, on his way to Missouri.[31]

In January 1848, Bicknell was back at Natchez. In an interesting bit of salesman-speak he related to Meredith that where 700 boxes of medicine had been sold two years earlier, the past season's sales were only 471 boxes, still *the sales have increased in the average,"* [emphasis added]. Having decided to expand into Texas, Meredith's investment in the partnership increased over the winter. Bicknell now had a new heavy-duty wagon bought in Cincinnati and shipped down the Ohio and Mississippi Rivers to Memphis, and he was testing a new batch of quinine sent from Philadelphia, relating that it showed traces of vegetable matter. He was leaving soon for Alexandria, Louisiana, the jumping-off point for Texas. "My load," he wrote Meredith, "is very heavy," and his horse would suffer.[32]

Six weeks later, Bicknell was back in Natchez and reporting to Meredith on his trip. "I wrote to you upon the eve of my starting to Texas. I found Geo. M. Hogan upon the Trinity [River] about 450 miles from this place. I made a contract with him. Term, substantially as follows: He is to distribute the medicines in that part of Texas north of the San Antonio Road & west of the Trinity, excepting Houston, Galveston, and the counties of Houston, Cherokee, Rusk & Shelby north of the San Antonio Road. After deducting commission, he is to have 25 percent for his services, and is not to allow in any case without our consent more than 33⅓ percent. ... He pays his own expenses, and we are chargeable only with frt. [freight] to Shreveport or other designated port."[33] (George M. Hogan was a collection agent who worked for Dr. Sappington in the early 1840s and was known to Meredith. The date of Hogan's relocation to Texas is unknown; however, many Missourians went there after the Republic joined the Union in 1846. Meredith had an interest in Texas and invested in land there in the 1840s. Bicknell forwarded with his letter one from Hogan to Meredith "about yr. land.")

A disturbing facet of George T. Bicknell's enigmatic personality surfaces in this letter when he tells Meredith that he is withholding forwarding to Dr. Sappington a letter from George Hogan, "so that Dr. Bradford may not be apprised of our doings in Texas. I desire that Dr. Bradford should by no means whatever learn further our intentions about Texas."[34] As manager of the trust established by Dr. Sappington in 1844 for the benefit of Eliza Sappington Pearson's children, Dr. C. M. Bradford would expect to receive a portion of the income that would result from the sale of Sappington's Anti-Fever Pills in Texas. George Bicknell's clumsy attempt to hide the knowledge of Marmaduke and Bicknell's venture into that state, and thereby circumvent the payment of money to the trust, was — like his suggestion that impure quinine be substituted in the manufacture of the pills — an imposition on the Sappington family to which Meredith could not acquiesce. In addition to entering into an illegal conspiracy to defraud the trust, the eventual revelation of his dishonesty would destroy Meredith's relationship with his father-in-law and the entire Sappington family.

Faced with the knowledge that his partner was willing to engage in an illegal activity that could discredit his own reputation, Meredith decided, rather than recall Bicknell at once and end the partnership, to leave him in the field for the remainder of the season. Debts could perhaps be collected and the sale of the pills in Mississippi and Louisiana could continue, but it is clear that their relationship was strained.

In a letter written the first day of October 1848, the normally ebullient Bicknell, previously confident he could sell medicine in the South and full of optimistic plans for the future, whose letters to Meredith had always filled several pages, is constrained to a single sheet of paper on which he briefly reports his recent activities and then writes a short passage about political matters in Mississippi, something he had not previously done. Even his handwriting, when compared to his previous correspondence, is subdued, cramped and restrained where before it was open and lively. The sale of medicine during the summer he reports as being "fully equal to my expectations. There is little money in this country and I am not so successful in making collections as I could wish." His expenses for the past 20 days were $12.82, he notes, while the sale of medicine during the same time amounted to only $6.65. It is apparent in this letter that Bicknell had lost interest in what he was doing. He expected to be in Missouri by the middle of November.[35]

"I announce to you in this that the firm of Marmaduke and Bicknell is virtually dissolved," Bicknell advised George M. Hogan in late January 1849. "Col. Marmaduke will purchase my interest in the firm, tho' the arrangement at this date is not definitely settled." Bicknell asked Hogan to acknowledge receiving pharmaceutical items Bicknell had purchased for him so a settlement could be effected with Meredith. A note of desperation is apparent in Bicknell's pleading: "I cannot pay for these articles, as portions were contracted for in N. Orleans, Vicksburg & St. Louis, and I may never see those places again."

In addition to half a dozen items listed in Bicknell's letter, the partnership sent to Hogan 85 different drugs, ointments, oils, and other preparations, including two pounds of Turkish opium, two pounds of blue mass (a mercury-based medicine), 18 vials of strychnine, a pound and a half of ipecac, 12 dozen bottles of castor oil, calomel (a purgative) in various amounts, laudanum, and turpentine.[36]

A final judgment of George T. Bicknell as Meredith's business partner is difficult to make because not all is known about his activities, since they occurred so far away from Saline County, but a report in 1850 from Meredith's agent in the South at that time offers a clue. After following Bicknell's route through Mississippi's northern counties, John P. Jackson told Meredith that "Mr. Bicknell's rascality has been very well concealed in many places. I have only procured one certificate, which is the only case I believe of positive proof against his villainy; yet it is to be perceived with all agents that have any recollection of the business transactions where Mr. Bicknell has had an opportunity of defrauding, that he has played a high-handed game."[37]

Time to Quit

The problems inherent in Meredith's long-distance pill business — lackadaisical and thieving field and sub-agents, poor roads, bad weather, flooded streams, and communication lapses caused by slow delivery and occasional loss of letters — did not improve over the years. In 1854, Francis Tymony was again in Mississippi attempting to straighten out Meredith's accounts. Visiting the northern counties first, he found that where there was a need for the medicine "there was none there and as Mr. Gregory [a previous agent] scarcely ever changed any I find where he left it was where there is no sale, besides he has left any amount of difficulties for me to settle." Tymony's exasperation is evident as he chides Meredith for his poor choice of a representative. "I do wish that you would never employ such blockheads again to transact your business. I have no doubt you have lost fully a thousand dollars by him."[38] His opinion of the people of Mississippi hadn't improved over the years, either. "These difficulties which has been left for me to settle has several times jeopardized my life, among some of these overbearing, tyrannical southern people." Tymony's letter arrived in Saline County six weeks later. Writing to his disgruntled agent, Meredith admitted that he was "very confident" when he employed Gregory that he "was not qualified to do my business as it ought to have been done," but implied he had already hired him before he realized his mistake, "and had I known it before he came to my house to start, certainly would not have employed him. ... He is good for nothing at any business."[39]

Meredith trusted Francis Tymony's judgment as he tried to settle the delinquent accounts, telling him he was "perfectly willing for you to do as you think best in the matter." What Tymony did not know until he received this letter was that Meredith intended to end his involvement in the pill business. "I hope you will be able to arrange my business in such a manner as to render it necessary to make but a few more trips *to close it up* [emphasis added]."[40] Meredith's closure of the pill business in Mississippi and Louisiana preceded the end of the Sappington family enterprise by only a few years; the residue dissolved by the advent of the Civil War.

Notes

1. "It is my misfortune this day to be afoot": Sylvester Hall to Marmaduke, April 17, 1839. Folder 12, Marmaduke Papers C1021, SHSMO. Buffalo gnats, more commonly known as black flies, are aquatic insects up to 1/8-inch long. Major hatches occur in spring from eggs laid the previous fall in running water. Female black flies require a blood meal for development of their eggs. They are attracted to people and livestock, attacking eyes, ears, nostrils, biting any exposed body parts, causing extreme pain, itching and localized swelling. Swarms are known to sometimes kill the host animal, death occurring as toxemia, a result of bites; from anaphylactic shock; or occasionally suffocation by inhalation of the flies themselves.

2. "there was not one Commissioned officer, non Commissioned or Private man": Madge Pickard and R. Carlyle Buley, *The Midwest Pioneer, His Ills, Cures, & Doctors*, 11.

3. "Sciatic, weak lungs, fits, inward weakness and nervous affections": Pickard and Buley, *The Midwest Pioneer*, 36.

4. "a variety of spices": Max A. Goldstein, ed., *One Hundred Years of Medicine and Surgery in Missouri*, 20. Doctor Farrar, like Dr. John Sappington, engaged in a number of business ventures, one being a St. Louis drugstore owned in conjunction with Joseph Charless, "the first printer in St. Louis and the father of journalism west of the Mississippi River." John Neal Hoover, "Joseph Charless (1772–1834)," *Dictionary of Missouri Biography*, 162. Farrar and Charless dissolved their partnership in the drugstore in May 1812.

To Make a Fortune in Missouri

Farrar then entered into partnership with another doctor and they opened a drug and medicine store "on Main Street below Maj. Christie's tavern, adjoining Dugen's silversmith shop." Goldstein, 20. Like John Sappington, Farrar invested heavily in real estate, his widow credited with owning property worth $200,000 in 1850. Roland Lanser, "The Pioneer Physician in Missouri 1820–1850," *MHR*, Vol. 44, No. 1 (October 1949), 47. Joseph Charless remained in the drug and paint store business. His son, Joseph Jr., operated the store at the corner of Main and Pine streets until his death by murder in 1859. Charless Jr. was shot and killed by Joseph W. Thornton, former bookkeeper of Boatman's Savings Association, in retaliation for testifying against Thornton in a criminal proceeding for embezzlement. Joseph Charless invoice to W. B. Sappington, March 19, 1840. Folder 26, John Sappington Papers C1027, SHSMO. An account of Joseph Charless Jr.'s death is in the *Weekly Jefferson Inquirer*, June 11, 1859, Reel 16357, Newspaper Archives, SHSMO.

5. Dr. Sappington designated the states lying within the major watersheds: Lynn Morrow, "Dr. John Sappington: Southern Patriarch in the New West," *MHR*, Vol. 90, Issue 1, (October 1995), 50. Morrow's monograph on Dr. Sappington is a source of considerable information about the organization and operation of the pill company. Dr. Price's role in the company's financial affairs is found in: Jackson & Miller to Doct. Price, July 20, 1837. Folder 26, John Sappington Papers C1027, SHSMO.

6. States east of the Mississippi River: The assignment of the large territory east of the Mississippi River to William and Darwin Sappington is shown in: Affadivat of John Sappington, September 21, 1836. Folder 1, Sappington Family Papers C2889, SHSMO.

7. "An oppy [opportunity] now offers to write you by Mr. Carson": Marmaduke to Sappington, February 12, 1838. Box 2, Folder 3. Sappington-Marmaduke Papers, MHS. An example of sales in Louisiana is reported by an agent in Natchitoches Parish who received 250 boxes of pills from field agent Tussey, selling 22 boxes for which he received "four dollars and fifty cents and the Remainder I have credited out." Thomas Ford to John Sappington, August 23, 1837. Folder 26, John Sappington Papers C1027, SHSMO. Marmaduke recruited agents from nearby counties when possible. Jonathan Tussey lived in Howard County, Missouri, and in Pettis County: 1830 U.S. Federal Census Howard County p. 139; 1840 U.S. Census Pettis County p. 35. William Carson lived in Moniteau Township, Howard County, 1830 U.S. Census p. 187; 1840, Ibid., p. 23.

8. "creditors have had the land and plantation seized and sold": Henderson Taylor to Marmaduke, April 20, 1842. Box 3, Folder 2, Sappington-Marmaduke Papers, MHS.

9. "to engage your services in the case I have against the estate of Joseph H. Boon": Marmaduke to Mathias Bingham, July 1, 1845. Box 3, Folder 6, Sappington-Marmaduke Papers, MHS. Meredith's letter details actions taken by himself, Dr. Sappington, and Darwin Sappington over a six-year period and contains the text of the Boone promissory note.

10. Although he was generally meticulous in the management of his financial affairs: Appraisal of M. M. Marmaduke estate dated May 23, 1864. Saline County Probate Estate Files, Estate CE-1710, Reel C8250, Missouri State Archives.

11. a man "of industry and honesty of purpose": Tymony to Marmaduke, January 10, 1840. Folder 12, Marmaduke Papers C1021, SHSMO.

12. "I am a little fearful of Mr. Tymony. I tell you, he takes a large dram": Heathman to Marmaduke, March 24, 1840. Folder 12, Marmaduke Papers C1021, SHSMO.

13. Tymony profusely thanked Meredith "for the many tokens of your kindness and confidence": Tymony to Marmaduke, October 9, 1841. Box 3, Folder 1, Sappington-Marmaduke Papers, MHS. Tymony was poetic in his letter, speaking of his departure from Missouri as "over the hills and far away." He said that he might take a job in St. Louis if he "should meet a favorable offer," but what he really wanted was to return and work for Meredith.

14. despite an occasional tour through the two states by other members of the company": E. D. Sappington to Marmaduke, January 25, 1841. Ibid. Sappington told Marmaduke that Dr. Price was on his way to Natchez to "meet his hands" with the boxes of medicine, "all the medicine sold out" from there to Memphis.

15. "I am here and I will try to relate as briefly as possible how I have got here": Tymony to Marmaduke,

If Life and Health Last

January 9, 1844. Box 3, Folder 4, Sappington-Marmaduke Papers, MHS.

16. "I have been in my regular round of business": Tymony to Marmaduke, October 27, 1844. Box 3, Folder 5, Sappington-Marmaduke Papers, MHS.

17. "found your books, got waggons to convey them to Holy Springs": Tymony to Marmaduke, March 12, 1845. Box 3, Folder 6, Sappington-Marmaduke Papers, MHS. The book was opposed by some members of the company who believed divulging the formula would harm their interests. Publishing it was "a move not supported by the younger men of his family. Sappington challenged readers to 'make your own' according to the formula." Morrow, *Dr. John Sappington, Southern Patriarch in the New West*, 55.

18. "thank God after the narrow escape for life by the burning of the Central House [hotel] of Memphis": Tymony to Marmaduke, April 17, 1845. Box 3, Folder 5, Sappington-Marmaduke Papers, MHS. Life as a traveling salesman was not as glamorous for Tymony after his marriage to Caroline Elizabeth Prewitt in Howard County a few weeks before he left for Memphis, and he was anxious to return to Missouri.

19. "fifty pounds of quinine, with the other ingredients": Memo of an agreement made and entered into, November 13, 1845. Box 3, Folder 6, Sappington-Marmaduke Papers, MHS. The Marmaduke and Bicknell partnership agreement was drafted by Marmaduke using quasi-legal phraseology similar to that found in agreements he had written 20 years earlier for the Santa Fe trade. In the agreement, Bicknell is listed as a resident of Saline County; however, a search of U.S. Census records for 1840 through 1850 failed to identify him.

20. George Bicknell appeared to be an ideal manager for Meredith's pill business: Little is known about him. He perhaps was from Texas. A William Bicknell was selling pills in Texas in 1840 and owed Dr. Sappington money. His September 12, 1840, letter explaining why he can't pay his debt is in Folder 12, Marmaduke Papers C1021, SHSMO. The Sappington-Marmaduke collection held by the Missouri Historical Society contains a letter to Marmaduke from H. L. Williams of Lamar County, Texas, who reports that he has "kept up a diligent inquiry as regards the situation of Bicknell's property. All tell me that there is no doubt of it being in some embarrassment and that B. has transferred all to his son. Some are of the opinion that the money could be made by indemnifying the Sheriff." Williams to Marmaduke, February 26, 1841. Box 3, Folder 1, Sappington-Marmaduke Papers, MHS. In 1855, Marmaduke obtained a judgment in Red River County, Texas, against "Col. T. J. Shannon for the recovery of your land bought of William Bicknell." On appeal, the judgment was upheld by the Texas Supreme Court. Morrils & Dickson to Marmaduke, April 18, 1855. Box 5, Folder 5, Sappington-Marmaduke Papers, MHS.

21. "to the extent that it has been [because] other preparations have got the public fast by the coat button": Bicknell reported his early activities and presented his thoughts in a series of letters to Marmaduke written February 3, March 8, and April 5, 1846. Box 4, Folder 1. Sappington-Marmaduke Papers, MHS. Even before the formula for Dr. Sappington's Anti-Fever Pills was published in Dr. Sappington's book, many druggists sold similar pills, some of which were genuine medicine containing quinine, while others were counterfeit copies carrying the doctor's name. A case of the latter arose in Jefferson City, Missouri, in 1840 when a Dr. Mansur was reported to have "boiled white walnut bark in his house that he made the pills with," intending to sell his product as Dr. Sappington's pills. Handbills advertising the counterfeit medicine were seen on the druggists' counter and reported to Meredith. L.S. Eddins to Marmaduke, November 21, 1840. Box 2, Folder 6, Sappington-Marmaduke Papers, MHS.

22. "not that Sappington's Pills might be sold, but to prevent their sale": Bicknell to Marmaduke, February 3, 1846. Box 4, Folder 1, Sappington-Marmaduke Papers, MHS.

23. "6 or ten thousand boxes of Gottlieb Feuchtwhanger's German Cathartic Pills." Bicknell to Marmaduke, April 5, 1846. Box 4, Folder 1, Sappington-Marmaduke Papers, MHS. Bicknell's lively imagination is seen in his fictitious Gottlieb Feuchtwhanger, a name drawn from a private token coin, the Feuchtwanger Cent, widely circulated in the United States during the 1830s and '40s by Lewis Feuchtwanger, a German immigrant, mineralogist, and chemist, who practiced medicine and operated a pharmacy in New York.

24. "to make a few suggestions relative to the next Campaign": Bicknell to Marmaduke, May 19, 1846. Box 4, Folder 1, Sappington-Marmaduke Papers, MHS.

25. Ibid.

26. Ibid.

27. Bicknell's argument for posters was favorably received: Bicknell to Marmaduke, January 11, 1847; Price to Marmaduke January 30, 1847; Bicknell to Marmaduke, February 21, 1847: Box 4, Folder 2, Sappington-Marmaduke Papers, MHS.

28. "This country has been remarkably healthy the past year": Bicknell to Marmaduke, April 4, 1847. Box 4, Folder 2, Sappington-Marmaduke Papers, MHS.

29. "It has of late occurred to me that if the coming season in Mississippi be comparatively healthy": Bicknell to Marmaduke, April 25, 1847. Box 4, Folder 2, Sappington-Marmaduke Papers, MHS. Powdered tragacanth is a natural gum obtained from dried sap produced by several species of Middle Eastern legumes. Mixed with water, it makes a thick paste. Bicknell doesn't say who will carry the tin of paste and post the show cards. In the winter of 1847, Bicknell wrote to "Dr. Keucklehan of Boonville relative to his wormpowders" offering to distribute the medicine. Bicknell to Marmaduke, January 16, 1848. Box 4, Folder 4, Sappington-Marmaduke Papers, MHS.

30. "and unless Mississippi is extremely unhealthy they will not be needed in this country": Bicknell to Marmaduke, May 21, 1847. Box 4, Folder 2, Sappington-Marmaduke Papers, MHS. While in Louisiana, Bicknell reported finding 2,576 boxes of Sappington's and Dr. Price's pills (valued at $1,053) sent to Natchez and New Orleans had been damaged while aboard the steamboat *Champlain* from St. Louis. Upon his return to Missouri later that year, the St. Louis law firm of Todd & Krum was retained to sue the owners of the *Champlain*. The suit was eventually settled out of court for the actual cost of the medicine. Todd & Krum to Bicknell, January 21, 1848. Folder 17, Marmaduke Papers C1021, SHSMO; Marmaduke to Todd & Krum, July 9, 1848. Box 4, Folder 5, Sappington-Marmaduke Papers, MHS; Todd & Krum to Marmaduke, September 19, 1848. Folder 18, Marmaduke Papers C1021, SHSMO.

31. "Mobile, Charleston, & Tennessee. If you wish Gold or Silver or Missouri paper, immediately": Bicknell to Marmaduke, July 30, 1847. Box 4, Folder 4, Sappington-Marmaduke Papers, MHS.

32. "the sales have increased in the average": Bicknell to Marmaduke, January 16, 1848. Box 4, Folder 4, Sappington-Marmaduke Papers, MHS.

33. "I wrote to you upon the eve of my starting to Texas": Bicknell to Marmaduke, March 3, 1848. Ibid.

34. "so that Dr. Bradford may not be apprised of our doings in Texas": Ibid.

35. "fully equal to my expectations. There is little money in this country": Bicknell to Marmaduke, October 1, 1848. Box 4, Folder 5, Sappington-Marmaduke Papers, MHS. This appears to be the last letter between Bicknell and Marmaduke. Any others written in the period between March 3 and October 1, 1848, have not been discovered, their absence unusual in that it appears most of Bicknell's correspondence was retained by Marmaduke.

36. "I announce to you in this that the firm of Marmaduke and Bicknell is virtually dissolved": Bicknell to George M. Hogan, January 20, 1849. Box 4, Folder 6, Sappington-Marmaduke Papers, MHS. Undated statements listing medicinal items, Marmaduke and Bicknell to Geo. M. Hogan, Folder 1, Marmaduke Papers C1021. SHSMO.

37. "Mr. Bicknell's rascality has been very well concealed in many places": John P. Jackson to Marmaduke, February 9, 1850. Folder 18, Marmaduke Papers C1021, SHSMO.

38. "there was none there and as Mr. Gregory scarcely ever changed any": Tymony to Marmaduke, March 1, 1854. Box 5, Folder 4, Sappington-Marmaduke Papers, MHS. Meredith was preceded in exiting the pill business by Dr. Price, who dissolved his manufacturing operation in 1851, having on-hand more than 24,000 boxes of pills. Statement of number of boxes of pills in possession of the late firm of Wm. Price & Co., May 7, 1851. Folder 1, Sappington Family Papers C2889, SHSMO.

39. "was not qualified to do my business as it ought to have been done": Marmaduke to Tymony, April 11, 1854. Box 5, Folder 4, Sappington-Marmaduke Papers, MHS.

40. "perfectly willing for you to do as you think best in the matter.": Ibid.

CHAPTER 14

AN ELUSIVE EMPIRE

The first Marmaduke to settle in Virginia (Richard, in 1637) was one of thousands of English colonists who undertook the difficult and dangerous crossing of the Atlantic Ocean hoping to get a share of the abundant free (or nearly so) land that awaited them on the American continent. These early arrivals had little understanding of the breadth and depth of the land that lay beyond the forest rimming Chesapeake Bay. Indeed, they had no need to look past the trees. Once ownership had been settled (willingly or forcefully) with the native tribes who already lived there, the fertile land of Virginia sustained their needs. As farmers, merchants, tradesmen, and family builders, Virginia's colonists established a plantation system of agriculture that flourished for the next 150 years, enriching them and their descendants. By the end of the American Revolution, however, much of the former colony's soil was worn out from a repetitive cycle of tobacco and corn cultivation, and the state's populace had outgrown the land's ability to accommodate its expansive nature. To resolve this, Virginia's native sons looked westward, finding new land across the Appalachian Mountains in Kentucky, Tennessee, and beyond.

By the early 1820s a great flood of land seekers, following the rivers of the heartland, were in Indiana and Illinois, and spreading north and south along the Mississippi River and west into Missouri. Always, their goal was the land and the resources it held that could be exploited. The planters wanted the soil of the bottomlands and open prairies for the crops they could grow in it. Others sought the rock, coal, salt, lead, iron, and other minerals trapped within the dirt (or below it), while some figured to prosper from the water in the thousands of rivers and small creeks that drained the land. Such resources, when properly developed, could make a man rich, but he had to have a good title to the land, one that would prove his ownership in any future contest.

In deciding to go west in 1823, Meredith Marmaduke acted no differently than had his colonial ancestors who settled on Virginia's Northern Neck. He wanted land and viewed it as a way to increase his wealth through long-term ownership, by exploiting its resources, and as an asset to be sold when its value increased. Missouri's plentiful federal lands were his primary target, and he had no problem with buying cheap and selling high. In 1829, Meredith wrote to Missouri lawyer Edward Bates, then serving in the U.S. House of Representatives, to inquire about an issue in which he had an interest. Legislation to establish "graduation" — reducing the cost of public land that did not sell at the minimum price, so it was more affordable — had languished in

Washington for several years, and Meredith sought Bates' opinion about the status of a graduation bill now pending consideration. Meredith's friend and political ally Senator Thomas Hart Benton favored graduation as a means to promote migration to the West, thereby spreading Jacksonian Democracy and the concept of manifest destiny. Bates, a Whig, saw a problem with graduation as it was presented to the Congress, telling Meredith he "never heard an objection to the graduation of the price of lands, according to their real quality factual value." His concern was how to assure that the land went to people who would actually live on it. "I will go as far as any man in providing homes for the needy. I would give a tract of land to all such as would improve the country by actually inhabiting ... the gift. But I would neither give nor sell at a normal price to speculators, and all are speculators who buy for any purpose but actual use."[1]

Measuring America

Prior to 1785, surveyors in colonial America relied upon natural, geographical, and cultural features to locate and define the boundaries of a tract of land. Called a survey by metes and bounds, this method presented difficulties in the later identification of a specific parcel of land because the descriptive features frequently changed or disappeared. The description of a farm in the Virginia Military District of Ohio illustrates the problems inherent in a metes and bounds survey: "Located on the waters of Brush Creek ... Beginning at a Stone in the line of Levi Broadstones thence with the line of William Mooney Sen. south 81 degrees East 125 poles to a stone corner to William Mooney Sen. and in the line of Henry Heock thence with his line south 9 degrees west 77 poles to a gum tree corner to said Henry Heock and in the line of James Forsythe & Findley Lyle thence with the line of said James Forsyth & Lyle north 81 degrees 125 poles to a white oak tree in said Lyle's line and corner to Levi Broadstone thence with Broadstone's line north 9 degrees to the beginning. ..."[2]

If a gum tree was struck by lightning and split in two, an oak was cut for firewood, a stone slid downhill, or a neighboring landowner died and his heirs sold the property, the accuracy of a metes and bounds survey was in peril. With such fluid boundaries and descriptions, disputes and litigation were common. Faced with the challenge of satisfying the seemingly insatiable appetite of westward traveling Americans for land, the federal government had to find a better way to identify the land it wanted to sell them.

In the fall of 1785, Thomas Hutchins, the first geographer of the United States, set a stone marker into the ground on the west bank of the Ohio River, near the present city of East Liverpool, Ohio, and established "The Point of Beginning" for a new system of surveying land. Early that year, the U.S. Congress had decided to sell some of the nation's public lands in order to generate income for the national treasury. It was apparent to the lawmakers that the metes and bounds system, with its hodgepodge of shapes, changeable markers, and attendant problems, was not adequate to survey the public domain. Influenced by the thinking of Thomas Jefferson, George Washington, and others, Congress adopted a new, more precise and sustainable method of measuring America — the Public Lands Survey System. Hutchins' task was not easy. The terrain along the Ohio River was rugged, difficult to survey, and the report of a nearby Indian attack ended his initial attempt to establish a base line leading west from The Point of Beginning. In coming years he would continue his work with help from other surveyors; however The Seven Ranges of Townships, as this survey came to be called, would not be finished until 1806, some 17 years after the nation's first geographer had died.

Thomas Hutchins probably had no idea of the role his survey would play in the growth of the United States in coming years, but the influence of his work is significant. His survey is the model on which future surveys of the nation's public land are based. And with the wilderness properly measured, the government could sell land with assurance that its title was defensible. As America's populace moved west, government surveyors were out ahead establishing townships similar to those surveyed by Hutchins.

The Public Lands Survey System would eventually encompass almost 1.5 billion acres, and with some modifications is still in use today. It is founded on a grid of 36-mile-square townships surveyed from a principal meridian line (north-south) and a baseline (east-west) that intersect at an arbitrary point of beginning. The First Principal Meridian, which forms the border between Ohio and Indiana, approximates a line of longitude as measured from Greenwich, England. In November 1815, a team of government surveyors crossed the Mississippi River to establish the beginning point for the Fifth Principal Meridian in a swamp in northeast Arkansas. The site is memorialized today by a stone marker at the end of a boardwalk in the Louisiana Purchase State Park, and it is from here that land in Arkansas, Missouri, Iowa, Minnesota, and much of the Dakotas was laid out in townships. The survey crew establishing the Fifth Principal Meridian finished their task two months and 317 miles later at a point on the Missouri River in Franklin County. The Fifth Principal Meridian is the benchmark from which subsequent surveys in Missouri were made. In 1816, contract surveyors began laying out townships east and west of the meridian, setting corner stones every six miles to form a grid of square boxes. Each square mile within a township was staked and numbered (1–36) and termed a "section," each about 640 acres in size. Sections could be further subdivided into halves and quarters, a quarter-section being the standard 160-acre plot sold in Missouri by federal land offices. Land unsold after being offered at auction could be bought in a lesser amount.[3]

In July 1817, William Rector, surveyor general for the territories of Illinois, Missouri, and Arkansas, reported nearly 6 million acres of public land in eastern and central Missouri surveyed and ready to be sold. A federal land office was already located in St. Louis. Two others, at Franklin and Jackson, opened in 1818. Eventually, 14 such offices would open in the state as the survey expanded. A horde of land seekers (Missouri's population grew from 7,000 to 20,000 in the first two decades of the century) awaited the opening of the offices. "Come one, Come all, we have millions of acres to occupy," promised the editor of a St. Louis newspaper in 1816.[4] The terms of sale had been set by Congress in 1804. Tracts could be purchased at public auction in minimum lots of 160 acres. Land not selling when first offered could be bought by private entry. Offering extended credit proved unworkable, and in 1820, full cash payment was required on the day of purchase. Now, too, land not sold at public auction could be privately entered in any amount above 80 acres, at $1.25 an acre. In coming years,

Meredith Marmaduke would do a great deal of business with land offices in Franklin, Fayette, and Springfield as he expanded his holdings across the state.

The Lure of Speculation

Meredith's purchase of 160 acres in western Chariton County in 1819, four years before he set out for the Booneslick country, could be viewed, in one sense, as a trial balloon, a personal test of his willingness to leave Virginia for an uncertain future. But it also could be seen as a speculative investment that was most likely sold after he arrived at Franklin, the money helping to finance his Santa Fe expeditions. Chariton County, as was most all of Missouri in the early 1800s, was ripe for speculation. (The Missouri State Archives in Jefferson City holds among its documents a nonresident filing of ownership for 2,500 acres in Chariton County by Henry Clay, Kentucky's formidable politician and a future presidential candidate.) In later years, Meredith speculated with another Chariton County tract, a quarter-section where the city of Salisbury now stands. In 1856, Lucius Salisbury approached him, asking if Meredith would sell the 160 acres of land for $500.[5]

Like many others who came to Missouri during the first half of the 19th century, the siren call of speculative land investment was too inviting for Meredith to overlook. Property in the right place, bought at the right price, was guaranteed to turn a tidy profit when sold, given the state's population doubled (or better) each decade from 1820 to 1860, rising during that time from 66,586 residents to nearly 1.2 million. New towns rose from bare ground in every county, some becoming significant trading centers in a short time as the surrounding land was taken up and put under cultivation.

The birth of Arrow Rock gave Meredith his first opportunity to invest in a developing town. He did so with the encouragement of his father-in-law, Dr. Sappington. In late May 1829 the doctor, Joseph and Benjamin Huston, the Reverend Peyton Nowlin, Joseph Patterson, and a handful of other Saline County residents whose homes and farms were in the eastern part of the county, gathered at the Arrow Rock ferry landing to talk about building a town on the hill that gave rise to the site's name. They believed the town, attracting commercial interests and trade with Boone's Lick Road travelers who joined the Santa Fe Trail at the Missouri River, would "tend to the mutual advantage" of themselves and the county in general. Enthusiasm for the venture was high, and when the group adjourned later that day 50 acres had been donated for the new town by two families who held title to the land.

As the surveyor for Saline County (appointed in 1827), Meredith was called upon to lay out the nascent village to be called Philadelphia, symbolic of the wealth in the East that was financing Booneslick merchants and the expansion of the West. (Philadelphia — sometimes called New Philadelphia — was renamed Arrow Rock in 1833).[6] Setting up his equipment, Meredith platted the town in square blocks, each 1 acre in size, subdivided into quarter-acre lots. These were auctioned July 24, 1829, with proceeds to be used for town improvements. With money gained from recent trading at Santa Fe, Meredith and Lavinia bought one of the lots as an investment and held it until 1853 when they sold it to the town's Baptist Church, whose members had been a brush-arbor congregation for a number of years, meeting in the open.

Betting on a New Town

Ten years after buying a lot at Arrow Rock, another new town drew Meredith's interest. In 1838, the Saline County Court (with Meredith as one of its members) petitioned the state legislature for permission to establish a new county seat. The village of Jonesboro had held that distinction for the past seven years, but throughout this time the room provided for sessions of the circuit court — the upper floor of a log building whose lower rooms housed a grocery store and a stable — left something to be desired. In his upstairs courtroom, Judge William Scott worried over the thought of sending members of a jury downstairs to the horse barn to deliberate after hearing a trial. It was his opinion that the smell of manure and the agony of biting flies did not contribute to making good decisions. By the fall of 1838, he was "exceedingly anxious that the court should be removed to some place by next term."[7]

Another reason to relocate the county seat was the fact that its present location did not comply with state law, which required that the seat of government be placed at the center of the county. This issue had been raised back in August of 1829 when Meredith was asked by the county court to "meet the commissioners at 12 o'clock at Harrises Lick (with your instruments)," to aid in finding the center of the county so a new county seat could be established.[8] The hamlet of Jefferson, in the Missouri River bottoms, was the county seat at that time. The commissioners failed to understand that it would take Meredith more than one day to locate the center of the county, an omission that may partially explain why the county seat was instead moved to Jonesboro two years later.

In mid-December 1838, Saline County Court Presiding Judge W. A. Wilson related to Meredith a discussion he had the previous week "with our Representatives [in Jefferson City] in regard to our County Seat matter."[9] Wilson reported that Dr. George Penn, Saline County's state senator, and Thomas B. Harvey, the county's state representative, were unsure about the steps they should take to obtain the required approval of the General Assembly. They concluded that the county's residents should first vote to select a temporary county seat, so the circuit court could be moved before its next session. Penn and Harvey would then introduce bills to support the county's petition. As it worked out, the General Assembly granted the petition in February 1839, although it would be the following August before voters selected Arrow Rock as their interim county seat. The legislation also established a commission comprised of five men from counties near Saline who were charged with selecting a site for the new town, yet to be named Marshall.

Meeting in a Saline County home on April 11, 1839, the site-selection commission, aided by a map obtained from the Fayette land office, determined that the center of section 10, township 50, range 21, was the center of the county. After some deliberation, the commissioners concluded that this site was not a suitable place for the county seat. In a later report to the county court, they did not explain the reason for their decision, but it was probably because it would have been too difficult and too expensive to obtain the land. Every square foot of soil in section 10 had recently been bought up and was owned by one of seven individuals. Two men owned 40-acre tracts, two owned 160 acres each, and the remaining three owned 80 acres apiece. Four different men owned the land that encircled the center of section 10. It was obvious to the commission that in the five months since the county court had decided to move the seat of government, speculators had pin-pointed the center of Saline County, and had hurried to buy up all of the land it contained, as well as land in surrounding sections. With section 10 eliminated from their inquiry, the commission "proceeded to examine the lands generally around the center of section ten ... and found ... the most suitable place nearest the said center of section ten to be upon the lands of Jeremiah Odell" in section 15, immediately south of section 10. Odell must have been waiting in a rocking chair on the porch while the commission was meeting for "being satisfied that Odell's title was good" its members struck a deal with him that day to locate the new county seat on 65 acres that he generously donated to the cause. (Donating land for a county seat was not unusual in Missouri, especially when the donor had other property nearby. Odell still owned 15 acres adjoining the land he gave away, and another 80 acres in the adjoining section 11.)[10] Two days after ending their meeting, on April 13, the site commission presented its decision to Circuit Judge William Scott. The Saline County Court received the deed to the site three months later, and today the courthouse square and surrounding city blocks stand on the Odell property.

Although a patent for the 80 acres from which the donated land was carved was not issued by the General Land Office in Washington City until January 1840, Odell supported his ownership with a receipt from the Fayette land office for a certificate binding the land to him while his application for a patent was being approved. The General Land Office was often so far behind in its work that it was not unusual for an interval of six months to three years to pass following their receipt of land-entry papers before a patent was issued. When a request for a cash-entry patent was received at a district land office, a certificate was prepared and forwarded to the General Land Office in the U.S. Treasury. There the over-burdened clerks reviewed the application for accuracy, availability of the land, and suitable payment. Applications were often returned to the issuing land office for corrections. When the review was completed a patent was issued and sent to the office of the President for his signature. In 1948 this duty was delegated to the Secretary of the Interior.

Of particular interest to the speculators betting on land in the center of Saline County were nine sections (10–15, and 21–23) that might be considered by the site commission. During late 1838 and early 1839, five of these square-mile sections, in which no patents had previously been issued, were quickly bought and applications were filed for most of the land in the other four. Meredith's position on the county court, coupled with his intention to campaign for the lieutenant governor's office in 1840, forced him to be cautious in his dealings with regard to acquiring land at the site of the new county seat. Once the location was determined, however, he could entertain a speculative venture there without being accused of improper behavior. Meredith waited for three weeks after the commission's report to the circuit court before he visited the Fayette land office. There he applied for patents on 1,000 acres of land, 240 of which he bought for himself and 760 acres purchased in partnership with his brother-in-law Claiborne Jackson.[11] This included all the land in section 22, 120 acres in section 15, another 80 in section 21, and 160 acres in section 23. Meredith later bought additional land for himself in sections 11 and 21.

The surrounding land in Marshall also attracted Meredith's attention, and on

September 23, 1839 — the first day town lots were sold — he purchased at auction Lot 3 in Block 9, a corner parcel on the north side of the courthouse square. He paid $185 for the lot, the most money any of the 100 lots sold that day brought, giving Cornelius Davis, who managed the sales process for the county court, half in cash and a note for the remainder.[12]

If Meredith and Jackson were betting on Marshall rapidly growing to encompass their land in the near future, increasing its value as pressure for acreage to develop took hold, disappointment was their reward. The town was slow to grow, and in the mid-1860s its population was less than 300. Despite an influx of settlers after the Civil War, 30 years after its founding Marshall housed only 924 people. As late as 1876, the land in section 22 that Meredith and Jackson had bought 36 years earlier was still a half mile from the town's southern edge. Why they selected this particular section for investment is not clear. It offered no significant inducement other than as property suitable for development as the town expanded, yet it was far enough away from the courthouse square, around which the town grew, that it would take years for that to happen. The Santa Fe Trail was north of Marshall, so Meredith could not have viewed the land as commercial property along a major roadway. And there was plenty of land suitable for cultivation closer to home, where he had slaves available for labor, if that was his intention. As Marshall and the surrounding area failed to develop into the larger town imagined, the coming years saw Meredith and Jackson divide the land into small tracts and sell. As late as 1852, however, Meredith still held title to 480 acres in sections 11, 20, and 22. By the time of his death 12 years later, this too had all been sold. As speculators, doing what Edward Bates had found so distasteful, Meredith and Claiborne Jackson had to accept a long-term return from their investment in the Marshall land. Today all of section 22 is fully developed, primarily residential, and contains churches of the Presbyterian, Catholic, Lutheran, and Baptist faiths, as well as part of the campus of Missouri Valley College, a four-year liberal arts school affiliated with the Presbyterian Church. The belief that Marshall would grow to encompass his land may not have been realized in Meredith's lifetime, but it's unlikely that he lost money by investing in the center of the county. He would soon do it again.

A New Opportunity

In June of 1839 Augustus Stevenson, Meredith's agent in the sale of Dr. Sappington's Anti-Fever Pills, then in Arkansas, received a letter from Meredith directing him to "collect all money you can in Fayetteville in metal. Then go to Springfield, Missouri, and deposit all with Joel H. Hayden … . it will not be out of your way."[13] Joel Hayden was the registrar for patent applications at the federal land office in Springfield, a friend of Meredith's and a fellow Democrat whom he trusted. Augustus Stevenson had been sent south some time previously to collect money owed by sellers of Dr. Sappington's Anti-Fever Pills and was on his way home when he received Meredith's letter. Hayden would hold the $2,390 Stevenson delivered to him until September 15, 1839, when Meredith's agent, C. Jones, delivered an additional $1,698.20. Hayden then applied all the money he had received to the purchase of 3,800 acres of federal land in St. Clair County, Missouri. Additional expenses amounting to $229.55 resulted in Meredith determining that the "amot. to be charged on acct. land speculation" for the St. Clair acreage came to $4,317.55.[14]

Thus began the most ambitious speculation scheme that Meredith would initiate in his lifetime. On land he owned, he envisioned creating a new county seat town with a store from which staples and general merchandise would be distributed throughout southwestern Missouri. The presence of dense forests on some of the parcels he bought indicates an interest in producing lumber for shipment by steamboat to St. Louis and beyond. And his purchase of open fields near the two principal towns in the county shows an intention to raise livestock — and perhaps other farm produce — for local and distant consumption. As he did with the land he and Claiborne Jackson had acquired at Marshall, he again involved family members, keeping faith with his father-in-law's belief that money earned from the collective business ventures of the extended family should stay in the family. In this investment, Meredith brought on board Claiborne Jackson and both Sappington brothers, Darwin and William. Different this time was that they were silent partners. The entire 4,000 acres (termed the "western lands") would be patented in Meredith's name only. Records do not inform us of why they did it this way. It's possible that, to facilitate their overall scheme, they wanted less exposure of Jackson and the Sappingtons, whose wealth and position were known around the state.

Meredith's interest in St. Clair County, through which runs the Osage River, surfaced at the same time as steamboats were becoming an important element of commerce in Missouri. By 1839, improvements in design and machinery made it possible for packets carrying 300 tons of freight to make regular runs on the major western rivers. At the close of the decade, 39 steamboats were operating on the lower Missouri, off-loading their cargo at Jefferson City, Boonville, Arrow Rock, and other river towns, where it was transferred to the interior regions of the state in freight wagons. Operating on the Osage River was risky for steamboats. An 1840 survey found 98 shoals in the river from its mouth to Osceola, 25 of them in the stretch of river between Warsaw and Osceola. One of the worst shoals was the Gravois Bar, at the mouth of Gravois Creek in Morgan County. During the annual spring rise there would be as much as five feet of water over the Gravois Bar, and steamboats could pass upstream without trouble. But during the low water of summer, boats that ran aground there had to wait for the next rise of the river to continue. The first steamboat to venture into the Osage, the *North St. Louis*, in July 1837, went only 30 miles before being stranded when the river level dropped. But that voyage was enough to encourage others to try. In the spring of 1838, the steamboat *Adventurer* went 160 miles to the town then known as Osage (later named Warsaw) before returning to St. Louis. The *Osage Packet* became a regular traveler on the river in 1840, and the following year the steamer *Leander* carried 200 tons of freight to Warsaw. An example of the transfer of goods from large to small steamboats for transport up the Osage River is seen in the *Maid of Osage*, built in 1840 expressly for Osage River navigation, and the *James H. Lucas*, a Missouri River packet that made regular runs from St. Louis. Both were owned by Captain Nansen Bennett who operated out of Cote Sans Dessein in Callaway County, nearly opposite the mouth of the Osage River. A few miles upstream, steamboats with freight consigned to merchants at Jefferson City discharged their cargo on a wharf at the foot of Jefferson Street now known as Lohman's Landing. Traffic on the Osage River increased in coming years with as few as two and as many as 16 steamboats in a season making regular stops to discharge and pick-up freight at Lisletown, Tuscumbia, Linn Creek, Warsaw, Osceola, Taberville, and Papinville in Bates County.[15]

Hoping to enhance the state's streams for navigation, Missouri's legislature established a Board of Internal Improvements in 1839, only to abolish it in 1841. As a candidate in 1840 for lieutenant governor, Meredith spoke in favor of spending money to improve navigation on "tributary streams ... which penetrate far into the interior of the State."[16] Certainly he had the Osage River in mind at this time, owning land upstream in St. Clair County. During his four years in office, he kept the subject of internal improvements active; however, it was not until 1847 that legislators again addressed the Osage River. This time, they incorporated a company known as the Osage River Association to begin improvements on that stream. (No document has been found to show Meredith's hand in this, but perhaps it was there.) Inadequate funding left little money to correct the problems until 1855, at which time the General Assembly appropriated $50,000 for dredging, removal of snags, and other work, going as far upriver as Osceola in St. Clair County.

A Growing Populace

Settlement patterns in the early 1800s show that newly arrived Missourians favored living along and near the Missouri and Mississippi Rivers. Few roads existed then to provide access to interior areas; that began to change, though, as the state's population increased, rising from 140,455 in 1830 to 383,702 in 1840. Another 300,000 settlers would swell Missouri's population to nearly 700,000 by 1850. St. Clair County's population would double during this same period and triple by 1860. By 1830, interior counties were starting to lay out roads to attract new arrivals in the state. Local road districts were organized in eastern St. Clair County by 1837. During this time, the southwest corner of Missouri became accessible by two roads, the "Springfield Road" from St. Louis to that town and a route that linked Boonville with Springfield. The latter road entered Benton County and passed through Cole Camp and Warsaw, where as many as 100 wagons a week crossed the Osage River and went on to Bolivar and Springfield. At Warsaw, a road west across the prairie crossed a corner of Henry County to enter St. Clair County and continued west to eventually intersect a road coming from Clinton. That road went south "crossing the Osage River at Crow & Crutchfield's store [in Osceola], to the county line of Polk County, in the direction of Bolivar." Meredith may have traveled this route from Warsaw in 1839 to locate the St. Clair County land he intended to buy, or he may have found his way to a trail that linked Warsaw to a road "from Crow & Crutchfield's store ... to the Benton County line, in the direction of [Warsaw]," (roughly today's state Route 82).[17] This latter route would have taken him through the township where a C. Jones then lived, who may be the person Meredith sent to Springfield with instructions about which parcels of land to purchase.

Prior to the 1830s, St. Clair County was sparsely settled. Tradition credits Jacob Coonce, a frontiersman who is reported to have first visited the region in 1827, with erecting the county's first cabin in 1831 on land near the Sac River (which enters the Osage west of Osceola). Born in St. Louis (or Pennsylvania) in 1803, Coonce, who "ranged from Gasconade" to the Sac River as he hunted and trapped, found the uninhabited western region of Missouri well supplied with the wild animals that provided his livelihood.[18]

Arriving on the upper Osage soon after Jacob Coonce were several brothers of the Waldo family, lately from Gasconade County, Missouri. Originally from western Pennsylvania they had migrated to Missouri 20 years earlier and settled on the lower Gasconade River where they farmed, operated a saw and grist mill, and became active in county government. A younger brother, David, arrived in Missouri in 1820 to join his siblings in Gasconade County where he served as sheriff, assessor, clerk of the circuit court, and treasurer, all before he was 23 years old. Not satisfied with being a county official, he left the Gasconade country for Lexington, Kentucky, in 1826 to study medicine. A year later, he was back in Missouri working as a doctor. In the summer of 1828, he joined a caravan going to Santa Fe and changed his life forever. Arriving at Taos in July, he met traders Ceran St. Vrain and Richard Campbell who were planning a trading expedition into the northern Mexican states of Chihuahua and Sonora and wanted Waldo to join them. It's not clear if he brought trade goods from Missouri. Historian David Lavender believed he did, saying, "Waldo was loaded with goods" when he met St. Vrain and Campbell.[19] He also may have obtained his merchandise from other traders then in Santa Fe, Meredith being one of them. He had arrived in Nuevo Mexico's capital city only a week or so before Waldo came to Santa Fe seeking permission to trade. Certainly the two men would have run into each other in the small village as Waldo sought out the more experienced traders to help him deal with the Spanish bureaucracy. This is the year Meredith sold his trading stock quickly, probably at wholesale prices. Although in coming years Meredith preferred to outfit other traders going to Santa Fe, David Waldo persisted in the Mexican trade, going so far as to become a citizen of Mexico in order to ease his business operations there. He eventually settled at Kansas City where he built a financial empire founded on freighting and merchandising. He also speculated in land, had numerous farms he operated and rented to others, and became a banker. At his death in 1878, he was said to be one of the wealthiest men in Jackson County.[20]

Other hopeful settlers, many from Virginia, the Carolinas, Tennessee, and Kentucky, flocked to St. Clair County in the 1830s. Drawn by the land and the prospect of bettering their lives, they tended to group together, forming neighborhoods that were supported by local tradesmen. The Gash brothers, Ebenezer and William, came from North Carolina to settle on Coon Creek six miles west of the Sac River in 1833. Within a year, five other families had joined them there. Opposite the mouth of Coon Creek, on the north bank of the Osage River, a store and blacksmith shop sprang up in a hamlet called Roscoe to serve these nearby settlers. Patrick Shields owned the store and in addition to hardware, cloth, and staple goods, he sold "pork, cows and calves … and three and four-year-old steers. … The merchants hauled their goods from Boonville." David Huffman began operating a ferry at Roscoe in 1839, charging 25 cents for a man and horse to cross, 12½ cents if you were walking, or 50 cents for a two-horse wagon.[21]

Today, the few houses that comprise the town of Roscoe are scattered among trees on the south side of the river since the village moved to higher ground after the Civil

War. Today's Roscoe sits in the heart of Meredith's hoped-for empire in southwest Missouri. Nearly half of the 1839 "western lands" purchase — 1,520 acres, the Roscoe acreage — lies in a two-mile-long strip along the Osage River that begins seven miles west of Osceola and ends at Coon Creek. The channel of the Osage runs tight against a series of low bluffs on the south bank of the river for the entire length of the Roscoe acreage. The bluffs are clothed today (as they were in 1839) with an oak-hickory forest that extends a half mile inland before open ground is seen, while the north bank of the river is bottomland subject to overflow during high water. If the man-made structures on the Roscoe acreage were to be removed, the area would look familiar to Meredith although the trees on both sides of the river in 1839 would have constituted old-growth forest.

In addition to the Roscoe acreage, Meredith bought 880 open-prairie acres on a plateau a mile southeast of the town's present site. Part of that purchase included two carefully chosen tracts that added nearly a half mile of spring-fed creek with trees along its course, ideal for watering livestock and providing shade during summer. He also bought 240 prairie acres a mile southeast of the village of Osceola that had a small, spring-fed stream on one side of the tract. Although nothing has been found (if it ever existed) that can definitively tell us Meredith's plans for his St. Clair County lands, there can be little doubt that he intended to use the two prairie sites as pasture on which to marshal cattle for sale locally, shipped downriver to St. Louis, or driven to Springfield and elsewhere in the Southwest.

Along with the Roscoe acreage and the two prairie sites, the western lands purchase included six forested tracts in the eastern part of the county that ranged in size from 120 to 400 acres. Examination shows that none of these were suitable for cultivation (although the mast produced by the trees could be used as forage for swine). Meredith's interest in the land was probably the value of its trees as lumber. One tract fronted on the Osage River, another was on the Sac River, while the remainder were within a mile of the Osage, making them all accessible to the river for rafting timber. Whether he intended to build a sawmill is unknown. There was one on the lower Sac River at this time, and others were soon at work in the county making dimension lumber, barrel staves, and other wood products for local consumption and shipment down the river. Lumber was a major commodity produced in counties bordering the Osage River. Before the Civil War "the bulk of downstream traffic [included] pork ... lumber, staves ..." St. Clair County in 1850 had two water-powered sawmills employing eight people. Their combined inventory at the time of a census taken that year was 800 "stacks" of milled lumber valued at $1,800. After the war, an 1870s Jefferson City newspaper reported that in one month a local warehouse shipped a carload of lumber that had come down the Osage River.[22]

The Best Investment a Man Could Make

Livestock production and logging formed part of Meredith's plan for the western lands, but he had additional projects in mind when he invested in St. Clair County. Evidence for this is disclosed in several letters written by Darwin Sappington, the first penned in late December 1839. In it, he reveals that he and Meredith intended to open a mercantile store. Meredith's participation in the Jonesboro store ended in 1834 partly because the head of the Santa Fe Trail had moved up the Missouri River and the endless stream of wagon trains each spring — many of which bought their stock of goods at Jonesboro — no longer passed through Saline County. The number of people traversing Saline County also decreased as more affluent travelers booked passage on steamboats to Independence and beyond. What had been a lucrative business for the two partners had become less profitable, and it made sense for Meredith to withdraw. Now, in 1839, a new wave of "wagons" was on the horizon as western Missouri's population was poised to double and triple in coming years. Operating a general merchandise store on the upper Osage River looked promising when the partners agreed to invest in the western lands. However, by December 1839 Darwin had cooled to the idea. Writing from his home in Russellville, Kentucky, he told Meredith he was of the opinion "our mutual interest would be promoted by postponing for the next 12 months the mercantile house on Osage we had contemplated when I left Mo." He blamed his feeling on "the moneyed affairs of this government [which are] tremendously deranged at this time." Darwin's reluctance to open a store reflected the general mood of the country as a result of the 1837 panic, an economic depression that had spread across the nation that year and was still in place, a time when profits, wages, and crop and land values declined. But Darwin was not pessimistic about the western lands venture. His next thoughts reveal another aspect of the partners' plans.

"Our western lands ... must ultimately prove to be the best investment a man could make of his spare cash." Predicting a profit of "20 to 25 per cent from their sale," Darwin's optimism lay in "the tremendous tide of emigration to the west, or in other words to Mo, for the last six months say 50 or 60 thousand. And too look how the states Ohio Inda Ill are taxing their citizens on the score of internal improvements. it [sic] is time this state as yet has not taxed her citizens." He had "little doubt" but that if the legislature would call for such a tax the governor would approve it.[23] Internal improvements included, of course, aiding navigation on the Osage River as well as creating new roads and improving existing routes, all of which could only serve to enhance prospects for the rapid settlement of St. Clair County and the sale of the western lands.

Vote Early and Often
By legislative act on February 15, 1841, St. Clair County was severed from Rives County and became independent. (Rives County was renamed Henry County that same year.) Meredith probably influenced this action, given his interest in the region's future development. The legislature also appointed a commission of three St. Clair County residents to select a site for a new county seat. Almost immediately proponents for two competing sites, Osceola and Roscoe, began a "heated campaign" to win over the commissioners to their particular location. The village of Osceola was an obvious choice. With a handful of cabins and Crow and Crutchfield's store perched on the hill above the river, a ferry carrying traffic across on the Clinton to Bolivar road, plus the junction of roads leading to Warsaw and Roscoe, Osceola possessed the makings of a seat of government with one exception — it was not in the center of the county. Residents of the Roscoe neighborhood thought they could do better. Their village — also blessed with a store, a ferry, and a blacksmith, plus a settlement nearby on

Coon Creek — might lack the crossroad advantage Osceola had, but Roscoe was seven miles farther west, placing it nearer the center of the county. This hamlet also had one drawback: the flood-prone bottomland on the north side of the Osage wasn't the best place to build a courthouse. Correspondence between Darwin Sappington and Meredith supports a conclusion that when they acquired the western lands the partners had every intention of getting the county seat placed on property they owned south of the river at Roscoe. Four years after he bought the western lands, Meredith asked Darwin for his thoughts about selling some of it. Darwin believed it best to make arrangements to "let those Gentlemen ... have the land on some terms if it can be done. So as not to interfere with our previous seling [selling] to the County *as an inducement to get the County Seat on our land* [emphasis added] I presume we should have something for the lots."[24]

Meredith's effort to obtain the county seat on the Roscoe acreage got underway in January 1841 when he and Claiborne Jackson contemplated relocating to St. Clair County so they could oversee and influence the selection process, as well as promote their other interests. Meredith invited Darwin, still living in Kentucky, to join them. He responded with his thoughts, positive and otherwise: "You informed me in your last letter that Mr. Jackson and yourself expect to visit the Osage Country in the Spring and if pleased to move out there. It is butiful [sic] Country with a climate at times preferable to that of Saline and probably many other advantages. Notwithstanding, I cannot give my own consent to move to that Country under its present situation. No society but what you may take with you, nor can you have for several years. Saline I consider far enough out of the world."[25]

Accustomed to a level of comfort and social life in Kentucky not found in the hinterlands of Missouri, Darwin was not opposed to investing in St. Clair County land but he was not interested in moving there. And, as it turned out, neither were Meredith or Claiborne Jackson.

The Intermediary

As Missouri's lieutenant governor in 1841, Meredith was in a delicate position with regard to the commission appointed to select the site of St. Clair County's new seat of government. Any visible attempt by him to influence its members could have adverse political consequences in Jefferson City. Nor could Claiborne Jackson openly lobby the commissioners. As a member of Missouri's House of Representatives, he too faced political reaction if he was discovered trying to intervene in the selection process. Realizing this, Meredith had little choice but to secure an agent to vigorously argue for a site on the Roscoe acreage without disclosing the ownership of the land. To do this, he needed someone living in St. Clair County who commanded the attention and respect of its citizens. He found his man in the person of Jesse A. Applegate and promptly recruited him as the "front man" in organizing the campaign to place the county seat in Roscoe.

Born in Kentucky in 1811, Jesse Applegate was 10 years old when his family left there and moved to western Illinois, near St. Louis. Seemingly precocious, at some time during the 1820s he became acquainted with Missouri's first attorney general, the lawyer Edward Bates, in whose St. Louis office he briefly worked as a clerk. Bates "took a deep and personal interest" in the young man, the law office becoming "in a sense Jesse Applegate's high school, college and university" where he "laid the foundation" for his later life (although he never practiced law). Applegate also learned surveying during this period and by age 20 was employed in St. Louis as a deputy surveyor in the office of Missouri's surveyor general.[26] Sent into the field in 1832, he moved with his new wife to St. Clair County "and surveyed a good part of this country ... finishing in 1838."[27] His survey work completed, Applegate remained in St. Clair County, settling on land alongside Coon Creek. He turned to agriculture and the raising of livestock, was elected a justice of the peace, and became a respected member of the Roscoe community. He also patented 1,640 acres of St. Clair County land, much of it along the Osage River, some of it adjoining Meredith's Roscoe acreage. (Having surveyed the county, Applegate would have been an invaluable aide in Meredith's selection of land to buy and this may have led to their later collaboration. Again, there is a connection in Meredith's life to Edward Bates.)

The intensity of Meredith's desire to secure the county seat is apparent in his actions to assure that it would be on the Roscoe acreage. The particular tract he and Applegate eventually put forth for the site-selection commission's consideration was already owned by James Wilson. Wanting that land, early in 1841 Meredith sought out Wilson and bought all of the 480 acres he owned in the section. (Meredith already owned the remaining 160 acres. To keep his involvement secret, Meredith delayed recording the purchase of Wilson's acreage until the following year.) As a result of this purchase, Meredith controlled nearly four square miles of land in the heart of the Roscoe acreage without disclosing his involvement in the fight for the county seat. If the commission wanted it located in the center of St. Clair County, it would be on land Meredith owned.[28]

The opposition favoring Osceola was led by Phillip Crow, an owner of the Crow and Crutchfield grocery. History records that Applegate, "early in the contest ... made the discovery that a majority of the people were against him." By early May of 1841, the squabble had become so heated that the site-selection commission asked the county court to hold an election so residents could choose either Roscoe or Osceola. Election Day was set for early in August. As it approached, Applegate — with help from others favoring the Roscoe site — was accused of attempting to pack the voter list by going "to other points and importing a vast array of voters." In return, the Applegate forces claimed that the Crow faction "imported between thirty and forty hands to make brick for the new court house," but who truly were there "principally to vote" and had instructions to "Vote early and vote often."[29] The result of the election favored Osceola, offering little consolation to the Applegate contingent as it lost by either 17 or 7 votes, depending upon who did the counting. In a last ditch effort to change the outcome, the Applegate force filed a motion in circuit court to withhold naming Osceola as the county seat, claiming the site-selection commission lacked authority to do so. At the August 1841 session of the circuit court, their appeal was quickly overruled and the battle was over.

Or was it? Five months after the court's finding against the Roscoe enthusiasts, Meredith told Darwin Sappington, in a letter written the last day of January 1842, that their quest for the county seat was still alive. Darwin responded saying he was

An Elusive Empire

"gratified to learn that there is a probability of the center of St. Clair Coty getting the Coty Seat, and in order to carry out and consummate the propositions submitted by you to Jesse Applegate on this subject I hereby authorize you to act in this matter for me and as far as I am able to on the part of my Brother Wm. B. Sappington, also." Darwin also related that he had written Applegate to tell him Meredith had their power of attorney. He finished his letter to Meredith with the thought "that justice must and will ultimately prevail in this matter."[30] What prompted Meredith to conclude that he and Jesse Applegate were still engaged in the county seat fight in January 1842 is a mystery not unveiled in county records or history. Osceola has always been the seat of government for St. Clair County.

Jesse Applegate left St. Clair County in 1843, taking his family to Independence, where they joined a wagon train bound for Oregon organized by Peter H. Burnett. Following a division of the train into two sections on the Kansas River, Applegate was elected captain of the so-called "Cow Column" comprised of emigrants whose herds of cattle moved more slowly on the trail. He remained in Oregon for the rest of his life as a progressive farmer and businessman who achieved a degree of political fame, and helped frame the state's first constitution. In 1851, Meredith wrote to Jesse Applegate asking for information about a land transaction. He also inquired about the potential in Oregon for a young lawyer, with his son John Sappington Marmaduke's future in mind. Applegate's response portrays the depth of the relationship between him and Meredith. "I think … a young man of talents coming here with undoubted evidence of his responsibility as a son of yours must come would have a fair field for his exertion and an almost certain harvest of wealth and honor. It is needless for me to add that it would afford me the greatest pleasure to show every attention to the son, as a testimony of the respect with which I regard the father."[31]

Was the western lands venture profitable for Meredith? Did he wrongly interpret the prospects for making a fortune by speculating in land when he bought 4,000 acres in St. Clair County?

The loss of the county seat took the steam out of Meredith's bid to establish an empire in St. Clair County. In coming years he failed to exploit the western lands investment, his time and energy given to other business, political, and farming interests. After the county seat fight, there is nothing to indicate that he gave the western lands much thought, nor that any of the land was utilized in any way. No receipts for lumber sales exist, no accounts of cattle sold or barrels of pork shipped, no contracts for lands rented, not even any correspondence relating to the western lands is found in the Marmaduke and Sappington papers held in archives. Reasons for the partners' neglect of the western lands are many. Darwin Sappington was in Kentucky, not inclined to devote time to the project. William Sappington was busy growing cotton (and buying and selling land and slaves) in Mississippi, and Claiborne Jackson had business and political interests in Howard County and Jefferson City. And they all were heavily involved in the pill business during much of this time. From time to time, Meredith bought and sold small amounts of St. Clair County land, although tax receipts show that no effort was made to increase his holdings; the number of acres on which taxes were paid varied little from year to year.[32]

At St. Louis in April 1857, the partners dissolved their western lands enterprise.

To Make a Fortune in Missouri

The land was divided among the partners based upon the amount of money each had provided for the original investment, with the current value of the land taken into consideration when allocating the tracts. Of the 4,037 acres held by Meredith as the principal agent, he retained 1,496, deeding to Claiborne Jackson 1,000 acres, Darwin Sappington 861, and William Sappington 680. Meredith still owned his portion of the acreage at the time of his death. Hanging on a wall in the St. Clair County Historical Society Museum in Osceola, a plat map shows members of Meredith's family, who received St. Clair County land in the division of his estate, still owned land there in 1870.

Osceola did become a distribution center for a large area of southwest Missouri and eastern Kansas. Its rows of warehouses stored goods brought upriver by steamboats. Contemporary accounts tell of a hundred wagons lined up there each morning waiting to load merchandise for transport to small towns and remote villages. But population growth in the region slowed as the nation drifted toward Civil War in the 1850s. In the end, the western lands venture did not produce the wealth Meredith had imagined; the acreage he owned after the partnership ended became his reward for reaching too far.

Notes

1. "I will go as far as any man in providing homes for the needy": Bates to Marmaduke, February 2, 1829. Box 1, Folder 5, Sappington-Marmaduke Papers, MHS.

2. "Located on the waters of Brush Creek": William Mooney Survey, Deed Book 30, p. 401, Highland County Ohio Recorder, Hillsboro, Ohio. Copy in author's possession.

3. The Public Lands Survey System: Information about The Public Lands Survey System, and surveying in general, may be found in Andro Linklater, *Measuring America*. In First Principal Meridian; Fifth Principal Meridian; Seven Ranges, http://wikipedia.org. For information about public lands in Missouri, see: Gary W. Beahan, *Missouri's Public Domain: United States Land Sales 1818–1922*: Lemont K. Richardson, "Private Land Claims in Missouri," three parts in *MHR*, Vol. 50, Nos. 2, 3, 4 (January, April, July 1956).

4. "Come one, Come all, we have millions of acres to occupy": Lemont K. Richardson, "Private Land Claims in Missouri," *MHR*, Vol. 50, No. 4 (July 1956), 396.

5. In later years, Meredith speculated with another Chariton County tract: Salisbury to Marmaduke, February 25, 1856. Folder 20, Marmaduke Papers C1021, SHSMO. Lucius Salisbury bought Meredith's land and in 1858 established there the town named for him. *Historical, Pictorial and Biographical Record, of Chariton County, Missouri*, 218–19.

6. Meredith was called upon to lay out the nascent village to be called Philadelphia: Information about the survey of Arrow Rock is described in Michael Dickey, *Arrow Rock: Crossroads of the Missouri Frontier,*71–72; *1881 History of Saline County, Missouri*, 475.

7. "exceedingly anxious that the court should be removed to some place by next term": W. A. Wilson to Marmaduke, December 14, 1838. Folder 11, Marmaduke Papers C1021, SHSMO. W. A. Wilson is probably William A. Wilson, a resident of Marion Township (no longer existing) in the northeast corner of Saline County. He was appointed postmaster at Old Jefferson (former county seat) in 1853. 1840 U.S. Federal Census, Saline County, Schedule 4, p. 92; Record of Appointment of Postmasters, 1832–1971. NARA Microfilm Publication M841, Record Group 28.

8. "meet the commissioners at 12 o'clock at Harrises Lick (with your instruments)": Asa Finley to Marmaduke, August 12, 1829. Folder 5, Marmaduke Papers C1021, SHSMO. Asa Finley settled near the mouth of the Salt Fork in 1819. *1881 History of Saline County, Missouri*, 198. Harrises' Lick was one of the many salt licks that existed in Saline County. The "Harrises ventured up Edmondson's Creek in 1824," Ibid., 198. Salt Fork and Edmondson's Creek are in northern Saline County, east of the town of Miami.

An Elusive Empire

9. "with our Representatives [in Jefferson City] in regard to our County Seat matter": W. A. Wilson to Marmaduke, December 14, 1838. Folder 11, Marmaduke Papers C1021, SHSMO.

10. Meeting in a Saline County home on April 11, 1839, the site selection commission: Details of the meeting in Saline County are contained in "Commissioner's Report To The Honorable Circuit Court of Saline County," reproduced in *1881 History of Saline County, Missouri*, 225–27. Jeremiah Odell retained 15 acres on the southern edge of the tract on which Marshall was founded. The next nearest piece of land he owned was a half mile northeast of where the county courthouse was built. Bureau of Land Management, General Land Office Accession records MO2710_.324, MO2710_.049, MO1750_.236.

11. Meredith waited three weeks after the commissioner's report went to the circuit court before visiting the Fayette land office: Record Group 49, Land Patents 1789–2012, Fayette Missouri Land Office Tract Book Vol. 001, entry 8597, National Archives and Records Administration, Kansas City, Mo. Applications for patents were recorded at land offices in "tract books." More than 2,000 tract books contain records pertaining to transactions in the eastern states. Today these are held by the National Archives and Records Administration, Washington, D.C., with copies at some regional NARA offices. Information in a tract book includes the date of initial filing, name of applicant, and amount paid. Unfortunately, Volume 001 for the Fayette, Missouri, office during this period is incomplete. To determine a general period when entries were made for land in the sections listed, reliance has been placed on interpretation of data contained in Bureau of Land Management General Land Office Records for those sections: The Missouri State Archives has an abstract of federal land sales applications at offices in Missouri between 1818 and 1903 that provides some information.

12. The surrounding land in Marshall also attracted Meredith's attention: IOU note Marmaduke to Cornelius Davis, Commissioner, September 23, 1839, Folder 12, Marmaduke Papers C1021, SHSMO. Meredith executed the note (marked paid) the day of the sale to Cornelius Davis for $92.50.

13. "collect all money you can in Fayetteville in metal": Marmaduke to Augustus Stevenson, June 24, 1839. Box 2, Folder 4, Sappington-Marmaduke Papers, MHS.

14. "amot. to be charged on acct. land speculation": Duplicate statements etc., of land entered in Springfield Land District 1839. Folder 32, John Sappington Papers C1027, SHSMO. C. Jones is unidentified. The 1840 U.S. Census for Rives County, Missouri, from which St. Clair derived in 1841, lists a "C. Jones" in Weaubleau Township, the eastern half of St. Clair County. There was also a Louis C. Jones "employed in commerce" in nearby Polk County at the same time. Either could have been Meredith's agent.

15. Thirty-nine steamboats were operating on the lower Missouri: Information about steamboats operating on Missouri's rivers before the Civil War is found in: Adam Isaac Kane, *The Western River Steamboat*, and Robert L. Dyer, *A Brief History of Steamboats*. Steamboat information specific to the Osage River can be found in Gerard Schultz, "Steamboat Navigation on the Osage River Before the Civil War," *MHR*, Vol. 29, No. 2 (April 1935). Jefferson City's early role in steamboat commerce is in Eldon Hattervig, *Jefferson Landing, Commercial Center of the Steamboat Era*, Missouri Department of Natural Resources, Jefferson City 1980.

16. "tributary streams … which penetrate far into the interior of the State": To The People of Missouri, *Jeffersonian Republican*, June 13, 1840. SHSMO Newspaper Archive, Reel 16360.

17. "crossing the Osage River at Crow & Crutchfield's store:" *History of Henry and St. Clair Counties, Missouri*, 837, 839, 865.

18. Coonce, who "ranged from Gasconade": *History of Henry and St. Clair Counties*, 107.

19. David Lavender, *Bent's Fort*, 85.

20. Arriving on the upper Osage … were several brothers of the Waldo family: Early accounts of the Waldo brothers' activities in Missouri and David Waldo's rise to prominence in Missouri and the Santa Fe trade are portrayed in James W. Goodrich, "In the Earnest Pursuit of Wealth," *MHR*, Vol. 66, No. 2 (January 1972). Jeremy Neely, "A Pure Son of Missouri," *MHR*, Vol 109, No. 4 (July 2015), offers information about the Waldo brothers on the upper Osage, while their activities on the Gasconade River are recounted in Lynn Morrow, "Piney Sawmillers at Gasconade Mills," *Old Settlers Gazette*, No. 26 (July 26, 2008).

21. "pork, cows and calves ... and three and four-year-old steers. ... The merchants hauled their goods from Boonville:" *History of Henry and St. Clair Counties*, 832–35, 840.

22. "the bulk of downstream traffic [consisted of] pork ... lumber, staves": Gerard Schultz, "Steamboat Navigation on the Osage River Before the Civil War," *MHR*, Vol. 29, No. 2 (April 1935), 178. U.S. Census, Schedule 5, Products of Industry in the County of St. Clair during the year ending June 1, 1850, 203. "Osage River Commerce in the 1870's, History Not Found in Textbooks," *MHR*, Vol. 51, No. 4 (July 1957), 447.

23. "Our western lands ... must ultimately prove to be the best investment a man could make of his spare cash:" Sappington to Marmaduke, December 27, 1839. Box 2, Folder 4, Sappington-Marmaduke Papers, MHS.

24. "let those Gentlemen ... have the land on some terms if it can be done": E. D. Sappington to Marmaduke, October 12, 1843. Folder 14, Marmaduke Papers C1021, SHSMO. Sappington's use of the word "seling" offers two interpretations, one being the sale of land, the other being "selling" in the promotional sense. Since none of the western lands were sold to the county, it is reasonable to accept the latter.

25. "You informed me in your last letter that Mr. Jackson and yourself expect to visit the Osage Country in the Spring and if pleased to move out there:" E. D. Sappington to Marmaduke, January 25, 1841. Box 3, Folder 1, Sappington-Marmaduke Papers, MHS.

26. "took a deep and personal interest:" Joseph Schafer, "Jesse Applegate: Pioneer, Statesman and Philosopher," *The Washington Historical Quarterly*, July 1907, 219–221. Schafer's biography of Applegate presents an extensive review of his life in Oregon as he rose to social and political prominence in the territory, eventually becoming a delegate to the conference that wrote the state's first constitution. More about Applegate is found in: Floyd C. Shoemaker, "Osceola, Land of Osage River Lore," *MHR*, Vol 54, No. 4 (July 1960). Marmaduke knew Edward Bates, corresponded with him about federal land policy and other issues, and may have consulted him prior to collaborating with Applegate. See Bates to Marmaduke, February 2, 1829. Box 1, Folder 5, Sappington-Marmaduke Papers, MHS.

27. "and surveyed a good part of this country ... finishing in 1838." *History of Henry and St. Clair Counties*, 834.

28. The intensity of Meredith's desire to secure the county seat: Meredith's purchase of James Wilson's land is found in: M. M. Marmaduke & Wife Deed to William B. Sappington, April 10, 1857. Folder 67, John Sappington Papers C1027, SHSMO. The location of the land for the county seat that was proposed by Jesse Applegate is described in: *History of Henry and St. Clair Counties*, 857. It is the James Wilson tract purchased by Marmaduke and described in the above mentioned deed.

29. "imported between thirty and forty hands to make brick for the new court house": *History of Henry and St. Clair Counties*, 857.

30. "gratified to learn that there is a probability of the center of St. Clair Coty getting the Coty Seat": Sappington to Marmaduke, February 22, 1842. Box 3, Folder 2, Sappington-Marmaduke Papers, MHS.

31. "I think ... a young man of talents coming here with undoubted evidence of his responsibility as a son of yours": Applegate to Marmaduke, November 16, 1851. Box 5, Folder 1, Sappington-Marmaduke Papers, MHS.

32. the number of acres on which taxes were paid varied little from year to year: Marmaduke and Co. land tax receipts, 1851, 1852, 1857. Folders 60 and 65, John Sappington Papers C-1027, SHSMO.

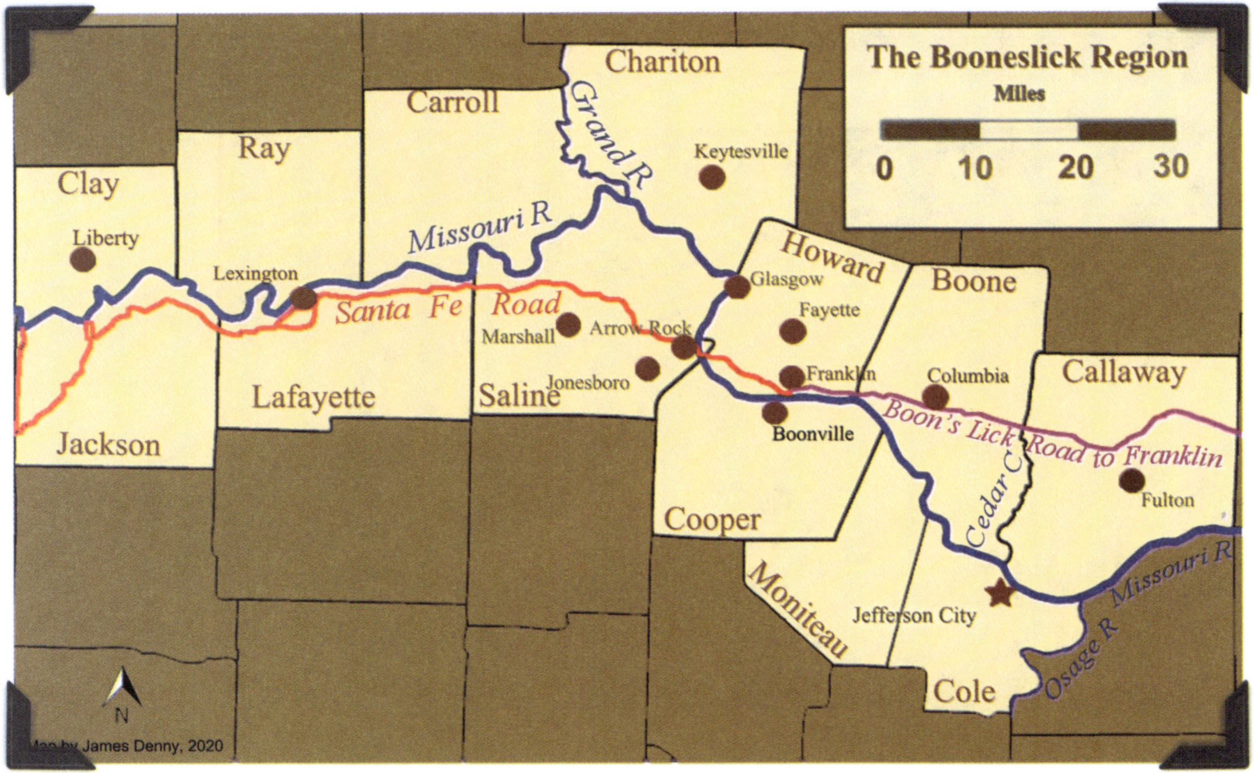

River and road transport, inexpensive land, and bountiful soil attracted settlers from Upper South states to the Booneslick region. Marmaduke arrived in Franklin, Missouri, in the fall of 1823 and the following year traveled the Santa Fe Trail as a trader. (Map courtesy of James Denny.)

Meredith Miles Marmaduke, 1834 portrait by George Caleb Bingham. The two men later clashed over the artist's uncomplimentary portrayal of Meredith as a corpulent politician in a painting titled *Stump Speaking*. (Courtesy of Missouri Historical Society, St. Louis.)

Lavinia Marmaduke, 1834 portrait by George Caleb Bingham. Whether intentional or not, Bingham's stiff, unsmiling woman is not the attractive young wife the family recalls. Years later, upon seeing the portrait, a great-granddaughter said she was "sorry that Lavinia looks so sad. I'm told that she was lovely. In those days they didn't smile." (Courtesy of Missouri Historical Society, St. Louis.)

Dr. John Sappington, 1834 portrait by George Caleb Bingham. As the father of Meredith Marmaduke's wife, Sappington used his political and financial influence to assist his son-in-law on a path to wealth and political office. (Courtesy of Missouri Department of Natural Resources.)

Jane Breathitt Sappington, 1834 portrait by George Caleb Bingham. A daughter of the influential Breathitt family in Kentucky, Jane Sappington was the mother of two sons and seven daughters — three of whom married the same man. (Courtesy of Missouri Department of Natural Resources.)

Claiborne Fox Jackson, 1861. Meredith Marmaduke's brother-in-law and business partner was instrumental in ousting Senator Thomas Hart Benton from office. As governor, Jackson sought to align Missouri with the Confederacy. (Courtesy of the State Historical Society of Missouri.)

Elizabeth (Eliza) Sappington Jackson, circa 1860. Her marriage to bigamist Alonzo Pearson ended in 1831 by an act of the General Assembly; in 1838, she became the third of Dr. John Sappington's daughters to marry Claiborne Jackson. His first two wives — Eliza's sisters — had died, one of malaria and the other in an accident. These marriages connected Jackson to his prestigious father-in-law, which helped fuel his financial and political ambitions. (Courtesy of the State Historical Society of Missouri.)

THE OLD MARMADUKE

The Marmaduke homestead, shown in the *Hand-Book of Saline County, Missouri*, an 1889 pamphlet promoting the area, depicts the second house Meredith and Lavinia built on land obtained from her father, Dr. John Sappington. The couple's first home, a single-story building behind the newer home, became the

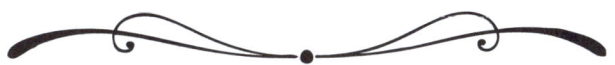

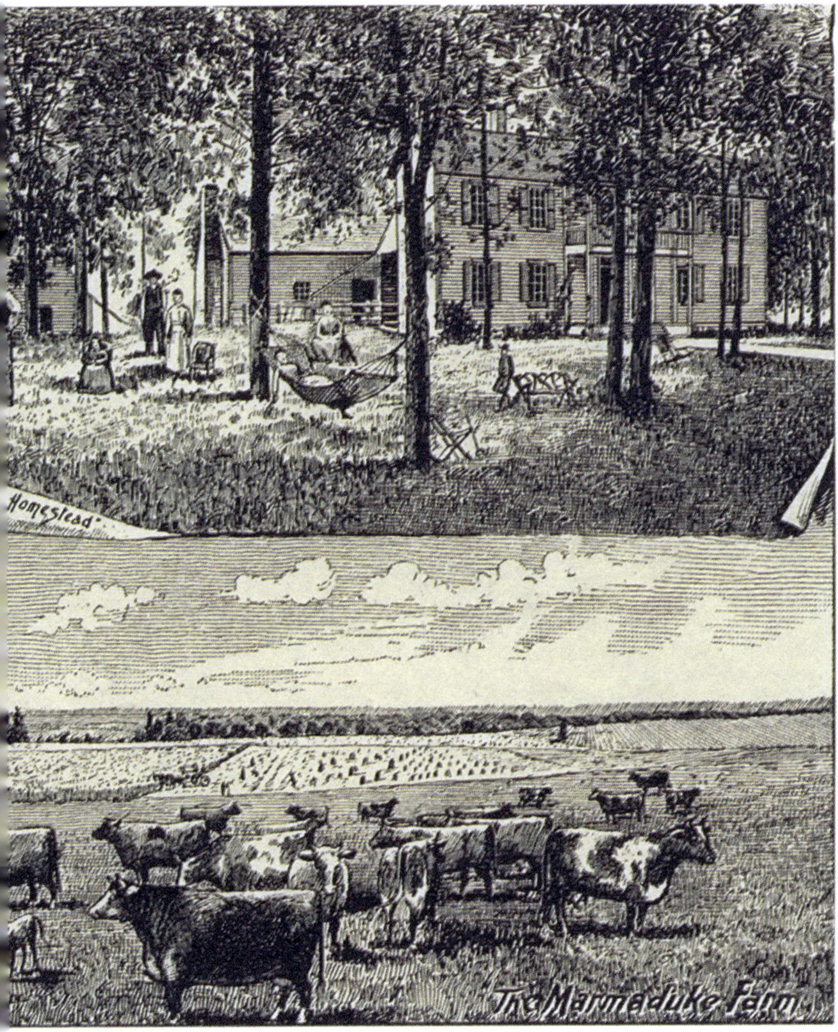

:STEAD, NEAR NAPTON.

farm overseer's residence. After Meredith's death in 1864, Lavinia continued to occupy the large house until sometime before 1870, when she moved to nearby Marshall.

The Marmaduke house is no longer standing. This is the last known image of the property, taken in 1973, when the house had been relegated to use as a hay barn. (Courtesy of Friends of Arrow Rock.)

Thomas Hart Benton, shown here in a portrait by Alonzo Chappel, circa 1858. Benton represented Missouri in the U.S. Senate for 30 years, from its first days of statehood. His support of policies favoring the sale of federal lands at low rates benefited Meredith Marmaduke. As members of Missouri's Democratic Party and the Central Clique, the state's first political machine, the two men often collaborated to influence political activities. (Courtesy of the State Historical Society of Missouri.)

Mystery surrounds the origin of this portrait of Governor Meredith Miles Marmaduke, on display in the Missouri State Museum. Painted after circa 1920, the artwork is believed to have been created by a St. Louis artist working from a crayon likeness. (Courtesy of Missouri Department of Natural Resources.)

The Marmaduke brothers in a photograph believed taken circa 1865–1866. From left: Meredith Jr. (seated), Darwin William, Henry Hungerford, John Sappington (seated), Leslie, Vincent (seated). (Courtesy of Michael Dickey.)

The entire village of Arrow Rock was designated as a National Historic Landmark in 1963 because of its location near the head of the Santa Fe Trail and the town's prominence during the period of westward expansion. In 1965, the Arrow Rock home of artist George Caleb Bingham, pictured here, was also designated a National Historic Landmark. (Courtesy of Friends of Arrow Rock.)

The J. Huston Tavern was established in 1834 to provide meals and lodging for travelers coming to the area on riverboats or via the Santa Fe Trail. It also served as a site for social events and political meetings. A restoration effort led by the Daughters of the American Revolution in 1926 sparked a preservation movement in Arrow Rock that eventually led to the founding of the Friends of Arrow Rock in 1959. (Courtesy of Friends of Arrow Rock.)

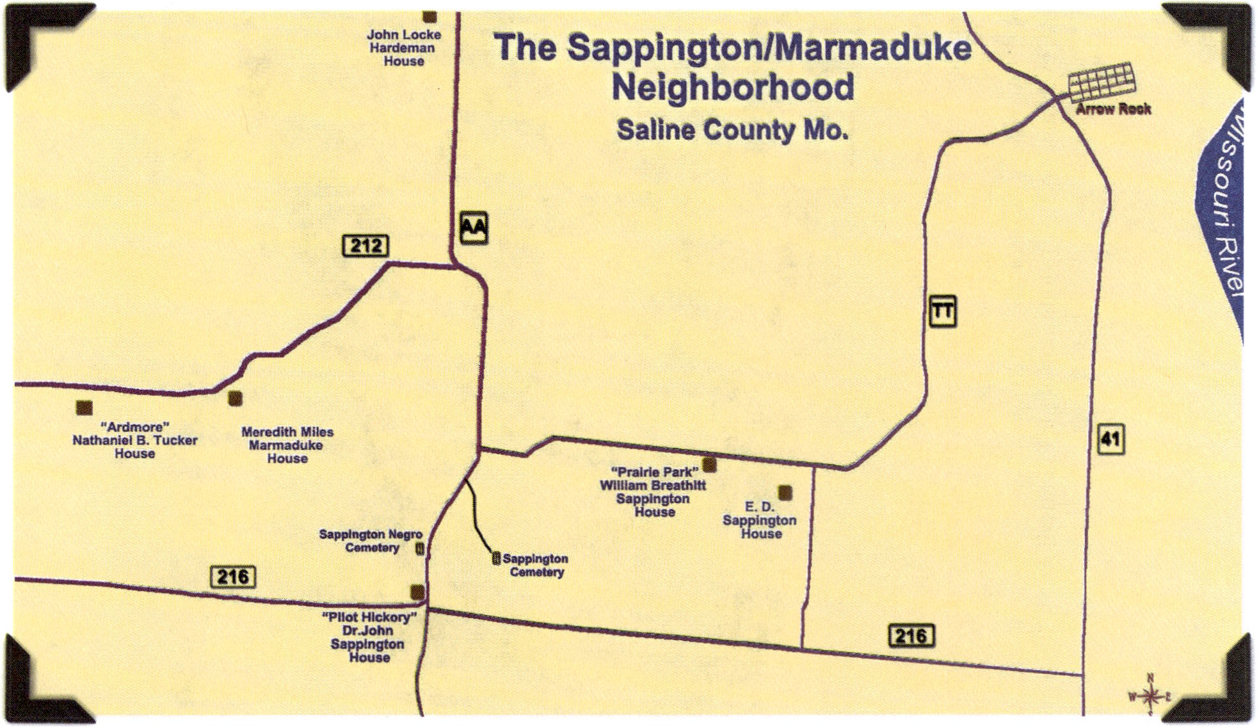

Of the sites shown on this map of the Sappington/Marmaduke neighborhood southwest of Arrow Rock, only four remain: the Sappington Cemetery State Historic Site, the Sappington Negro Cemetery State Historic Site, William B. Sappington's mansion "Prairie Park," and "Lo Mismo," the John Locke Hardeman home. (Map courtesy of James Denny.)

CHAPTER 15

DIRT IS DESTINY

To make his fortune in Missouri, Meredith Marmaduke invoked a path to wealth and power that had its roots in a Southern plantation society whose members prospered on a synthesis of capital, land, and slaves. When he arrived in the state in 1823, the substantial farms owned by the Hardeman family, Dr. Sappington, General Thomas A. Smith, and others in the Booneslick region were ample testimony to the validity of this three-legged model for prosperity succeeding on the frontier. To emulate the success of these planter-farmers, Meredith engaged first in the uncertain and dangerous business of trading at Santa Fe, wagering what money he had in order to obtain capital to finance the acquisition of land (in addition to his Chariton County property). Despite his losses on the trail, his five-year trading venture was successful and provided him with the cash he required (credit sales were forbidden) to buy federal land. Over a period of 30 years, he followed this formula — using surplus capital earned from the Santa Fe trade, the mercantile store at Jonesboro, and the pill business in Mississippi and Louisiana — to acquire land in Saline County and elsewhere. He began by expanding his home farm, the genesis of which was the 160 acres west of Arrow Rock he obtained from Dr. Sappington in 1826. By 1845, he had added 2,000 acres to the home farm and could look west from his house and know that for three miles he owned all the land he could see. At places along this stretch, his property was a mile and a half wide, north to south. To the north of his home farm, Dr. Sappington owned 2,040 acres, giving the two families control of 6½ contiguous square miles of fertile prairie.

Aside from his home farm expansion, Meredith spent the two decades preceding the Civil War acquiring an additional 1,280 acres of federal land in other areas of Saline County (excluding the Marshall land discussed in the preceding chapter). Several of these tracts were bought in partnership with Darwin Sappington (they also purchased 760 acres of federal land in Pettis County) and Claiborne Jackson. At the minimum price of $1.25 an acre, Meredith paid $4,100 for 3,280 acres of federal land. In contrast, improved private land in the region was selling for $6 to $8 an acre during the 1830s.[1] He also bought 16 tracts from private owners (six from family members) that added another 3,220 acres to his Saline County holdings. Meredith seldom sold any of his land, even during the 1850s when demand for farm commodities drove prices up, promising a sizeable profit by selling his federal land for $20 to $40 an acre. In addition to the town lot in Arrow Rock that he sold to the Baptist Church in 1853 and the 160 acres in Chariton County, Meredith sold five other tracts during his lifetime, and one of these was deeded to his son, Vincent. By the early 1850s the amount of land Meredith had acquired in Saline County was approaching 4,000 acres (although he claimed fewer acres when interviewed by a census marshal that year). Saline County tax records for 1852 show he was assessed $107.90 on 3,796 acres in 44 parcels. During the next eight years, he added 601 acres to his Saline County holdings, paying taxes on 4,397 acres in 45 tracts in 1860. His interest in acquiring land never waned although acquisition slowed as the nation slid into civil war. An appraisal of his estate at the time of his death in 1864 showed he owned 5,500 acres in Saline County.[2]

It was not feasible for Meredith to actively farm all of the land he owned. He had slaves (probably not enough) to work some of the 2,160 acres that comprised his home farm, but his other holdings, scattered as they were across Saline, Chariton, and Pettis Counties, were too distant to be managed in this way. How much of his home farm and the outlying tracts was rented to other farmers is unknown, but judging from Dr. Sappington's success in placing tenants on more than 5,000 acres in 1848, it's clear there was a demand for rentable land.[3] Meredith rented some of his land to newly arrived families who would cultivate it until they saved enough money to buy their own. The 760-acre farm north of Marshall that he bought from James Story in 1848 is an example of this. W. S. Wilson, already established in the county, rented the Story farm from Meredith in 1850 to hold it for his brother-in-law, who was expected to arrive from Kentucky that fall. In November, Wilson told Meredith he had been contacted by someone who wanted to know "if I still wished to rent your Story Farm. I expect my Brother in law [sic] soon ... but he has not yet arrived. I do not wish to deprive you of an opportunity to rent your farm, therefore if you have a chance to rent, do not keep it for me."[4]

The amount of farmland available for rent in Saline County by 1848 appears to have been enough to offer prospective tenants a choice. John Locke Hardeman (a ward of Meredith's for several years after his father, John, died in New Orleans in 1829) managed Nathaniel Beverley Tucker's large Saline County farm, Ardmore, and his other properties in 1848. Tucker lived in Williamsburg, Virginia, at the time. Hardeman, acting as agent to lease Tucker's farms, was concerned about finding reliable tenants telling Tucker that "One great obstacle in the way of getting good tenants here is the fact, that, there are too many land renters [landlords]. Doct. Sappington & his family laid out large sums in farms for rent — much to the injury of this community." Locke also reported an offer to lease Ardmore Farm for a year, with the rent to be paid as "four thousand pounds of bacon (sides & hams) with two thousand barrels of lard."[5] Farm rent was often paid with the produce derived, giving the landowner an opportunity to speculate on favorable market conditions with the grain, meat, or other commodity, and thereby increase his income from the transaction.

Busting Sod

Almost all of the Saline County land that Meredith bought was prairie. Despite the fertility of the soil in the Missouri River bottoms, he eschewed purchasing land there, his preference for prairie acreage undoubtedly influenced by the Missouri River flood of 1826. Newly married that year and living in his father-in-law's house while his was under construction, he saw firsthand the devastation to families caused by the high water. Pioneer farmers had been attracted to the Saline County bottomlands as early as 1810, and by 1826 several hundred families had settled there. Some had prospered and were progressing from subsistence to commercial agriculture, selling corn and hogs to markets in towns along the river. Known as the "Big Rise," the 1826 flood forced many of these farmers out of the bottoms to high ground, leaving their property to be ravaged by water and mud. Homes, outbuildings, furnishings, and equipment, all obtained at great cost and labor, were heavily damaged or washed away, never to be recovered. Observing this, it was no great leap for Meredith to recognize the benefit of owning upland acres rather than river-bottom acreage, particularly when he saw what General Thomas A. Smith was doing to dispel any idea that the prairie was less fertile, by planting trees and crops on his Experiment Farm near Jonesboro.[6]

The prairie land Meredith sought to buy was clothed with a dense stand of tallgrass — switch grass, big and little bluestem grass, and Indian grass — flowers and other herbaceous plants, supporting a population of bison, elk, deer, prairie chickens, and a host of smaller birds and animals. Meredith's neighbor, William Barclay Napton, who arrived in the Booneslick country in 1832, was impressed by the height of the grass, saying it was "in most places, as tall as a medium sized man, and as high as the head of a man on horseback" in other places.[7] Scientific measurement of the fertility of the Missouri prairie was not developed in the 1830s, but the comments of explorers and settlers present an intriguing image: "immense natural meadows, like a rich carpet," "fit for stock of all kinds," "deep black soil," "covered with luxuriant growth," "an unlimited supply of forage," "studded with innumerable flowers." Stockmen could turn their cattle and sheep loose on this nutrient-filled Valhalla, but before the soil could be tilled and planted in crops, the grass had to be destroyed. Sod-busting, as it was called, was hard work. The grass was first set afire to burn off dead leaves and stems, leaving a scorched turf that had to be turned over and left to decay. The lightweight plow settlers brought out from the east was not up to the task; its iron-tipped wooden share and moldboard didn't easily shed the sticky prairie soil. With such a plow it took a full day for three men behind a team of oxen (horses didn't have the stamina to "bust sod") to break one acre of ground — one to drive the team, one to handle the plow, and a third to clean dirt from the share. Needing a better implement, farmers often fabricated their own plows to be more productive. John Locke Hardeman discovered a homemade plow in Mississippi that he thought might suit Meredith's needs. "I am having made a plough which I intend to send you as a present. It is here called a 'V' plough. It is used for the purpose of making ridges for cotton and corn. I am so well pleased with its work that I wish you to make trial of it also. The stock I shall have to fashion myself, there being no mechanic in the vicinity. You may, I think, expect it about the first of May."[8]

The invention in 1837 of the large John Deere "grasshopper plow," with a cast-iron frame, steel share, and improved steel moldboard, made it possible to turn sod more quickly. Whatever plow farmers used, they had to wait most of a year before the overturned sod decayed enough to be scattered with a harrow. They could then plant seed in the exposed soil. Farmers did not harvest that first crop — usually corn used to feed the farmer and his animals — until 15 to 20 months after the sod was "busted." During this time, a prairie farmer needed reserve capital in order to survive, having already invested several dollars per acre for soil preparation and seed. Lacking such capital, several years might pass before a farmer could rise above the level of subsistence agriculture. In contrast, those prairie farmers who — like Meredith — had capital to draw upon for family survival, for the purchase of seed and improved implements, and as well enjoyed the benefit of slave labor, were able to enter the realm of commercial agriculture more quickly.

A Varied Harvest

Unlike modern industrial farmers who specialize in the production of only one or two grain crops, or who focus on a specific aspect of livestock or poultry production, Meredith and his Saline County neighbors (as well as most farmers in the Booneslick region) practiced diversified agriculture, producing a variety of crops and animals. Diversification allowed Meredith to optimize his investment in labor by allocating his slaves to a variety of tasks whose labor requirements were complementary in terms of time spent planting, cultivating, harvesting, feeding, rearing, and preparation for consignment and sale. On the other hand, labor (slave or otherwise) was a limiting factor in determining how much land he could put into production. Using horse-drawn implements, Saline County farmers could figure on needing one laborer for every 30 acres of land devoted to raising crops such as corn, wheat, or oats. Hemp cultivation was even more labor-intensive.[9] The amount of time Meredith's slaves spent tending to livestock isn't easy to determine, but with more than 300 animals on his farm in 1850 there's little doubt that a great amount of labor went into their care. Diversification also allowed Meredith to spread the risk of lost income in the event of a crop failure (or abundance, which invariably drove prices down). Another reason to produce a variety of crops and livestock was the continuing need for a certain amount of "subsistence" farming in order to provide food and products that his family and slaves needed for their consumption throughout the year.

The prevalence of diversified agriculture in Saline County is recorded as part of the 1850 census, which included the first attempt by the federal government to survey the production of America's farms. In Saline County, census marshal William H. Letcher — a 25-year-old lawyer who probably saw his census employment as a means of introducing himself and his law practice to everyone in the county — began his work on August 2, going from house to house in the towns and villages and traveling to each farm. When he completed his Herculean task four months later, he had visited 955 families, and had recorded the agricultural production of 633 farms in Saline County. The agriculture schedule of the census sought to determine the number of "improved" and "unimproved" acres each farmer owned, their cash value, and the value of his farm implements and machinery. Letcher also recorded the quantities of 36 grain, livestock, and other farm commodities that were present on each farm on the first day of June that year.

Slightly more than half (329) of the farms William Letcher visited reported having less than 100 acres of improved land, defined in the census instructions as acres "used for grazing, grass, or tillage, or which is now fallow," belonging to the farm. The land did not have to be contiguous. Another 276 farms reported 100 to 299 acres of improved land; only 28 farmers said they had 300 or more improved acres. Unimproved land, also recorded, was defined as not necessarily contiguous, "but may be a wood lot or other land at some distance, owned in connection with the farm."[10] These definitions must have caused William Letcher some grief, since he was instructed to list all the improved and unimproved land "owned or managed by the person named." It appears that the government's intent was to record all the land a farmer owned, whether it was part of the farm being surveyed or not. But what about land rented to others; who should claim that? Meredith chose to report only a portion of the land he owned in the county. More ambiguity appears in the instructions given the census taker for determining the value of a farm. He was to list the "actual cash value" of all improved and unimproved acres but was not told if this included the home, outbuildings, and slave quarters. Meredith's 1850 agriculture census (Schedule 4) lists the value of his farm as $7,000, while in that year's household census (Schedule 1) his "real estate" is valued at $30,000.

When William Letcher visited Meredith's farm on November 23, 1850, he recorded 11 people in the home including Lavinia and seven of their children, 23-year-old Polly Oliver (born in Kentucky, she may have been related to Lavinia's Breathitt family in that state), and Samuel W. McCorkle, a 20-year-old school teacher (born in Missouri), there to instruct the children. To complete the agricultural production census, Letcher listed Meredith's holdings as 400 acres of improved land and 900 acres of unimproved land. Only four other Saline County farmers had more land in production. The largest improved acreage, 1,000, belonged to Cynthia B. Smith, the widow of Thomas Adams Smith. Thomas H. Harvey reported 700 acres improved; Meredith's friend, John Locke Hardeman, listed 600 acres; and Abraham Van Meter had 500 improved acres. (Dr. Sappington reported 300 improved acres.) Letcher recorded Meredith's produce on hand, as of June 1, 1850, as 800 bushels of wheat, 2,500 bushels of "Indian" corn, 150 bushels of oats, 20 tons of baled hemp, 100 bushels of Irish potatoes, 500 pounds of butter, 500 pounds of wool, $375 worth of orchard produce, and 50 tons of hay. In addition to horses, of which he stabled 30 in 1850, he pastured 40 mules, 21 "milch" cows, 14 working oxen, 60 head of beef cattle, and 200 sheep, and was feeding 121 pigs. Only one significant crop that was grown in much of the Booneslick region was missing from Meredith's agricultural production that year — tobacco. Although a major product of neighboring Howard and Lafayette Counties, tobacco was cultivated by only 13 percent of Saline County's farmers, and Meredith was not one of them. His experience in Virginia, where as a young man he had witnessed the deterioration of his family's plantation as the soil's fertility declined under intensive tobacco cultivation, apparently gave Meredith a lifelong aversion to the cultivation of tobacco as a commercial crop, and no document has been found to show that he ever grew tobacco in Missouri.[11]

The Middlemen

Before the establishment of a national telegraph system, which reached mid-Missouri in the 1850s, Saline County farmers found it difficult to stay abreast of current commodity prices in the major market towns of St. Louis, New Orleans, Cincinnati, and the Tidewater region of Virginia. Relying on untimely information in local newspapers and in letters they received, they often missed opportunities to sell their products at the right time for the best price. To overcome this as his farm production expanded in the 1830s, Meredith sought a reliable consignment agent, someone who monitored commodity prices at the major trading centers and would store his produce until it could be sold at the best price. The St. Louis Merchants Exchange was organized in 1836 to provide such services. Its members were a "who's who of the region's political and economic elite," trading in such products as corn, hogs, buffalo hides, cotton, hemp, barrels of whiskey, and barge freight.[12] Housed in an "elegant" building a few blocks west of the riverfront, the exchange also served as a clearinghouse for cash notes issued by banks in the Mississippi and Ohio River valleys, an important service in the late 1830s when out-of-state banks were prohibited by law from operating in Missouri. Among the exchange's members were many friends and supporters of Senator Thomas H. Benton, including Edward Walsh, a partner with his brother, James, in the firm known as J. & E. Walsh, "wholesale grocers and commission merchants."

Raised in County Tipperary, Ireland, the Walsh brothers migrated to the United States in 1818 and eventually settled in St. Louis. Edward Walsh, entrepreneurial by nature, a "lead, flour and steamboat magnate," owned his first flour mill in the city by 1831, eventually acquiring several more. An early investor in steamboats working the western rivers, he was a member of a company that specialized in the transportation of lead from the mines at Galena, Illinois, to St. Louis. He also owned stock in, and served on the board of directors of, several of the city's banks and insurance companies. By 1850, his wealth was great enough to allow him to own a large house on the western edge of the city where he lived with his wife, Isabelle, and their five children. Edward's brother, James, on the other hand, was content with managing their co-owned grocery and commission business, and is believed to have been a bachelor, living in a boarding house in 1850. Aware of Thomas Benton's many contacts within the St. Louis business community, Meredith may have asked him to recommend a consignment agent and the senator immediately thought of his "warm and personal friend," Edward Walsh.[13] This occurred after 1834, probably in the closing years of that decade. Instructions Meredith gave Darwin Sappington, on a buying trip to the east in 1834 for their mercantile store in Jonesboro, directed him to purchase at St. Louis on his return there, "such other articles ... as you may not buy in Phil. or Pittsbg." In his letter Meredith made no mention of the firm of J. & E. Walsh — something he would have done if a relationship had existed with that company at the time.[14]

Although fidelity in business dealings was important to Meredith (his relationship with J. & E. Walsh lasted for nearly a quarter century), he occasionally corresponded with other St. Louis consignment houses. The firm of Blain, Thompkins & Barrett responded to his request for market information in 1846, advising that "Good wheat now commands pretty easily from 65 to 68 cts. ... However we regret to inform you that our market for hemp is rather discouraging," their best offer having been $50 per ton. Another St. Louis consignment house seeking Meredith's business was Yeatman, Pittman & Co. Their hand-written letter (termed a "circular") sent him in May 1853 quoted current market prices for hemp, pork, bacon, wheat, corn, flour, bale rope, pig lead, and dry hides that were "firm at 10-1/2 cts." A lengthy explanation of market conditions accompanied the price for each commodity. Raw whiskey was "in good demand at 19 $." The circular also advised Meredith of a change in management of the firm, which would in the future be known as Yeatman, Robinson & Co., adding that "we are satisfied that all business intrusted … will be promptly and satisfactorily attended to as heretofore."[15]

Meredith occasionally consigned his produce to a local agent, particularly if prices at St. Louis were low and he wanted to avoid the cost of shipping. James L. Watson, in Boonville, received a consignment of pork in October 1847. A letter acknowledging its receipt was sent to Meredith with the slave who had delivered the meat. "Your note of this day per your boy is recd. and with it 36 Bacon Sides weighing in bulk 693#, 25 Bacon Hams weighing 273#. … It shall have my close attention." Watson reported that day's market price for hams and sides, and went on to relate a news item from the *New York Sun* newspaper he thought might interest Meredith. Two months later, he reported that all the hams had been sold but only half the sides. Demand was down "from the stopage [sic] of the steam boat," and Watson feared "being able to close out the remainder, but will use every endeavour [sic] to do so."[16]

Hemp — The Money Crop

Although the products that Meredith sent to the J. & E. Walsh company on consignment included hams, bacon, lard, wool, hides, and wheat, hemp was his primary commercial product that annually produced a significant income. A February 1853 statement from the Walsh firm detailing the sale of his hemp crop during years 1851–1853 illustrates the importance of hemp in Meredith's agricultural scheme. It also demonstrates the value of having a consignment agent and illuminates the services the Walsh firm provided. Meredith had a surplus of capital at this time, which allowed him to withhold his hemp from the market until its sale price increased to an acceptable level. In February 1851, J. & E. Walsh received, on the steamboat *Corn*, 117 bales of Meredith's hemp, which they placed in a warehouse near their Levee Street office; there it remained for the next 23 months. Another 101 bales arrived in October of that year on the steamer *Campbell*. These, too, were placed in the warehouse. And in October 1852, Meredith sent another 143 bales to St. Louis aboard the *Martha Jewitt*, to join those already in storage. Citing an oversupply of hemp early in 1851, which drove the market price below $100 a ton, the Walsh firm did not sell any of Meredith's hemp that year. In November 1852, with hemp prices increasing, three bales — weighing a total of 1,120 pounds — were sold by the warehouse (to cover storage charges) for $107 a ton, giving Meredith's account a $59.80 credited at J. & E. Walsh. Anticipating a further increase in price, the firm held the remainder of Meredith's hemp off the market until January 1853, at which time they sold 276 of the stored bales at prices ranging from $108 to $118 a ton. The remaining 82 bales were sold in early February for $115 a ton. In all, J. & E. Walsh traded 63,182 pounds of Meredith's hemp for $7,231. Steamboat freight charges (paid by the Walsh company), drayage fees in St. Louis, plus warehouse and commission fees, amounted to $1,231, giving a net return to Meredith of $6,000 [equivalent to $173,000 in 2018]. Relating the company's transactions, agent J. P. Willard told Meredith they had "watched the market … and lost no opportunity after our market had become scarce of the article and demand increased … to mark it off at best prices as orders would come in."[17] Later that spring, Meredith sent the Walsh firm five barrels of lard, five dry hides, and one barrel of tallow, delivering the items to the firm of Major W. D. Bayer & Co. of Arrow Rock for forwarding. The shipment arrived in St. Louis on May 5 aboard the steamer *Kate Swinney*, owned by Capt. W. D. Swinney and named for his only daughter, and was sold the following day for $122.84. Freight charges amounted to $3.05 and the commission deducted by J. & E. Walsh for selling the hides, 1,268 pounds of lard, and 131 pounds of tallow was $3.07, netting Meredith $116.72.[18]

J. & E. Walsh's handling of a shipment of Meredith's hemp in 1854 shows other aspects of their relationship, and reinforces the importance to Meredith of having in St. Louis a reliable consignment house with up-to-date information about markets and transportation. In June he sent the firm 197 bales of hemp, produced the previous year, with a suggestion that they forward them to the New York house of Morris & Co. for final sale. In response, the Walsh firm telegraphed Meredith "respecting Messrs. Morris & Co. in consequence of our not knowing anything of that house, as to its solvency, & of whom we could not procure satisfactory information here, consequently have consigned your hemp to Messrs. E. D. Morgan & Co., a house of undoubted solvency. This precaution was taken solely for your interest." The Walsh company also noted receiving four bales of hemp more than the 193 listed on the bill of lading that had accompanied them from Arrow Rock aboard the *Kate Swinney*, saying they had shipped all "to New Orleans to be forwarded by our agents there, Messers. J. Connally & Co., to New York on best terms possible. We considered this route the most expeditious in consequence of breakage in the Illinois Canal & the very low state of water in the Ohio River. We have insured your hemp from St. Louis to New York at $200 per ton & will instruct the parties to whom we have consigned same at New York ... to effect insurance also against fire until sold."[19] Freight, insurance, commission, and other fees incurred for this transaction amounted to $442.30.

Despite a decline in hemp processing at St. Louis in early 1855, the downriver demand for rope and bagging remained high, generated by a doubling of cotton production during the decade to nearly 5 million bales in 1860. The price Meredith received for his 1854 and 1855 hemp production was considerably more than the $118 a ton paid by New Orleans buyers in 1853. In four shipments sent to St. Louis during 1855, Meredith transferred 272 bales of hemp to J. & E. Walsh. The first reached the city in May and June, and the last arrived in October and November. Held by J. & E. Walsh until late March of 1856, all of these were sold to New Orleans buyers on one day for prices ranging from $160 to $170 a ton, netting Meredith $6,860 [$197,796].[20]

Risks and Quality

Transporting products to St. Louis by steamboat presented a risk each time a shipment left Arrow Rock. Although steamboat loss records are not complete, it is estimated that more than 300 boats were sunk, burned, or otherwise wrecked on the Missouri River during the period 1819–1848. Robert Dyer, historian and for many years editor of the journal, *Boone's Lick Heritage*, cataloged 16 boats lost in the 40-mile stretch from Rocheport to Glasgow between 1820 and 1860. One was the *Wenona* which struck a snag and sank a few miles above Jefferson City on November 11, 1855. On board were

40 bales of hemp belonging to Meredith. The cargo had been insured by J. & E. Walsh with the Glasgow Insurance Company of Glasgow, Missouri, for $150 a ton, and they were expecting settlement after a 60-day period "for adjustment of losses." A month previously, Meredith had shipped 50 bales to St. Louis on the *Wenona*.[21] Another 150 bales of Meredith's hemp were lost in the Missouri River August 28, 1859, when the 221-foot-long side-wheeler *Duncan S. Carter* sank at Augusta Bend below Washington, Missouri. Writing from St. Louis to his mother, Lavinia, Darwin Marmaduke reported the loss two days later, saying, "We are unfortunate"; the bales had not been insured.[22]

The quality of the baled hemp affected its value and J. & E. Walsh often reminded Meredith of this. Reporting on the hemp market in August 1855, they noted that it was gradually improving "for good qualities of hemp, and prices range from $115 to $126." However, "the arrival within a few days of some very inferior hemp has produced a depression ... from $3 to $5 a ton, but the good qualities still hold their price."[23]

Quality control began on Meredith's farm in late August when the stalks of the mature crop were cut and the plants left on the ground to wilt. Later the crop was gathered into bundles and stacked until late autumn when the bundles were opened and the stalks again spread on the ground, this time to absorb moisture. This step, termed "dewrotting," softened the woody stems so the fibers would separate as the stalks passed through the rollers of a hemp "brake." The released fiber was then placed in a press and compacted into bales for shipment. Care had to be taken during this entire process to assure that no dirt, weeds, or other debris contaminated the bale. Buyers often sampled the interior of bales to look for hidden, low-quality, or loosely packed hemp. An alternate process, wet-rotting, required the stalks to be submerged in a pond or tank prior to being "broken" and baled. Although wet-rotted hemp produced a stronger fiber desired in the maritime industry for making rope, and hence brought a higher price when sold, most Booneslick farmers — unfamiliar with the process, lacking an adequate supply of water, and disliking the added labor cost — produced dewrotted hemp.

Other Services

Produce brokerage wasn't the sole service J. & E. Walsh provided to Meredith. His cash account with the firm was in effect a checkbook from which he would direct withdrawals to pay for goods or services, or provide cash to members of his family. When his son John was attending college in the east during the 1850s, Meredith occasionally transferred money to him via the company. After making one such payment in February 1853, the firm reported that John "was well pleased & stated there was no longer a necessity for such remittances." That same month, J. & E. Walsh also paid $11.50 on Meredith's behalf for his subscription to an agricultural publication, and $2 for a subscription to the *Missouri Weekly Democrat* newspaper.[24]

Meredith also relied upon the firm of J. & E. Walsh as a forwarding agent and banking house for transactions involving his Dr. Sappington's Anti-Fever Pill business. Agent George Bicknell was in St. Louis in February 1846, about to board the steamboat *Julia* for a sales and collection swing through Mississippi and Louisiana, when he wrote a quick note to Meredith advising him that he, "left in store with Messr's J. & E. Walsh the boxes of medicine for Natchez & N. Orleans." Sending the anti-malaria pills ahead spared Bicknell the problem of carrying them in his saddlebags or in a wagon, but also ran the risk of loss incurred by poor handling on the part of the steamboat operator. One such shipment sent aboard the steamboat *Champlain* in 1847 arrived at New Orleans with 264 boxes of anti-fever pills and 1,654 boxes of Price's Anti-Bilious Pills, damaged in transit. The following year Meredith, represented by the St. Louis law firm of Todd & Krum, sued the boat's owners in an effort to recover nearly $500, the value of the damaged goods. The suit was eventually settled out of court in Meredith's favor.[25]

Meredith used the trusted J. & E. Walsh Company to help transfer pill business money collected by field agents to a bank in Fayette. The multistep process required to accomplish this illustrates another aspect of his relationship with the St. Louis commodity firm and demonstrates the difficulty interstate businesses encountered when attempting to move money from one city to another prior to the establishment of a secure banking industry. Pill salesman Francis Tymony, at New Orleans in March 1850 with $1,762.86 in his handbag, obtained a draft for that amount on the commodity-trading house of "Messr's Small & McGill," payable at "Messr's J. Small and Co." in St. Louis. Forwarding the draft to J. & E. Walsh, Tymony explained, "I am now travelling as the collecting agent for Col. M. M. Marmaduke ... and have been instructed ... to forward any drafts I may wish — payable to your orders at St. Louis with such instructions as I may think proper to give you with regard to its disposition." Tymony directed the Walsh firm to present the draft to J. Small & Co., then deposit the money in the Bank of St. Louis and obtain a draft from that institution payable at their branch in Fayette. J. & E. Walsh was then to send the Bank of St. Louis draft to Meredith at Arrow Rock.[26]

At any time during the years of his expanding farm operations Meredith could have sold his hemp and other produce locally to commission firms located at Glasgow, Boonville, Lexington, Miami, Columbia, Rocheport, or any of several other towns along the Missouri River. Although some of these firms were active for many years, they failed to attract Meredith's interest; instead, he preferred selling in St. Louis where the urban firms specialized in routing products to New Orleans and the East Coast. His long-term connection with the commission house of J. & E. Walsh was predicated on the firm's ability to safely warehouse his hemp and other commodities in St. Louis and provide access to communication and transportation that made it possible to market his produce for the best price.

The Progressing Farmer

Northern Missouri's abundant grasslands and water early on made the state an important producer of beef cattle. Farmers had no trouble finding markets for their livestock locally and elsewhere, sometimes selling to drovers who trailed large herds to eastern states to be resold and then slaughtered. Some 3,000 head of livestock crossed the Mississippi River at Clarksville in northern Missouri in 1834, destined for consumption by residents of cities in Ohio and Pennsylvania. This type of activity persisted for a number of years. Meredith may have sold livestock in this manner, prompted by inquiries from drovers seeking cattle to buy. In 1850, George Glascock, writing from Warren City, Tennessee, asked Meredith for help in finding cattle that he could purchase. Glascock intended to drive a herd to Virginia and "not finding the market in Tennessee sufficiently supplied to select from I have turned my attention [elsewhere] ... and seeing some fine droves in Virginia last fall from your state I have observed it probable that Missouri could furnish me. I wish to purchase a thousand head of three or four years old or some even older, say five or six."[27]

Drovers were not the only outlet for Missouri livestock. There were stockyards in St. Louis by 1845, buyers bidding for cattle to send down the Mississippi to New Orleans. This trade grew over the years, and 15,000 head went down the Mississippi in 1852. Many of these cattle were probably sent on to the East Coast. The New Orleans market, eastern-oriented drovers, and a demand for cattle to be driven west to feed the growing number of settlers in California and Oregon (where Missouri cows bought at $10 were selling for $100 to $150) benefitted Booneslick farmers in the late 1840s and 1850s. It seemed they could find markets for their cattle in almost any direction they looked.

This abundance of outlets plus easy access to new land had a downside, though, in a lack of interest in advanced breeding and land management techniques. Although some farmers in the Booneslick counties sought to improve their land and livestock as they moved from subsistence to commercial agriculture, they lacked general interest in selective breeding and maintaining soil productivity through fertilization. Too, interest in enhancing agricultural production by using such techniques initially found little support in the state's General Assembly. Contrarily, Missouri newspapers often encouraged farmers to improve their practices. An article in the January 22, 1830, issue of the *Missouri Intelligencer* suggested farmers could increase crop yield by using manure as fertilizer on land that had been cropped for several years.[28] Cooper County farmer James R. Hammond, writing in the summer of 1849 to the editor of a popular agricultural magazine, bemoaned the attitude taken by many of his neighbors, saying "Farming here is conducted on the regular *skinning* system — taking everything and returning nothing. ..." He said the area's livestock was "exceedingly scrubby" and that his neighbors were indifferent to "procuring the improved breeds ... [and] as to manuring, the idea is looked on as preposterous!"[29]

Not all farmers were as backward as Hammond's neighbors. Selective breeding in England during the last quarter of the 18th century had produced separate strains of improved beef and milking animals known as Durham or Shorthorn cattle. Descendants of these animals were in the United States by the 1820s, and the breed's popularity grew as knowledge of its superior qualities spread westward. By 1834 Shorthorn cows and bulls were in Boone County, and in 1835 the county fair featured livestock as one of its premier exhibits, urging local farmers to "breed up" for better profits. As a result, during the next two decades the area's farmers became a locus in Missouri for improved stock breeding. An early appearance of Shorthorn cattle in Saline County occurred in 1839 when William Lewis, who lived 10 miles west of Jonesboro, advertised a "fine 2 year-old" Durham bull for sale. That same year Nathaniel Leonard introduced Shorthorns to Cooper County.[30] Another early Shorthorn promoter in Missouri was John O'Fallon of St. Louis, who by 1843 is reported to have had the largest herd of Durham livestock in the state. He also experimented with cross-breeding domestic cattle and the American bison for dairy purposes but abandoned the program after several years of failure. Meredith Marmaduke's neighbor, Thomas Adams Smith, acquired "a fine Durham bull and two cows," sent up the Missouri River by steamboat in 1843, a gift from John O'Fallon.[31]

Meredith's acquisition of improved livestock probably occurred about the same time, as he became aware of the growing movement toward herd improvement across the state during his term as lieutenant governor and then chief executive. His interest in breeding better cattle ultimately led to his appointment in 1855 as one of 22 directors of the Central Missouri Stock Importing Company, one of several such regional groups incorporated by the state's General Assembly in December that year. The organization's board of directors represented Boone, Callaway, Cole, Howard, Saline, and Cooper Counties in the Booneslick region, plus nearby Randolph and Monroe counties. Meredith's friend James S. Rollins was a representative on the organization's board of directors for Boone County, while John Locke Hardeman joined Meredith as a second Saline County representative. The corporation was supposed to buy and import "improved breeds of horses, cattle, Jacks, Jennets, hogs and sheep." It was capitalized at $25,000 (limited to that amount) with shares selling for $50 each and had a 10-year life before dissolving.[32] Seeking Meredith's involvement in early 1856, Boone County farmer Thomas Jenkins wrote asking him "to meet with us ... in order to insure that an early organization of the company may be effected. Let me have your valuable experience, aid, and cooperation in giving this highly important enterprise such a start as will insure its success."[33] Unfortunately, the corporation's demise occurred after only two years, as interest in buying the shares waned following a downturn in the nation's economy.

Rise of County and State Fairs

The development of agricultural societies in Missouri had a rocky start in 1822 when farmers in Chariton County organized the Agricultural and Commercial Society of Missouri to promote communication between themselves and the region's business community. The effort failed after a brief run. Two years later, in the fall of 1824, what was billed as a state agricultural fair occurred at the St. Louis home of William C. Carr. Sponsored by the St. Louis County Agriculture Society, that event also failed to generate enough interest for its continuation. Though erratic in their development, local agricultural societies continued to arouse interest among the state's farmers during the 1830s and '40s. In 1838, the Saline County Court instructed the sheriff to post notices advising citizens of a meeting at the log courthouse in Jonesboro on June 17 to organize a county agricultural society. It is likely that Meredith had a hand in convincing the court to explore the possibility of forming the organization. Evidently this initial effort failed for nothing more is heard about a Saline County farmers' society for 18 years. Elsewhere along the Missouri River, Boone County is reported to have had an agricultural fair in 1835. Its success is unknown; however, the formation there of an Agriculture and Mechanical Society in 1848 led to the presentation of a fair in 1852. Cooper and Callaway Counties held farmer's fairs in 1839, and although they generated some local interest both events failed for lack of financial support. Money issues plagued almost all early efforts to create county agricultural fairs. Historian R. Douglas Hurt described these ventures as "admirable" in concept but denied success by the "parsimonious" attitude of farmers. They wanted the fairs, but they didn't want to spend money to support them. Despite setbacks, central Missouri farmers continued to show interest in holding county fairs. Farther up the Missouri River, Howard and Lafayette Counties created agricultural societies in 1853, and Saline County finally got on board, incorporating an Agriculture and Mechanical Association in March 1857. Meredith's experience organizing a state fair several years earlier no doubt helped put him in office as the county association's president. He held the post for two years, during which fairs were presented on 15 acres a quarter-mile south of Miami, a town on the river at the county's northern border.[34]

The 1854 constitution of the Howard County agricultural society demonstrates a community-inclusive approach adopted by the organizers. The document likely became a model used for the development of similar societies. Its 17 articles and 23 bylaws attempt to address every aspect of a fair's operation and the awarding of prizes. The constitution called for "the development of agriculture, including ... the great staples of industry and trade but also fruits and vegetables; the promotion of the mechanical arts ... the improvement of the races of all the useful and domestic animals ... the general advancement of rural economy household manufactures, and the dissemination of useful information on those subjects." All this was to be accomplished "by fairs for the exhibition and sale of all such articles ... and by the periodical award of premiums. ..." In planning for the fair, the Howard County society sought to increase interest among the county's citizens, both rural and town, and thereby ensure the event's financial success. The first fair, in 1854, took place over three days during which judges, one of whom was Meredith's brother-in-law L. S. Eddins, awarded premiums ranging from $1 to $10 in 20 categories of exhibits. Awards of $10 went to the largest yield of hemp per acre and the best Missouri-raised bulls, cows, and oxen, plus mules and "blooded, harness and saddle" horses. Categories for exhibit ranged from orchards and gardens to "Flowers, Paintings, and Drawings," typically women's contributions that garnered awards from $1 to $5. Men and boys focused their contributions on agricultural implements, carriages, buggies, wagons, and the expected farm crops and livestock.[35]

The increasing interest in sponsoring local agricultural societies was acknowledged by Missouri's legislators in February 1853 when they enacted — at the urging of farmers from several Booneslick counties — a bill to incorporate The Missouri State Agricultural Society, an early effort to establish a state fair. The act empowered the society to buy 20 acres of land and erect buildings for "an exhibition of various breeds of horses, cattle, mules and other stock, and of agricultural, mechanical and domestic manufactures and productions." Meredith's appointment as president of the society indicates his influence in securing the legislative action. Appointed with him as directors were influential farmers from central Missouri (many of whom he knew) including James S. Rollins from Boone County and Nathaniel Leonard from Cooper County. Also represented were Howard, Callaway, Osage, and Randolph Counties. The General Assembly added to the directors, most likely at the urging of Meredith, two Boonville men who would have important roles in establishing the society. Joseph L. Stephens, named recording secretary, was an attorney and later manager of a branch Bank of St. Louis, and William H. Trigg, who established the first bank in Boonville in 1847, was named treasurer. Meredith was soon able to obtain the appointment of John

Locke Hardeman as vice president of the society.[36]

In early May 1853, the members of the Cooper County Agricultural Society, led by William Trigg and Joseph Stephens, voted to join the new state society and agreed to work as a committee to develop a constitution and bylaws for the new organization. The document was completed by mid-July, and Stephens sent Meredith and John Locke Hardeman copies for review, along with a request for the names of potential financial supporters of the society. As well, the Boonville group agreed to organize and put on the first state fair later that year. Although the act establishing the society did not specify Boonville as the site for the new fair, language in the bill pointed in that direction. Perhaps reflecting the General Assembly's lack of confidence in the idea of a state fair, legislators provided a meager $1,000 of funding annually from the state treasury for four years to help get the organization on its feet. Otherwise the society had to fund itself through contributions and fees. By the summer of 1853 Meredith, Stephens, and Trigg had already raised enough additional money to purchase 14 acres of land overlooking the Missouri River "just below Boonville" known as the Rupell property. News of the state fair's scheduled opening on Monday, October 3, appeared in newspapers across the state that summer and aroused a great deal of interest. Joseph Stephens was so pleased with the response that he wrote Meredith to say that he was "happy to see the very favorable notices the Society receives from the press. ... Some of them publish the list of premiums [and] rules" in entirety."[37]

More than 4,000 visitors attended the four-day event, viewing exhibits and displays provided mostly by Booneslick area farmers and their families. Some agriculture-related St. Louis business houses were also present. Boone County residents took home the most premiums, while Cooper County led in swine prizes and Howard and Audrain in mules. Callaway County produced the best draft and saddle horses, and Boone County the best tobacco.

Financial problems plagued the fledgling state fair following the 1853 event. Organizers spent $6,000 buying the fairground and erecting the buildings; receipts from the event were half that.[38] Contemplating the 1854 state fair, Meredith and Stephens canvassed potential sponsors and donors in St. Louis in the spring and commissioned "Mr. Schoolfield of Columbia" to travel east and see what financial support he could raise among implement and other farm equipment manufacturers. The society raised enough money to open the fair again in the fall of 1854 with expanded fairground facilities to accommodate more exhibitors. But the event continued to be weak financially, and there was a growing feeling among state legislators that it was essentially a regional fair. Their concern was bolstered by the distribution of premiums — 156 of 205 awards went to exhibitors from Boone, Howard, and Cooper Counties. Heading into 1855, it appeared that the event might not survive, and there is no evidence that the state fair took place that year.[39] In January 1856, John Locke Hardeman (Saline County's legislative representative at the time) notified Meredith that "The fate of our Agricultural Society is decided so far as this House can do it. The House decided by a large majority to repeal the State Act and charter five district societies with 500 [dollars] to each."[40] The state Senate concurred in the House's action, and as a consequence Missouri had no state fair for the next 45 years.

Notes

1. Aside from his home farm expansion: Federal acreage purchased by Marmaduke in Saline County can be found by searching Bureau of Land Management, Government Land Office records online at www. glorecords.blm.gov. Prices for private land during the 1830s are from R. Douglas Hurt, *Agriculture and Slavery in Missouri's Little Dixie*, 56–59. Marmaduke's purchases of private land in Saline County, and land sales, are found in Saline County Index to Deeds 1821–1862, Microfilm Roll C6219, Missouri State Archives.

2. Records from the Saline County tax collector's office: 1852 receipt for State and Saline County tax, Folder 19, Marmaduke Papers C1029. SHSMO. M.M. Marmaduke, Assessment of personal property and real estate for Saline County, Mo., 1860, C1238. SHSMO. Meredith reported owning 400 acres of improved land and 1,100 acres of unimproved land in the 1850, first-ever, Productions in Agriculture (Schedule 4) census, *1850 U.S. Federal Agricultural Schedule, Saline County, Missouri*. His father-in-law claimed 300 acres of improved land and 1,500 acres of unimproved land. Both men reported far less than they owned at the time. Instructions for entering data on Schedule 4 defined improved and unimproved land, in essence seeking to record all agricultural land owned by a farmer, not necessarily contiguous, whether in production, fallow, or otherwise.

3. Hurt, *Agriculture and Slavery in Missouri's Little Dixie*, 61.

4. "if I still wished to rent your Story Farm. I expect my Brother in law [sic] soon": W. S. Wilson to Marmaduke, November 12, 1850. Folder 18, Marmaduke Papers C1021, SHSMO.

5. "One great obstacle in the way of getting good tenants here": John L. Hardeman to N. B. Tucker, March 27, 1848, and September 15, 1848. Folder 6, John Locke Hardeman Papers C2337, SHSMO. More insight into farm rental is found in R. Douglas Hurt, *Agriculture and Slavery in Little Dixie*, 63–64.

6. Early settlements in Saline County are described in *History of Saline County*, 144–150.

7. "in most places, as tall as a medium sized man, and as high as the head of a man on horseback": William Barclay Napton, *Past and Present of Saline County, Missouri*, 84. Meredith's Saline County neighbor acquired his property, Elk Hill, in 1840. Louis S. Gerteis; Napton, William Barclay (1808–1883), in Christensen, et al., *Dictionary of Missouri Biography*, 568. Missouri's prairie and agricultural practices of the early 19th century are described in Donald Christisen, "A Vignette of Missouri's Native Prairie," *MHR*, Vol. 61, No. 2 (January 1967).

8. "I am having made a plough which I intend to send you as a present": John L. Hardeman to Marmaduke, March 19, 1836. Box 2, Folder 2, Sappington-Marmaduke Papers, MHS.

9. Saline County farmers could figure on needing one laborer for every 30 acres: Hurt, 69. *1850 Saline County U.S. Census, Schedule 2, Slave Inhabitants*, Reel F50; *Schedule 4, Productions of Agriculture*, Reel S948, Missouri State Archives. Harrison A. Trexler, *Slavery In Missouri 1804–1865*, 196. Baltimore: The Johns Hopkins Press, 1914. The ratio one slave per 30 acres of improved land is derived from analysis of six slave-holding Saline County farmers reported as having 300 or more acres of improved land. Male and female slaves aged 15 to 60 years, less 10 percent of the female slaves thought to be household workers, comprised the labor force for each farm. Acres farmed per slave ranged from 14.5 to 43.75, averaging 27.2. Type of crop, age, and health of slaves, their duties, environmental factors, and slaveholder demands on labor contribute to the variation. Examples in Hurt and in Trexler were also examined and found to be consistent with the sample derived from data in Schedules 2 and 4 of the 1850 census.

10. "but may be a wood lot or other land at some distance, owned in connection with the farm": Instructions to Schedule 4, 1850 U.S. Federal Agricultural Census.

11. When William Letcher visited Meredith's farm on November 23, 1850: *1850 United States Federal Census Schedule 1*, 140, 148; and *Schedule 4*, 377. Saline County, Mo., Reels S458 and S948, Missouri State Archives. Polly Oliver and Samuel M. McCorkle have not been identified. She may have been Lavinia's cousin, perhaps from the Breathitt family in Kentucky. McCorkle may have been the son of Samuel M. McCorkle of Greene County, Missouri. The 1840 U.S. Census lists two sons aged 10 through 14 in his household. Indications are the family moved to Saline County sometime prior to 1850. Abraham Van Meter is the father of Abel J. Van Meter, for whom Van Meter State Park in northern Saline County is named. Abraham and his family arrived in Saline County in 1834, settling near the town of Miami, where

he became "the most extensive cattle dealer in northwestern Missouri." An interesting history of the Van Meter family is found in Jean Tyree Hamilton's "Abel J. Van Meter, His Park and His Diary," *The Bulletin of the Missouri Historical Society*, Vol. 27 (October 1971).

12. "who's who of the region's political and economic elite": Merchants Exchange of St. Louis, Early Commodity Market, https:scripophily.net/merexofstlou1.hml. Still active, the St. Louis Merchants Exchange is the oldest organized cash commodity market in the nation.

13. "lead, flour and steamboat magnate": William Hyde, and Howard L. Conard, eds. *Encyclopedia of the History of St. Louis, Vol. 4,* 2396. James N. Primm, *Lion of the Valley, St. Louis, Missouri,* 200. John A. Paxton, *The St. Louis Directory and Register, 1821,* np. Edward and James Walsh may have come to America with their parents. In 1821, P. Walsh was engaged as an auctioneer and commission merchant at 29 North Main Street. That same year, Hester Walsh had a grocery at 70 South Main Street.

14. "such other articles ... as you may not buy in Phil. or Pittsbg.": Marmaduke to Darwin Sappington, February 3, 1834. Folder 7, Marmaduke Papers C1021, SHSMO. Meredith's relationship with the firm of J. & E. Walsh was a firmly established aspect of his business and farm activities until 1861, when it was disrupted by the Civil War.

15. Although fidelity in business dealings was important: Blain, Thompkins & Barrett to Marmaduke, April 2, 1846, Folder 16; Yeatman & Pittman, May 18, 1853, Folder 19. Marmaduke Papers C1021 SHSMO.

16. "Your note of this day per your boy is recd. and with it 36 Bacon Sides": Watson to Marmaduke, October 16 and December 15, 1847. Folder 17, Marmaduke Papers C1021, SHSMO.

17. Produce Meredith sent to the J. & E. Walsh company on consignment: J. & E. Walsh to Marmaduke, February 1, 1853. Box 5, Folder 3, Sappington-Marmaduke Papers, MHS. J. & E. Walsh to Marmaduke, February 15, 1853. Folder 19, Marmaduke Papers C1021, SHSMO. The relative value in 2018 of a $6,000 commodity sold in 1853 was determined using an inflation calculator. Samuel H. Williams, *Seven Ways to Compute the Relative Value of a U.S. dollar Amount, 1774 to Present.* (electronic document: www.measuringworth.com/calculator/uscompare.)

18. The shipment arrived in St. Louis on May 5 aboard the steamer *Kate Swinney*: J. & E. Walsh to Marmaduke, May 7, 1853. Box 5, Folder 3, Sappington-Marmaduke Papers, MHS.

19. "respecting Messrs. Morris & Co. in consequence of our not knowing anything of that house": J. & E. Walsh to Marmaduke, June 15, 1854. Folder 20, Marmaduke Papers C1021, SHSMO.

20. Despite a decline in hemp processing at St. Louis in early 1855: Hurt, *Agriculture and Slavery in Missouri's Little Dixie,* 121; J. & E. Walsh to Marmaduke, March 31, 1856 (four letters). Folder 20, Marmaduke Papers C1021, SHSMO. For Missouri River towns with rope walks see: Miles W. Eaton, "The Development and Later Decline of the Hemp Industry in Missouri," *MHR*, Vol. 43, No. 4 (July, 1949), 351–52.

21. Transporting products to St. Louis by steamboat presented a risk: J. & E. Walsh to Marmaduke, January 10, 1856. Box 5, Folder 6, Sappington-Marmaduke Papers, MHS. Lawrence Giffen, *Walks on Water — The Impact of Steamboating on the Lower Missouri River,* 84–88. Vols. 1–2. Glasgow Insurance Company Books 1855–1870, Collection C2313, SHSMO.

22. Another 150 bales of Meredith's hemp were lost in the Missouri River: Darwin Marmaduke to Lavinia Marmaduke, August 30, 1859. Box 5, Folder 6, Sappington-Marmaduke Papers, MHS. Phil. E. Chappel, "Missouri River Steamboats," *Transactions of the Kansas State Historical Society, 1905–1906*, Vol. 9, 301.

23. "for good qualities of hemp, and prices range from $115 to $126": J. & E. Walsh to Marmaduke, August 23, 1855. Folder 20, Marmaduke Papers C1021, SHSMO.

24. "was well pleased & stated there was no longer a necessity for such remittances": J. & E. Walsh to Marmaduke, February 28, 1853. Folder 19, Marmaduke Papers C1021, SHSMO.

25. "left in store with Messr's J. & E. Walsh the boxes of medicine for Natchez & N. Orleans": Bicknell to Marmaduke, May 21, 1847. Box 4, Folder 2. Sappington-Marmaduke Papers, MHS; Bicknell to Marmaduke, January 16, 1848. Box 4, Folder 4. Sappington-Marmaduke Papers, MHS; Todd & Krum to Marmaduke, January 21, 1848. Folder 17, Marmaduke Papers C1021, SHSMO; Marmaduke to Todd &

Dirt is Destiny

Krum, July 9, 1848. Box 4, Folder 5, Sappington-Marmaduke Papers, MHS; Memoranda (2), Marmaduke & Bicknell vs Owners of S.B. Champlain, undated. Box 4, Folder 2, Sappington-Marmaduke Papers, MHS.

26. Meredith used the trusted J. & E. Walsh company to help transfer pill business money: Tymony to J. & E. Walsh, March 20, 1850. Folder 18, Marmaduke Papers C1021, SHSMO.

27. In 1850, George Glascock, writing from Warren City, Tennessee, asked Meredith for help in finding cattle: Glascock to Marmaduke, March 8, 1850. Box 4, Folder 7, Sappington-Marmaduke Papers, MHS. Glascock had moved to Tennessee from Westmoreland County, Virginia, following an altercation with his father that Meredith, in later years, tried to ameliorate. His letter mentions mutual friends in Virginia.

28. Contrarily, Missouri newspapers often encouraged farmers to improve their practices. George F. Lemmer, ed. "Agitation for Agricultural Improvement in Central Missouri newspapers prior to the Civil War." *MHR*, Vol. 37, No. 4 (July 1943), 372.

29. "Farming here is conducted on the regular *skinning* system": George F. Lemmer. "Missouri Agriculture as revealed in the Eastern Agricultural Press 1823–1869, Letter of James R. Hammond August 7, 1849 to the editor of the *Cultivator*." *MHR*, Vol 42, No. 3 (April 1948), 234.

30. An early appearance of Shorthorn cattle in Saline County: George F. Lemmer. "Early Leaders in Livestock Improvement in Missouri." *MHR*, Vol. 37, No. 1 (October 1942), 30. Nathaniel Leonard Papers, C2525, SHSMO.

31. "a fine Durham bull and two cows," sent up the Missouri River by steamboat in 1843, a gift from John O'Fallon. Napton, *Past and Present of Saline County*, 131.

32. "improved breeds of horses, cattle, Jacks, Jennets, hogs and sheep": "The Central Missouri Stock Importing Company;" *Local Laws and Private Acts of the State of Missouri at the Adjourned Session of the 18th General Assembly*, 336.

33. "to meet with us … in order to that an early organization of the company may be effected": Jenkins to Marmaduke, February 16, 1856. Box 5, Folder 6, Sappington-Marmaduke Papers, MHS.

34. Historian R. Douglas Hurt described these ventures as "admirable": Hurt, 166. 1881 History of Saline County, 397–98, 451.

35. The 1854 constitution of the Howard County agricultural society: Constitution of the Howard County Agricultural and Mechanical Society. Box 5, Folder 4, Sappington-Marmaduke Papers, MHS.

36. The increasing interest in sponsoring agricultural societies was acknowledged by Missouri's legislators: An Act to Incorporate The Missouri State Agricultural Society — approved February 24, 1853. *Laws of Missouri, 1852–1853*. Jefferson City: Vol. 10 (1854).

37. In early May 1853 the members of the Cooper County Agricultural Society: Stephens to Marmaduke, May 7 and July 13, 1853. Box 5, Folder 3, Sappington-Marmaduke Papers, MHS.

38. More than 4,000 visitors attended the four-day event: First State Fair at Boonville. State Historical Society of Missouri, compiler. *This Week in Missouri History*, Vol. 5, np.

39. "Mr. Schoolfield": Stephens to Marmaduke, June 10, 1854. Folder 19, Marmaduke Papers C1021, SHSMO

40. "The fate of our Agricultural Society": Hardeman to Marmaduke, December 10, 1855. Folder 20, Ibid.

CHAPTER 16

MISSOURI AND NO RESTRICTIONS

In March of 1820, news of Missouri's admission to the Union as a state where slavery was allowed reached St. Louis the last week of the month, the information traveling across the country in only a few days' time. The town's citizens responded to their newly acquired status with "the ringing of bells, the firing of cannons, and ... joyful congratulations." A few days later, St. Louis's newspapers called for an illuminated celebration with lighted candles on display in the windows of homes. That night, as flaming tapers appeared in windows throughout the town, one house exhibited a candlelit paper transparency depicting a black slave "dancing joyously" because "Congress had voted to permit the slaves to come and live in such a fine country as Missouri."[1]

Statehood for Missouri did not come easily. Debate over the territory's admittance to the Union had begun in earnest in 1818 when the U.S. Congress, following the territory's request for statehood, considered a bill to authorize the calling of a state constitutional convention, a required step toward full recognition. Problems soon arose over Missouri's desire to be admitted as a slave state. With opposing views about the extension of slavery into new states, legislators conducted a "bitter debate" for much of the next two years that focused national attention on the issue. The Missouri Compromise, approved in early March of 1820, preserved the balance of power in Congress by admitting Maine as a free state and Missouri as a slave state while prohibiting the expansion of slavery north of the parallel 36 degrees, 30 minutes north latitude (the southern boundary of Missouri, excluding the Bootheel). As a result, Missouri became a thumb of slavery bordered on the east by the "free" state of Illinois, and on the north and west by Indian country that eventually became the states of Iowa, Nebraska, Kansas, and Oklahoma. To the south lay the proslavery Arkansas Territory. The admittance of Missouri as a slave state settled in Meredith Marmaduke's mind any doubt he may have had about leaving Virginia. His journey with five slaves in 1823 was predicated upon the knowledge that he could transfer them halfway across the nation to a slave-holding state where they would continue to be an economic asset. Like the Virginia planters who preceded him, Meredith held cultural and social beliefs about slavery that guided his actions until his death. To understand this aspect of his life — and its effect upon his family, his slaves, and his farming, political, and business activities — it is helpful to know how slavery generally operated in Missouri.

Some of the earliest black slaves known to be in Missouri entered in the 1720s as miners working lead deposits along what became known as the "Negro Fork" of the Meramec River in Washington County. At about the same time, black slaves began to appear on farmsteads along the Mississippi River south of St. Louis. By the time of Louisiana's transfer to the United States in 1804, nearly 1,500 slaves lived in eastern and southern Missouri. Six years later, the population had doubled and by 1820 more than 9,000 slaves were in the Territory of Missouri, many of them brought from Virginia, Kentucky, and Tennessee. The importation of enslaved black human beings continued through the next four decades as the state's white slave-owning population increased. This, coupled with native-born children of slaves, brought the slave population in Missouri to nearly 115,000 (13 percent of the state's population) by 1860. Their owners considered them personal property, the same as real estate and personal goods, and Missouri's legislature concurred. Meredith's attitude and practices regarding the men, women, and children who were his slaves were guided by this authority, as well as by personal belief in a right to own such property.[2]

Missouri Laws Governing Slaves

Missouri's first territorial legislature, meeting in 1804, recognized the right of slave owners to import their bondsmen into the new territory. To enable them to control the lives of their slaves (and perpetuate enslavement, itself) the legislature enacted a law respecting slaves; its 35 articles were based upon the slave code of Virginia, with many of the provisions similar to those in the Code Noir, a document dating to 1685 that governed slavery in French Louisiana. Under Missouri law, Meredith's slaves could not travel without permission; they could, however, possess firearms (living, as they were, on a "frontier plantation" where guns were deemed necessary for protection and hunting). Violators were subject to "ten lashes on his or her back for every such offence." His slaves could not gather in meetings, incite violence, make seditious speeches, or testify in court against a white person. To discourage social contact, slaves could visit a neighboring plantation for only four hours at a time, and no more than five slaves could visit a plantation at one time. Slaves could meet "at a public mill" when there on business for their owners, so long as it wasn't at night or on a Sunday. Meredith occasionally allowed slaves to travel for business purposes. In 1847, he sent a slave to Boonville with a wagon carrying nearly 700 pounds of hams that were consigned to a merchant there.[3]

Slaves were also prohibited from trading "any commodity" without permission. Anyone who traded with such a slave could be fined and might "receive on his or her bare back thirty-nine lashes well laid on." Illicit trading was more serious than raising a hand against a master. A slave who did that was subject to having just 30 lashes "well laid on." A judge could waive the penalty if the slave was "wantonly assaulted, and [had] lifted his or her hand in ... defense."[4] This section of the code apparently caused plantation owners some discomfort because if their slaves were flogged they might become unable to work. As a result, the article was modified in 1822 to prohibit flogging as a penalty.

The 1804 slavery laws, with modifications from time to time, remained the basis for the regulation of Missouri's slaves and their white masters and free black citizens for the next 60 years, abandoned only at the close of the Civil War. Many of these laws were difficult to enforce and likely were ignored, nevertheless during this period the lives of black men, women, and children in Missouri were closely governed.

The Marmaduke Slaves

An early settler in northern Missouri recalled that the prairie sod was too tough to break without a team of oxen to pull the plow. He should have added that the strength of animals had to be matched by a healthy and strong human work force. To achieve this, many farmers removing from Virginia, Kentucky, and Tennessee to settle along the Missouri River brought their slaves with them. As property, they had economic value in the form of their labor, and their presence allowed the efficient production of hemp and tobacco, major sources of income.

As a member of the planter class (defined by historian R. Douglas Hurt as someone who owned at least 20 slaves and 500 acres of land), Meredith Marmaduke was not the man behind the plow laying out rows for sowing corn, or the worker drenched in gritty sweat cutting hemp stalks in the humid August fields of Saline County. To perform such activities, he used slaves. This also allowed him to pursue other interests that began with his appointment to various county posts during the late 1820s, continuing with his partnership in the store at Jonesboro, management of his portion of Dr. Sappington's pill business, and his various land speculation schemes. Too, slave labor maintained his agricultural interests while he served as lieutenant governor, then governor, in the period 1841–44.

By 1840, the number of people Meredith held in bondage had increased from the five he brought from Virginia in 1823 to 13. Seven of these slaves were males, four of them old enough to be used as farm labor, and Meredith classified them as "agricultural workers" in the 1840 federal census. Three of the males were younger than 10 years of age. Four of his female slaves in 1840 were old enough to be employed as household labor under Lavinia's supervision; two others were younger than 10. By 1850, Meredith's slave force had doubled in number to 27, making him the eighth-largest of 509 slaveholders in Saline County and among the top 364 slave owners (based on the number of slaves held) out of 19,148 in the state. Eleven of his slaves in 1850 were females ranging in age from 3 to 65 with three of them age 11 or younger. Five of the female slaves were mulattos, all children aged 9 to 13. The parentage of the mulatto children is unknown; they were, however, not sired by any of Meredith's sons who would have been too young. His male slaves in 1850 numbered 16. Two were in their 30s, the oldest of which was 38. Only one, aged 21, was a mulatto. Nine were considered prime — or approaching prime — fieldworkers aged 15 to 22 years old. Five of the males were 7 years old or younger (one was a 1-year-old baby).[5]

During the late 1840s and throughout the 1850s, the demand in Missouri for commercial agricultural products increased with corn, hemp, and tobacco leading the way. In these same years, the desire for Oregon land and the discovery of gold in California in 1848 created a stream of migrants traversing the state who needed flour, corn, beef cattle, and draft animals as food and transport during their months-long journey west. One estimate has the number of wagons departing from western Missouri in the spring of 1849 at nearly 12,000, an early wave of migration that would continue over the next decade. Locke Hardeman noted the flow of westward-bound migrants in a letter to Beverley Tucker, saying "The 'Californians' have been detained on account of cholera, which is havoc in our midst."[6] Missouri's farmers, particularly those in the Booneslick region and along the state's western border, were quick to take advantage of the opportunity laid before them by increasing both crop production and animal husbandry. Meredith responded by opening new ground to cultivation, more than doubling the number of acres of improved land (from 400 in 1850 to 900 in 1860), with much of this going to the production of corn (from 2,500 bushels in 1850 to 7,500 in 1860); and by doubling swine production from 161 to 300 during the same decade. To do this, he needed more slaves, and the 1860 federal census found him with 54 — once again double the number from 10 years earlier. His 1860 slaveholdings consisted of 23 females and 31 males. One of the female slaves was a gray-haired grandmother who had seen 80 summers come and go. Two other older women, ages 50 and 47, plus 11 whose ages ran from 14 to 37, were capable of working as domestic or field labor. Nine girls on the plantation were aged 10 years and younger. Only one female, aged 35, was a mulatto. Twenty of the male slaves Marmaduke held in 1860, ranging in age from 16 to 47, were old enough to work in the fields. Three of them were mulattos. Of the remaining 11 males, one boy was 14, two were 12, and eight were 8 years old or younger.[7]

During 24 years of record (1840 to 1864), Meredith kept only one adult male slave over the age of 50, an indication that he believed older males to be less productive as field hands and more likely to be suitable for only light chores. Missouri plantation owners sometimes purged their slave rosters of older men by selling them while they still could command a good price. Slave values rose in Missouri during the two decades preceding the Civil War. An indication of what Meredith might have received from the sale of his older slaves can be seen in an 1859 Saline County estate appraisement where the probate court accepted a property schedule that valued a male slave age 17 at $1,300, and a 36-year-old male at $1,200. Other slaves in the same estate included an 8-year-old boy valued at $650 and a 5-year-old at $440. Females in the estate were valued from $50 for a 6-month-old to $1,250 for a mother and 14-month-old child.[8] Slaves advertised for sale during the same period in Booneslick newspapers had comparable or higher prices.

In both 1850 and 1860, the preponderance of prime-age male slaves on Meredith's plantation reflected his need for a labor force that could endure the stress of producing the hemp and other crops that were the plantation's primary source of income. The value of these older boys and men, however, depended upon a stable or increasing economy that would absorb the plantation's commercial products, and this became less sure as the nation slid irreversibly into civil war. By 1864, the year of Meredith's death, the age composition of his slaves had changed considerably. An estate audit filed with the Saline County Probate Court contains the names of 51 slaves he owned at the time of his death. Only six of them were adult male field hands (aged 22 to 46), a reduction of 10 males in the same age range from four years earlier.[9]

The general disarray of transportation and markets that accompanied the Civil War affected Meredith's ability to access normal distribution channels. From 1861 until the defeat of the entrenched Confederate force at Vicksburg in 1863, the Mississippi River below the confluence of the Ohio was closed to most steamboat traffic, shutting off that important market for Meredith's products. With no need for their labor, Meredith compensated by selling most of his valuable male slaves, turning unproductive "property" into cash. He also lost two male slaves who ran away in 1863 and joined the Union Army. Twenty-eight-year-old Bateman Brown slipped away from the plantation to enlist at Lexington, while 33-year-old Patrick Marmaduke walked undetected to Sedalia, where he enlisted.[10] The reduction of prime male slaves on the plantation was offset by an increase in the number of slave children during the same period. In addition to the six adult males mentioned above, his estate appraisal listed 18 boys 1 to 16 years old, six of whom were 2 years old or younger; 11 women ages 18 to 40; and 16 girls aged 1 to 14 of which six were 6 years old. With a large number of slaves on his plantation in 1864, including 34 children younger than 16, Meredith was either hoping for a favorable outcome of the nation's conflict, whereby ownership of his slave property would continue, or he was sheltering slaves from the violence that ravaged Missouri as a border state. If he anticipated having slaves as property when the war ended, he was positioned to either sell young slaves and use the income to purchase prime-age field hands or keep them until they were old enough to become field hands. On the other hand, paternalistic feelings toward his slaves may have directed his decisions during these difficult years. Further examination of Meredith's actions as a slaveholder in the decades preceding the Civil War may shed some light on his intentions.

Life on the Plantation

In January of 1841, when Meredith was in Jefferson City as lieutenant governor, the welfare of the plantation's slaves was on Lavinia's mind as she penned a letter to him. "Minny's leg as I mentioned some time ago being sore, is getting better and I believe will nicely heal. I believe it has been — weeks he has been unable to do anything. With that exception, the Negroes have been healthy."[11]

Four years later, another letter Meredith received from home while in Jefferson City again reminded him that the responsibilities of a plantation owner were not left behind when he was gone.

> My dear Father, The workmen were here to work last Monday. They think that they will have the granary ready to raise by next Tuesday if the weather keeps warm as it now is all of the timbers that are not up will be hauled up tomorrow. There will be no more than enough flooring for one floor.
> Mr Hurt killed thirty two of our hogs yesterday and has cut them out and salted them.
> The hands are pulling of some corn that was left in the far fields. I have got seventy four ewes and fifty four withers at home making in all 128, and I think I know where there is one or two more of ours and if they are I get them home in a day or two we have as yet but one lamb. Ulysses had the distemper very bad but is getting over it. The stock looks pretty well every thing goes on pretty much as it did when you were at home. Lewis got his leg very badly cut by a hog at grandfathers in attempting to kill it.

Mr. Hurt has killed only four of our wild hogs this winter. We have put up none.
I believe I have given you all the news.
I remain your affectionate Son, Vincent Marmaduke.[12]

Fourteen-year-old Vincent's letter to his father provides a glimpse into the diversified activities that characterized the life of the slaves on the Marmaduke plantation. A new building was being erected, and slaves were helping hired carpenters in its construction. It was midwinter, a time for slaves to butcher hogs, salt the meat, and pack it into barrels. Wild hogs were killed, the meat probably given to the slaves on the plantation. Slaves were being sent to "far fields" to harvest corn before the withered stalks lodged, grinding the dry ears in the dirt. A lamb was born to be followed by many more in coming weeks. Unless cared for by slaves, they could die in the bitter cold of a windy winter night. In the barnyard, distemper — a nasty viral infection — has laid low one of the farm dogs and could spread to others. And a hog's filthy tusk has opened an ugly wound in a slave's leg. The limb may become infected. Sepsis could spread throughout the man's body, eventually causing his death and the loss to Meredith of valuable property.

Meredith relied on his family to keep him apprised of farm activities, but he looked to Ossumus Hurt, an overseer, to manage the farm and direct the work of the slaves. With business and political interests requiring his frequent absence from the plantation, an overseer was a necessity. Meredith employed three during the period 1840–1860, each a young man with a small family who migrated to Missouri from an Upper South state, each experienced to some degree with the management of slaves. Ossumus Hurt, a 28-year-old Virginian, oversaw Meredith's slaves and home farm in 1840 and for some years thereafter. At the same time, he also served as overseer for Dr. Sappington. Hurt lived with his wife, two girls under the age of 5, and two slaves of his own in a house on the doctor's plantation. Ten years later Ossumus Hurt was a landowner himself with five slaves and real estate worth $4,000. James M. Valdenar, born in Maryland, was Meredith's overseer in 1850. He and his family occupied Meredith and Lavinia's first house, built in 1826 and replaced by a new home in 1847. In 1860, another young Virginian, James H. Huffman, was working as Meredith's overseer. He, too, lived with his wife and two young children in the original Marmaduke home.[13]

The use of overseers was not widespread in Missouri because nearly 90 percent of the state's slaveholders, the majority of whom were small-scale farmers, owned 10 or fewer bondsmen. To employ a manager for such a small workforce was an economic disadvantage. Too, by sharing work and family life, white and black residents of small-scale farms often formed relationships that reduced the need for strict oversight. This was unlike the South where large gangs of slaves, of no particular interest to the plantation master other than their labor, received close and sometimes brutal management. In 1850, there were 509 slave owners in Saline County. Most were small-scale farmers, with a scattering of business and tradesmen. Nineteen other slaveholders qualified as planters (500 acres and 20 or more slaves). That same year only 18 men in the county identified themselves as overseers (excluding several road overseers) when questioned by a census auditor. Some worked for Meredith's neighbors, among them Dr. Sappington, his sons William and Darwin, Thomas H. Harvey, General Thomas

A. Smith's widow Cynthia, Pink D. Booker, John Gravens, Minor W. O'Bannon, and Reuben McDaniel — all living in the vicinity of Arrow Rock.

A slave's life was never easy. Long hours of field and house labor were required of men, women, and often children. William Wells Brown, a Missouri slave who escaped bondage in 1834 to become a noted novelist, playwright, and historian, published a narrative in 1847 that told of slaves on the farm where he lived in St. Charles County being awakened daily by an overseer at 4 a.m. to begin work a half hour later, and not returning to their quarters until after dark. It was not solely men who were subjected to long hours and hard labor. Black women, other than those assigned duties in the master's household, were expected to labor in the fields, and their children from age 6 or 7 were given work on the farm doing light duties, feeding animals, and keeping the kitchen kindling box stocked with wood. Jane Simpson, a slave in southwest Missouri, recalled that as a little girl she worked to "pick up chunks in de field, set brush heap afire, burn up rubbish, pull weeds and de like." A former Saline County slave, Richard Bruner, said he "remembered being a water boy to de field hands before I were big enough to work in de fields." He soon was put to work hoeing tobacco.[14]

Slaves sometimes left Meredith's plantation and traveled to Boonville or Arrow Rock, delivering farm produce or running errands. These trips provided opportunities to run away without being detected for some time. An "underground railroad" was active in Boonville in 1853. F. H. Moss, a Canadian citizen, "decoyed" three slaves from the town that year. Apprehended and returned to Cooper County, where he was accused of "running off slaves," Moss provided his accusers with "names and other information connected with the 'underground railroad' system as practised [sic] in Missouri." That same year, two runaway slaves from John Nowlin's farm passed through Meredith's plantation, perhaps on their way to Boonville, and stayed long enough to speak with other slaves. When later questioned, Meredith's slaves acknowledged the incident to a member of Nowlin's family. Nowlin then reported the episode in a letter to Meredith, asking his help in locating the fugitives. In addition to two slaves who ran away to join the Union Army in 1863, one other instance of slaves fleeing Meredith's plantation is known, occurring during a time of increasing abolitionist influence in the region. In November 1856, five male slaves fled the plantation as a group. Meredith's search for them in Randolph County was unsuccessful and it is not known if they were ever recovered. Their loss was a significant economic blow. Replacing them with five prime-age male slaves would cost him at least $6,000 ($173,000 in 2018).[15]

Brutality and Benevolence

In Missouri as elsewhere, mistreatment of slaves existed; scholars are divided, however, over the question of whether or not slaves in the state lived less-brutal lives than those in the cotton states of the South. Philip V. Scarpino, in his study "Slavery in Callaway County, Missouri 1845–1855," concluded that most masters regarded their slaves as "both human beings and valuable property," noting that the wills of deceased slave owners often showed humane or paternalistic feelings toward their bondsmen, sometimes allowing them to select their new master rather than be sold as part of the estate property. Unfortunately, benevolence wasn't always present. Author Diane Mutti Burke, in her book *On Slavery's Border*, contends that historical evidence shows benign slavery in Missouri was not true "in most cases." William Wells Brown relates in his memoir: "Though slavery is thought, by some, to be mild in Missouri, when compared with the cotton, sugar and rice growing States, yet no part of our slave-holding country, is more noted for the barbarity of its inhabitants, than St. Louis."[16] As a child, Brown witnessed numerous instances of cruelty while living on a farm adjacent to that of Daniel Boone in St. Charles County, including his mother being flogged with a whip. (The events Brown describes in his writings, and as a popular speaker on the abolitionist circuit, are thought to be authentic, although recent scholarship by biographer Ezra Greenspan — who portrays Brown as "the leading African American man of letters" for his era — casts doubt on whether he actually experienced all that he related. Instead, Greenspan argues, Brown often incorporated the experiences of others into his writings and presentations, claiming them to be his own.)[17]

Meredith's sentiments toward his slaves is reflected in a letter to John Hardeman, written in 1824 from Santa Fe. He had left his bondsmen in Hardeman's care to be hired out while he was gone. His concern for their welfare in the coming winter in Missouri reveals a disposition that appears to surpass measuring them solely as property. "I have 3 or 4 boys with whom I am well pleased, and will thank you in hiring them to use such caution as will prevent them from being exposed to violent cold or in any wise abused, as also all my negroes. This request ... I presume however is unnecessary as I well know your attention to your own slaves. ..." Meredith worried about not just "3 or 4 boys," but "also all my negroes," and the care they received while he was gone. His appointment of John Hardeman to look after his slaves was made on the basis of Hardeman's humane treatment of his.[18]

An interesting anecdotal story that involves a Marmaduke slave bears out the fact that a slave's quality of life depended upon the moral character of a master or overseer. In 1936, Edward Craddock, born in 1864 to Saline County slaves, told an interviewer that the stories his father told him were vivid. "One especially," he said, "because of its cruelty. A slave right here in Marshall angered his master, was chained to a hemp-brake on a cold night and left to freeze to death, which he did." Edward's father was owned by J. H. Craddock, who farmed with his father in Saline County's Marshall Township in 1860. Their farm was only three properties removed from that of Vincent Marmaduke, Meredith's son. Vincent owned 25 slaves at the time, one of them a 17-year-old mulatto girl named Ophelia. She became Edward Craddock's mother. She and Edward's father (also named Edward) had married while they were still slaves living separately on the Craddock and Marmaduke farms. Brutality and compassion for slaves in the form of death and marriage lived side by side within the same Saline County township. (The elder Edward Craddock was the mulatto son of a plantation slave named Rachell and her master's son "Paschall the Rascal" Craddock, born in 1791 on the Craddock plantation in Amelia County, Virginia.)[19]

Trading "Likely" Men and Women

In the spring of 1836, John Locke Hardeman was farming cotton in Madison County, Mississippi, and selling slaves at New Orleans. To finance the slave trade, he had empowered Meredith to sell some of his land in Pettis and Saline Counties, and now wanted him to invest the proceeds "in negro property. I need four or five women to equalize my force, males and females. Dr. Mitchell showed me a likely girl for whom I would give a good price. I could stand $600 or $800 for the very likeliest men and women. Should an opportunity offer you would do me a favor by taking any bargains for me that may offer in likely negroes. I mean strong under 23 & over 15 years old. ... I do not yet know that it will do to speculate largely in negroes this year. I can determine [that] before I leave this country. ... I would not like to establish a higher price for negroes than is given in this neighborhood. But could go as far as mentioned above. Has Walker sold his fellows?" By September, Locke Hardeman had acquired a "stock in trade, say 12 negroes." A month later, he wrote Meredith about "this year's negro adventure," in which he was now partnered with "Esq. Plemmons" [Thomas], whose brother was James G. Plemmons. Locke Hardeman said that he and the Plemmons brothers had left St. Louis with "16 negroes" and wanted to buy "eight or ten more." Locke spent nearly $2,500 to finance his share of their "stock" and he was anxious about the investment. The cotton market was weak, and he feared "that negro traders will have to Squat this season. It seems almost impossible to make sales, the merchants in N. Orleans will not accept for Planters until after January."[20]

Despite the stagnant slave market, Locke said he would not sell at less than 50 percent profit. At New Orleans, "Likely men had been sold for $1,600 or $1,700," while "Likely women" were fetching $1,000 to $1,200. It was Locke's opinion that "the selling price will be $2,500 pr. pair & that sales will be brisk when Planters can silence their old debt by sales of the new [cotton] crop." Three months later Locke told Meredith he was getting out of the slave-trading business. "... my last purchase of negroes — I think it will be my last! for purposes of speculation. I wind up that business with about $1,000 profit, perhaps a little less."[21]

Locke's letters raise an interesting question. As well as buying slaves for Locke Hardeman, did Meredith engage in slave trading as a commercial venture? In July of 1829, he paid Jacob Nave of Saline County $200 for a "Negro girl" named Lucy. She was only 7 years old.[22] The sale of slave children, although not prolific in the Booneslick country, was not uncommon. A Howard County farmer in 1830 wanted to sell nine boys and girls, all under age 10. Two months after buying Lucy, Meredith contacted Robert P. Clark of Boonville wanting to sell a young girl and boy. Clark's reply shows Meredith's intention: "Col. Marmaduke. In answer to your communication on the subject of purchasing negroes for the cotton market, I have only to add that Judge Briscoe & myself are engaged in purchasing young and likely negroes for that market. Yours will suit I suppose from your description, both the boy and girl. Mr. Briscoe will be to see you in the latter part of this month on his way up to Lexington, and of him you can learn as to terms. I will only say we purchase on a credit." Robert Clark and Judge John Briscoe were not major slave traders. Both were Democrats holding offices in Cooper County at the time the letter was written, Clark as clerk of the circuit court and Briscoe as a county administrative judge. Both men also owned farms and slaves; Clark had 10 bondsmen, Briscoe 11. The two were opportunists seeking to profit from a demand for slaves in the rising cotton market of the late 1820s and early 1830s.[23]

Meredith may have been influenced to consider selling slaves south by information about their value that came in letters he received from friends and relatives in Virginia and elsewhere. Such letters were not unusual. His nephew, John McClanahan, wrote from Louisville, Mississippi, to tell him that "Negros are very high here men is worth from 12 to 15 hundred dollars current." A niece, Elizabeth, wrote Meredith telling of slave hiring costs in Westmoreland County, Virginia. Such news added to his knowledge about the trade in slaves. Whether Lucy was the girl Meredith was trying to sell into the Southern slave trade — or that he even engaged Clark and Briscoe on his behalf — is unknown; however, it is clear that he was buying and selling children, separating them from their mothers and family members.[24]

In the two decades preceding the Civil War, the state's slave population more than doubled with the greatest increase occurring along the Missouri River from Cole County to the Kansas line. (Elsewhere in the state, the slave population remained stagnant, even decreasing slightly in counties south of St. Louis.) Saline County's slave population tripled during this period, rising from 1,615 in 1840 to 4,876 in 1860, while the number of slaveholders only doubled from 261 to 506.[25] The increase in the number of slaves in the Booneslick counties, coupled with a growing demand for labor in the Southern states, attracted the attention of traders and advertisements seeking slaves to buy began appearing in the *Missouri Statesman* newspaper in 1848. Published in Columbia, the paper had wide circulation in central Missouri and was read by slave owners. Subsequently, traders established themselves and conducted an active business in a number of the area's towns including Lexington, Fayette, Moberly, and Waverly, and farther to the west in Liberty in Clay County. John R. White, of Fayette, is thought to be the region's most active trader, employing agents who scoured the countryside buying slaves that he would resell in Alabama, Mississippi, and Louisiana. At Lexington, trader J.J. Bentis accepted a slave on consignment from Meredith in 1850. He sold "the boy you left with me for $750. James Hicklin was the purchaser." Meredith had ample opportunity to sell slaves that would be sent south to labor in the cotton fields.[26]

Boonville had an active slave market at one time. Joseph Higgerson, born a slave in 1845 on a farm "just below the Lamine and Missouri Rivers" in Cooper County, when interviewed for the Federal Writer's Project series, *Slave Narratives*, was asked if he remembered seeing slaves sold at Boonville. "Yes, ma'am. Why down at Boonville, woman and a baby was put up to be sold, and de buyer he want de woman, but he don't want de baby, so they separated 'em, and was gettin' ready to put 'em on de boat for Noo Orleans, and ship 'em down de river, and de woman she ran back to kiss de baby goodbye, and de trader picked up a whip and cracked it and shouts, 'A bellerin cow will soon forget its calf!' She was sold down de river an never saw de baby again."[27]

Although slave coffles (gangs of slaves chained together for transport) were not normally seen in Missouri, some traders did employ that practice. Marilda Pethy, a slave in Montgomery County, recalled she had "seen people handcuffed together and driv' long de Williamsburg road like cattle."[28] What is perhaps the largest movement of slaves within the state occurred aboard a steamboat on the Missouri River in December 1858. John G. Haskell, an early Kansas architect, recalled that after boarding at Leavenworth he realized that traders were embarking with slaves as the boat traveled downstream. By the time the paddle-wheeler reached Jefferson City, where Haskell got off, there were 350 enslaved black passengers onboard for transport to St. Louis and then south to the cotton states. Hastening the sale of slaves in Missouri's western counties late in that decade were incidents of violence over the extension of slavery into Kansas, most notably the proslavery raid on Lawrence in 1856, and John Brown's murderous retaliatory raids elsewhere in the state. Increasingly, Missouri slave owners worried about the possible loss of their human property to abolitionist influence in the region.[29]

Trading Within the Family

For his own labor needs, whenever possible Meredith bought slaves from family members and neighbors or at estate sales where he knew the deceased slaveholder's reputation as a master. In this way, he was assured of acquiring bondsmen whose health and submissiveness were known, and who were apt to remain on his plantation because they had nearby family members whom they could occasionally visit. Slaves purchased from traders might be misrepresented (older slaves were disguised to look younger and told to lie about their age), or perhaps had undetected chronic illnesses, and were more apt to run away and return to their former neighborhood or escape slavery altogether. The purchase and sale of slaves within the extended Sappington-Marmaduke family was a common occurrence. In 1837, Meredith's future son-in-law, Levin Harwood, wrote to say he had "learned ... that you were disposed to let me have Aphilia. ... If it is not subjecting yourself to inconvenience I will give you the $600 for [her]." Another time William Eddins of Howard County offered to sell Meredith a family of slaves "which I got by my wife." William's brother, Layton, was Meredith's brother-in-law, having married Susan Sappington. At the time, Meredith declined, but several months later he contacted William to see if the slave family was still for sale. "At one time I would have sold them to you low, but you were not disposed to purchase at that time," Eddins replied. "From what I had been told of the character of the woman I anticipated a great deal of trouble but thus far I have been agreeably disappointed. I am so much pleased with her at present I do not wish to sell her. Were I to sell him, I would run many risks in suiting myself as well. I will say in a word that she is not for sale so long as she continues as she is at present and if even I part with her I will never sell any of her children. I presume from this you will see that I am not at all disposed to sell."[30]

The largest transfer of slaves within the extended family occurred in 1853 several months after the death of Dr. Sappington's wife, Jane, when 25 slaves listed in the estate were sold to various family members. Meredith bought two, paying $1,000 for 20-year-old Washington, and $470 for an 8-year-old girl named Caroline. The proceeds from the sale, nearly $51,000, were later divided among Dr. Sappington's children and their spouses and his grandchildren.[31]

Wanting to add to his slave force in 1849, Meredith asked George Penn, at the time managing the federal bank in St. Louis, about slaves for sale in that city. Penn inquired locally and told Meredith very few were available and prices were high. "For boys 12 years old $450 & for men 20 years old $700. ... These are the prices for what are called No. 1. Messrs. McAfee & Blakely who buy & sell largely inform me that they have increased their number of agents who are purchasing in the County. I think it quite likely they can supply you."[32]

Meredith occasionally acquired a slave on a trial basis. In 1826, he paid John Smith

$300 for Tennessee, a "negro girl," with the right to return her for a refund if she was found unsatisfactory. At the end of six months, he sent her back to Smith. He, however, had no money at the time and instead gave Meredith a promissory note due in six months.[33] The task of finding the right domestic help was shared with Lavinia, who managed the house servants. Writing to Meredith at Jefferson City in 1841 she inquired if he had "heard of a servant girl yet that you think would suit us? Margaret Burke has lately come over. She says there is a very valuable girl about 18 years of age for sale in the neighborhood ... belonging to a Mrs. Wilson (a widow lady) and the same that Mr. Burke purchased his of. I believe they are compelled to sell her. If you think proper you could write to Mr. Burke for the particulars respecting her. If you write you had best write immediately."[34] She also told him that she had hired "Eliza Christmas," a slave they had been considering for domestic work, exposing again her influence over household issues.

Slave children were a highly desired commodity in the Booneslick region and were sometimes used instead of money in financial transactions. In 1847 George Penn offered to settle a debt with Meredith by giving him six young people from one family. Penn was himself being asked to take the children as payment for a debt owed him. "John Deadrick has a family of Negroes which he proposed to sell to me for debts due me in Saline," he wrote. "One girl 17 years old, & one 16, & one 9. Three boys, one 14, one 12, & one 10 years old, the six for $2,000. If you will take them at the same price I will close the contract with him. He states he can get $200 more for them in cash from a Negro trader than what he offers them to me, but is unwilling to sell them in that way. I am desirous of disposing of my debts so as to make them pay you and will let him have it if you desire this property. They are of good ages and Mr. Deadrick states of good family."[35]

Providing Necessities

Sheltering and provisioning slaves was an expense owners had to bear, and they generally provided only enough food, clothing, and housing to assure their bondsmen's survival. Comfort was not a consideration. Housing his slaves was a significant concern for Meredith as their number grew over the years until in 1860 there were 54 people on his plantation (not including his family) who needed shelter. Unfortunately, none of the structures in which they lived have survived; the site of Meredith's home was abandoned and eventually cleared of all buildings. At the time his first house was being built in the late 1820s, he also had to build a cabin for the few slaves he owned at the time. Judging from evidence of slave houses on nearby plantations, the cabin was sited behind and some distance from Meredith's house. The style of slave dwellings in the Booneslick region ranged from a small cabin in which as many as 10 or 12 people lived in one room, to a rare, two-story house holding as many as 40 persons. The 54 slaves on Meredith's farm in 1860 were crowded into four houses, probably — like Meredith's home — made of lumber. The rough-sawn boards that comprised their frame and siding may have come from Alexander Gilbraith's sawmill on Salt Fork Creek at Jonesboro, established in 1821.[36]

Although Missouri's 1804 slave code did not address the subject, clothing their bondsmen was the responsibility of slave owners. Louisiana Colony law had required that slaves have "a shirt and trousers of linen in the summer, and a great coat and trousers of wool for the winter." Because ready-made clothing was costly, slave owners often bought inexpensive bulk cloth to be cut and sewn into dresses, trousers, shirts, and blankets. Masters dressed their slaves in clothing that would protect them from adverse climate and assure their health and ability to work. Contracts for hired slaves usually included a clause that specified certain items of clothing be furnished during the term of the contract, as well as at the end when the slave would be returned to an owner. A Boone County female slave hired out in 1842 was to be provided with two shirts, two dresses and two aprons for summer wear, and a new dress and woolen stockings for use in winter. Lewis Mundy, a former slave in northeast Missouri, said he "never wanted for clothes very bad. We wore long shirts that reached to de knees until we was twelve or fourteen years old. Dem Wool shirts sure was warm. We had one pair of shoes a year." Shoes were usually purchased from local merchants. In October 1845, Meredith outfitted some of his slaves for the impending winter season with 24 pairs of "Thick Brogans, Hip Brogans, Hip Boots, [and] Woman's Boots" in adult and children's sizes. He bought them from the mercantile store of D. Ballantine Jr. in Boonville, to whom he paid $22.90.[27]

In addition to providing shelter and clothing, Meredith also had to feed his slaves. This was no small concern considering the number on the plantation in 1860. Studies have shown that Southern plantation slaves existed on a diet of corn, sweet potatoes, molasses for sweetening, rice, and occasionally, a bit of meat. Meredith's agricultural production in the 20 years preceding the Civil War included corn, "Irish" potatoes, milk, butter, honey, and wheat for flour. These, with the produce of small gardens the slaves tended and what consumables they obtained by foraging and hunting, and perhaps occasional meat from the plantation's swine herd, made up the foods eaten by Meredith's slaves. His challenge was the efficient and economic production of enough consumables to keep them healthy and working.

Each time the number of slaves Meredith owned doubled in the years 1830 to 1860, there had to be a concomitant doubling in the amount of housing, clothing, and land and labor for food, invested for their support. Across the plantation, more slaves meant more acres in production; however, without the benefit of mechanical implements and the use of advanced fertilizers, the larger slave force did not translate into more production per slave. In 1850, Meredith had 14 slaves (men and women) old enough to be considered field hands. They produced crops (hemp, grain, livestock, and food) on 400 acres, a ratio of 28 acres per slave. In 1860, 32 slaves old enough to work in the fields produced crops on 900 acres, again a ratio of 28 acres per slave. Balancing the size of his labor force with the investment he made in its acquisition and support was a juggling act made more difficult by fluctuating markets and national economic conditions.

Reasonable and Practicable

Two impressions appear to be valid when judging Meredith Marmaduke's actions as a slaveholder. First, he behaved no differently in his attitude toward his slaves than did the majority of slaveholders in Missouri. He viewed them as people living in a society in which they had no voice in the conduct of their own affairs. Backed by

Missouri law, he could do with them as he pleased — with limitations. Nothing exists to indicate that he was cruel, or otherwise abused his slaves; however, their history on his plantation is incomplete and will never be fully known. His principle objective in their treatment was to feed, clothe, and house them, and treat their illnesses, in a manner sufficient to assure their survival. This was a reasonable and humane thing to do. On the other hand, Meredith's practical side dictated that he view his slaves as property whose exploitation would increase his personal wealth. This is shown in his sale of prime male slaves in the early 1860s, when they were surplus to his needs and their value was still high. This act was a financial consideration based on the loss of a market for his produce, and was not related to any concern over the future well-being of his slaves.

The worst form of the slave-as-property ethos was slave trading. Always alert for a new financial opportunity, Meredith almost entered into the business of buying and selling slaves in 1829. His failure to do so probably reflects an awareness of the potential for adverse consequences, rather than a decision made solely for financial reasons. Harrison Trexler reported that Missouri slave traders "held no enviable position," usually viewed as despicable sellers of human flesh, the nature of the business making it contemptible.[38] As a rising merchant and political figure in the 1830s, Meredith needed to avoid the stigma that accompanied the image of slave traders. He may have aided Locke Hardeman by quietly buying slaves for him that would eventually be sold in Mississippi and Louisiana where the transactions were unnoticed, but even this is unlikely given Hardeman's brief tenure in the business.

Agricultural production on Meredith's plantation in the two decades preceding the Civil War is the most apparent example of benefit directly traceable to slave labor. Not as clearly seen, but certainly as potent a factor in his drive to become wealthy, is that slave labor allowed him to pursue other business and political interests that contributed significantly to his financial well-being.

The death of Meredith's son, Vincent, on March 25, 1904, offers an interesting view into the feelings of the Marmaduke family slaves toward their former masters. The long funeral cortege that carried Vincent from his home in Marshall to Ridge Park Cemetery included a horse-drawn hearse accompanied by eight pall bearers. Three of these men had been slaves on Vincent's farm and were probably known to Meredith, perhaps had even lived at one time on his plantation. Two others were descendants of Marmaduke slaves. The willingness of these five men to participate in the funeral of a former master, bearing his coffin on their shoulders from the hearse to the grave, speaks positively to an assumption that in general, Marmaduke family slaves were not ill-treated.[39]

Notes

1. In March of 1820 news of Missouri's admission to the Union in 1820 as a slave state reached St. Louis: Meyers, *The Heritage of Missouri: A History*, 154–55. St. Louis *Inquirer*, March 25, 1820, Newspaper Collection, Reel 39318, SHSMO.

2. "Some of the earliest black slaves known to be in Missouri entered in the 1720s": Louis Houck, *A History of Missouri*, Vol. 1, 281–82. For more about early slavery in Missouri see: Arvarh E. Strickland, "Aspects of Slavery in Missouri, 1821." *MHR*, Vol. 65, No. 4, (July 1971); Harrison A. Trexler, *Slavery in*

Missouri and No Restrictions

Missouri 1804–1865; and Raymond D. Thomas, "Missouri Valley Settlement, St. Louis to Independence," *MHR*, Vol. 21, No. 1, (October 1926). Missouri's slave population in 1860 was about half that of the older, eastern slave-owning states and would almost certainly have grown to equal them if the practice had not been ended by the Civil War.

3. Missouri Laws Governing Slaves: *Laws of A Public and General Nature, of the District of Louisiana, of the Territory of Louisiana, of the Territory of Missouri, and of the State of Missouri, up to the Year 1824*. Vol. 1, 27–33. *Missouri's Early Slave Laws: A History in Documents*. sos.mo.gov/archives/education/aahi/earlyslavelaws. Watson to Marmaduke, October 16 and December 15, 1847. Folder 17, Marmaduke Papers C1021, SHSMO.

4. *Laws of A Public and General Nature*, 27–33.

5. By 1840, the number of people Meredith held in bondage: 1840 U.S. Federal Census, Saline County, Missouri. D. D. Bellamy. Slavery, Emancipation, and Racism in Missouri, Table 4, Classification of Slaveholder in Missouri in 1840, 39. PhD. dissertation. Ann Arbor: University of Michigan, 1971. Schedule 2, 1850 U.S. Federal Slave Census for Saline County. The top eight slaveholders were: Cynthia Smith, widow of Thomas Adams Smith, owned 79 slaves; Pink Booker, 41; John Deadrick, 36; Robert Thompson, 34; John L. Hardeman, 31; James McDowell, 29; William Gillam, 28; Meredith Marmaduke, 27. Trexler defined prime workers as males 18 to 35 years of age. Trexler, *Slavery in Missouri 1804–1865*, 37.

6. "The 'Californians' have been detained on account of cholera, which is havoc in our midst": Hardeman to Tucker, June 13, 1849. Folder 6, John L. Hardeman Papers C3227, SHSMO.

7. Meredith responded by opening new ground to cultivation: 1850 & 1860 U.S. Federal Census, Schedule 4, Productions of Agriculture (Saline County); Reel F948; 1850 & 1860 U.S. Federal Census, Schedule 2 , Slave Inhabitants (Saline County).

8. "During 24 years of record": Meredith Marmaduke, Schedule 2, 1850 and 1860 U.S. Federal Slave Census, Saline County, Mo. Estate of John Eustace. Probate Records, Saline County, Mo., Inventories and Appraisements, 1855–61, Vol. 1, 602–03, Reel C6296, MSA. A transplanted Virginia farmer, Eustace owned 17 slaves in 1850; at his death in 1859, he owned 15. Seven prime-age males were sold during this period, leaving him with only two male field hands. Five of his female slaves were old enough to work as field hands. The remaining slaves on the plantation were all younger than 13. Trexler, "The Value and the Sale of the Missouri Slave," *MHR*, Vol. 8, No. 2 (January 1914), 73.

9. By 1864, the year of Meredith's death, the age composition of his slaves had changed considerably: Meredith Marmaduke will and estate appraisal, Saline County Probate Estate Files, Reel C8250, Estate CE-1710, MSA.

10. He also lost two male slaves who ran away in 1863 and joined the Union Army: *Index to descriptive lists of volunteers for the United States Colored Troops for the state of Missouri, 1863–1865*, 84. Patrick Marmaduke's surname was probably assigned by the official who enrolled him in the army. The Index, compiled from NARA records, shows that many newly enlisted former slaves either took or were given their master's surname.

11. "Minny's leg as I mentioned some time ago being sore, is getting better": Lavinia to Marmaduke, January 25, 1841. Box 3, Folder 1, Sappington-Marmaduke Papers, MHS.

12. "My dear Father, The workmen were here to work last Monday": Vincent Marmaduke to Meredith Marmaduke, December 17, 1845. Box 3, Folder 6, Sappington-Marmaduke Papers, MHS.

13. Meredith relied on his family to keep him apprised of farm activities: Meredith Marmaduke, 1840 U.S. Federal Census, 1850 & 1860 U.S. Federal Census Schedules 1 & 2, Saline County, Mo.

14. Jane Simpson, a slave in southwest Missouri, recalled that as a little girl: Jane Simpson interview. *Slave Narratives: A folk history of slavery in the United States from interviews with former slaves*, Vol. 10, 312. Richard Bruner interview, Ibid, 59.

15. Slaves sometimes left the plantation and traveled to Boonville: "The 'Underground Railroad' in Boonville," *MHR*, Vol. 30, (January 1936), 213. Columbia weekly *Missouri Statesman*, December 19, 1856. Reel 7548, Newspaper Archives, SHSMO. Nowlin to Marmaduke, January 1, 1853. Box 5, folder

To Make a Fortune in Missouri

3, Sappington-Marmaduke Papers, MHS. In terms of relative value (1856–2018), the loss of Marmaduke's five slaves in today's dollars is $173,000 as a commodity; $1,180,000 as unskilled wage labor. measuringworth.com/uscompare.

16. William Wells Brown relates in his memoir: William Wells Brown, *Narrative of William Wells Brown, A Fugitive Slave*, 14–15.

17. Ezra Greenspan, *William Wells Brown, An African American Life*, 4, 49.

18. "I have 3 or 4 boys with whom I am well pleased": Marmaduke to Hardeman, October 13, 1824. Folder 5, Hardeman Collection C3655, SHSMO.

19. An interesting anecdotal story that involves a Marmaduke slave: Jacob Hatfield, "Craddock family roots extend deep into county," *Marshall Democrat-News*, August 14, 2008. Reel 54262, Newspaper Archives, SHSMO. Ed Craddock interview, *Slave Narratives. A folk history of slavery in the United States*. Vol. 10, 96–97. 1860 U.S. Federal Census, Saline County, Mo., Schedules 1 and 2. Slave marriages, though permitted by owners and usually performed by black ministers, were not legally recognized in Missouri until 1865.

20. Trading "Likely" Men and Women: Affidavit, Locke Hardeman to Marmaduke, March 18, 1836; letters, Hardeman to Marmaduke, March 19, September 21, October 22, 1836. Box 2, Folder 2, Sappington-Marmaduke Papers, MHS. Thomas Plemmons, born in North Carolina in 1802, lived in Cole County, Missouri, in 1832 and served as a county judge for several years. In 1850, he was farming in Carroll County, Missouri. *History of Cole, Moniteau, Morgan, Benton, Miller and Osage Counties, Missouri*, 227. 1840 U.S. Federal Census, Cole County, Missouri; 1850 U.S. Federal Census, Carroll County, Missouri.

21. Despite the stagnant slave market: Hardeman to Marmaduke, January 27, 1837. Box 2, Folder 3, Sappington-Marmaduke Papers, MHS.

22. Locke's letters raise an interesting question. Did Meredith engage in slave trading as a commercial venture: Bill of sale, Jacob Nave to Marmaduke, July 6, 1829. Box 1, Folder 5, Sappington-Marmaduke Papers, MHS. The transaction between Nave and Marmaduke was witnessed by Josiah Gregg, who would soon become a Santa Fe trader and later an accomplished author whose book, *Commerce of the Prairies*, enjoyed international success. Jacob Nave lived in Arrow Rock Township with two other family members and nine slaves in 1830.

23. "Col. Marmaduke. In answer to your communication on the subject of purchasing negroes": Clark to Marmaduke, September 1, 1829. Box 1, Folder 5, Sappington-Marmaduke Papers, MHS. Robert P. Clark, born Bedford County, Virginia, 1791, later moved with his parents to Clark County, Kentucky. In 1816, he resigned as County Clerk of Estill County, Kentucky, moving with elder parents to Franklin, Missouri, then to Boonville in 1818. Appointed Clerk of the Circuit Court for Cooper County (original), he served from 1819 to 1841. Elected delegate to Missouri Constitutional Convention 1820. Cooper County's first administrative county court met at his home on High Street in Boonville, January 8, 1821, at which time he was appointed county clerk, a position he held for several years while still clerk of the circuit court. "Judge" Briscoe was John M. Briscoe who arrived in Cooper County in 1818. He ran for sheriff (unsuccessfully) in 1820, was elected county assessor 1822 for one year, served as county judge for nine months 1825–26, and again from 1834 until 1842. *A History of Cooper County, Missouri*, 72, 56, 76, 138, 181,196–97, 224.

24. Meredith may have been influenced to consider selling slaves south: John McClanahan to Marmaduke, December 22, 1836. Folder 10, Marmaduke Papers C1021, SHSMO. Elizabeth Marmaduke to Marmaduke, January 13, 1838. Folder 11, Ibid. William Dozier to Marmaduke, July 25, 1831. Box 1, Folder 7, Sappington-Marmaduke Papers, MHS.

25. In the two decades preceding the Civil War, the state's slave population more than doubled: Hurt, Table IV 218, 308–310; Burke, Table 1, 309; U.S. Federal Census manuscripts, Saline County 1840, 1850, 1860.

26. "the boy you left with me for $750. James Hicklin was the purchaser": Bentis to Marmaduke, May 14, 1850. Box 4, folder 7, Sappington-Marmaduke Papers, MHS. John R. White account books. R. B. Chinn Collection A0272, MHS.

27. Boonville had an active slave market at one time: Joe Higgerson interview, *Slave Narratives*, Vol. 10, 176.

Missouri and No Restrictions

28. Although slave coffles (gangs of slaves chained together for transport) were not normally seen in Missouri: Marilda Pethy interview, *Slave Narratives*, Vol. 10, 277.

29. What is perhaps the largest movement of slaves within the state: John G. Haskell, "The Passing of Slavery in Western Missouri," *Transactions of Kansas State Historical Society*, Vol. 7, 36, 38.

30. Within the Family: L. B. H[arwood]. to Marmaduke, November 22, 1837. Box 1, Folder 7, Sappington-Marmaduke Papers, MHS. W. S. Eddins, November 27, 1847. Box 4, Folder 3, Sappington-Marmaduke Papers, MHS.

31. The largest sale of slaves within the extended family: List of slaves sold, September 10, 1853. Folder 61; Statement, division of proceeds. Folder 62; "Ages of Negroes." Folder 94; John Sappington Papers C1027, SHSMO.

32. Wanting to add to his slave force in 1849, Meredith asked George Penn: Penn to Marmaduke, September 20, 1849. Box 4, Folder 6, Sappington-Marmaduke Papers, MHS.

33. Meredith occasionally acquired a slave on a trial basis: Smith to Marmaduke, January 26 and July 25, 1826. Box 1, Folder 3, Sappington-Marmaduke Papers, MHS.

34. "heard of a servant girl yet that you think would suit us": Lavinia to Marmaduke, January 12, 1841. Box 3, Folder 1, Sappington-Marmaduke Papers, MHS.

35. Slave children were a highly desired commodity in the Booneslick region: Penn to Marmaduke, April 26, 1847. Box 4, Folder 2, Sappington-Marmaduke Papers, MHS. Hurt, *Agriculture and Slavery in Little Dixie*, 232–33, notes that "at best" slave mothers with small children could expect them to be sold at a young age.

36. Alexander Gilbraith's sawmill on Salt Fork Creek: *1881 History of Saline County*, 178, 198–99.

37. "never wanted for clothes very bad": Lewis Mundy interview, *Slave Narratives*, Vol. 10, 258. "Thick Brogans, Hip Brogans, Hip Boots, [and] Woman's Boots": Statement, D. Ballantine Jr. to Marmaduke, October 25, 1845. Folder 16, Marmaduke Papers C1021, SHSMO.

38. "held no enviable position": Trexler, *Slavery in Missouri, 1804–1865*, 45.

39. The death of Meredith's son, Vincent: Col. Marmaduke Dead. Marshall, Missouri, *Weekly Democrat-News*, April 2, 1904. Reel 28066, SHSMO.

CHAPTER 17

A RISING GENERATION

During the early years of Missouri's development as a state, gender and family prosperity played significant roles in determining the future of children as they matured beyond adolescence. In the early to mid-1800s the children of farm and working-class families might receive some basic schooling (reading, writing, "ciphering") if money was available to pay for a teacher. But education beyond the elementary level remained elusive for many. Too, girls — no matter how well educated — were expected to marry and devote their lives to children, husband, and home. Few options existed for their employment outside the home. Boys from less prosperous families could work on the family farm or in a family's trade or business, apprentice themselves to a merchant or tradesman, hire on with a passing steamboat, or seek adventure by running away. On the other hand, the children of more prosperous families, such as the Marmadukes and the Sappingtons, usually received more than a basic education and might even attend college, although the girls of such families still faced limited choices for their futures.

Widespread public school education did not exist in Missouri for the first half of the 19th century. Legislative and administrative features were slow to evolve, despite an 1812 act of Congress that granted the state trusteeship of Section 16 in each township of surveyed land for the purpose of public education. With this in mind, the drafters of Missouri's 1820 constitution called for the establishment of one or more schools in each township, as need dictated. From 1825 on, Missouri's General Assembly struggled with school policy, passing acts every session in the 1830s in an effort to provide guidance and clarify the responsibilities of the state's counties. Seemingly oblivious to state policy, many county administrators felt no strong sense of responsibility for public education. As a result, during the first half of the 19th century, Missouri's families educated their children without government assistance, relying on home schooling, an occasional tutor, private schools, or community-organized subscription schools. In 1839, legislation to fund schools was voted by the General Assembly with the first money (16 cents per pupil in 13 counties) distributed in 1842. Independent township schools were prominent in Missouri's rural counties until 1872, when legislators mandated establishing a Superintendent of Education in each county and the organization of county-funded school districts.[1]

That Saline County families wanted their children schooled is evident in the opening of two subscription schools in 1817 in the newly settled bottomlands along the Missouri River. Laban Garrett taught a subscription school in Edmondson's

Bottom that year, charging $1 per pupil each month. Probably because of irregular attendance and subsequent reduced income, the school closed after four months. Another subscription school in the Big Bottom shared a similar fate. Elsewhere, Peyton Nowlin, who officiated at Meredith and Lavinia's wedding, taught school in the Arrow Rock vicinity in the early 1820s. His interest in education led to his appointment as commissioner to oversee Saline County's school lands. The county's first boarding school, a private facility operated by John and Frances Duggins on their farm west of present-day Marshall, opened in 1834 and was active for 10 years.[2]

Meredith and Lavinia combined home teaching with hired tutorship and boarding schools when their children were young. The task of home schooling fell on Lavinia when Meredith was away, although her interest in teaching occasionally lagged. Writing to him in Jefferson City, she admitted she had "neglected the children's books very much lately, but will commence with them today — am lazy, to improve."[3] Their oldest daughter, Jane, sometimes assisted Lavinia in those years, telling her father, "The children say their lessons almost every day. I intend to have Meredith reading by the time you come home." As his daughters grew older, Meredith wanted to send 14-year-old Jane and her younger sister, Sarah, to a boarding school to finish their education. In the winter of 1841, Lavinia, her protective instincts aroused, was preparing for their departure, asking Meredith to write "and let me know what time you wish our little girls to leave for school. I shall have a great deal of sewing to do for them. ... Please let me know who you expect to board them with."[4]

Meredith's drive to become wealthy brought educational and financial advantages for his children that were unavailable to those of less fortunate families. How this played-out over the years is seen in the lives of the children as they grew from adolescence into young adulthood.

The Daughters

The Marmaduke children all began to leave home during the late years of their second decade of life. Sent away for advanced schooling, the girls readied themselves for society and marriage. The eldest daughter, Jane, at age 19, in 1846 married Levin B. Harwood, a distant Kentucky cousin of the Breathitt family to which Jane's grandmother, Jane Breathitt Sappington, wife of Dr. John, belonged. Jane and Levin Harwood operated a farm near Miami in Saline County in their early years of marriage. By 1852, Jane had given birth to three children (losing a son in 1848). Knowing her mother's years of seemingly endless child-bearing and raising, Jane was determined to not let additions to her family restrict her life, telling Lavinia that she was resolved to "run about, at least, but I reason in this way, that I enjoy it now while young more than when old, and never expect to have less to keep me at home. On the contrary, every eighteen months will add another to the list, and between having and nursing them I don't see much pleasure. Let me take all I can get, and take it I intend, at every nook & corner."[5]

In 1860, the Harwood family lived in St. Louis, with Jane's brother Darwin as a member of the home. Levin Harwood obtained a position in 1857 as a broker in the commission house of J. & E. Walsh. A year later, he and Darwin Marmaduke formed a partnership, advertising themselves as "Wholesale Grocers, Forwarding and Commission Merchants ... in J. & E. Walsh's stand at the corner of Washington

Avenue and Levee."[6]

Meredith and Lavinia's second child, Sarah, was born in 1830. She became ill when she was 13 years old, open sores developing on her head, and the glands in her neck swelling and becoming tender to the touch. Worried when she failed to improve, Meredith wrote to Dr. James Curtis Welborn (most likely recommended by Dr. Sappington, who no longer practiced medicine), an "ardent Democrat" of Pike County, Missouri, describing Sarah's symptoms and asking for his help in curing her affliction.[7] Citing the difficulty a doctor faces when "making up his opinion without Seeing and examining the patient," Welborn, with Meredith's description of his daughter's symptoms in hand, said he believed she suffered from "Scrofula Fugax, it often arises from the absorption of matter from sores upon the head." His diagnosis was no doubt influenced by a recent edition of *Hooper's New Medical Dictionary*, first published in 1817, which described Scrofula Fugax as "… of the simplest kind; it is seated about the neck, and for the most part is caused by absorption from sores on the head."[8] To effect a cure, Dr. Welborn recommended that Meredith apply "local applications" of a "weak solution of carbonate of potash thrown into the discharging tumor from a small silver syringe … together with dietitic [sic] regulations & proper exercise."[9]

Whatever the treatment that Meredith decided upon, it worked! In November 1845, Sarah was attending a boarding school in Lexington, Missouri, run by "Dr. Long" and "Miss Jane" and wrote her father telling him that she was "very well, and have been so since you left. I can discover no symptoms of the disease returning and am very careful not to take cold and particular about taking my medicine," which consisted of "two bottles of Panacia." Sarah's only wish was that Meredith would come and get her next month so she could be at home for Christmas.[10] Cured of scrofula, Sarah eventually married Thomas J. Yerby, a farmer in Lafayette County, and in 1860 she was living there with her husband and their two children.

A handful of letters tell something about the life of Meredith and Lavinia's third daughter, Lavinia, affectionately named "Bena" by the family. Born 12 days before Christmas Day, 1838, Bena became the family's stay-at-home daughter, looking after her aging parents and not marrying until she was nearly 30 years old. As a teenager, Bena attended school in Lexington, living with her sister and brother-in-law, Sarah and Thomas Yerby. After seeing her through a spell of illness in the winter of 1852–53, Sarah wrote her parents that 15-year-old Bena was "beginning to recover her natural colour [sic] and is now pretty much out of danger, & with the exception of some restraint upon her appetite needs no particular attention."[11] She was in Lexington again during the fall of 1855, staying with the Yerby family for three months before going downriver to Miami to spend a few days with her sister, Jane Harwood. Perhaps Bena was in Lexington to finish her schooling. At home by the third week of January 1856, her return was noted by her grandmother, Jane Sappington, who said she "had not had sight of her since the first of Oct."

In St. Louis on the first day of August 1859, "election day when Lager Beer will flow in large streams through the River of excited candidates and … unflinching friends," a poetic Darwin wrote to Bena asking her to accompany him that fall on a journey to Memphis and New Orleans, a trip that he expected would last several weeks.[12] She declined and instead went to Philadelphia, Pennsylvania, with her sister, Jane

Harwood, who was fleeing St. Louis in hopes of recovering from frequent periods of malarial fever. Accompanied east by Jane's husband, the sisters found lodging in Mrs. Franklin's boarding house on Sixth Street, from where they could see "a very pleasant line of street rail coaches" that the adventurous Jane intended to ride every day. After helping his wife and sister-in-law settle at Mrs. Franklin's house, L. B. Harwood left them in the care of "Mr. Price [who] comes around every day & yesterday he was here three times. He seems to take as much interest in us as if we were near relatives instead of strangers."[13] Under the care of a Dr. Wilson, Jane wrote her mother that she was confined to her bed for much of the time, while "Bena is sewing as hard as if she was working for wages. She goes out walking every day, and then to her work. ... You may expect to see her looking very fine and fashionable."[14]

The usually decorous Bena had a brush with romance while in Philadelphia. Aboard a steamboat on a day-trip on the Delaware River, she met someone to whom she was attracted, and her reaction was noticed by her companions. Later, at home that winter, Jane wrote her father to tell him that "Mr. Price asked to be remembered to you & family. He wants to know of Bena, what it was in the stateroom of the steamer that caused so much blushing & heart-throbbing? Says he left to escape the contagion, & that she must recollect it is Leap Year."[15]

A lasting romantic engagement failed to materialize for Bena while she was in Philadelphia, placing her on the threshold of spinsterhood at age 22. In this respect, she joined her brother, John, whose interest in the opposite sex was thwarted by his military duties in 1860. Stationed at a remote camp in Utah Territory, John (who never married) wrote to Bena a few days after the beginning of the new year to complain, "if I don't get into civilization soon I will be a confirmed old bachelor, even now have a strong lean that way."[16] With no prospective husband in sight, Bena was living with her parents on the home farm near Arrow Rock in 1860. Marriage would not come her way for another eight years.

The Sons

After giving birth to two daughters, Lavinia quickly produced two sons. Vincent, born in April 1831, was named after his paternal grandfather, Vincent Marmaduke (also the name of Meredith's older brother); and John, born in March 1833, was named for his maternal grandfather, Dr. John Sappington. Being so close in age, and as the eldest of Meredith and Lavinia's seven sons, the two boys undoubtedly shared many experiences growing up in Saline County. Meredith assured that they followed similar educational paths; however, as they matured Vincent and John differed significantly in their interests. As a young boy, Vincent reacted to his father's absences from home (while serving as lieutenant governor and governor in the early 1840s) by assuming the role of "man of the farm." Writing to Meredith in Jefferson City, Vincent related news about the animals and crops and shared information about the slaves, an early interest in agriculture that he retained as he matured. John, on the other hand, found little of interest in the farm. The greater world of military and political events was more to his liking. In a letter to Meredith, John mentioned a "Nicaraguan revolution" and asked "Is not the state of parties in the U.S. H. of R. [House of Representatives] truly alarming?" He also wondered about the "two wings of the democratic party" in

Missouri. The farm and its activities were not mentioned. He closed his letter by asking Meredith to send him $50.[17]

In the spring of 1846, Meredith enrolled 15-year-old Vincent in Masonic College, a new school in rural Marion County in northeast Missouri, originally established to educate orphaned children of deceased Masons. Meredith's decision to send Vincent to Masonic College was probably influenced by the presence in the area of other Marmaduke family members, one of whom, a first cousin, was a Mason in the Hannibal Lodge. These nearby kinfolk gave Meredith some assurance that his young son would be among friends. Also at Masonic College was a nephew, Darwin Pearson, son of the dissolved marriage between Elizabeth Sappington and Alonzo Pearson. Young Pearson would be a companion to Vincent, who previously had not lived away from home. In a letter, Darwin told his uncle that he was "very well pleased with this college indeed I am getting along finely with my studies." The student body, only 40-some scholars, came "from every direction, some from Mississippi, Illinois, New Orleans & there is several from Jefferson City."[18] Masonic College pleased Vincent as much as it did his cousin. Three weeks after arriving he wrote his mother to reassure her that he was well despite having had a toothache (the offending tooth pulled by Dr. Johnson, in the nearby hamlet of Philadelphia). Vincent's most important news, however, concerned his appetite, which had not suffered by the absence of home-cooked food: "We have fine eating here all the time. We have Puddings and Pies Ice crem [sic] and all those fine things, and plenty of study too."[19]

Masonic College's major asset was ownership of 1,270 acres of rich farmland 12 miles southwest of Palmyra, Missouri. The site, purchased in 1844 by the Grand Masonic Lodge of Missouri (Meredith was a member in St. Louis), had formerly housed a failed school named Marion College. Masonic College's future may have been foretold when a few days after the first teachers were hired a violent storm tore through the campus and blew out almost all windows in the college building. Within a year after opening, it was apparent that the school would not prosper at its remote site, and in 1848 the Masons moved the college across the state to Lexington in Lafayette County, in hopes that students and revenue would increase. Unfortunately, the move failed to attract the financial backing needed to assure the school's success. After selling its Marion County land, Masonic College struggled for another nine years before permanently closing its doors in 1857.[20]

Meredith chose not to enroll Vincent in the new Masonic school at Lexington, instead sending him to Chapel Hill Academy in western Lafayette County. Archibald Ridings, a graduate of the University of North Carolina at Chapel Hill, opened the Missouri school in 1840. Many of central Missouri's wealthy families sent their children to the coed academy to prepare them for college. Educator Robert Anthony O'Bryan-Lawson's study of Chapel Hill Academy (the subject of his thesis for a Master of Arts degree in history from the University of Missouri-Kansas City) noted that among the school's graduates were "generals, lawyers, doctors, Wall Street bankers, politicians, teachers, engineers, ministers, as well as the wives of prominent Missouri men [representing] the elite class of Missouri's small slave-holding society."[21]

Masonic College and Chapel Hill Academy served as preparatory schools for Vincent, who entered Yale College at New Haven, Connecticut, as an upperclassman in January 1851, graduating in 1852. Biographer Nathaniel Hughes Jr., author of *Yale's Confederates: A Biographical Dictionary*, concluded that Vincent was "not a creditable student" yet he "proved to be a leader" in later life.[22] Skull and Bones, the secret society limited to a select few Yale undergraduate seniors, tapped Vincent for membership in his final year at the school. Following Yale, Vincent briefly studied law, then in 1853 married Julia Eakin and tried his hand at farming in Saline County. In 1856, his interest in farming faltered. Unsure of what to do, he wrote to his father seeking his advice. It was a matter, he said, that had him "troubled and perplexed. ... unable to arrive at a conclusion as to what is best and right for me. ... My individual feeling prompts me to Texas, as the theatre [sic] of my future action, but to that course several prominent & very natural obstacles oppose themselves." He wanted to speculate on land, and Texas was the place to be. But he was reluctant to take his wife and two young daughters so far away from other family members. "As to farming here again, that is out of the question," he told Meredith. "I have neither the taste, talent or heart for it, unless on a larger scale which I have no means to do." (The "larger scale" would eventually attract Vincent back to the farm.) An alternative to speculating in Texas land was to be a commodities agent in St. Louis where, "if I could, by your influence, become associated with Mr. Walsh [J.& E. Walsh]. It strikes me that if he had some young & active man his business in that line might be greatly increased. ... an association with Mr. Walsh now appears to me desirable, if thr'o you it could be affected."[23]

Meredith's response to Vincent's uncertainty about his future is not known; however, Meredith also had Texas land fever and may have been interested enough to finance a speculative venture there. Within two months, Vincent was in Texas accompanied, not by his wife and children, but by his younger brother, Meredith Miles Marmaduke Jr. Upon learning that they were in Texas, Sam McClure (Meredith's former partner in the Santa Fe trade) wrote to ask for their help. John M. Cade, formerly of Mississippi, now living in Texas near the mouth of the Trinity River, owed McClure $2,000, which he hoped the Marmaduke brothers could collect for him. Their success as debt collectors is unknown, but as land speculators they made good money for within two years they were back in Saline County, where Vincent bought a farm near Marshall, paying Moses White $17,500 for 1,013 acres, "one of the best, if not the very best, improved farms in the county."[24]

Meredith and Lavinia's second son, John Sappington Marmaduke, who also attended Masonic College and Chapel Hill Academy, entered Yale College in 1850 at age 17. He remained there two academic years, his tenure overlapping with that of his older brother, Vincent, who graduated in the spring of 1852. In the fall of 1852, John unexpectedly transferred to Harvard College at Cambridge, Massachusetts. The change of schools caused some wringing of hands at home as Meredith and Lavinia sought to learn their son's intentions. Then came a letter from John proposing an extended visit at home that would stretch beyond the year-end holidays. When this idea failed to receive a positive response from Meredith, John replied that he would "of course defer my visit," but he was not happy with his father's decision to let him remain at Cambridge during the holiday season. "You seem to think that my object [in coming home] was to travel about, kill time, and evade books. My visit was altogether of a contrary nature. It was to save money, save time & to apply myself in such a manner to my books as to benefit myself in the greatest possible degree in the shortest time. ... My intention was to go among a people who know you well, and who (if I conducted myself properly) would interest themselves in my behalf, find myself a quiet, compatible, cheap place of living where I could give instruction to 10 or 12 pupils ... until the latter part of July."[25]

John felt that staying at Harvard for the upcoming semester was unnecessary, that he could independently study and then pass examinations. It was just a matter of applying oneself. "From the 19th of this month until the last of July I have nothing to keep me here. ... in one week I can master Logic, Natural & Moral Philosophy as to pass a fine examination. Then I have nine weeks ... to study Spanish & German alone. Say that I average 9 hours a day on them, that is 54 a week (excepting Sunday) or in all 486 hours. Now how many hours are employed by the student in the study of these two languages who remains at college the 22 weeks. ... By taking such a course it would have required greater exertions on my part, and would have debarred me from many enjoyments & pleasures which are to be met with here." John did not specify the "enjoyments & pleasures" he had in mind, but the possibilities were known. "There is less dissipation here, as far as I have been able to learn, than at Yale, although the opportunities here are much greater."[26]

Sensing his son's restlessness, worried he might leave school altogether, Meredith in December 1853 wrote U.S. Representative John Phelps of Springfield, Missouri, seeking an appointment for John to the U.S. Military Academy at West Point, New York. In response, Phelps wrote to John with a challenge. Wanting to be sure that his first appointment to West Point went to someone genuinely interested in the army (and perhaps aware of John's unhappiness with college) he offered John the appointment with one condition. "Probability is in your favor upon the condition that if you receive the appointment you make arms your profession for life." John doubted whether making such a commitment was necessary. He told his father, "It is not a mistake when he says 'Make arms your profession for life.' I had always heard and supposed that after three years [sic] service one was at liberty to withdraw or not. I still think so."[27] Still, the condition placed on the appointment rattled John enough that he failed to respond to a second inquiry from Phelps. With John remaining silent, Phelps obtained the appointment and sent it to Meredith, with a caveat: "I requested him to write me ... but I recd' no letter from him. If your son shall not accept this appointment please inform me ..." Otherwise, Phelps would select someone else.[28]

In early June 1853, West Point admitted John Sappington Marmaduke as a new cadet. A letter John had promised his 13-year-old brother Darwin arrived at the Saline County farm not long thereafter.

> My Dear Darwin,
> I promised to write you shortly after my arrival here. I now fulfill it. I reached this place last Friday (Wednesday). Made known my name to the officers on Monday last. Am now regularly at work, studying, reciting and drilling, all going in pretty well.
> Every thing is [done] according to military rules. Each cadet is required to attend strictly to his duty, or leave the academy. Many do leave, perhaps one third

of those that enter.

On the 20th of this month all new cadets are examined mentally and physically. We are stript [sic] stark naked and examined by an intelligent medical board. What think you of that?

We have about 250 cadets in all. We rise at 5 a.m., breakfast 7-1/2 a.m., dine at 1, sup at 7-1/2 p.m., go to bed at 10 p.m., thereby giving us seven hours to sleep. We sleep on the floor, or rather on a blanket which is spread on the floor, cover with a comfort. It went hard first night, but is equal to a bed of down now. I am exceedingly tired tonight, so I expect a capital sleep.

The new cadets look exceedingly sad as if they would like to get home. Poor little fellows I pity them. Some of them are not much larger than you. You doubtless know more than some of them. ... the drum & fife are sounding 1/2 past nine o'clock at night before my window, indicating that I must fix my pallet & c. so as to be in bed by 10 o'clock. So good night. Your affectionate Brother, John S. Marmaduke.[29]

In 1854, Meredith and Lavinia traveled east to visit his family in Virginia. They also planned to see John at West Point. He suggested they come during June when the cadets would be undergoing annual examinations "attended by citizens, and to those acquainted with the subjects, very interesting. Your early arrival will give you choice of rooms at hotel, which is no inconsiderate thing in a crowded house."[30]

John Marmaduke graduated from West Point on June 28, 1857. His performance as a cadet was not outstanding. Rated on academic, leadership, and athletic achievement, he ranked 30th in a graduating class of 38. Forty cadets admitted with him in 1853 failed to complete the rigorous four-year course of study and drill. Among John's classmates graduating in 1857 was Marcus Reno, whose conduct in 1876 as the senior officer under General George Custer during the Battle of the Little Big Horn (in which Custer and five companies of men with him were killed) is still being debated. (Reno was later accused of cowardice and drunkenness as Custer and his men were being massacred.) Another of John Marmaduke's graduating classmates was Henry M. Robert, a career soldier who had a scholarly bent and would later author *Robert's Rules of Order*, a parliamentary procedure manual widely used in the United States.[31]

Newly commissioned Lieutenant John S. Marmaduke was assigned to the United States Mounted Rifles Regiment, commanded by Colonel William W. Loring. First formed in 1846, the regiment, with John Marmaduke as a member, was sent to New Mexico in 1857 where — from its home base at Fort Union, now a National Monument — the soldiers were tasked with protecting settlers from raids by Indians. The following year, Lieutenant Marmaduke and the Mounted Riflemen were reassigned to Camp Floyd in Utah, joining an expeditionary force sent by President Buchanan to effect change in the territory's Mormon administration. There, John was transferred to the 7th Infantry, at the time commanded by Colonel Albert Sidney Johnston.[32]

Writing home from a temporary camp on the Bear River in Wyoming Territory, John told his parents that he was "about 140 or 150 miles north of Camp Floyd," and instead of fighting Mormons he was chasing Indians "who have and are now committing murder and theft on the emigrants going west. ... As yet one fight ... has taken place. No troops killed, 6 or 8 wounded."33 In January 1860 John was at Camp Floyd 50 miles southwest of Salt Lake City, "where things are moving in the usual military monotonous way. We can't get a chance to fight the M's [Mormons], and are too good natured to fight one another."34

Born in 1835, Meredith Jr. was the third son Lavinia delivered in five years. He undoubtedly followed the footsteps of his older brothers as they traipsed around the family farm and went away to school. Twenty-three years old when he returned from speculating on Texas land, Meredith Jr. soon married Mary Bruce and also bought a large farm in the vicinity of Marshall. He lived there for the next 30 years, he and his wife raising a houseful of children, one of whom they named Meredith Miles Marmaduke III.35

When their fourth son was born in 1840, Meredith and Lavinia faced a dilemma. They wanted to name him after one of her brothers, William and Darwin, but which one was to be honored? Meredith was close to both, but Darwin Sappington had been his partner in the Jonesboro store. Should it be his name that carried forward in the Marmaduke family? Hoping to please both brothers, the newborn child was christened Darwin William Marmaduke. But familial rivalry was not to be settled so easily. Darwin Sappington was in Russellville, Kentucky, when he learned about the new Marmaduke in Missouri. He was pleased that the boy's first name was Darwin, "knowing that the latter one [William] is hard to wear in any country."36

In 1853, when Darwin was 13, a family friend was traveling to Virginia, where he was a student at Randolph-Macon College, and stopped in to visit the Marmaduke home at Arrow Rock. The young man later wrote Meredith to say, "You spoke of being at a loss (when I was at your house) to know what to do with Darwin. As you are very much opposed to him studying the dead languages, I could recommend to you the scientific courses as very thorough indeed, but I do not think that you would send him here."37 Knowing his son's interests and aspirations Meredith realized that the study of "dead languages" might not be appropriate for Darwin, who needed a more practical course of study. Of course he could go to one of the two colleges in Lafayette County; however, the curricula at Chapel Hill College included "ancient languages, mathematics, mental and moral philosophy, and music." Masonic College's required courses (in addition to geology, mineralogy, chemistry, civil engineering, and botany) included Cicero's Orations, Greek Testament, Horace's Satires, Epistles, and Arts Poetic, as well as Greek translations and composition, and composition in English and Latin.38 Dead languages it seems were in abundance at both schools, yet sending young Darwin far from home and his mother was not an option Lavinia would accept. Wherever he ultimately went to complete his education (probably Masonic College), Darwin undoubtedly had his father's assurance that he need not worry about proficiency in the study of dead languages. In July of 1860, Darwin worked as a commission broker in St. Louis where he lived in Jane and Levin Harwood's home. That fall, he married Jane Caroline (Jennie) Sappington, a first cousin, the daughter of his namesake, Darwin Sappington. It is recorded that "Both families opposed the marriage."39

After Darwin, Lavinia gave birth to three more sons. Layton Price Marmaduke, born the first day of August 1841, died in infancy and was buried in the Sappington family cemetery. A year later, Lavinia delivered her ninth child, Henry Hungerford, named for Meredith's uncle in Virginia. In 1858, at age 16, Henry (Hank, to his siblings) entered the U.S. Naval Academy at Annapolis, Maryland, as a midshipman. His older brother's experience at West Point may have interested Henry in the potential of a military school. More likely, a lackadaisical temperament prompted Meredith to send him to a school where order and discipline were enforced. Like his brother John at West Point, Henry was a mediocre student at Annapolis, often failing to rise above the bottom third in class ranking in his studies. In his third year at the academy, he placed 34th of 57 midshipmen in Seamanship, 42nd in Ethics and English, 37th in French, and 57th in Drawing and Draughting. During Henry's time at Annapolis, Lavinia and Meredith worried about the number of demerits reported home each semester by the authorities at school. In an attempt to deflate their concern, Henry depicted his misconduct as "trifling offenses," telling his mother he had been at the school 16 months "during which time the Superintendent has never said a word to me as regards bad conduct, a thing which the majority of the Students cannot say."[40]

Lavinia was 39 years old when her last child was born; Meredith was 55. Their daughter Jane's observation, "every eighteen months will see another added to the list," had mostly proven true for Lavinia and Meredith except for this son, whom they named Leslie. Born in June 1846, four years had elapsed between his birth and that of his nearest-in-age sibling, Henry. Two years after Leslie's birth, Lavinia miscarried her 11th child, causing ill health that persisted. Twelve months later, she was still suffering from the miscarriage, her lingering illness forcing Meredith to consider an unusual treatment to improve her health, one that would require traveling to Philadelphia where she would receive magnetic healing therapy. He sought the advice of family friend George Penn, a doctor and at the time the director of the federal bank in St. Louis. Penn responded, saying he felt that Lavinia could travel "provided she has sufficient strength to stand it. Whether she would derive much benefit from being magnetized I am unable to say. It would be an experiment from which no injury could result & possibly some benefit."[41]

In midsummer of 1860, 14-year-old Leslie Marmaduke lived with his parents and his sister Lavinia in the family home. The other children, scattered across the country from Annapolis, Maryland, to Camp Floyd in Utah Territory, were engaged in occupations that ranged from student to soldier, from housewife and mother to commodities broker and commercial farmer. They were the beneficiaries of their father's determination to become wealthy, and they had every expectation that they would continue to prosper in the future. Within a year, they would find their lives turned upside-down as the nation sundered in the early days of the Civil War, a conflict that had already touched Meredith.

Notes

1. Widespread public school education did not exist in Missouri for the first half of the 19th century: Claude A. Phillips, *A History of Education in Missouri*, 3-10.

2. That Saline County families wanted their children schooled is evidenced in the establishment of two subscription schools: *History of Saline County*, 157-58, 177-78, 231.

A Rising Generation

3. "neglected the children's books very much lately, but will commence with them today — am lazy, to improve": Lavinia to Marmaduke, December 29, 1842. Box 3, Folder 3, Sapping and Marmaduke Papers, MHS.

4. "The children say their lessons almost every day. I intend to have Meredith reading by the time you come home": Jane Marmaduke to Marmaduke, December 4, 1840. Box 2, Folder 6, Ibid.

5. "run about, at least, but I reason in this way": Jane Harwood to Lavinia Marmaduke, November 7, 1852. Box 5, Folder 2, Sappington & Marmaduke Papers, MHS.

6. "Wholesale Grocers, Forwarding and Commission Merchants": Advertisement, *Marshall Democrat*, September 9, 1859. Reel 28061, Newspaper Collection, SHSMO.

7. an "ardent Democrat" of Pike County, Missouri: *The History of Pike County, Missouri*, 418.

8. "... of the simplest kind; it is seated about the neck": Robert Hooper, *New Medical Dictionary*, 729. Modern medicine knows scrofula as a form of tuberculosis affecting the lymph nodes, especially of the neck, most commonly in children and usually spread by unpasteurized milk from infected cows. It can be treated by antibiotics or by surgery. *The American Heritage Science Dictionary*. Houghton Mifflin Company, electronic document, np.

9. "Scrofula Fugax, it often arises from the absorption of matter from sores upon the head": Welborn to Marmaduke, April 26, 1843. Box 3, Folder 3, Sappington-Marmaduke Papers, MHS.

10. "very well, and have been so since you left": Sarah Marmaduke to Marmaduke, November 22, 1845. Box 3, Folder 6; December 13, 1845. Box 3, Folder 5, Sappington-Marmaduke Papers, MHS.

11. "beginning to recover her natural colour and is now pretty much out of danger": Yerby to Marmaduke, January 15, 1853. Box 5, Folder 3, Sappington-Marmaduke Papers, MHS.

12. "election day when Lager Beer will flow in large streams through the River of excited candidates and … unflinching friends": Darwin to My Dear Sister, August 1, 1859. Folder 20, Marmaduke Papers C1021, SHSMO.

13. "Mr. Price [who] comes around every day & yesterday he was here three times": Lavinia Marmaduke to My Dear Ma, September 2, 1859. Box 5, Folder 6, Sappington-Marmaduke Papers, MHS. Mr. Price has not been identified.

14. "sewing as hard as if she was working for wages. She goes out walking every day, and then to her work": Jane Harwood to My Dear Ma, September 14, 1859. Ibid.

15. "Mr. Price asked to be remembered to you & family": Jane Harwood to Marmaduke, January 22, 1860. Box 5, Folder 7, Ibid.

16. "if I don't get into civilization soon I will be a confirmed old bachelor, even now have a strong lean that way": John Marmaduke to Lavinia, January 4, 1860. Ibid.

17. In a letter to Meredith, John mentioned a "Nicaraguan revolution": John S. Marmaduke to Meredith Marmaduke, December 30, 1855. Box 5, folder 5, Sappington-Marmaduke Papers, MHS. At the time John wrote to his father, his class of cadets at West Point was studying mercenary adventurer William Walker's recent armed rise to power in Nicaragua. C. W. Doubleday, *Reminiscences of the Filibuster War in Nicaragua*. New York: G. P. Putnam's Sons, 1886.

18. "very well pleased with this college indeed I am getting along finely with my studies": Darwin Pearson to Marmaduke, December 3, 1845. Box 3, Folder 6, Sappington-Marmaduke Papers, MHS. James Bragg Marmaduke, a resident of next-door Shelby County, had campaigned for Meredith in northeast Missouri during his bid for the lieutenant governor's office. William Daniel Marmaduke, then a merchant at Hannibal, was Master of St. John's Masonic Lodge No. 28. Grace Sharp. Letters from a Missouri "Forty-Niner," Col. William Daniel Marmaduke. *Missouri Historical Review*, Vol. 20, No. 1 (October 1925), 129.

19. "We have fine eating here all the time. We have Puddings and Pies Ice crem and all those fine things, and plenty of study too." Vincent Marmaduke to Dear Mother, May 26, 1846. Box 4, Folder 1, Sappington-Marmaduke Papers, MHS.

20. Masonic College's major asset was ownership of 1,270 acres of rich farmland 12 miles southwest of

To Make a Fortune in Missouri

Palmyra, Missouri. *History of Marion County, Missouri*, 233-34. *History of Lafayette County, Missouri*, 248-49. Young's *History of Lafayette County*, 207-210.

21. "are generals, lawyers, doctors, Wall Street bankers, politicians, teachers, engineers, ministers, as well as the wives of prominent Missouri men": Robert A. O'Bryan-Lawson. *Chapel Hill, Missouri: Lost Visions of America's Vanguard on the Western Frontier, 1820-1865*, 69. Chapel Hill College's success prompted directors of the Missouri Synod of Cumberland Presbyterian Church South to affiliate with the school and Archibald Ridings in 1847, a position they maintained until purchasing the property from Ridings in 1860. Declining enrollment during the late 1850s and the onset of the Civil War forced its closing in 1861.

22. "not a creditable student" while attending Yale, yet he "proved to be a leader": in later life. Nathaniel C. Hughes Jr., *Yale's Confederates: A Biographical Dictionary*, 132. Closely engaged in business, speculating in lands and hemp": Charles Ives, *Statistics of the Class of 1852, of Yale College*, 45. Skull and Bones Society is known for "crooking," stealing keepsakes and mementos from other Yale societies or from campus buildings, and is said to possess the skulls of Geronimo and Pancho Villa. Zach O. Greenburg, "Bones May Have Pancho Villa Skull." *The Yale Herald*, Vol. 32, No. 2 (January 23, 2011).

23. "troubled and perplexed. ... unable to arrive at a conclusion as to what is best and right for me": Vincent Marmaduke to Meredith Marmaduke, February 10, 1856. Box 5, Folder 6, Sappington-Marmaduke Papers, MHS.

24. Sam McClure (Meredith's former partner in the Santa Fe trade) wrote to Meredith in April in hopes that his sons might be able to collect $2,000 owed him by John M. Cade: McClure to Marmaduke, Box 5, Folder 6, Sappington-Marmaduke Papers, MHS. In 1860, John M. Cade, age 43, farmed 1,000 acres of land in Liberty County, Texas, 30 miles northeast of present-day Houston, through which runs the Trinity River. He had a 14-year-old son who was born in Mississippi. 1860 U.S. Federal Census, Liberty County, Texas, Schedule 1, 344.

25. "You seem to think that my object was to travel about, kill time, and evade books": John Marmaduke to Marmaduke, January 14, 1853. Box 5, Folder 3, Sappington-Marmaduke Papers, MHS. John Marmaduke's six-page letter to his father is a lengthy justification of his decision to enroll at Harvard, as well as a discussion of the classes he was taking and why he believed he could pass exams in most of them with little difficulty. To offset his father's concern about increased costs, John conceded that "Board & Room bill, fuel & c is greater. To counterbalance such expenses there ought to be great advantages, and great improvement, improvement which could be made no where else at less cost."

26. Ibid.

27. "Probability is in your favor upon the condition that if you receive the appointment you make arms your profession for life": Ibid. Phelps condition was contained in a letter sent to John.

28. "I requested him to write me ... but I recd' no letter from him. If your son shall not accept this appointment please inform me": John Phelps to Marmaduke, March 12, 1853. Folder 19, Marmaduke Papers C1021, SHSMO.

29. "My Dear Darwin, I promised to write you shortly after my arrival here. I now fulfill it": John Marmaduke to Darwin Marmaduke, June 8, 1853. Box 5, Folder 3, Sappington-Marmaduke Papers, MHS. John Marmaduke's comment "Poor little fellows I pity them," reflects his status as an older cadet who already had three years of college experience. Cadets who entered West Point with him in 1853 and graduated four years later (38), ranged in age from 16 to 21. John and one other were age 21, five cadets were age 20, the remainder ages 16 to19. Ages of cadets who failed to complete the four-year course aren't known.

30. "attended by citizens, and to those acquainted with the subjects, very interesting": John Marmaduke to Marmaduke, March 25, 1854. Box 5, Folder 4, Sappington-Marmaduke Papers, MHS. The letter concludes with questions and observations about current political affairs, demonstrating again where John's interests lie.

31. John graduated from West Point on June 28, 1857: 1965 *Register of Graduates and Former Cadets of the United States Military Academy*, 245-46.

32. Newly commissioned Lieutenant John S. Marmaduke was assigned to the United States Mounted Rifles Regiment: John Lee, "John Sappington Marmaduke," *Missouri Historical Society Collections*, Vol 2,

A Rising Generation

26-28. "The Army at Camp Floyd," *The New York Times*, January 17, 1860. *William Wing Loring 1818-1886*, thelatinlibrary.com/chron/civilwarnotes/loring.

33. "about 140 or 150 miles north of Camp Floyd": John Marmaduke to Parents, August 27, 1859. Box 5, Folder 6, Sappington-Marmaduke Papers, MHS. John Marmaduke's location, "Camp on Bear River," places him in the vicinity of present-day Cokeville, Wyoming, on the Oregon Trail where two cut-offs (Sublette and Dempsey) joined the main trail coming from Fort Bridger. Mountain man Jim Bridger served as guide for General Johnston's expedition. The destruction of Bridger's Fort by Mormon militia was a factor leading to the army entering Utah in 1857. For more, see Hebard & Brininstool, *The Bozeman Trail*, Vol. 2, 224.

34. "where things are moving in the usual military monotonous way": John Marmaduke to Sister Bena, January 4, 1860. Box 5, Folder 7, Ibid.. "Bena" is a family name given to John's 22-year-old sister, Lavinia. The Utah War (Mormon War, or Buchanan's Blunder) as the Utah Expedition is called produced a skirmish or two but no battles, and was ultimately settled peaceably.

35. 1860 U.S. Federal Census, Schedule 1, Saline County, 249; 1870, 154.

36. "knowing that the latter one is hard to wear in any country": Darwin Sappington to Marmaduke, March 24, 1840. Box 2, Folder 5, Ibid.

37. "You spoke of being at a loss (when I was at your house) to know what to do with Darwin": Unknown to Marmaduke, August 28, 1853. Folder 19, Marmaduke Papers C1021, SHSMO.

38. "ancient languages, mathematics, mental and moral philosophy, and music": Paul D. Porter, "History of Chapel Hill College" provides look at state's higher education. *Democrat-News*, Marshall: October 13, 1987. Reel 28220, Newspaper Collection, SHSMO. Henry C. Chiles, *The Masonic College of Missouri*, 14-16, 25. Chiles characterizes the college as a "prep" school in 1855-56, although completion of the four-year course of study resulted in a Bachelor of Arts Degree.

39. "Both families opposed the marriage." Undated newspaper clipping. Folder 15, Sappington Family Papers C2889, SHSMO. Jane Sappington Marmaduke died five years after the marriage. In 1870, Darwin married Mary Crawford of Mobile, Alabama.

40. Like his brother at West Point, Henry was a mediocre student at Annapolis: G. S. Blake, Superintendent Naval Academy, report, December 1859. Box 5, Folder 7, Sappington-Marmaduke Papers, MHS. Henry Marmaduke to Dear Ma, January 13, 1860. Ibid.

41. Two years after Leslie's birth, Lavinia miscarried her 11th child: L. S. Eddins to Marmaduke, May 28, 1848. Box 4, Folder 4, Sappington-Marmaduke Papers, MHS; George Penn to Marmaduke, June 2, 1848, Ibid; Penn to Marmaduke, March 27, 1849. Box 4, Folder 6, Ibid. Magnetic healing, or "animal magnetism" as it was called, was popularized in Europe during the latter years of the 18th century by Franz Mesmer, a German physician. A 1781 French scientific inquiry (Benjamin Franklin was a member of the French commission) into Mesmer's claims concluded there was no scientific evidence of animal magnetism. Magnetic healing gained a following in the United States during the first half of the 19th century, with many books about the subject being published. Practitioners claimed they could heal all kinds of afflictions.

CHAPTER 18

MARMADUKE'S CONFLICTION

September 1863. Forty years after he arrived at the frontier town of Franklin, Meredith Marmaduke could honestly say he had achieved what he set out to do when he left Virginia in 1823 — make a fortune. Looking west from his house in Saline County, he owned all the land he could see and more beyond. As one of the earliest to travel the Santa Fe Trail, he had prospered in the dangerous and risky business of trading in Mexico. At home, the store he opened in Jonesboro, serving neighbors and western traders alike, had put money in his pocket. Peddling medicine that brought relief to malaria sufferers in the South had made their lives easier and his richer. As a land speculator with large ideas and a farmer who combined dirt and slave labor with marketing acuity, Meredith had generated great wealth.

Beyond these pecuniary accomplishments, political savvy and personal integrity had earned him the respect of Missouri's citizens, who responded by electing him to the state government's second-highest office and trusting his leadership in other capacities. His personal life had prospered as well. Marriage to Lavinia Sappington connected him with one of pioneer Missouri's leading out-state families whose political connections provided access to the nation's highest offices. And the marriage had given him nine children who lived to this time.

Now at age 72, Meredith should have been able to relax and enjoy the fruits of his labor. Sadly, nearly every aspect of his life, including his hard-won fortune and his family, was conflicted by a great quarrel — America's Civil War.

An Ambitious "Fox"

Meredith's discordance in 1863 was rooted in a chain of political events that began 20 years earlier and led to the downfall of Missouri's most powerful senator and the rise to power of the man who helped tear him down. The years-long struggle between these two men hung Meredith on the horns of a dilemma: should he be faithful to his friend and political ally Senator Thomas Hart Benton, or should he support his business partner and brother-in-law Claiborne Fox Jackson?

Born in 1806 in Fleming County, Kentucky, Claiborne Jackson came to Franklin in 1825 and entered the mercantile business. In 1831, he married 18-year-old Jane Sappington, one of Dr. John Sappington's daughters, and soon thereafter opened a store in Arrow Rock. Marriage into the Sappington family may have been more than a romantic gesture on Jackson's part; although his political aspirations were as yet unspoken, he certainly was aware of Dr. Sappington's influence in advancing the political and economic circumstances of his other son-in-law, Meredith Marmaduke. Unfortunately, Jane Jackson died of "ague" (a term then used to describe malaria) not long after her marriage. His first wife buried in the Sappington family cemetery, Jackson waited two years before remarrying, this time to Louisa, another 18-year-old daughter of John Sappington. She, too, suffered an early death, dying of injuries incurred in a "runaway" accident in the spring of 1838. Not wanting to lose his toehold in the influential Sappington family, six months after Louisa's death Jackson wed another of the doctor's daughters, this time 32-year-old Eliza, the former wife of bigamist Alonzo Pearson. Unlike her sisters, Eliza would survive her new husband, dying in Texas of malaria in 1864.[1]

Claiborne Jackson made his first political bid in 1836, winning a House seat in Missouri's General Assembly as Saline County's representative. As a reward for campaigning for Martin Van Buren in that year's presidential election, Senator Benton secured Jackson's appointment as the first postmaster at Arrow Rock. The following year, Jackson resigned both positions to accept appointment as cashier of the Fayette branch of the Bank of the State of Missouri. An ardent supporter of Benton's hard-money policy, Jackson lost the bank position in 1840 when he was ousted in a legislative upset engineered by soft-money anti-Benton Democrats. In 1842, Jackson regained a House seat, this time representing Howard County, and with the support of his central Missouri friends was elected House majority leader. Using the power of this office, in coming months he forcefully drove disputed bank and monetary policy bills through the state legislature, and later sidelined an effort to call a constitutional convention for the purpose of redistricting the state, a move that would have reduced the Central Clique's power in the General Assembly.[2]

Not content with a state office, Jackson saw an opportunity in October 1843 to advance his political standing when Lewis Linn, Missouri's other U.S. senator, unexpectedly died. Knowing that Governor Thomas Reynolds would appoint someone to the highly coveted position, Jackson quickly made known his candidacy. Believing he had the ear of the governor, the support of his brother-in-law as lieutenant governor, and the likelihood of approval by Senator Benton, Jackson pressed his case. Letters of endorsement for favorite candidates began arriving at the governor's office and among them was one from Meredith, written two weeks after Linn's death. In an unspoken rebuke to Claiborne Jackson, he endorsed John G. Miller, a former Missouri governor and member of Congress from the state's Second District.[3]

In rejecting his brother-in-law, Meredith followed the lead of Senator Benton who, having worked with John Miller in Congress for three terms, favored the more experienced man whose judgment and sensibilities were known. Although respected for his work in the Missouri House, Jackson's "confrontational style" drew criticism and enemies.[4] He was at times possessed of an explosive nature. In 1827, he was sued by a competing Franklin merchant for assault, charged with beating him with fists and a stick. In 1838, Meredith witnessed Jackson's animosity toward those who disagreed with him when he jumped onto a table and threatened Judge James Birch with a large knife at a gathering of Democrats in Fayette. And in 1840, Jackson had agreed to a duel (even though the practice was illegal in Missouri) with the Whig candidate for governor, specifying rifles as the weapons. Known for his shooting skill, Jackson would probably have killed his opponent. Fortunately, the deadly encounter was derailed by friends of both men. These incidents, coupled with observation of Jackson's driving ambition as a politician, undoubtedly raised Meredith's eyebrows when considering his brother-in-law's suitability for such a powerful position as U.S. senator. Jackson's bid for the Senate ended in failure when Governor Reynolds instead chose David Rice Atchison, a non-Clique Democrat from Platte County. Undaunted, Jackson next campaigned in the spring of 1844 for nomination as his party's candidate for U.S. representative. Here, too, he failed to gain Meredith's support and the bid ended in failure, as would Jackson's other efforts in coming years to gain federal office, a goal he would never achieve.

Meredith maintained a friendly relationship with Jackson in coming years; however, his refusal to support his brother-in-law's political aspirations was a contributing factor to a growing disaffection between the two men. Where previously they had visited as family members, partnered in business arrangements, and corresponded about political interests, after 1844 these communications ended. Jackson's ruffled feathers were probably not smoothed by rumors in 1847 that Thomas Benton might be appointed General of the United States Army and sent to Mexico to oversee the current war with that country, and that Meredith was being promoted as his successor in Congress. In March that year, Dr. George Penn — then in St. Louis as agent for the federal treasury — wrote Meredith saying that Benton's possible military appointment was feared by the Whigs "lest it should place him in a position to make his military equal to his civil reputation and open his way to the presidential chair. … Governor Edwards I understand will be here in a short time. I shall take occasion whilst he is here to name you to him as the successor of Genl. Benton. If you desire the situation I would suggest to you the propriety of having some communication with your confidential friends upon the subject." Any interest on Meredith's part in replacing Thomas Benton as one of Missouri's senators was short lived; the Mexican-American War drew to a close without Benton's rumored military appointment getting off the ground.[5]

Conflict Over Texas

Senator Thomas Benton's influence over Missouri's Democratic Party had given him 23 years in the U.S. Senate, and if at times he felt omnipotent, that was understandable. His decision, however, in early 1844 to oppose a treaty between the United States and the Republic of Texas that would admit Texas to the Union as a state where slavery was permitted fueled a political feud that would eventually destroy the Central Clique's power and lead to the senator's loss of office. The treaty was strongly supported by President John Tyler, Secretary of State John Calhoun (who negotiated the document with Texas), and senators from the South, some of whom favored secession if the treaty failed to gain approval in Congress. Calhoun advocated the nullification of the Missouri Compromise and the expansion of slavery into new territories and states. Benton believed the treaty reflected Calhoun's views and justified his resistance, saying the document was designed to sever the South from the Union. His opposition was viewed with alarm among Missouri's slaveholding Democrats, who accused him of changing his position from his earlier years in office when he was favorable toward slavery, though inclined to "temporize on the issue."[6] For Meredith, Benton's opposition ran contrary to his interests as a slaveholder and created a conflict of interest that shadowed their association in coming years. The events that came to surround the issue added tinder to the smoldering fire that was affecting Meredith's relationship with Claiborne Jackson.

In the spring of 1844, as governor and titular head of Missouri's Democratic Party, Meredith heard rumblings of discontent with Benton, even speculation that the senator might not be reelected when the General Assembly met in the fall. Fearing that Benton was out of step with his political base, Meredith corresponded with David Rice Atchison, voicing his concern. Responding in April, Atchison told Meredith that Benton had not acted yet; the Texas treaty had been signed "but it has not been laid before the Senate for ratification [.] upon this treaty we will have thunder. The Yankees will I fear oppose it. ..." Atchison, though, was not convinced that the South would secede, saying, "The northern men swear that the annexation of Texas will bring about an immediate dissolution of the Union, but this I think is a bug bear and nothing more."[7]

To gauge the feelings of central Missouri's Democrats, Meredith also wrote to John J. Lowry, a Howard County banker and physician who "appeared at times to be more politician" than either.[8] In June, Lowry expressed support for Benton's position on Texas, but he also believed that the senator's support among Central Clique Democrats was weak. "Benton is for Texas but he wants business done properly! ... I fear that some of our friends may be imprudent, by unnecessarily drawing Col. Benton into the Texas question & thereby injure him."[9] Among the "friends" Lowry referred to was Claiborne Jackson. Yet another correspondent, Thomas H. Harvey, in St. Louis, told Meredith in July that he regretted "doubly that Col. Benton's course should operate as it does & will to 'undercut' the Democratic party. ..."[10] Harvey's comment underscored a contentious meeting of Missouri's Democrats in Jefferson City two months earlier at a convention to nominate candidates for election that summer. Disagreement over Benton's stand on Texas, Congressional redistricting, and banking practices had already split the party into several factions. (Missouri faced a federal mandate to establish Congressional districts that provided equal representation. Redistricting would reduce Clique power in the state and therefore was delayed as long as possible.)

As summer approached in 1844, Senator Benton's policy toward the annexation of Texas continued to plague the members of Missouri's Democratic Party. In speeches at Boonville in mid-July, he attempted to explain why he opposed the treaty. Its design, he contended, "was not to get Texas into the Union, but to get the southern states out of it ... to pick a quarrel with Great Britain, and also with the non-slaveholding states on the subject of slavery." (Benton saw Texas's annexation as a slave state as opening the way for secession by the South.) His remarks, he said, were "meant for the prime movers and negotiators of the Treaty," who "meant to make dissension, discord, and mischief between the north and south."[11]

Benton also directed his ire at "land speculators and stock jobbers," who he said were based in Washington, the city "a buzzard's roost ... defiled and polluted by the foul and voracious birds ... who saw their prey in the treaty." Throughout his long Senate career, Benton championed policies that made it possible for people of limited financial means to obtain federal land. Speaking before the Senate in 1837, in support of a graduation bill that would reduce the price of public lands to speed their sale, Benton said the legislation was "emphatically a measure for the benefit of the agricultural interest." He noted that in the previous year 20 million acres of public land were sold to speculators, allowing them to profit at the public's expense. Now, in 1844, he wanted to prevent this from happening in Texas, where more than 225 million acres of land were still public domain, owned by the Republic of Texas. Benton's position on the speculation of public lands did not sit well with Missourians, many of whom — including Meredith Marmaduke — favored the practice. (The senator's efforts on this issue paid off; the annexation treaty signed by President John Tyler in 1845 provided that Texas would extinguish its own debt. To do this, Texas became the only state to retain control of her own public lands, although ultimately relinquishing 67 million acres to the federal government in 1850 in return for cash that wiped out the debt.) In March 1846, despite Benton's efforts to derail the Tyler-Calhoun treaty, Congress voted to admit Texas as a state where slavery could exist, if the populace desired.[12]

Texas In Mind

On both counts, the extension of slavery and the prevention of land speculation, Benton's position differed greatly from that held by Meredith. Slavery and land were prime elements in Meredith's bid to become wealthy, and Texas had long been on his mind. His interest in the future state dated back to 1836, when he briefly thought about relocating to there. He mentioned that possibility in a letter to John Locke Hardeman, then in Mississippi. "You still speak of Texas," Locke Hardeman replied. "It is doubtless a fine country, good soil and all that, but of doubtful health." Some 25 members of the Hardeman clan had recently moved from Tennessee to Texas, including John Locke's uncles, Bailey and Thomas James Hardeman, who were "well pleased" with what they saw there. The real problem with Texas, Locke Hardeman believed, was, "The country now in a state of revolution that may or may not succeed. …"[13] Despite Locke Hardeman's concerns, Meredith wrote to Bailey Hardeman for information about "the soil and climate of Texas, its natural advantages, together with the prospects of trade and speculation." Bailey responded with a nine-page, detailed letter that painted a positive picture of the region.[14]

Although Meredith ultimately decided to forego moving to Texas, he did acquire land in Red River and Lamar Counties (adjacent, in northeast Texas on the Oklahoma border). His venture there did not turn out well as long-distance speculating proved difficult to control. In 1841, he hired Paris, Texas, attorney H. L. Williams in an effort to collect money that was owed him from the sale of the Lamar County tract. Fourteen years later, in 1855, he received a favorable state Supreme Court judgment in a bid to recover Red River County land for which he had not been paid.[15]

Oregon Bound?

Texas land was not Meredith's sole speculative, long-distance allurement. In early 1847, the settlement of a long-standing boundary dispute between the United States and Britain established the Oregon Territory, an area that roused his interest. The possibility of being appointed governor for the vast expanse of land that now constitutes the states of Washington, Oregon, Idaho, and parts of Montana and Wyoming, led Meredith to make his interest in the territorial governorship known. His letter seeking the appointment (Benton would have delivered it to President James K. Polk) was a secret kept from his friends in Missouri. Writing to Meredith on Christmas Day 1847 from his home in Howard County, Dr. John Lowry said he "had never heard that you were an applicant for the appointment of Gov. of Oregon, until you mentioned it. No person believes that you are." Lowry was in the dark about Meredith's interest in Oregon because he, himself, wanted the appointment. The previous January, he had written to Meredith expressing his appreciation "for your letter to Col. Benton in my behalf. When I had the pleasure of an interview with you last, it was my determination not to trouble my friends any more respecting my appointment as Gov. of Oregon. They had as I thought said enough."[16]

The prospect of moving west to govern a brand-new territory that bordered on the Pacific Ocean appealed to Meredith's sense of adventure much as his move from Virginia to Missouri did in 1823, as well as his subsequent journeys to Santa Fe. Too, there were practical and financial considerations. With an abundance of federal land available for purchase at low cost, Oregon's potential for agricultural development and land speculation was great. Meredith also saw an opportunity to enhance his political credentials, something that had so far eluded him in Missouri, notwithstanding his tenure as lieutenant governor and a scant year as governor by default. The rationality of Meredith's thinking at this time in his life can be called into question. He was now 56 years old and Lavinia was 40. The average life span for men and women in the United States at the time was just less than 40 years, so statistically the Marmadukes were not in the prime of life.[17] Twenty years of good living had broadened Meredith's girth, and repeated child-bearing had weakened Lavinia's body. It's doubtful if Meredith told his family about the possibility of going to Oregon; with seven children at home, one of whom was only a year old, Lavinia would likely have balked at the prospect of a 2,000-mile, six-month-long wagon ride. And she would not have wanted to leave her mother and father for the prospect of a lonely existence half a continent away from her family. Dr. Sappington was 80 years old at this point and his wife was 69. Lavinia knew their lives were drawing to a close.

There was also the question of what Meredith would do with his Missouri lands and his slaves. The real estate could be sold at a profit and replaced in Oregon over time, but could he give up his slaves whose labor contributed so greatly to his wealth? Africans, whether slave or free, were not welcome in the Oregon country at the time. A provisional government established by settlers to oversee their affairs until the region was accepted into the Union had enacted, in 1844, the first of a series of exclusion laws designed to free slaves, expel them from the country, and prohibit the entry of black immigrants into the region. Any freed slave who stayed in the Oregon Territory was subject to being whiplashed, a harsh act that was repealed in 1845. Replacement legislation allowed black residents already there to remain but banned the entry of others, whether free or enslaved. Similar legislation existed over the next decade and despite the end of the Civil War, and passage of the 14th and 15th Amendments to the United States Constitution, a black exclusionary clause remained in Oregon's constitution until it was repealed in 1929.[18] In any event, Meredith's bid to become governor of Oregon Territory came to nothing when President Polk appointed Joseph Lane, a veteran of the Mexican-American War, to the post.

The Fox Again Denied

While Meredith was secretly considering leaving Missouri, friends and political acquaintances were urging him to get into the governor's race for the 1848 election. A Jefferson City acquaintance, speaking for Democrats there, said "We want here, a Farmer for a Governor. Col. Benton has made us a visit this summer. You, I am informed, would be his choice for Governor." Another friend, writing from Huntsville, told him that the most influential Democrats of Randolph County were beginning to ask who might be their next governor. "You Sir, are favorably spoken of by the Democracy of this county." A St. Louis contact told Meredith he had "for some months noticed with satisfaction that the public are looking to you as one of several candidates for the office of Governor." And from his home in Howard County, John Lowry asked Meredith about "your probable strength in the contemplated Jefferson Convention for the nomination of Gov. of Missouri. … Col. Price says that he has just returned from St. Louis & that you will be the first choice of the Democracy of that place, & that Jackson is the second choice. … Col. Price is a friend of Jackson's."[19]

Whatever hope Claiborne Jackson had of support for his candidacy from St. Louis's Democrats was dashed in early January of 1848 at a meeting of the city's faithful to elect delegates to the state nominating convention later that spring. Challenged by anti-Benton, soft-money Democrats to elect delegates who would favor a gubernatorial candidate of their choice, the pro-Benton Democrats succeeded in electing a slate that was instructed to support Meredith's nomination, ignoring Claiborne Jackson. The day after the St. Louis meeting closed, a friend who was there wrote Meredith to say that "Mr. Jackson was present and his name was not even mentioned."[20] George Penn, who was also at the meeting, told Meredith that Claiborne Jackson had arrived in St. Louis a few days prior to the gathering. "He told me that he had been informed that the democrats [sic] here were under the impression that he was hostile to Col. Benton and opposed his reelection to U.S. Senate. With the view of disabusing the public mind upon this subject, he visited the city. The number here in his [Jackson's] support is much smaller than I had anticipated, nor do I believe his reported friends have done much to advance his prospects."[21] Despite the favorable showing for him in St. Louis, Meredith was doubtful he would be nominated at the state convention. John Lowry acknowledged Meredith's concern and warned him again about Jackson. "You say, that Judge King will come to the convention with more counties than any other aspirant! I had thought that Mr. Jackson would, of this however I may be mistaken." Austin King, a Democrat, was Circuit Judge for Caldwell County and had previously served two terms as Boone County's representative to the General Assembly.[22]

As the time for the state convention approached, Meredith was chided by friends for not being more aggressive in securing the support of delegates. Claiborne Jackson, on the other hand, was actively canvassing for delegates. Francis Tymony wrote Meredith in mid-March, warning him that Jackson was working against him. "Mr. Jackson has made great exertions [at] meetings in different counties in his favor, and had you but made half the exertions you would have gained the nomination with ease. ... Mr. Jackson seems to be courting the favor of friends and has taken Judge King to be his special favorite."[23]

A Rowdy Affair

William Switzler, publisher and editor of the *Missouri Statesman* newspaper, published in Columbia, was on hand when the 1848 Democratic Party state convention opened in the Capitol building at Jefferson City on Monday, March 27. Reporting on the event several days later, Switzler described the gathering as "loud and discordant" with "all sorts of wire pulling" taking place among the delegates.[24] Split between pro-Benton "Hards" and anti-Benton "Softs," many of the delegates had instructions from their county committees about whom to support. The convention promised to be a rowdy affair as candidates and their supporters strode the halls of the Capitol, exchanging promises for votes. The details of the scheme used to empower the delegates are not recorded, but in total they had 37,750 votes to cast for candidates. A candidate needed a simple majority of 18,876 votes to win the nomination. As the convention progressed, 20 ballots would occur before one man would be declared the winner.

Disposing of lesser issues on Monday, the next morning found the delegates taking up the business that was the major reason for their coming together — the nomination of a candidate for governor in the upcoming statewide election. The names of six men were put forward and accepted: Claiborne Jackson, Meredith Marmaduke, Austin King, J. M. Hughes, P. H. McBride, and J. H. Relfe. Austin King and J. M. Hughes arrived at the convention late on Monday. Traveling together from western Missouri, they were aboard the steamboat *Little Missouri* when it "wrecked," and had to transfer to the *Bertrand*, which brought them to Jefferson City. Using a political strategy that was common at the time, each of three candidates — Relfe, from central Missouri; McBride, from northeast Missouri; and Hughes, from western Missouri — were favorite sons with little chance of winning the nomination, but they held votes that would be delivered to a preferred candidate when needed.[25]

The horse race began after dinner on Tuesday as delegates cast votes for their favorite candidates. Although with each succeeding ballot the tally shifted a bit among the six men, the first three ballots saw little movement as Jackson led the pack with nearly 10,000 votes. At the end of the third ballot, King closely trailed Jackson. Meredith was in third place, some 3,000 votes behind Jackson. Hughes, McBride, and Relfe rounded out the field in that order. Relfe withdrew ahead of the seventh ballot, some of his votes going to King, which gave him an 800-vote lead over Jackson; Meredith remained in third place, not really in contention and unable to improve his tally. On the eighth and ninth ballots, no votes exchanged among the candidates. At this point, with the contest at an impasse, it was late into the evening and the delegates voted to adjourn until the next day.

When the convention reconvened Wednesday morning, the 10th ballot revealed that only a few delegates had changed their minds overnight. The first break in the deadlock came on the 11th ballot. McBride withdrew, and the votes he held split, some going to Jackson, others to Meredith. King now led with 13,692 votes, Jackson trailed him with 13,012 votes, and Meredith ran a distant third with 5,822 votes. Hughes remained alive with 4,596 votes. The race began to change on ballot number 12. While Jackson and King sparred, neither man gaining or losing significantly, the number of votes Hughes received more than doubled, jumping to 10,600, while Meredith's tally fell to only 2,001 votes. The 13th ballot ended with no changes. On the 14th ballot, Meredith's vote tally suddenly jumped to 8,986. On the 15th ballot, Meredith received 11,273 votes, putting him on a footing to challenge King at second place with only 500 votes separating them. Jackson now had 13,508 votes. What brought about the abrupt change in Meredith's fortune? Was he going to seriously challenge his brother-in-law for the nomination?

As the balloting had continued Wednesday afternoon and Meredith's support had dwindled away, it became apparent — after the 12th ballot — that he could not expect to win the nomination and the best he could do was influence the outcome of the contest. With that in mind, someone from Meredith's camp — probably his manager, 27-year-old Francis (Frank) P. Blair Jr. — approached the Hughes camp with the offer of a deal.[26] If Hughes would release his delegates to vote for Meredith he would consolidate them with his support, which was expected to increase even more with the show of strength, and then withdraw from the race after instructing all of his supporters to shift their allegiance to Hughes. Although the full circumstances behind Meredith's move never have been revealed, it's possible that he believed Hughes would surge to the front and challenge Jackson and King. It is also possible that Hughes was in the race as a blind-proxy candidate holding votes for Austin King. In either case, it's apparent that Meredith did not want Claiborne Fox Jackson to win the nomination.

When the roll was called for the 16th ballot, Meredith withdrew and most of the delegates supporting him immediately moved to Hughes's camp, giving him nearly 11,000 votes. Jackson, with slightly more than 14,000 votes, held a 300-vote lead over King. Hughes, sitting with 4,500 votes behind Jackson, remained in the race for three more ballots, during which the tally among the three contenders wobbled slightly but never enough to propel a winner into the ring. Hughes, if he was a serious contender, certainly now realized that he was positioned to control the outcome of the contest. Withdrawing his bid at the end of the 19th ballot, he threw his support to Austin King. On the 20th ballot, King bested Jackson by 3,000 votes, giving him a clear path to the nomination.

An expert at "wire pulling," Meredith, by making a deal with Hughes, avoided openly betraying Claiborne Jackson and adroitly stepped away from creating a conflict within his extended family. But his failure to support his brother-in-law was not overlooked. Two months after the nominating convention ended, Meredith's other brother-in-law, Layton Eddins, warned him that Jackson was nursing a grudge. In late May, Eddins had attended a meeting at Glasgow of Howard County Democrats where Austin King was the key speaker. Afterward, Eddins invited King and several others to spend the night at his home. Eddins's suspicion about Jackson was aroused from their conversation that night, which revolved around the events that occurred during the recent Jefferson City meeting. Reflecting what he had learned from his guests, Eddins told Meredith that "Jackson and his friends are dead against you ... that he blamed you for how things [were] done at that convention. ... Be not surprised to see Mr. C. F. Jackson a candidate for one of the honors to be conferred on some one from our County and district."[27]

Legislative Shackles

If he could not be the governor, Claiborne Jackson would settle for something else. Twice shunned in bids for federal office, and with his term as Howard County's representative ending, Jackson spent the summer of 1848 campaigning for a seat in the state Senate. On Monday, December 25, he was in Jefferson City for the opening session of the 15th General Assembly as the newly elected senator from Missouri's 10th district. He was sworn into office and spent the next week participating in the routine business matters that occupied the Assembly. Unseen, however, he caucused behind closed doors with a group of men who were drafting a document about slavery that would eventually become a key element in Claiborne Jackson's dispute with Thomas Benton, and thus further strain the relationship between Jackson and Meredith Marmaduke. The first draft of what came to be called the Jackson Resolutions was presented to members of the state Senate on January 1, 1849, by Carty Wells of Lincoln County, chairman of the Senate Judiciary Committee. This was soon followed by the reading of an amended version in the Missouri House on January 5, presented by Representative John B. Henderson of Pike County. On January 15, Jackson himself stood before the combined General Assembly and introduced the joint resolutions that came to bear his name.[28] As approved by the General Assembly, the Jackson Resolutions declared that the U.S. Congress had no constitutional power to regulate or limit slavery. Taking aim at Thomas Benton, the resolutions instructed Missouri's Congressional delegation to initiate and support legislation that would ensure the expansion of slavery into new territories. In Washington, having already opposed the admission of Texas and the Oregon Territory on terms that would allow slavery, Benton ignored the legislature's instructions and advocated the admission of California as a state without slavery. Missouri's legislators also used the Jackson Resolutions to censure Benton for failing to support the Calhoun treaty. The senator fought back. Believing he could galvanize support among Missouri's citizens for his position, he returned to Missouri intent on traveling the state seeking approval of his actions. Prior to Benton's return, Meredith told George Penn that he was concerned about the senator's antislavery activities, but he would withhold judgment for the time being. Penn replied that, "I fully agree with you that it will be necessary for the Col.'s old friends to determine upon their course after he [Benton] has fully defined his position. ... I shall however still hope until I hear it from Col. Benton himself that he is with the great body of our party. ..."[29]

On Monday, May 21, Benton was in Jefferson City preparing for a speech the following Saturday. Observing the senator on Tuesday, George W. Hough wrote Meredith that day to tell him that Benton's "appeal" had caused some "strictures to be made upon him. It is a strange thing to see Col. Benton appealing from his own party."[30] At the time, Benton was accused of being a "Free Soiler," referencing a short-lived political party active during the 1848 and 1852 presidential elections that sought to halt the expansion of slavery. In St. Louis, members of the Free Soil Party, some of whom were disaffected Democrats, hoped to attach Senator Benton's name to their movement. Meredith viewed this as worrisome, and George Penn agreed. "Your views in regard to the free soil question as it is called entirely accord with mine." Penn told Meredith that if Benton rejected the Free Soilers, "the democracy in this state will have nothing to fear. But the ground is opened by the free soil party here that they are the true expression of his views." If Benton sided with the Free Soilers "it will break up the [Democratic] party in St. Louis, that is the division will be so great as to give the Whigs the decided ascendency in the city."[31]

Benton continued his campaign for support among the populace of the state. Speaking in Clay County in July 1849, he compared the Jackson Resolutions to the Calhoun treaty, saying they were intended to mislead Missouri's citizens into abetting the dissolution of the Union.[32] Despite his tour around the state, public acceptance of the senator's position was weak. Thomas Benton headed into 1850 a damaged candidate for reelection to the U.S. Senate. When the members of the state Senate convened that fall, of the 33 men who took their seats in the chamber only 13 could be counted as Benton supporters.[33] In January 1851, a coalition of those opposed to Thomas Hart Benton — Democrats and Whigs alike — elected Henry S. Geyer, a Whig, as the new U.S. senator from Missouri. Whether or not Meredith faulted his brother-in-law for his part in Benton's defeat is not recorded, yet he could not have ignored the succession of anti-Benton events that were orchestrated by Claiborne Jackson during his years in Missouri's General Assembly. Ten years hence, Meredith and Jackson would find their relationship strained even more.

Throughout this difficult period, Meredith had remained committed to Thomas Benton, both as a friend and as the state's leading political figure. Although he disliked the senator's anti-extension (of slavery) posture and his opposition to land speculation, he disliked even more the possibility of the breakup of the Union by secession of the Southern states and believed that Benton's presence in Congress would work to hold back this threat. Benton's loss of the U.S. Senate seat in 1850 did not keep him out of Missouri's turbulent political scene. Two years later, he was elected to the U.S. House of Representatives from the state's First Congressional District (St. Louis and nearby counties). Claiming victory, his supporters hoped this win would turn out to be a path back to the Senate in 1856. Early in 1854, Frank Blair Jr. encouraged Meredith to stand for election to the Missouri legislature as a representative. "My object," Blair wrote, "is to induce you if possible to take the field as a candidate for the Legislature in order to restore the true Democracy to power and place Col. Benton again in the Senate." Meredith's candidacy, Blair believed, "would give proof of your estimate of the importance" of the crisis surrounding the Democratic Party in Missouri, and would encourage other Democrats to show their support for Benton.[34] Writing to James Lusk in Jefferson City several days after receiving Blair's letter, without disclosing his purpose, Meredith sought Lusk's view of the political scene around the state. As the publisher of the daily *Jefferson Inquirer* newspaper, James Lusk was a clearinghouse for information about the Democratic Party. "The antis [anti-Benton]," he responded, "are now begging for union and harmony — conventions, and caucuses, but I hope our friends will keep their hands clear of them." Not finding encouragement for his candidacy beyond Frank Blair and loyal friends, and with his interests at this time focused on farming, agricultural advancement, and the establishment of a state fair, Meredith was reluctant to commit himself to another political race. Despite his faith in the former senator, he chose to not involve himself in a fight to put Benton back in the Senate. To the disappointment of his friends, in 1854 Thomas Hart Benton lost his bid for reelection to the U.S. House and never again held public office. After a losing attempt in 1856 to become Missouri's governor, Benton retired to the nation's capital to write a two-volume history of American government from 1820 to 1850. He died there in 1858 and was returned to Missouri for internment in St. Louis's Bellefontaine Cemetery.[35]

The Lexington Proslavery Convention

In July of 1855, Meredith traveled to Lexington to attend a gathering of Missouri slave owners. The passage of the Kansas-Nebraska Act the year before, which in effect repealed the Missouri Compromise and allowed settlers in those two territories to determine whether they would be free or slave states, was the impetus for the convention. Also on the minds of the attendees, but not openly admitted, was the fact that three months earlier many of them had fraudulently declared themselves to be residents of Kansas Territory in order to vote there. Among these were Meredith's son-in-law Levin Harwood, and Claiborne Jackson. (The previous November, Harwood had also fraudulently voted to elect the territory's first delegate to Congress, traveling to the home of Isaac R. Titus in Kansas's First District — today's Osage, Shawnee, Lyons and Waubaunsee Counties.).[36] In March 1855, the two had been part of an organized, armed force that swept into Kansas determined to prevent the election of a free-state legislature in the new territory. In this the Missourians were hugely successful, overwhelming legitimate Kansas voters to elect men whose devotion to slavery could assure that institution's establishment on the prairie and perhaps beyond. For those interloping Missourians who had gone to Kansas, the outcome of the Lexington convention might put a better public face on their illegitimate venture while discrediting the detested Free Soilers from Massachusetts and elsewhere who also went to Kansas with the intent to settle there and vote in the March election.

Among the delegates, confusion existed about the purpose of the Lexington meeting, although it was generally agreed that they should create a document that would represent what they believed were the true feelings of the citizens of Missouri with respect to slavery. Not all were in agreement as the convention opened. Robert H. Miller, publisher and editor of the *Liberty Weekly Tribune*, later expressed his regret that "greater harmony did not characterize the proceedings." Recognized as delegates were 223 men, most all of whom were slave owners, from 24 counties in central and western Missouri, plus two men who represented St. Louis city and county. A "Mr. Ralston" of Kansas Territory attempted to be admitted as a delegate but was met with opposition. This was a convention of "Missouri pro-slavery men" he was told, "gentlemen from abroad would not be recognized" although he could stay and observe.[37] Saline County sent a delegation of 18 men that included Meredith, his son Vincent, his brother-in-law William Sappington, brother-in-law Claiborne Jackson, and his son-in-law Levin Harwood. Jackson managed to be appointed to a select group to oversee the event and was assigned to work on a committee drafting resolutions. Meredith, recognized as a former governor (Austin King was there, too, as was sitting Governor Sterling Price) and a leading slave owner in the region, received no office or responsibilities during the meeting. This may have been his choice, finding it more productive to quietly work to assure that the report of the resolutions committee, while condemning abolitionism, did not advocate Missouri's separation from the Union.

An attempt on the first day of the meeting to prevent debate, which editor Miller noted served "no valuable purpose whatever ... but will most certainly lead to heated and unprofitable excitement," was defeated, although delegates were restricted to making only one speech unless permitted to do otherwise by a vote of the assembly. That night the resolutions committee, working under the direction of Missouri Supreme Court Judge William B. Napton, prepared its report.[38] Presented to the conference the next morning, its 10 resolutions expressed strong support for the proslavery provisions of the Kansas-Nebraska Act, "especially with reference to Kansas" where "already laws have been passed upon that specie of property"; decried the intervention of "organized bands of colonists shipped from Massachusetts and other quarters ... for the purpose of colonizing Kansas, and thus force the territory to become free territory"; and closed with an appeal to the "good sense and patriotism of the entire North" to put down "fanatical aggressors ... such as the Emigrant Aid Societies." Approving the document with no opposition, the delegates voted to present it to the audience in the hall who, according to the *Liberty Weekly Tribune*, responded by "every man in the house rising to his feet and greeting the result with a loud cheer."[39]

Summarizing the meeting, editor Robert Miller noted that some of Missouri's "best men ... very wisely adopted no fire-eating, nullification, disunion, or disorganizing resolutions, but made a platform upon which all pro-slavery men can stand." Meredith's influence on the convention was felt behind the scenes working with individual delegates. For 20 years he had been a leading figure on Missouri's political stage and personally knew many of the county officials and leaders who attended the convention. Their respect for him and high regard for his opinions helped keep the more militant delegates at the convention — such as Claiborne Jackson — at bay.

Divisive Decade

In 1853, Claiborne Jackson (previously a resident of Howard County) became Meredith's next-door neighbor, the new owner of Pilot Hickory, Dr. Sappington's home farm. The doctor, widowed and advanced in age, divided his estate that year into seven equal shares he assigned to his children, with one share going to the children of Eliza's marriage to Alonzo Pearson. (When Jackson refused to fund the Pearson children's maintenance, Dr. Sappington did so.) In order to acquire Pilot Hickory, Jackson had to bargain with the doctor's children for their shares of the home farm.[40] This accomplished, Eliza took up the care of her ailing father, and Jackson took up farming. (Jackson also partnered with William B. Napton in 1858 to establish the *Marshall Democrat* newspaper at Saline County's seat of government.) Within a few years, Jackson was among the county's wealthiest farmers and slave owners. Meredith's dealings with his neighbor at this time were cordial. With adjoining farms, they had similar interests — crops, markets, and slaves — and when together discussed these and other issues, but Jackson's treachery in ousting Benton doubtless lay on their relationship with the coldness of a gravestone.

Throughout the 1850s, Jackson's thirst for political power never waned, yet — as he was to discover — he could not escape what he had done. Four years after losing his state Senate seat in 1852, he tried to return to the political stage. Missourians, however, remembered his role in the downfall of Thomas Benton and his campaign in

1856 for a seat in the U.S. House of Representatives failed. A later effort to win a seat in Missouri's General Assembly was similarly turned aside. Undaunted, in the fall of 1859 he pronounced himself a candidate for governor, a move that ultimately would add to the growing conflict in Meredith's life.[41]

The future of slavery held center stage in the Missouri political scene in 1860 and as well was an issue that divided the Democratic Party at the national convention that year. There, Northern Democrats favored Stephen A. Douglas, U.S. senator from Illinois, as their candidate for the presidency. Douglas, who opposed secession, had resisted Southern efforts in Congress to enact a federal slave code and as well had opposed the Lecompton Constitution, a document that would have established Kansas as a slave state and excluded free black people from residency there. Southern Democrats responded to Douglas's candidacy by leaving the convention to form the Southern Democrat Party and nominate their own presidential candidate, Kentuckian and current vice president of the United States, John C. Breckinridge. Although a proponent of slavery, Breckinridge was also opposed to secession. A third presidential candidate, Tennessean John Bell, a respected Whig politician who had served seven terms in the U.S. House and most recently was a U.S. senator, ran under the banner of the Constitutional Union Party. As the upcoming election showed, Bell's proslavery credentials and opposition to secession appealed to Missouri's slave owners. Like them, he believed that the U.S. Constitution protected the ownership of slaves as property.

The national party's quarrel spread among Missouri's Democrats that spring and summer, presenting Claiborne Jackson with a problem in his quest for the governor's office. Which of the three (excluding Republican Abraham Lincoln) presidential candidates should he endorse? Realizing that choosing any one of them would lose him the support of voters favoring the others, he initially ignored the question before eventually aligning himself with Douglas during a speech in Fayette about a month before the August state election. His choice of Douglas was aimed at St. Louis where he needed to attract Republican as well as Democrat voters. Several days after the election, Jackson learned that he would soon travel to Jefferson City, having won the governor's office with 47 percent of the votes cast. (He failed to carry his home county in the election. Saline County voters favored maverick politician Sample Orr by 69 votes.)[42] Left unanswered were the new governor's true feelings about secession. (His endorsement of Douglas had earned him the sobriquet "a Douglas man with Breckinridge tendencies" among disgruntled Missouri voters.).[43] If the South left the Union (as was expected if Lincoln won the presidency), would Jackson side with the Southern states and try to join them, or would he take a more moderate course in an effort to preserve slavery and remain in the Union, the path favored by Meredith and his Saline County neighbors? Jackson did not have a mandate for secession.

The results of the November election showed, by virtue of their support for Douglas and Bell, that the majority of voters in Missouri preferred to remain in the Union. Statewide, each received slightly more than 35 percent of the votes cast, with Douglas finishing ahead by two-tenths of a percent. Breckinridge got less than 20 percent, and Republican Lincoln received 10 percent of the votes. In Saline County, the majority of voters saw John Bell as someone who mirrored their interests and favored him over Douglas. Breckinridge ran a poor third, and no one in the county voted for Lincoln.

Who Meredith voted for in 1860 remains unknown, but he probably favored John Bell. In coming months, as the likelihood of secession increased, Meredith spoke to the citizens of Saline County on several occasions "from the stone steps of the old hotel in Marshall," exhorting them to remain in the Union. An 1881 history of Saline County recounted Meredith's life, saying that "While sympathizing deeply with the southern people, he had no affection for the Confederate cause and remained a *constitutional Union man* to the end of his days."[44]

Meredith's Confliction Escalates

The blanket Claiborne Jackson had laid during his campaign over his conviction that Missouri should be allied with the Southern states, in the event of secession, was thrown aside in his inaugural address at Jefferson City on January 3, 1861. Standing before a packed house of incoming and outgoing legislators and members of the public, he aroused his audience by attacking the Republican Party, saying that its soul was "hostile to slavery," and then proceeded to lay the groundwork for aligning Missouri with the Southern states. "So long as a State continues to maintain slavery within her limits, it is impossible to separate her fate from that of her sister States who have the same social organization. … Missouri will not shrink from the duty which her position on the border imposes; her honor … and her sympathies point alike in one direction and determine her to *stand by the South*." Not wanting to play his hand all at once, Jackson tossed a bone to those who, like Meredith, favored the South but didn't relish secession; Missouri would stay in the Union if the North recognized state sovereignty on the issue of slavery. "The issue of present embarrassment [South Carolina had voted to secede two weeks earlier; five other states would follow by the end of January] depends entirely upon the sentiments and actions of the North." Jackson finished his remarks, hedging his bet by calling for a convention to determine "by the expression of the people … what is to be the ultimate action of the State."[45]

Established by an act of Missouri's General Assembly in late January 1861, what came to be known as the Missouri Constitutional Convention of 1861–1863 opened its first meeting at Jefferson City on February 28, 1861, and moved to St. Louis the following week. Delegates to the convention had been selected February 18 in a statewide election. Of the 140,000 votes cast that day, 110,000 went to candidates who had made known their intention to keep Missouri in the Union. Among the 104 delegates was Meredith's son Vincent, former governor Sterling Price (elected chairman of the convention), and Sample Orr, Claiborne Jackson's recent campaign opponent.[46] Charged with determining Missouri's status in the Union, after two weeks of debate the delegates (with one dissenter) overwhelmingly voted to not secede.

Though discouraged by the convention's outcome but not defeated in his attempt to move Missouri toward secession, Governor Jackson engaged in a series of anti-Union actions, refusing President Lincoln's call for Missouri troops after the April 12 Confederate attack on Fort Sumter, South Carolina. On May 2, at a special session of the legislature, Jackson restated his belief that Missouri should ally itself with the South and ordered the state militia to assemble in four days' time for training. Most alarming to pro-Union Missourians, Jackson appealed to Confederate States President Jefferson Davis for help in arming the militia. In St. Louis on May 10, what became known as the Camp Jackson Affair pitted an 800-man state militia force against a much larger Union force (augmented by a Union militia group called the Home Guards organized by Frank Blair Jr.) commanded by Captain (later General) Nathaniel Lyon. Believing that Jackson's militia would attempt to capture the federal arsenal south of the city (a secessionist militia force had already seized the federal arsenal at Liberty in Platte County), Lyon first securing its weapons by sending them to Illinois, then surrounded the Jackson militia encampment and forced its surrender. Later, while the captured militiamen were being moved through the city, residents upset by Lyon's action precipitated a riot in which 15 bystanders and two soldiers were killed.

The tragedy that occurred after Lyon's controversial move at Camp Jackson resulted in Missouri's General Assembly enacting a "Military Bill" that reformed the state militia into the Missouri State Guard and divided the state into nine military districts, each commanded by a general. The bill required all able-bodied men to join the new organization, and appropriated $2 million for support and training. Sterling Price was appointed the Guard's commander. A month after the Camp Jackson affair, Governor Jackson and General Price met with Captain Nathaniel Lyon and Frank Blair Jr. in St. Louis, seeking an agreement about the political and military management of the state. After five hours of discussion, in which no suitable plan was found, Lyon ended the meeting by telling Jackson and Price they had an hour to leave town, and that he intended to seize control of the state to ensure its retention in the Union. The governor and Price then sped by train to Jefferson City, destroying bridges at the rivers behind them in an effort to slow Lyon's advance on the capital. That day, June 12, the Civil War reached almost to Meredith Marmaduke's doorstep. Little did he know that within weeks the conflict would tear into the heart of his family.

Notes

1. Phillips, *Missouri's Confederate*, 68, 91, 276.

2. Claiborne Jackson made his first political bid in 1836: *History of Saline Co.*, 219; Napton, *Past and Present*, 110; Phillips, *Missouri's Confederate*, 72-73, 76, 140; Morrow, "Dr. John Sappington," *MHR*, 50.

3. Letters of endorsement for favorite candidates: Marmaduke to Reynolds, October 16, 1843. Folder 58, Box 2, Record Group 3.7, Thomas Reynolds Papers, MSA. Phillips, 149.

4. "confrontational style": Phillips, *Missouri's Confederate*, 143.

5. "lest it should place him in a position to make his military equal to his civil reputation": George Penn to Marmaduke, March 13, 1847. Folder 17, Marmaduke Papers C1021, SHSMO.

6. "temporize on the issue.": Merkel, "The Slavery Issue and the Decline of Thomas Hart Benton, 1846-1856," *MHR*, Vol. 38, No. 4 (July 1944), 388-89.

7. "but it has not been laid before the Senate for ratification": Atchison to Marmaduke, April 11, 1844. Box 3, Folder 4, S&M, MHS.

8. "appeared at times to be more politician": McCandless, *A History of Missouri*, Vol. 2, 1820-1860, 218.

9. "Benton is for Texas but he wants business done properly!": Lowry to Marmaduke, June 12, 1844. Box 3, Folder 4. Sappington-Marmaduke Papers, MHS.

10. "doubly that Col. Benton's course should operate as it does & will to 'undercut' the Democratic party": Harvey to Marmaduke, July 9, 1844. Box 3, Folder 5. Ibid.

Marmaduke's Confliction

11. "was not to get Texas into the Union, but to get the southern states out of it": News From Boonville, *Daily Missouri Republican*, July 30, 1844. Reel 41323, Newspaper Archives, SHSMO.

12. "land speculators and stock jobbers": Thomas H. Benton, *Thirty Years View*, 126-127. www.tsl.texas.gov/exhibits/annexation.

13. "You still speak of Texas": Locke Hardeman to Marmaduke, March 19, 1836. Box 2, Folder 2, Sappington-Marmaduke Papers, MHS. Nicholas Hardeman, *Wilderness Calling*, 121-22.

14. "the soil and climate of Texas, its natural advantages": Bailey Hardeman to Marmaduke, May 19, 1836. Box 2, Ibid.

15. In 1841 he hired Paris, Texas, attorney H. L. Williams: Williams to Marmaduke, February 26, 1841. Box 3, Folder 1, Sappington-Marmaduke Papers, MHS. Merrill & Dickson to Marmaduke, April 28, 1855. Box 5, Folder 5, Ibid.

16. "had never heard that you were an applicant for the appointment of Gov. of Oregon": John Lowry to Marmaduke, January 5, 1847. Box 4, Folder 2, Sappington-Marmaduke Papers, MHS. Lowry to Marmaduke, December 25, 1847. Folder 17, Marmaduke Papers C1021, SHSMO.

17. The average life span for men and women in the United States at the time was less than 40 years: J. David Hacker, *Decennial Life Tables for the White Population of the United States, 1790 - 1900*. Table 1. Washington: National Institutes of Health, 2010. ncbi.nlm.nih.gov/pcm/articles.

18. Any freed slave who stayed in the Oregon Territory was subject to being whiplashed: The Black Laws of Oregon, 1844-1857. blackpast.org/perspectives/black-laws-oregon-1844-1857.

19. "We want here, a Farmer for a Governor": G. Gunn to Marmaduke, August 29, 1847. Box 4, Folder 3, Sappington-Marmaduke Papers, MHS; Robt. Blaking to Marmaduke, September 8, 1847. Ibid; John M. Krum to Marmaduke, September 6, 1847. Ibid. Lowry to Marmaduke, December 25, 1847. Folder 17, Marmaduke Papers C1021, SHSMO.

20. "Mr. Jackson was present and his name was not even mentioned": Thomas Gray to Marmaduke, January 9, 1848. Box 4, Folder 4, Sappington-Marmaduke Papers, MHS.

21. "He told me that he had been informed that the democrats": Penn to Marmaduke, January 11, 1848. Ibid.

22. "You say, that Judge King will come to the convention with more counties than any other aspirant!": Lowry to Marmaduke, January 14, 1848. Ibid.

23. "Mr. Jackson has made great exertions": Tymony to Marmaduke, March 17, 1848. Folder 17, Marmaduke Papers C1021, SHSMO.

24. "Loud and discordant" with "All sorts of wire pulling": Democrat Convention, *Missouri Statesman*, March 31, 1848. Reel 7546, newspaper archives, SHSMO.

25. The names of six men were put forward and accepted: Attorney Austin A. King served two terms as Boone County's representative to the state legislature and in 1848 lived in Caldwell County from where he served as a circuit judge. *Dictionary of Missouri Biography*, 459. J. M. Hughes is probably James M. Hughes, a Clay County Democrat who was a candidate for state representative in 1838. *History of Clay and Platte Counties, Missouri*, 761. Priestly H. McBride, Monroe County Circuit Judge, 1831-33 and 1836-44, judge of Missouri Supreme Court 1845-49. Also served one year as Secretary of State under Governor John Miller. *History of Monroe and Shelby Counties, Missouri*, 194 and 208. James H. Relfe, of Howard County, served in U.S. House of Representatives, 1842-46. *History of Howard and Chariton Counties, Missouri*, 40. Captained by Bob Wright, the *Little Missouri* struck a snag and sank near Frankford about the year 1850. Listing of Steamboats Operating on the Missouri River; from Phillip E. Chappell, *History of Steamboating on the Missouri River*, kchoc.org/cultural/boatinfo/steamboating. The steamboat *Bertrand* sank in 1865, some 25 miles above Omaha. Found in 1968, the wreck's cargo is in a museum located at DeSoto National Wildlife Refuge, near Missouri City, Iowa.

26. With that in mind, someone from Meredith's camp: Frank Blair Jr., a devotee of Thomas Benton, studied law in the senator's office and in the 1850s served as a Missouri congressman. In May of 1861 he conspired with Union General Nathaniel Lyon to prevent Claiborne Jackson's takeover of the federal

armory at St. Louis. Blair later served as a general in the Union army, and was elected a senator from Missouri in 1870. *Dictionary of Missouri Biography*, 79-81.

27. "Jackson and his friends are dead against you": L. S. Eddins to Marmaduke, May 28, 1848. Box 4, Folder 5, Sappington-Marmaduke Papers, MHS.

28. The first draft of what came to be called the Jackson Resolutions was presented to members of the state Senate on January 1 by Carty Wells of Lincoln County: *Journal of the Senate of the State of Missouri, First Session of the Fifteenth General Assembly*, 64-65, 111, 178; *Journal of the House of Representatives of the State of Missouri, First Session of the Fifteenth General Assembly*, 82. Carty Wells was a circuit judge in northeast Missouri and as senator represented Missouri's Third Senatorial District. *History of Marion County, Missouri*, 275.

29. "I fully agree with you that it will be necessary for the Col.'s old friends to determine upon their course": Penn to Marmaduke, March 27, 1849. Box 4, Folder 6, Sappington-Marmaduke Papers, MHS. In 1850, the Jackson Resolutions were presented to the U.S. Senate by David Atchison, who asked they be recorded and printed. Benton immediately objected, saying they were not the "true sentiments" of Missouri's populace. Benjamin Merkel, "The Slavery Issue and the Political Decline of Thomas Hart Benton, 1846-1856," *MHR*, Vol. 38, No. 4 (July 1944), 396.

30. "It is a strange thing to see Col. Benton appealing from his own party": G. W. Hough to Marmaduke, May 22, 1849. Folder 18, Marmaduke Papers C1021, SHSMO.

31. "Your views in regard to the free soil question as it is called entirely accord with mine.": Penn to Marmaduke, March 27, 1849. Ibid.

32. Speaking in Clay County in July 1849, he compared the Jackson Resolutions to the Calhoun treaty: *History of Clay and Platte Counties, Missouri*, 149-151.

33. of the 33 men who took their seats in the chamber only 13 could be counted as Benton supporters: Merkel. "The Slavery Issue and the Political Decline of Thomas Hart Benton, 1846-1856," *MHR*, Vol. 38, no. 4 (July 1944), 398.

34. "My object is to induce you if possible to take the field as a candidate": Blair to Marmaduke, February 5, 1854. Box 5, Folder 4, Sappington-Marmaduke Papers, MHS.

35. "The antis are now begging for union and harmony": Lusk to Marmaduke, February 18, 1854. Box 5, Folder 4, Sappington-Marmaduke Papers, MHS. William Lusk founded the *Jefferson Inquirer* at Jefferson City in 1838 as a pro-Benton publication. Frank Blair was the newspaper's first editor. A daily in 1854, the *Inquirer* became a weekly thereafter and ceased publication in 1861. *About Jefferson Inquirer (Jefferson City, Mo.) 1838–1854*. chroniclingamerica.loc.gov/lccn/sn84020038. McCandless, *A History of Missouri*, Vol. 2, 183.

36. Among these were Meredith's son-in-law Levin Harwood, and Claiborne Jackson: L. B. Harwood was included in a list of voters in the Seventh District at an election for delegates to Congress on November 29, 1864. *Congressional Series of United States Public Documents, Vol. 869, Kansas Affairs*, 50. *Special Committee to investigate the troubles in the Territory of Kansas*, 34th Congress, 1st Session, U.S. House of Representatives, Report No. 200; 8, 21. Hurt, *Agriculture and Slavery in Missouri's Little Dixie*, 289. Meredith's neighbor William Napton Jr., noted in his history of Saline County, "A number of prominent men from [Saline] County were in Kansas from time to time, giving advise … provisions, such as bacon, flour, potatoes, etc., together with arms. … Among the leaders were … Claiborne F. Jackson and others." Napton, *Past and Present of Saline County, Missouri*, 137.

37. "greater harmony did not characterize the proceedings": *Liberty Weekly Tribune*, July 20, 1855. Reel 26661, Newspaper Archives, SHSMO.

38. working under the direction of Missouri Supreme Court Judge William B. Napton: *Liberty Weekly Tribune*, July 20, 1855. William B. Napton, ardent slave owner, served on Missouri's Supreme Court for 27 years. First appointed in 1838, political considerations removed him from the bench in 1852. Reappointed in 1856, he was again ousted in 1861. He served a third term from 1872 until retirement in 1880.

39. "every man in the house rising to his feet and greeting the result with a loud cheer": Ibid.

40. The doctor, widowed and advanced in age, divided his estate that year: Claims in Notes, money and medicines [for] Children of Daughter Eliza Jackson, December 30, 1843. Folder 11, Sappington Family papers C-2889, SHSMO. List of notes due Dr. John Sappington, September 1, 1853; Sale bill of the Negroes, September 10, 1853; Affidavit regarding division of notes owed Dr. Sappington, September 23, 1853. Folder 61, John Sappington Papers C-1027, SHSMO.

41. Throughout the 1850s, Jackson's thirst for political power never waned: For an in-depth look into Jackson's political activities during the 1850s, see Phillips, *Missouri's Confederate*, 219-230.

42. Jackson learned that he would soon travel to Jefferson City, having won the governor's office with 47 percent of the votes cast: Election returns, 1860, Folder 16424, Capitol Fire Documents, Reel CFD-187, MSA. *History of Greene County, Missouri*, 257, 269-70. Sample Orr, a Democrat, was a probate judge in Greene County when he decided to enter the governor's race as a pro-Union candidate supporting John Bell for the presidency. His simple, down-home style of canvassing appealed to many Missouri voters and attracted the attention of men such as Frank Blair Jr. and James S. Rollins.

43. "a Douglas man with Breckinridge tendencies": *History of Greene County, Missouri*, 269.

44. "from the stone steps of the old hotel in Marshall": History of Saline County, 407.

45. "So long as a State continues to maintain slavery within her limits, it is impossible to separate her fate from that of her sister States": Jonas Viles, Claiborne Fox Jackson; *The Messages and Proclamations of the Governors of the State of Missouri*, Vol. 3, 330-35, 338-39.

46. Among the 104 delegates was Meredith's son Vincent: Although the number of convention delegates is often stated as 99, the names of 104 men are listed in the published record of the convention. *Journal and Proceedings of the Missouri State Convention, Held at Jefferson City and St. Louis, March 1861*, 5-7, 47.

CHAPTER 19

DIVIDED LOYALTIES

Although Meredith remained loyal to the Union during the Civil War, five of his and Lavinia's six sons allied themselves with the South. Only Leslie, who was 13 years old when hostilities broke out in 1861, was not active in supporting the Confederacy. The activities and events in which John, Vincent, Darwin, Meredith Miles Jr., and Henry were involved included combat on land and at sea, arms and provisions purchasing, negotiating with foreign powers, smuggling, local garrison duty that sometimes resulted in skirmishes with rebel guerrillas, and imprisonment. As well, Meredith's son-in-law, Jane's husband Levin Harwood, was implicated in a Confederate sabotage ring that destroyed more than 60 steamboats on the Mississippi River.

Scattered as the sons were from Missouri to Europe, with no means of communication most of the time, there was little hope that Meredith and Lavinia would know their sons' whereabouts or their well-being. Nothing exists to tell us of the worry and stress endured by the family at home in Saline County during the four years of war. In addition to daily anxiety about his sons' welfare, Meredith faced economic stress caused by the loss of income when farm products could not reach distant markets. And looming over his daily activities was the potential for violence that existed in the rural, less protected areas of Saline County. As a wealthy farmer, slaveholder, Unionist, and the father of sons identified with the Confederacy, he could easily be the target of lawless guerrillas or Union fanatics. Vigilance was paramount in order to prevent the destruction of property or the loss of life. The politically driven confliction that had been active in Meredith's life for the past 15 years now acquired a new dimension.

At Camp Floyd in Wyoming Territory on January 4, 1860, Lieutenant John Marmaduke wrote a letter to his sister Bena, knowing that outgoing mail was scheduled to leave the post the next day for the first time in three weeks. "The Christmas holydays [sic] are over," he wrote, "and things went off swimmingly I tell you, yet after all, Bena, let me spend my Christmas week at home with Father, Ma and my sisters & brothers. I have been away from home too long … Tis hard for me to say when again I will spend a Christmas at home or indeed any day. I want to visit home but I don't think I can — unless I resign which I don't wish to do at present."[1]

John's desire to remain in the U.S. Army would be tested and found wanting 15 months later. In April 1861, when news of the fall of Fort Sumter reached him in the West, accompanied by erroneous news that Missouri had seceded, John returned to Saline County and sought his father's advice about switching his allegiance to the

Confederacy. A member of the Marmaduke family later recalled that Meredith told his son, "There can be but one result. You will sacrifice your profession. Secession will fail. Slavery will be abolished. But you must decide for yourself, following your own convictions."[2] Ignoring his father's warning, within days John resigned his Army commission and offered his services to his uncle, Claiborne Jackson. In early May, he obtained a captain's rank in the newly formed Missouri State Guard and was charged with recruiting Saline County men for service as infantry militia.

Nathaniel Lyon's bold move against Camp Jackson in St. Louis and the subsequent violence in which 28 people were killed occurred on May 10. As if in response, on May 13 the Saline Jackson Guards organized at Marshall as a company of 110 county residents with John Marmaduke as their commander. Two days later, several hundred supporters of the Confederacy gathered at the Saline County seat to cheer on Captain Marmaduke and the new guard company as they paraded around the courthouse and received their company flag. Designed and sewn by ladies of the community, it contained their names embroidered in the corners of the blue and white banner. In a bow to his father, John invited him to address the men of the company before they departed Marshall. Meredith's remarks to the new soldiers, many of whom he knew or knew their families, reiterated what he had told his son several weeks earlier, that "secession would not succeed; that they had enlisted in a cause that was bound to fail. The speech was not well received."[3] The next morning the Saline Jackson Guards left Marshall in wagons, traveling first to Sedalia and from there to Jefferson City by train to join the muster of state militia ordered by Governor Jackson three weeks earlier.

Brothers in Arms
Leaving St. Louis on June 12, with Nathaniel Lyon's declaration of war ringing in his ears, Governor Jackson knew he could not prevent occupation of the state capital by federal troops. Although "about a thousand" volunteer State Guardsmen were at Jefferson City, they were deficient in both training and numbers to challenge the nearly 10,000 soldiers Lyon had in St. Louis.[4] Adding to Meredith's worries at this time was knowledge that among the guardsmen at Jefferson City were two of his sons — John, and 21-year-old Darwin who had joined his brother's company as a private when the unit organized in Marshall. On June 13, as part of Lyon's force neared the capital, Jackson and other state officials went to Boonville, believing it to be more defensible than Jefferson City. Jackson hoped support would come to his aid from the slaveholding Booneslick counties in the form of troops and supplies. In addition, the state armory had been relocated to Boonville, its stores augmented by munitions stolen earlier from the federal arsenal in Baton Rouge.[5] John Marmaduke with the Saline Jackson Guards and other guard companies followed Governor Jackson up the river. Sterling Price, however, was not with the guardsmen; he became ill and went to his home in Keytesville to recuperate.

Because of Price's absence, the senior military officer at Boonville was General John Bullock Clark of Fayette, a state military district commander who had earlier been ordered to proceed to Boonville with troops from his district.[6] A decades-long dislike existed between General Clark and Governor Jackson. They had clashed 21 years earlier when Clark's name appeared as a Whig candidate for governor on a fake Democrat Party ballot printed by Whig supporters during the run-up to the 1840 election. The perpetrators hoped to fool Democrats into voting for Clark. His participation in the scheme surfaced in a letter he claimed was stolen from him. Using the letter, Jackson publicly ridiculed Clark, and as a result Clark challenged Jackson — whom he characterized as a slanderer, scoundrel, and coward — to a duel. The prospect of the winner being prosecuted for the illegal act (and the loser being killed) caused both men to eventually reconsider; however, their relationship in 1861 was still poisoned by the affair. In a letter written afterward, George Penn told Meredith that in terms of public sentiment, Jackson had weathered the affair better than Clark.[7] Now facing an attack on the State Guard and himself, with General Price at home, abed and unable to lead the defense at Boonville, Jackson seemed unwilling to acknowledge General Clark's military experience and give him overall control of the guardsmen. Clark had commanded the Missouri State Militia during the Mormon War of 1838. As governor, Jackson assumed command of the State Guard and turned to now-Colonel John Marmaduke for help. Whether General Clark assented in the decision to appoint John as field commander is not recorded. Perhaps he deferred to Marmaduke's training at West Point and seven years' experience in the field.

With untrained and undisciplined troops who had never faced enemy fire, John Marmaduke realized he could not win a fight against Lyon's larger, more experienced force. (Lyon advanced on Boonville with 1,500 infantrymen and several artillery batteries; Marmaduke had less than half as many men and only one cannon, which was never fired.) Meeting with Jackson on June 16, Marmaduke recommended relocating the guardsmen and the state officials south of the Osage River, near Warsaw, where they could reorganize and train before having to stand in battle. At this, there was "considerable controversy among the officers and men whether ... a stand or retreat should be made," and a swell of bravado among the ranks caused many to declare that they "had come to fight, and they intended to do so."[8] Their enthusiasm swayed Jackson, who disregarded Marmaduke's advice and ordered him to confront the Union infantry east of the town. John did not record his feelings about the impending battle, but certainly in mind was the fact that his mother, father, and several younger siblings lived only 16 miles (as the crow flies) from Boonville. Might General Lyon impose restrictions on them as a consequence of John's role in opposing him?

On the morning of June 17, Lyon's force reached the river bottom eight miles below Boonville and moved onto the bluff east of the town. Marmaduke's pickets were driven in and overwhelming rifle and artillery fire pushed the guardsmen back. Three miles from town, they halted and "opened a galling fire" on Lyon's troops, but were again dislodged.[9] On seeing this, Governor Jackson realized the battle was lost and called for a retreat. Marmaduke tried to extract his troops in an orderly fashion, only to watch helplessly as the frightened men panicked and ran.[10] Less than a half hour had passed from the time Lyon's troops first fired on the guardsmen until the battle ended. Governor Jackson and his fugitive government escaped capture, never to return to Jefferson City. The State Guard troops headed for southwest Missouri to seek protection under a Confederate force operating in northwest Arkansas. Members of the Saline Jackson Guards subsequently fought in the battles of Carthage, Wilson's Creek, Dry Wood Creek (near Fort Scott, Kansas, sometimes called the Battle of

Mules), and at Lexington in September 1861. What remained of the company after Lexington retreated to Arkansas with Price.

Claiborne Jackson was not the only person discouraged by the outcome of the Boonville fight. John Marmaduke was less than enthused with the actions of his uncle. Jackson's submission to pressure from underlings in the dangerous situation brought into question his ability to make difficult, rational decisions when under stress. Believing that "politicians were controlling military affairs," John Marmaduke resigned his state commission and traveled to Richmond, Virginia, where he was commissioned a first lieutenant in the Confederate States Army and ordered to Arkansas for duty.[11] John may have been warned by his father about the flaw *he* perceived in Jackson's character, and after Boonville distrusted his uncle's ability to lead the state in the difficult struggle ahead. Rising to the rank of major general in the Confederate States Army, John Marmaduke distinguished himself as a leader of infantry and cavalry, fighting in 13 major battles in the Trans-Mississippi region, including the Battle of Shiloh in Tennessee where he was wounded and disabled for a month. Captured at the Battle of Mine Creek in eastern Kansas on October 25, 1864, he was imprisoned at Johnson's Island in Ohio, on Lake Erie, where a medical officer recorded him as being "in poor physical state."[12]

After the fight at Boonville, Darwin remained with the Saline Jackson Guards through the Battle of Lexington in September 1861; his six-month term of enlistment expired in early December.[13] On November 15, 1862, he enrolled as a private in Company H of the 71st Regiment, Enrolled Missouri Militia. The Enrolled Militia was a statewide Unionist defensive force, organized at the county level, whose members were governed by the U.S. Articles of War and Army Regulations. They were tasked with ending "robbery, plunder, and guerrilla warfare," protecting the state's law-abiding citizens; and securing state and country infrastructure (bridges, public buildings, roads) against destruction. At times, the Enrolled Militia engaged militarily with regular Confederate army troops. How Darwin managed to join the militia is a mystery, as the order establishing the force forbade membership by persons who had sympathized with the rebellion. For six months (November 1862 to his discharge in April 1863) Darwin served 155 days in Company H, under the command of Captain George Bingham. The company was on duty in Ray County and involved in "affairs in Jackson and Lafayette counties" in late November 1862. In April 1864, when about to be called on to serve again, Darwin was "Discharged by payment of Commutation tax."[14]

Despite his service in the Enrolled Militia, the federal authorities in St. Louis did not trust Darwin. In October 1864, he was spotted in that city with one of his brothers, their presence noted by J. H. Kemble, an informant who reported to the provost marshal that "one of the Marmadukes left the city yesterday for Quincy, Ill, the other one is still here. I learn from Co. Willson of Saline County, Mo., that they have both taken the oath & probably given Bond but still he regards them as being as strong Rebbles [sic] as their Brother the Rebble general." Informants were often used by Union authorities in St. Louis to keep track of suspicious persons in the city. In the same letter to Captain Tallon, Kemble reported the presence of another Saline County resident named Hunt, a former member of the Confederate army, who in company with a stranger "went to several sallons [sic] they walked from Market Street to the

River & back to 4th Street & got in to a carriage and drove up Market so fast that I could not keep up with them on foot."15

Two days after Fort Sumter was fired upon in April 1861, Vincent Marmaduke turned 40 years old. He was married, engaged in farming, and mining coal that he sent to St. Louis from the landing at Arrow Rock. His support of the Confederacy took a different form than that followed by his brothers who experienced combat. That said, Vincent's welfare during the war proved to be no less a worry for Meredith. Only months earlier he had been elected to serve in the Missouri State Convention, the body that ultimately would address the state's legislative needs for the first two years of the war.16 Even if he held thoughts about joining Sterling Price's army in south Missouri, Meredith would have advised against it, knowing that his son's presence at the 1861 State Convention would represent and advocate for the interests of the Booneslick region's slaveholders. Vincent was present at the convention's first meeting in St. Louis (transferred from Jefferson City) and would participate in three of the assembly's five meetings during its existence. Supporting his constituency, he voted against (and helped delay for three years) legislation that would have established a scheme for the gradual emancipation of slaves, and against a bill to disenfranchise persons who were engaged in rebellion against the United States. (The latter provision was enacted after considerable debate.)17

Vincent's presence at the June 1863 final meeting of the State Convention became a contentious issue. The previous October, Brigadier General Benjamin Loan, commander of the Missouri State Militia's central district headquartered at Jefferson City, had declared Vincent "a disloyal member of the State Convention." He ordered him to leave Missouri within 10 days and not return during the war. Communicating this to Major General Samuel Curtis, commander of the Department of Missouri, Loan also complained about Missouri's governor, Hamilton Gamble, releasing Sample Orr, "another disloyal member" of the Convention, from confinement "for uttering disloyal sentiments" during a speech at Jefferson City. In Loan's mind, Vincent and Sample Orr were "allowed to preach treason in the capital of the state," and it would require "active, zealous and energetic action" to preserve law and order.18 Somehow, Vincent avoided being sent out of Missouri at the time; confined to St. Louis, he was granted an extended parole.

When the convention opened in July 1863, Vincent was in St. Louis under the watchful eye of the provost marshal's office, forbidden to be anywhere in Missouri beyond the city limits. He needed a travel extension of his parole in order to attend the assembly in Jefferson City. Colonel James Broadhead, provost marshal general of the Department of Missouri, referred the matter to the convention for its approval, noting that Vincent was "under military arrest for disloyalty." Members of a committee appointed to determine Vincent's fate found no reason to disqualify him and in a resolution presented to the membership favored allowing him to travel to Jefferson City. Sensing an opportunity to rid the convention of a proslavery delegate, Unionist members voiced opposition. In an impassioned speech during the debate that followed, St. Louis attorney Charles D. Drake, newly elected to the convention, spoke in opposition to the resolution, telling his fellow members that "this body, representing as it does the entire people [of Missouri] should not, under any circumstances, call for the release of a prisoner of war ... that he may come here to attend this Convention." The resolution failed to gain approval of the convention's membership, setting the stage for Vincent's banishment from the state. He may have had time to tell his sister, Jane Harwood, then living in St. Louis, before he left the city under guard. In a memoir, Charles Drake recalled that the provost marshal sent Vincent "straightway to 'Dixie,' where I suppose he staid till the end of the war."[19] Drake's recollection was partially correct. In testimony before the U.S. House of Representatives in 1867, James O. Broadhead stated that at St. Louis on June 25, 1863, Vincent Marmaduke refused to take an oath of allegiance and was "under these circumstances, sent south, and was put through the lines at Vicksburg." [20]

From Vicksburg, Vincent went to Virginia and volunteered his services to Confederate President Jefferson Davis. Soon thereafter, he was in Europe assisting in the procurement of armaments and other material for Confederate forces.[21] His movements overseas are unclear, but in the summer of 1864 he returned to the United States, where he enlisted in the Confederate Secret Service. On November 6, 1864, Vincent was arrested by federal authorities in Chicago and jailed, accused of being a "rebel officer" affiliated with The Sons of Liberty, a secret organization planning an insurrection aimed at Illinois and Indiana. Arraigned before a military commission at Cincinnati in January 1865, he (with others) was tried for "Conspiring to release rebel prisoners of war confined ... at Camp Douglas" near Chicago, and for "Conspiring ... to lay waste and destroy the city of Chicago." In an interesting twist of fate, Lieutenant Colonel James O. Broadhead served at the trial as Vincent's legal counsel and also as a witness for him. Broadhead had been U.S. provost marshal for Missouri when Vincent was banished from the state in 1863. A Whig who later became a Democrat, Broadhead — an attorney from Pike County and a former state representative and senator — was well known to Meredith with whom he had served at the 1845 Missouri Constitutional Convention. His willingness to represent Vincent at the trial in Cincinnati is testimony to the high regard Meredith was accorded by former political associates. As a result of Broadhead's endeavors in Cincinnati, Vincent was found not guilty of all charges and soon thereafter returned to Missouri.[22]

"Ma what do you think of my going through Tennessee on my way home in June?"[23] Writing Lavinia from the U.S. Naval Academy in Annapolis, Maryland, in January 1860, Henry Marmaduke was unaware that after next summer's visit he would not see his mother for six years and never again see his father. He had entered the academy in September 1858, a month after his 16th birthday, and would study there until March 3, 1861, at which time he resigned and joined the Confederate States Navy. What prompted Henry to forego service in the United States Navy and give his allegiance to the Confederacy is unknown, but his decision came on the heels of Abraham Lincoln's election. He left the naval academy a month before his older brother, John, resigned his U.S. Army commission with the same purpose in mind.

During the next four years Henry would rise in rank from Midshipman to 1st Lieutenant, and serve as a gunner on at least six fighting vessels engaged in combat in locales ranging from the Mississippi River to the Atlantic coastal states. The most famous ship on which he served was the ironclad CSS *Virginia* (*Merrimac*) at the Battle of Hampton Roads, off the coast of Virginia, March 8–9, 1862. Commanding a crew of

14 on the *Virginia's* gun No. 2, he was wounded while fighting the U.S. Navy's frigate *Congress*, but continued to man his post throughout the two-day battle, including the duel between the *Virginia* and the federal ironclad USS *Monitor*. During the fight with the *Congress*, the muzzle of the gun manned by Marmaduke (and others) was struck by an enemy shell, "but they continued to fire as if it was uninjured. ... Midshipman Marmaduke, though receiving several painful wounds early in the action, manfully fought his gun until the close. He is now at the hospital."[24]

Three weeks after the battle, Henry was still recovering from his wounds at the naval hospital in Norfolk, Virginia, on March 27. Lavinia wrote to him in April and in hopes of delivery sent the letter to Thomas L. Price, a Missouri congressman in Washington. Because he could not forward Lavinia's letter directly to Henry, Price sent it to Union authorities at Fort Monroe, a Union stronghold at the southern tip of the Virginia peninsula that served as a mail transfer point during the war.[25] Although the Confederacy had established a postal department before war broke out, the United States, in August 1861, banned the exchange of mail between North and South by citizens except for letters from prisoners of war. These passed through Fort Monroe where they were opened, censored for objectionable content, and if deemed permissible resealed and sent on. Under such restrictions, the smuggling of mail between soldiers and citizens, North and South, became commonplace. It is not known if Henry received his mother's letter. On May 13, 1862, his wounds sufficiently healed, Henry was assigned to duty aboard the CSS *Chattahoochee*. He remained with the ship a year, leaving it on May 7, 1863.[26] Twenty days after his departure, a troublesome boiler on the *Chattahoochee* exploded, killing 18 of the vessel's crew.

In the summer of 1863, Henry traveled to Europe where representatives of the Confederacy were attempting to obtain war ships for the Confederate navy. He probably left Richmond the last day of August aboard the CSS *Florida* with Captain Samuel Barron who was going to Europe as flag officer in charge of all Confederate Navy vessels there.[27] (Unknown is whether or not Henry's posting was initiated by Vincent, who also went to Europe that summer, perhaps also aboard the *Florida*.) Professing neutrality, England, Ireland, and France prohibited the sale of armed vessels to both the United States and the Confederacy. To overcome this, Confederate agents covered their activities with a shroud of mercantilism, purportedly buying ships for commercial purposes. Once at sea, their civilian crews were to be replaced with Confederate naval officers and crew and armed for combat. Under construction (for the Confederacy) in France at the time were four wooden ships of the corvette class and two ironclad rams. The former were designated as armed merchants ships destined for service in the China Sea, and the ironclads were supposedly being built for Egyptian authorities. At the same time, Confederate warships were regularly sailing into French ports in need of provisioning and repair. When the *Florida* arrived at Brest, France, on August 23, Henry left the ship and went to Paris where he obtained housing with other Confederate naval officers, sharing a room with a former CSS *Virginia* shipmate, Hardin B. Littlepage.[28] While Henry's role in France is unclear, his experience on the *Virginia* and other warships was undoubtedly acknowledged by Flag Officer Barron, who relied on the cadre of naval officers stationed in France to carry out his mission.

Misfortune overtook the Confederate States' secret navy when a patriotic employee of a firm involved in the plot to build the ironclad rams revealed their true destination to the United States minister to France. The embarrassed French government seized all ships under construction for the Confederacy and sold them instead to foreign interests, thus assuring France's neutrality. During the summer of 1864, Confederate Secretary of Navy Stephen R. Mallory at Richmond, being "much in need of officers here," directed Captain Barron to send home all officers who were not required in Europe.[29] Henry Marmaduke left Paris on August 6, 1864, and was at Savannah, Georgia, on September 19 in temporary command of "Confederate steamer *Samson* ... and hold her in readiness for service."[30] Through the remainder of the war, he served on warships along the East Coast, and at Richmond in early April 1865 commanded a naval battery on the James River in a losing battle to prevent the fall of the Confederate capital. Several days later he commanded artillery at Sayler's Creek, Virginia, where he was again wounded. Captured there, he was imprisoned in Washington, then at Johnson's Island in Sandusky Bay on Lake Erie. (He was at Johnson's Island at the same time as his brother, Vincent. Whether the two met there is unknown, but it's difficult to believe that they didn't.) Released from custody on June 20, 1865, Henry H. Marmaduke went on to have a distinguished career with the United States government as a naval authority assigned to consular bureaus in South America.[31]

While Meredith worried about the welfare of his sons involved in combat and clandestine overseas activities, at home Meredith Marmaduke Jr. added to his distress. In the spring of 1862, Meredith Jr. and a friend, Thomas R. E. Harvey (son of the elder Meredith's friend Thomas H. Harvey, former Indian Affairs superintendent), were arrested in Saline County by provost marshal agents and jailed at Boonville. After taking the Missouri loyalty oath and posting a $2,000 bond (each), the two men were released. Soon thereafter they sought to have the bond money refunded and asked Weston F. Birch, a Glasgow businessman and banker, for his help. Birch appealed to career army officer General James Totten, at the time assigned to the Enrolled Missouri Militia. Birch told General Totten that Meredith Jr. and Thomas Harvey were "both highly respectable gentlemen. ... what we call Southern Men, but have never engaged in any way with the army or war." Birch asked Totten to remit the bond "as I know them to be well entitled to your kind consideration."[32] Totten forwarded the inquiry to the provost marshal general's office in St. Louis, who then queried the office in Boonville. From there, Lieutenant Charles Korh replied: "Thomas Harvey ... appeared before Lt. Col. Epstein charged with encouraging the Rebellion and giving aid and comfort to the enemy. He acknowledged the facts and still claimed to be a strong supporter with the southern cause. ... M. M. Marmaduke [Jr.] was charged with the same treasonable acts. ... Both men are as strong and active secessionists as can be found in Saline County. Lieut. Colonel Epstein thought it not more than right to put these men under $2000 dollars Bonds ... . He gave them at the same time a week for considering the matter and let them go on parole, but have not heard from them till your letter was received this morning." Little is known about the subversive acts the two men were accused of; however, horses found in their possession were identified as having been used by the U.S. Army during Sterling Price's attack on federal troops at Lexington the previous September. Although there is some question about Meredith Jr.'s activities, he is recorded as having gone to Colorado in 1863 (perhaps in response to pressure from local provost marshal authorities) where he reportedly remained until 1865.[33]

Why Five Sons for the Confederacy?

Meredith's firm belief in the legitimacy of the Union, as opposed to severing the nation over the issue of slavery, was rooted in both emotional and practical considerations. Growing to manhood in Virginia in the shadows of men who went to war with England to create the United States, and fighting English troops in 1812 to preserve the Union, Meredith's loyalty to the concept of an undivided nation was ingrained from childhood. As a slave owner, he continued to support the Union as the country engaged in civil war because he believed the major issue — the right to consider a class of people as property — could be resolved for his benefit by peaceful means. Why, then, did his sons cast their futures with the South? The answer to that question is, of course, difficult to determine with any accuracy, but several likely contributing factors come to mind. First, growing up on a farm where slaves were present in most aspects of family life, the sons understood the economic value they represented and could see their own futures threatened if slavery were abolished. Secondly, the sons were influenced by the racist attitudes regarding slavery expressed by friends and neighbors — many of whom were also slave owners — and other family members, in the latter case more specifically by the actions of Claiborne Fox Jackson, their uncle. And finally, they were influenced by the expressions of their father who, beyond secession, had no quarrel with the South.

A Saboteur in the Family

The political sympathies of Meredith's son-in-law Levin Harwood (known to have helped stir up trouble in Kansas) lay with the Confederacy, perhaps to the point of serving in the shadowy Confederate Secret Service, or at least supporting it financially. On May 9, 1865, he was arrested in St. Louis by Union authorities on suspicion of furnishing money to support the activities of Judge Joseph W. Tucker, a leading figure in the Confederate Secret Service, who organized a group of saboteurs on the Mississippi River known as "boat burners." Tucker's guerrilla force was responsible for the sabotage and sinking of more than 60 steamboats, many carrying military personnel and cargo as well as civilian freight and passengers, causing the death of hundreds of people. Harwood's arrest occurred as federal authorities swept the streets of St. Louis looking for Rebel conspirators, in response to suspicion that "boat burners" were involved in the explosion and sinking of the Union steamboat *Sultana* near Memphis 10 days earlier. More than 2,000 people died in that tragedy, most of them Union prisoners of war going home from Southern prison camps as they emptied at the end of the Civil War.

Charged with "conspiracy and violation of the laws of war," Harwood languished in the Gratiot Street Military Prison in St. Louis for nine months awaiting a decision on whether to prosecute him. Examined by Lieutenant Colonel E.E. Bryant, an investigator for the military judge advocate's office, Harwood admitted to "paying out moneys to boat burners," but claimed that he did it innocently. Colonel Bryant's report, submitted February 1, 1866, concluded that Harwood could not be convicted, despite his admission, because "The witness [Edward Frazer] on whose disclosures [Harwood] was implicated ... I am satisfied ... will favor the prisoner and so materially qualify his statements before [the military court] ... as to deprive the prosecutor of the resemblance of a case. ... I place so little reliance in the witness ... that I deem it doubtful whether the guilt of any one could be established on the basis of his testimony." Levin Harwood died in Kansas City, Missouri, two years after he was released from federal custody. He is buried there next to his wife, Jane, who died 21 years later.[34]

Booneslick's Economy Goes "South"

The Civil War devastated the Booneslick region's agricultural-based economy. Meredith's sale of farm commodities to St. Louis brokers decreased significantly in the summer of 1861 as Union authorities sought to deny the import of corn, wheat, and hemp into Southern states. The grains that were the staple food for slaves who tilled and harvested the cotton fields of the South, or that had passed downriver to New Orleans for shipment elsewhere, no longer could reach their ultimate destination. (The shortage of grain in the South had a ripple effect that ultimately resulted in thousands of starving women and children taking to the streets of Richmond, Virginia, in 1864, to strip merchants of bread and other meager staples.) Starting in April 1861, U.S. naval vessels began blockading ports from Virginia to Louisiana in an effort to halt the shipment of cotton, the South's most important commodity, overseas. At the same time, the cotton market was glutted with overproduction from recent years. England's cloth factories, the primary buyers of American cotton, had ample stocks on hand. (In coming years, as those stocks dwindled, England's cotton buyers encouraged its cultivation in other countries.) With America's cotton industry reeling, the hemp market — for cordage and bagging used in the cotton industry — was driven to its knees. Outside the South, the only other significant market for hemp was on the East Coast, where buyers wanted a high-quality product that cost more to produce and ship for the fabrication of naval cordage.

As a commercial planter, Meredith quickly felt the loss of these markets. In the decade preceding the Civil War, he had expanded hemp production by nearly 1,800 percent — from 20 tons grown in 1850 to 354 tons harvested in 1860. His corn production tripled during this same period to 7,500 bushels in 1860 — most of it was sold at St. Louis for resale as food for slaves working in the cotton fields of the South. Since hemp and corn formed the bulk of Meredith's saleable commodities at the start of the war, his income in 1861 and subsequent years suffered significantly. How much it decreased isn't known, but he acknowledged the loss in 1863, saying that it was "so large that I know not what calculation to make ..."[35]

The reduction of income from the sale of farm commodities created economic hardships for most Booneslick farmers. Some of them borrowed money to continue operating, only to lose their land when banks foreclosed on delinquent mortgages. Too, a number of the region's wealthier planters mortgaged their farms and later became defendants in lawsuits to recover unpaid loans as the result of their participation in a financial conspiracy, contrived by Claiborne Jackson, to get money out of Missouri's banks in order to finance Confederate military activities. Meredith's son Vincent and his brother-in-law William B. Sappington (president of the Bank of Missouri branch at

Arrow Rock) were players in the illegal scheme. During the first year of the war, banks in Saline, Cooper, and Pettis Counties issued $330,000 in promissory notes (backed by mortgages on land) for money that went to Confederate forces.[36] Financial records from this time in Meredith's life are scarce, but it is apparent from his estate papers that he had reserve capital that allowed him to continue limited farming without becoming indebted to the region's bankers.

"Squally Times"

Economic hardship was not the only distress burdening the citizens of Saline County during the war. Personal safety and the protection of property were daily concerns. Francis F. Audsley, a farmer who lived a few miles east of Miami, worried about the welfare of his wife and their property while he was serving as a member of Company A of the 44th Missouri Volunteers, a Union Army unit stationed upriver at Lexington. "I hear that the bushwhackers have been down among you again, and I am anxious to hear what mischief they did," he asked his wife, who remained on the family farm, in a letter written in October 1862. "There have been several skirmishes with them since they were down, but we cannot get the straight of it. ..." The situation did not improve during the next 10 months. Writing to his wife again in August 1863, he told her he was sorry that his company was not closer to Miami, for then "I could get to come down at any time, almost, if it would be safe for me to stop at Miami ... [but] some of the wretches might be lurking there, and I would hardly like for them to get hold of me. ..."[37]

Another Saline County farmer harassed by bushwhackers sent his wife east and wanted to follow her, but he could not because he had cows to dispose of and a tobacco crop that needed harvesting. Writing to her in Ohio, he said that "times have been so squally for the last week" that he was thinking about leaving, anyway.[38] Bushwhackers preyed not just on Unionists; they also "daily rode up to the houses of men of Southern inclination, demanding food for themselves and provender for their horses," taking what they wanted without compensation.[39]

As a farmer and slaveholder, Meredith was a potential target for roaming bushwhackers (and even Union or Confederate troops) seeking food, forage for their horses, horses for transportation, and livestock to be slaughtered and eaten. He was also at risk from his sons' military alliance with the South, his familial relationship with Missouri's renegade governor, Claiborne Jackson, and from his public assertion that secession was wrong. He lived with one foot in the Confederacy, the other in the Union. While this duality undoubtedly was uncomfortable, it may have resulted in his family and property not being molested by bushwhackers or troops from either side during the war. (Remarkably, the Marmaduke family's frame home stood until well into the 20th century.) Confederate sympathizers would not have wanted the wrath of General John Marmaduke to fall on them, and Union authorities, although suspicious of the family in Missouri, were respectful of Meredith's well-known decision to stand with the Union.

The fate of another politically prominent Saline County slaveholding resident, whose sons were also fighting for the Confederacy, lends credence to Meredith's duality as being at least partially responsible for his freedom from hostile acts. William Barclay

To Make a Fortune in Missouri

Napton, a twice-appointed Missouri Supreme Court judge, in office until December 1861 when he refused the loyalty oath, did not fare as well as Meredith. The two men, who lived in the same area southwest of Arrow Rock, knew each other well and were often allied in local and state affairs and enjoyed political brotherhood as members of the Democrat Party's "Central Clique." Writing in 1880 about his plantation named Elkhill, Napton said he viewed his Saline County home as a place endeared by his old associations, one of whom he noted was "Col. Marmaduke," describing him as "A man of earnest and purposeful life, he was one to be trusted and his integrity was never impeached nor his character blemished."[40]

Napton was known by federal authorities to be a Confederate sympathizer whose support of Governor Claiborne Jackson dated back to the 1840s, when Napton had authored the controversial legislation known as the Jackson Resolutions, attacking Senator Thomas Benton and his opposition to the expansion of slavery. During the early years of the Civil War, Napton was frequently harassed at Elkhill by federal authorities. Family stories relate that during one incident in the summer of 1862, Union militia troops put a noose around the judge's neck and pulled him from his house. Only the intervention of an officer who was a friend saved him from hanging. Finding no weapons, the soldiers took bedclothes and a mule for their own use. The intimidation continued through subsequent months, and in the late winter of 1862, while Union troops were searching Napton's house for contraband, his pregnant wife became ill and fell. Several weeks later, she died after giving birth to a dead child, the family blaming the incident at the house for her demise. In early 1863, federal authorities forced Napton to leave Elkhill and relocate to St. Louis, where presumably they could keep better watch over him. Entries in his journals from that period reveal that throughout 1863 he and members of his family who remained on the farm in Saline County were repeatedly harassed by Union authorities. For a brief period, Napton was jailed in St. Louis. Later that year, the army seized his slaves at Elkhill and put them to work building fortifications along the Missouri River.[41]

Although Meredith escaped open conflict on his home farm, he was seldom far from the hostilities occurring in Saline County. During the years 1862–1864, the county recorded 22 skirmishes and battles, five of them at or near Arrow Rock. During one of these, Meredith's family members found themselves on the edge of hostile action the afternoon of October 12, 1863, when Confederate Colonel Jo Shelby, on a recruitment and provisioning raid across the state, led a large force of cavalry and artillery troops from Boonville, passing along a road near Meredith's home on his way to Marshall. The presence of Shelby's troops — estimated to number 1,500 to 2,000 men — in close proximity to Meredith's farm, with the accompanying noise and dust generated by the passage of a like number of horses and the wheeled artillery, would not have gone unnoticed by the family. At 6 o'clock that evening, Union troops under the command of U.S. Army Brigadier General Egbert B. Brown caught up with elements of Shelby's force on Salt Fork Creek about two miles west of Meredith's home. Brown's report to Major General John Schofield in St. Louis said that Shelby was "forced to make a stand at Merrill's Crossing of the Salt Fork River, a point 8 miles southwest of Arrow Rock ... and commenced a skirmishing fight on the evening of the 12th. ..." Fighting a rear-guard action "in the midst of a cold, driving rain," Shelby went on toward Marshall where he hoped to capture the town and recruit more volunteers to his force.[42] The next day, after failing to dislodge the Union force protecting the town, Shelby divided his troops into two commands. He led one around Marshall and turned west, hoping to reach Lafayette County. The other command traveled east on the Marshall-Arrow Rock road (today's state Route 41), passing a few miles north of Meredith's home.

As 1863 drew to a close, Meredith struggled to maintain a semblance of normalcy at his farm in Saline County. With war separating him and Lavinia from their sons who were at risk for injury or death, a shroud of worry about their welfare hung over the family. The conflict also brought uncertainty to their daily life. Despite efforts by Union authorities in the county to establish stability, an atmosphere of disunity and violence prevailed, and Meredith did not know if his family and property were safe from harassment and plunder. Roaming bushwhackers, invading Confederate troops, or overzealous Union sympathizers who might view his sons' loyalty to the South as an excuse to foment trouble, might ride into the yard at any moment. In a letter addressed to Lavinia's cousin John B. Breathitt of Marshall, written in the summer of 1863, Meredith "represents life and property as very insecure in Saline."[43]

As the war moved toward its fourth year in 1864, Meredith faced the prospect of another season of lost income caused by the collapse of markets for hemp and corn, the farm's primary cash-generating products. An even greater concern was the potential loss of a major asset — the slaves whose cheap labor had contributed so greatly to the family's prosperity for the past 40 years. President Lincoln's Emancipation Proclamation, issued on January 1, 1863, freeing slaves in states that seceded from the Union, had set the stage for the end of slavery throughout the nation. In response, Missouri's Constitutional Convention (the state's legislative body during the Civil War) passed an ordinance that summer calling for the gradual emancipation of the state's slaves, to be completed by 1870. Meredith knew his slaves would eventually be freed. At question was whether or not the state would compensate him for the loss of his "property," as required by the state's constitution. But as a new year began, an even greater calamity to his family awaited. Looming over all of Meredith's worries in January 1864 was an insidious specter over which he had no control — death's shadow was creeping slowly forward.

Notes

1. "The Christmas holydays are over": John S. Marmaduke to sister Bena, January 4, 1860. Box 5, Folder 7, Sappington-Marmaduke Papers, MHS. Some sources claim that Lieutenant Marmaduke went to New Mexico with the United States Mounted Rifles Regiment when that unit returned to its assignment in the Southwest after the conclusion of the Mormon War in July 1858. The U.S. Army history of the Third Regiment of Cavalry, as the Riflemen became, records the unit, under Colonel William Loring, arriving at Fort Union in New Mexico on September 14, 1858, "direct from Salt Lake." Further, the regimental history names 12 officers of Loring's New Mexico command (including Loring) who resigned their commissions in 1861 to join the Confederacy. Marmaduke is not so named. His letter to Bena, written while he was in Wyoming Territory in 1860, shows that he remained on assignment with Col. Albert S. Johnston instead of returning to New Mexico with the Mounted Rifles. It is believed that he was at Fort Laramie when the war began. Charles Morton, Third Regiment of Cavalry, *The Army of the US Historical Sketches of Staff and Line with Portraits of Generals-in-Chief*, 200-201.

2. "There can be but one result": Walter B. Stevens. *Centennial History of Missouri: One Hundred Years in the Union 1820-1921*, Vol. 1., 742. Stevens did not identify the family member who related the conversation.

To Make a Fortune in Missouri

The date of John's resignation from the U.S. Army is recorded as April 1861 in *Register of Graduates and Former Cadets of the United States Military Academy, 1802-1963*, 246.

3. "secession would not succeed": *History of Saline County*, 275-76. For more on the attitude of Missourians after the Camp Jackson tragedy see Phillips, *Missouri's Confederate*, 252.

4. "about a thousand": Louis S. Gerteis, *The Civil War in Missouri*, 19. The call for muster of the state militia occurred soon after the Camp Jackson affair in St. Louis. A "Military Bill" passed by the General Assembly disbanded the Missouri Volunteer Militia and created the new Missouri State Guard. In Saline County, at least three other companies were forming at the time the Saline Jackson Guards departed for Jefferson City. Those units were also in Jefferson City and traveled with John Marmaduke to Boonville. *History of Saline County*, 276-77.

5. During the night of May 8, 1861, the steamboat *J. C. Swan* arrived at St. Louis with arms and ammunition seized by Confederate forces from the federal arsenal at Baton Rouge. Part of the cargo was later discovered by General Lyon's troops at the site of Camp Jackson while the rest had been sent to Jefferson City and then forwarded by Governor Jackson to the newly established state armory in Boonville. James W. Covington, "The Camp Jackson Affair," *MHR*, Vol. 55, No. 3 (April 1961), 203.

6. Brigadier General John Bullock Clark Sr. served as an officer in the Missouri Militia during the Black Hawk War in 1812 and was in command of state forces during the Missouri Mormon War of 1838. A U.S. senator in 1861, he was expelled from the U.S. Congress for taking up arms against the Union. He led State Guard troops in the battle at Carthage in 1861; served as senator, then representative, from Missouri in the First and Second Confederate States Congresses. Imprisoned after the war, he eventually returned to his Howard County law practice.

7. Penn to Marmaduke, October 4, 1840. Box 3, Sappington-Marmaduke Papers, MHS. For a more detailed account of the Clark-Jackson affair see Phillips, *Missouri's Confederate*, 98-100.

8. "considerable controversy among the officers and men": *A History of Cooper County from the first visit by White Men ...*, 99-100; *History of Saline County*, 279,

9. "opened a galling fire": Ibid., 98. Reports of the number of troops accompanying Lyon vary from 1,500 to 1,700. McElroy, *The Struggle for Missouri*, 123, gives the figure as between 1,700 and 2,000. Gerteis, *The Civil War in Missouri*, 35-36, writes that Lyon left St. Louis with "about two thousand men," and after leaving some at Jefferson City, moved against Boonville with "about seventeen hundred." The number of soldiers reported under Marmaduke's command ranges from 500 to 750.

10. Marmaduke tried to extract his troops in an orderly fashion: John McElroy, *The Struggle for Missouri*, 124.

11. "believing that politicians were controlling military affairs": *History of Saline County*, 412.

12. "poor physical state": Jack D. Welsh. *Medical Histories of Confederate Generals*, 154.

13. Darwin Marmaduke's service in the Saline Jackson Guards: Soldiers' Records, War of 1812–World War I. Record of Service Card, Box 107, Reel S00735, MSA. Darwin's role at Boonville is unclear. At Jefferson City, he was recorded as company quartermaster. As captain of the company, John Marmaduke, likely protected his brother by placing him in a position that would be away from the line of battle. Responsible for supplies at Boonville, Darwin would probably have been in town, three miles from the fight, perhaps loading wagons for transport to the battle site. *History of Cole, Moniteau, Morgan, Benton, Miller, Maries and Osage Counties, Missouri*, 257.

14. Despite having served in the State Guards: *History of Saline County*, 345; Soldiers' Records, War of 1812–World War I, 71st Regiment E.M.M., Office of Adjutant General, Record of Service Card 710, Box 54, Reel S0087, MSA. "Discharged by payment of Commutation tax": Ibid. The commutation tax paid by Darwin was $10, plus 1/10 of 1 percent of the value of taxable property owned, and had to be paid in advance of enrollment. "Affairs in Jackson and Lafayette Counties": Union Regimental Index, Missouri Infantry, civilwararchive.com/unionmo.htm.

More about the organization of the Enrolled Missouri Militia can be found in: *Missouri Troops in Service During the Civil War: Letter from the Secretary of War*, 48-52. George Bingham owned a wagon-making shop at Arrow Rock. His relationship to the artist George Caleb Bingham is not established, although they both were born in Virginia and were probably related. *History of Saline County*, 562-63.

Divided Loyalties

15. "One of the Marmadukes left the city yesterday for Quincy, Ill.": J. H. Kemble to Capt. Peter Tallon, October 19, 1864. Missouri Union Provost Marshal Papers: 1861-1866. Reel F1656, File 20846, MSA. Darwin was one of the Marmadukes reported to the provost marshal. By this time Meredith Sr. was deceased. It follows that Darwin's companion had to be Meredith Jr., although he is recorded (*History of Saline County*, 767) as being in Colorado at the time.

16. Missouri's new governor, Hamilton Gamble, on June 2, 1862, told members of the State Convention, "You have been called together because there is no other body in existence that can adopt the measures which the present condition of the state demands." *Journal of the Missouri State Convention, held in Jefferson City, June 1862*, 4.

17. His votes helped to sideline legislation: *Journal of the Missouri State Convention, held in Jefferson City, June 1862*, 72, 84. *Liberty Weekly Tribune*, June 13, 1862, 2. Reel 26664, Newspaper Archive, SHSMO. The Missouri State Convention of 1861–63 met in March, July, and October of 1861; June of 1862; and June of 1863. Further information about the activities of the assembly can be found in four volumes of the *Journal(s) of the Missouri State Convention, 1861-1863*.

18. "another disloyal member": *Official Records of the War of the Rebellion*, Series 1, Vol 13 (Serial No. 19), 807. Benjamin Loan was practicing law in St. Joseph when he was commissioned a brigadier general in the Missouri State Militia in 1861. As commander of the northwest and then the central military districts, he "participated in counter-guerrilla operations." Loan was discharged in 1863 and then elected to the U.S. Congress, serving three terms. *Annual Report of the Adjutant General of Missouri for the year ending December 31, 1865*.

19. "under military arrest for disloyalty": Folder 30, Charles D. Drake Autobiography C1003, SHSMO. Historian David D. March relates that "Seldom, if ever, has a Missouri politician been hated so intensely by so many Missourians as was Charles Daniel Drake." Drake, termed a "Radical Republican" has been held responsible for the drafting and adoption of the controversial 1865 Missouri Constitution, which included a widely despised loyalty test oath. Christensen, *Dictionary of Missouri Biography*, 253.

20. "under these circumstances, sent south": *Executive Documents Printed By Order of the House of Representatives, During the Second Session of the Thirty-Ninth Congress, 1866-67*, Vol 8, 247-48. Several biographical references contend that Vincent participated in the Battle of Corinth, October 3 and 4, 1862, where he supposedly earned the title "Colonel" for his command of a field artillery battery. No contemporary document to support this has been found, nor does anything support the idea that he was knowledgeable about artillery. Throughout the summer of 1862, he was in Missouri — farming, mining coal, and serving on slave patrols in Saline County. It is highly unlikely that he was in Mississippi that fall.

21. Vincent Marmaduke's service in Europe is referenced in: Nathaniel C. Hughes, *Yale's Confederates: A Biographical Dictionary*, 133. For more about Confederate arms procurement see: William Diamond, "Imports of the Confederate Government from Europe and Mexico." *The Journal of Southern History*, Vol. 6, No. 4 (November 1940), 470-503.

22. On November 6, Vincent was arrested by federal authorities at Chicago: *Official Records of the War of the Rebellion*, Series 1, Vol. 39/2 (Serial No. 79), 696; Series 1, Vol. 45/1 (Serial No. 93), 1077; Series 2, Vol. 8 (Serial No. 121), 502. James O. Broadhead as Vincent's trial attorney: Michael Dickey, *The Marmaduke Family of Missouri, A Family Divided*. Monograph (speech), November 5, 2018, to Boonslick Historical Society; Christensen, *Dictionary of Missouri Biography*, 116-117. Broadhead's involvement with the Marmadukes is worthy of further investigation.

23. "Ma what do you think of my going through Tennessee": Henry Marmaduke to Lavinia Marmaduke, June 13, 1860. Box 5, Folder 7, Sappington-Marmaduke Papers, MHS.

24. "but they continued to fire it as if uninjured": *Official Records*, Series 1, Vol. 9, Operations in Southeastern Virginia January 11 - March 17, 1862. Report of Flag Officer Franklin Buchanan, 11.

25. Lavinia's letter to Henry: Thomas L. Price to Meredith Marmaduke, May 14, 1862. Box 5, Folder 7, Sappington-Marmaduke Papers, MHS. Thomas L. Price, a Democrat, banker, and developer, the first mayor of Jefferson City, was elected Missouri's lieutenant governor in 1848 and served one term; a member of the state's House of Representatives 1860-62; and elected as U.S. representative to fill the vacancy caused by expulsion of John W. Reid. He served from January 1862 to March 1863.

To Make a Fortune in Missouri

26. Henry Marmaduke aboard the CSS *Chattahoochee*: John V. Quarstein, *The CSS Virginia: Sink Before Surrender*, np.

27. He probably left Richmond the last day of August: *Official Records*, Series 2, Vol. 2, Union and Confederate States Navy Department Correspondence 1861-1865, 813. Son of a U.S. Navy Commodore, Samuel Barron resigned from the U.S. Navy at the time of Lincoln's inauguration to join the Virginia Navy, later integrated into the Confederate States Navy. For more about the French connection with Confederate agents see *The Confederate Navy in Europe*, Chapter 6, Confederate Naval Operations in France, 147-176.

28. shared a room with a former CSS *Virginia* shipmate: Quarstein, *The CSS Virginia: Sink Before Surrender*, np.

29. "We are much in need of officers here": *Official Records*, Series 2, Vol. 2, Union and Confederate States Navy Department Correspondence 1861-1865, 516, 816-17, 673.

30. "Confederate steamer Samson ... and hold her in readiness for service": *Official Records*, Series 1, Vol. 15, South Atlantic Blockading Squadron, 771.

31. He had a distinguished career with the United States government: Historical Notes and Comments. *MHR*, Vol. 19, No. 2 (January 1925), 369-70.

32. "both highly respectable gentlemen. ... what we call Southern Men": Weston J. Birch to General James Totten, May 2, 1862. Missouri Union Provost Marshal Paper 1861-1866. Reel FD1585, File 1123, MSA.

33. "Thomas Harvey ... appeared before Lt. Col. Epstein charged with encouraging the Rebellion": Chs. Korh, Lt. & acting Provostmarshal [sic] to Colonel Barnard G. Farrar, May 6, 1862. Missouri Union Provost Marshal Papers, 1861-1866. Reel F1585, File 1191, MSA. M. M. Marmaduke (unknown whether father or son) posted a $2,000 bond in the provost marshal's office at Marshall, Missouri, on June 12, 1863; List of Bonds and Oaths Received from Marshall, Saline County, Mo., Ibid., File 1191. Meredith Jr. going to Colorado: *History of Saline County*, 767. Oaths and bonds were a means for local provost marshal authorities to identify persons suspected or known to be sympathetic to the South. Taking the loyalty oath sometimes resulted in reprisals from friends and neighbors in Missouri's close-knit rural communities. In addition to pressure from Union authorities, this may have been the reason for Meredith Jr. leaving the state. For more about oaths and bonds see Christopher Phillips, "Shadow War: Federal Military Authority and Loyalty Oaths in Civil War Missouri," *Civil War on the Western Border: The Missouri-Kansas Conflict, 1854-1865*.

34. The sympathies of Meredith's son-in-law, Levin Harwood, lay with the Confederacy: Receipt for prisoner, May 9, 1865, U.S. Provost Marshals' Papers, 1861-1867. Provo, UT: ancestry.com [online database], 366. Letter, E.E. Bryant to Col. J. L. Meline, February 1, 1866. Ibid., 363. From: *Union Provost Marshals' File of Papers Relating to Individual Civilians, 1861-1867*. Roll 121, Microfilm Publication MO345, Record Group 109, National Archives and Records Administration.

35. "so large that he knew not what calculation to make": Will of Meredith M. Marmaduke, 1864 Saline County Probate Estate Files, Estate CE-1710, Reel C8250, MSA. See also: Saline County Will Records, Vol. B, 81-84, Reel C-6301, MSA.

36. Some Missouri planters lost their land as the result of their participation in a financial conspiracy: Mark W. Geiger, *Missouri's Hidden Civil War: Financial Conspiracy and the Decline of the Planter Elite, 1861-1865*, 27, 36, 76-77. Geiger places the total amount raised by the scheme for Confederate forces in Missouri at $3 million.

37. "I hear the bushwhackers have been down among you": Francis F. Audsley to Elizabeth Audsley, July 31, 1862, August 16, 1863. Francis Fairbanks and Harriet Elizabeth Audsley Papers, C2374, SHSMO. Francis Audsley, born and educated in England, emigrated to Saline County in 1851 to join his family on their farm near Miami. Enlisting in the Union army, he was appointed a lieutenant and stationed at Lexington. He and Elizabeth owned property in Saline and Carroll Counties.

38. "times have been so squally": A. J. McRoberts to Mollie McRoberts, October 16 and 23, 1863. A.J. McRoberts Papers, C0375 SHSMO.

39. "daily rode up to the houses of men of Southern inclination": *History of Saline County*, 163.

40. "A man of earnest and purposeful life": Napton, *Past and Present*, 405.

Divided Loyalties

41. The fate of another politically prominent Saline County slaveholding resident: Christopher Phillips and Jason Pendleton, *The Union on Trial: The Political Journals of Judge William Barclay Napton*, 62-64, 66, 185, 191, 195, 197, 204, 212.

42. "forced to make a stand at Merrill's Crossing": Official Records, War of the Rebellion, Series 1, Vol. 22 (Part 1), 621, 623. Accounts of the number of men Shelby had with him on the Missouri raid vary. Brown's report was self-serving; Shelby had prepared an ambush at Merrill's Crossing. Instead of being forced to make a stand there, he was protecting the rear of his command from being overrun by Brown's troops. Shelby's advance into central Missouri was halted at Marshall by Union forces. Breaking his command into two groups, Shelby eventually returned to Arkansas.

43. "represents life and property as very insecure in Saline": *The Union on Trial*, 205. Judge Napton mentioned the letter in his journal entry for August 30, 1863, saying that John Breathitt was "now here as a refugee." Breathitt was from Kentucky, the nephew of Jane Breathitt Sappington (Dr. John's wife).

EPILOGUE

JOURNEY'S END

If Meredith Miles Marmaduke wanted to measure his success in attaining the life he had envisioned when he left Virginia, the summer of 1860 was the time to do so. He was at the pinnacle of achievement then, his fortune made, his family and finances not yet threatened by disruption in a civil war. He had come to Missouri in 1823 determined to create for himself a comfortable way of life — founded on ownership of land and slaves with the economic, political, and social advances such a life entailed — that was the birthright of a Virginia-born gentleman. Along with a wagon and five slaves, he brought with him a degree of affluence that on the first day in Franklin gave him a seat among the socioeconomic elites who were settling the Booneslick in the 1820s. He also brought the realization that, unmarried at age 32, he needed to find a wife and start a family if his dream was to be meaningful.

Some 37 years later, a census taker visited the Marmaduke farm in July 1860 to count all who lived there and to record the value of the family's real estate and personal property. How truthfully Meredith answered the questions about his wealth is unknown, but if the figures on the census form are trustworthy they show that he had done well. The value of his land is recorded as $110,000, his personal property he believed to be worth $65,500, and the few slaves he brought to Missouri had grown in number to 54, an 11-fold increase. Meredith could look at this aspect of his life and be satisfied that he was a wealthy man. His search for a wife, begun when he arrived in the Booneslick country, had also been successful. In 1860, he and Lavinia had been married for 34 years and she had delivered 10 children, nine of which lived to adulthood. As for engaging in the public duties expected of the wealthy planter class, Meredith had served as a county surveyor and judge, as lieutenant governor and governor, and in several other civic and political offices. He could be satisfied on that account, too.

Now, 41 years after leading his wagon of slaves into Franklin, Meredith was in his 73rd year of life and knew he was approaching death. On March 20, 1864, he called upon two of his neighbors, 67-year-old Andrew Brownlee and 23-year-old William H. Fenwick, to serve as witnesses to his prepared will and testament. His signature at the end of the document, "M. M. Marmaduke," with a characteristic flourished underline, was written without a sign of tremor. Meredith was overweight, described in a Saline County history as "five feet, ten inches in height, and inclined to corpulency." His body stressed by age and by the trials of travel on the Santa Fe Trail and elsewhere, his heart weak, he lingered six more days before dying on March 26. The cause of death was said to be "inflammation" of the stomach and bowels, perhaps a form of cancer, although it appears that he did not suffer a lengthy illness.[1] Missing from the family who gathered at the home after his death were three of his sons who had allied themselves with the Confederate cause in the Civil War. John was leading a cavalry brigade in Arkansas, Henry was aboard a Confederate ironclad ram ship in North Carolina, and Vincent was imprisoned at Camp Douglas in Chicago — all unable to enter Union territory to see their father or to attend his funeral.

Meredith wanted to be interred "without any ostentation in the burial ground set apart by Dr. John Sappington," five miles southwest of the village of Arrow Rock.[2] His body lies there today along with that of his wife and three of their children, his brother-in-law Claiborne Fox Jackson, Dr. John Sappington and his wife, and numerous other Marmaduke and Sappington family members. The cemetery — and a nearby black burial ground for the family's slaves — is now a state historic site. Today, visitors to Arrow Rock, the National Historic Landmark village on the bluff above the Missouri River, can step back in time to the mid-1800s, when Meredith Miles Marmaduke was a familiar sight on its streets. As for a lack of "ostentation," Meredith's grave site is marked by a large, arched monument. He was buried "according to the rites of Free Masonry. ... His funeral was largely attended."[3]

Provisions of Meredith's Will

Filed with the Saline County Probate Court a month after his death, Meredith's will names Lavinia as his executrix, an expression of confidence in her ability to deal with the complex family and legal issues that he knew would arise during settlement of the estate. He also named his son-in-law Thomas J. Yerby (daughter Sarah's husband) and his brother-in-law William B. Sappington as co-executors, although in coming years Yerby would take on the greater role. Fifteen years would pass before final settlement and distribution to the heirs occurred. Meredith gave detailed instructions for the settlement of his estate. The leading proviso, one that he described as "my duty, though a painfull [sic] one," excluded his sons Vincent and Darwin, and his son-in-law Levin B. Harwood (daughter Jane's husband), from any benefit in the estate.[4] The inventory of the estate, completed six weeks after Meredith's death, shows that Vincent owed his father more than $13,000 for money advanced him in recent years. Why Darwin is excluded isn't known, but he, too, may have owed his father for money advanced, although if so Meredith kept any such transaction to himself, as nothing relating to Darwin appears in a lengthy list of "Notes & Accounts" contained in the inventory. In contrast, the list shows small sums of money loaned to Meredith Jr. The inventory also lists notes for nearly $10,000 that Meredith had loaned Thomas Yerby.

From December 1855 until May 1861, Vincent was managing his father's money, making loans in amounts that ranged from $20,000 to as little as $270, and that in total amounted to more than $40,000. These transactions appear in the "Notes & Accounts" section of the inventory with the notation, "Assigned by V. Marmaduke."[5] The $20,000 loan went to Vincent's brother-in-law, 20-year-old James H. Eakin of Nashville, Tennessee, on May 1, 1861. (What Eakin did with the money isn't known, but the following September he repaid $2,000, and on May 29, 1866, he paid off the note.) In total, Meredith's estate inventory lists more than $71,000 in notes for loans — either made by Meredith or by Vincent on his father's behalf — and the interest the loans had accumulated.

Meredith wrote in his will that he had already given $3,000 each to his children Sarah, John, and Meredith Jr. How to distribute the balance of his estate caused him some concern. "In consequence of the disturbed condition of the country, growing out of the war, my losses have been so large that I know not what calculation to make," the will states, "but the residue of my estate after my debts are paid I wish divided into three equal parts."[6] Lavinia received one part; another went to his son Darwin, to hold as trustee for the benefit of his daughter, Jane Harwood, and her children. From the remaining one-third, daughter Lavinia and son Leslie, received $3,000 each, and son Henry received $2,000; these three bequests were delayed until April 16, 1875. Anything left after this last distribution was to be divided equally among all of his children except those he had specifically excluded, even though Darwin was entrusted with management of his sister Jane's portion.

Meredith's contrary treatment of his two daughters and their husbands — Levin Harwood specifically excluded as an heir and Jane's inheritance placed in a trust while her sister Sarah Yerby received her inheritance and her husband, Thomas, named a co-executor of the estate — raises a question about Harwood's relationship with his father-in-law. Meredith's treatment of Harwood indicates that there may have been bad feelings between the two men. Did he disapprove of Harwood's support of the St. Louis conspirators, among them the boat burners who were responsible for so much indiscriminate death and destruction in the Mississippi River Valley? Well-known in St. Louis, Meredith would have learned of his son-in-law's activities. As someone for whom personal bravery and honor — as a soldier, adventurer, merchant, and political figure — were lifelong qualities, it is difficult to envision Meredith sanctioning his son-in-law's support of subversive, quasi-military activities. Whatever the reason for his action, by stipulating that Jane's inheritance be held in trust by her brother, it is clear that Meredith wanted his daughter's money kept out of the reach of her husband.

Slaves, Goods, and Chattels

"An Inventory & appraisement of all and singular, the slaves, goods, chattels, notes, accounts, deeds & other personal property, and also the real Estate of Meredith M. Marmaduke deceased, produced before the undersigned ... this 23rd day of May 1864 by Mrs. Lavinia Marmaduke Executrix, & Thomas J. Yerby & W. B. Sappington co-executors. ...."[7]

Family friends Glen O. Hardeman, William Price, and Joel Scott, "appraisers duly qualified," began their lengthy inventory of Meredith's estate with an accounting of his slaves from information provided by Lavinia. Assisted by the farm's overseer, she had gathered the names and ages of 51 slaves living on the Marmaduke farms, a roster of human chattel that must have evoked in her some bitter feelings. Prior to the start of the Civil War, their slaves had constituted a significant part of the family's wealth. Now these unfortunate people were about to become a burden on their mistress as she saw the time for their release from bondage approaching. Although Abraham Lincoln's 1863 Emancipation Proclamation did not cover slaves in Missouri, the state's wartime legislature abolished slavery on January 11, 1865, without compensation to owners. The appraisers opened the Marmaduke list of slaves with the adult males — Luke, George, James, Philip, Wellington, and Branson; the oldest was 40 years old, the youngest 22. Beside each name, the appraisers entered a value. Wellington was deemed to be worth the most money at $100, Branson the least at $25. Altogether, these six men were thought to be worth $400. Before the war, any one of them would have brought that much money — or more — if sold. Adult females tallied in the inventory were Charlotte and Lucy, each aged 40, followed by Josephine, Harriette, Cicily, and Maria, all in their 30s; then descending in age from 26 were Cynthia, Ophelia, Caroline, Penelope, and Mary, at age 18 the youngest. The total worth of these women valued at $455. The appraisers listed 18 boys, ranging in age from 16 to 1½ years old, and 16 girls, the oldest 14 and the youngest 1 year old. These children were valued at $181.

A decade earlier, in the dissolution of a partnership between Saline County residents Claiborne Fox Jackson and Jesse M. Baskett, 16 slaves they owned (men, women, and children) were valued at slightly more than $5,000, or $312 each if averaged.[8] An indication of the value Meredith placed on his slaves prior to the start of the Civil War (he had 54 in 1860) is seen in the difference in the valuation of his personal property (which included slaves) in 1860 — $65,500, and in the inventory of 1864 that valued his personal property at only $12,786, of which the slaves were valued at a mere $1,036.[9] Based on an average value of $312 for the Jackson-Baskett slaves in 1853, the 51 slaves listed in Meredith's estate in 1864 should have been worth at least $16,000. It is apparent that a significant portion of the reduction in the value of Meredith's personal property in 1864 can be attributed to the decline in value of his slaves, and this, of course, would never be recovered. The balance of Meredith's personal property (excluding household goods and furniture, which were not shown in the inventory) consisted of farm implements, livestock, field crops, and two guns — a rifle valued at $20 and a double-barreled shotgun worth $15.

The Real Estate

The 7,959 acres of land Meredith owned in 1864 were not valued when the inventory was filed with the probate court in May of that year, although the land undoubtedly was the most valuable asset in the estate. The greater part of the property — 4,939 acres, was in Saline County — its value in 2018 estimated to be $5,000 to $8,000 an acre. He also owned 2,660 acres in St. Clair County, valued in 2018 at $1,800 to $2,200 an acre, plus land in Pettis and Howard Counties. The value of Meredith's property in 2018 would be $30 million to $45 million.[10] Whether for management purposes or simply for identification, the property was organized into 11 farms, listed in the estate inventory as: the Home Tract, 1,755 acres; Jones Tract, 864 acres; Salt Fork Tract, 575 acres; Logston Tract, 40 acres; Blackwater Tract, 240 acres; Story Farm, 760 acres; Lands of L. B. Harwood, 705 acres; Pettis County Land, 320 acres; Land in Howard County, 40 acres; Osage Lands, 1,496 acres; and the Applegate Lands, 1,164 acres. The latter two tracts are in St. Clair County. Each parcel of land within a named tract is listed in the inventory by its legal description — section, township, and range. Also listed in the inventory is Lot 3 of Block 9 in Marshall, Missouri. It is beyond the scope of this book to follow the disposition of these lands; however, their sale undoubtedly brought a great deal of money to the estate. Sometime prior to 1870, Lavinia moved from the home she and Meredith had built on their farm near Arrow Rock and settled in a house in Marshall, where she remained until her death in 1885.

Notes

1. "inflammation of the stomach and bowels,": *History of Saline County*, 408.

2. "without any ostentation in the burial ground set apart by Dr. John Sappington.": Will of Meredith M. Marmaduke, Missouri State Archives, Saline County Probate Estate Files, Microfilm Reel C-8250, Estate CE-1710; known hereafter as Will of Meredith M. Marmaduke.

3. "according to the rites of Free Masonry. … His funeral was largely attended.": *History of Saline County*, 1881, 408.

4. "my duty, though a painfull one": Will of Meredith M. Marmaduke.

5. "Assigned by V. Marmaduke": Saline County Probate Estate Files, Meredith M. Marmaduke Estate, Reel C-8250, Estate CE-1710, Missouri State Archives.

6. "In consequence of the disturbed condition of the country": Will of Meredith M. Marmaduke.

7. "An Inventory & appraisement of all and singular": Will of Meredith M. Marmaduke.

8. Claiborne Fox Jackson and Jesse M. Baskett, 16 slaves they owned: Settlement and division of slaves made between Jesse M. Baskett and Claiborne F. Jackson, on the first of January 1853. Folder 61, John Sappington Papers C1027, SHSMO.

9. An indication of the value Meredith placed on his slaves: 1860 Federal Census Saline County, Missouri, Schedule 2, Slave Inhabitants in Arrow Rock Township. Meredith M. Marmaduke Probate Estate Files.

10. Per-acre prices for comparable land in Saline and St. Clair Counties were obtained in November 2018 from local real estate brokers.

BIBLIOGRAPHY

BOOKS, MANUSCRIPTS, OTHER PUBLICATIONS, MAPS

Ambler, Charles Henry. *A History of West Virginia*. New York: Prentice-Hall, 1933.

———. *A History of Transportation in the Ohio Valley*. Glendale, CA: Arthur H. Clark, 1932.

Annual Report of the Adjutant General of Missouri for the year ending December 31, 1865. Jefferson City, MO: Emory L. Foster, Public Printer, 1866.

Baker, William B. "Roads West from St. Louis." In *Travelers on the Western Frontier*, edited by John Francis McDermott. Urbana: University of Illinois Press, 1970.

Banta, R. E. *The Ohio*. Rivers of America Series. New York: Rinehart, 1949.

Barile, Mary Collins. The *Santa Fe Trail in Missouri*. Columbia: University of Missouri Press, 2010.

Beachum, Larry. *William Becknell, Father of the Santa Fe Trade*. El Paso: Texas Western Press of the University of Texas at El Paso, 1982.

Beahan, Gary W., comp. *Missouri's Public Domain: United States Land Sales 1818–1922*. Jefferson City, MO: Missouri Secretary of State, Archives Information Bulletin, Vol. 2, No. 3, July 1980.

Bellamy, D. D. *Slavery, Emancipation, and Racism in Missouri*. PhD dissertation. Columbia: University of Missouri, 1971.

Benton, Thomas Hart. *Thirty Years' View*. New York: D. Appleton, 1856.

Biddle, Nicholas, ed. *The Journals of the Expedition under the Command of Capts. Lewis and Clark*. 2 vols. New York: The Heritage Press, 1962.

Brackenridge, Henry M. *Views of Louisiana; Together With A Journal of A Voyage Up The Missouri River, in 1811*. Pittsburgh: Cramer, Spear and Richbaum, 1814.

Bradley, John P., Leo F. Daniels, and Thomas C. Jones, comps. *The International Dictionary of Thoughts*. Chicago: J. G. Ferguson, 1969.

Brown, Lauren. *Grasses, An Identification Guide*. New York: Houghton Mifflin, 1979.

Brown, William Wells. *Narrative of William Wells Brown, A Fugitive Slave*. Boston: Anti-Slavery Office, 1849.

Burke, Diane Mutti. *On Slavery's Border*. Athens, GA: University of Georgia Press, 2010.

Butler, Stuart Lee. *A Guide to Virginia Militia Units in the War of 1812*. Athens, GA: New Papyrus Publishing, 2011.

Catlin, George. *Letters and Notes on the Manners, Customs, and Condition of the North American Indians*. 3rd ed. Vol. 2. New York: Wiley and Putnam, 1844.

Chiles, Henry C. *The Masonic College of Missouri*. Fulton, MO: Ovid Bell Press, 1935.

Christensen, Lawrence, et al., eds. *Dictionary of Missouri Biography*. Columbia: University of Missouri Press, 1999.

Crozier, William A., ed. *Virginia County Records, New Series*, Vol. 1, Westmoreland County. Baltimore: Genealogical Publishing, 1971.

To Make a Fortune in Missouri

Dary, David. *The Santa Fe Trail; Its History, Legends, and Lore.* New York: Alfred A. Knopf, 2000.

Davis, Walter B., and Daniel S. Durrie. *An Illustrated History of Missouri.* St. Louis: A. J. Hall, 1876.

Dickey, Michael. *Arrow Rock: Crossroads of the Missouri Frontier.* Arrow Rock, MO: Friends of Arrow Rock, 2004.

Dorman, John F., comp. *Westmoreland County, Virginia, Order Book 1690–1698.* 3 vols., pts. 1, 2. Washington, DC: 1962.

Doubleday, C. W. *Reminiscences of the Filibuster War in Nicaragua.* New York: G. P. Putnam's Sons, 1886.

Duffus, R. L. *The Santa Fe Trail.* Albuquerque: University of New Mexico Press, 1972, c1930.

Eslinger, Ellen, ed. *Running Mad for Kentucky.* Lexington: University of Kentucky Press, 2011.

Executive Documents Printed by Order of the House of Representatives, During the Second Session of the Thirty-Ninth Congress, 1866–67. Washington, DC: U.S. Government Printing Office, 1868.

Federal Writers' Project. *Missouri Narratives.* Vol. 10 of *Slave Narratives: A Folk History of Slavery in the United States from Interviews with Former Slaves.* Washington, DC: Library of Congress, 1941.

Fedric, Francis. *Slave Life in Virginia and Kentucky.* London: Wertheim, Macintosh, and Hunt, 1863.

Ferris, Robert G., ed. *Prospector, Cowhand, and Sodbuster: Historic places associated with the mining, ranching, and farming frontiers in the trans-Mississippi West.* Washington, DC: United States Department of the Interior, National Park Service, 1967.

Fischer, David H., and James C. Kelly. *Bound Away, Virginia and the Westward Movement.* Charlottesville: University Press of Virginia, 2000.

Foley, William E. *A History of Missouri, Volume 1, 1673–1820.* Columbia: University of Missouri Press, 1971.

Fothergill, Augusta B. *Wills of Westmoreland County, Virginia 1654–1800.* Baltimore: Genealogical Publishing, 1973.

Fothergill, Augusta B., and John M. Naugle. *Virginia Tax Payers, 1782–87.* Baltimore: Genealogical Publishing, 1986.

French, B. F., ed. *Historical Collections of Louisiana.* Vol 3. New York: D. Appleton, 1851.

———. *Historical Memoirs of Louisiana.* Vol. 5. New York: Lamport, Blakeman & Law, 1853.

Geiger, Mark W. *Missouri's Hidden Civil War: Financial Conspiracy and the Decline of the Planter Elite, 1861–1865.* PhD dissertation. Columbia: University of Missouri, 2006.

Gerteis, Louis S., *The Civil War in Missouri.* Columbia: University of Missouri Press, 2012.

Goetzmann, William H., and William N. Goetzmann. *The West of the Imagination.* New York: W. W. Norton, 1986.

Goldstein, Max A., ed. *One Hundred Years of Medicine and Surgery in Missouri.* St. Louis: *St. Louis Star*, 1900.

Goodwin, Doris K. *Team of Rivals: The Political Genius of Abraham Lincoln.* New York: Simon and Schuster, 2005.

Graham, Jean. *Tales of the Osage River Country.* Clinton, MO: Martin Printing, 1929.

Gray, Gertrude E., comp.: *Virginia Northern Neck Land Grants 1694–1742.* Baltimore: Genealogical Publishing, 1987.

Greenspan, Ezra. *William Wells Brown: an African American Life.* New York: W. W. Norton, 2014.

Gregg, Josiah. *Commerce of the Prairies.* Norman: University of Oklahoma Press, 1954, c1844.

———. *Scenes and Incidents of the Western Prairies.* Philadelphia: J. W. Moore, 1857, c1844.

Gregg, Kate L., ed. *The Road to Santa Fe: the Journal and Diaries of George Champlin Sibley.* Albuquerque: University of New Mexico Press, 1952.

Bibliography

Hafen, LeRoy R., ed. *Mountain Men and the Fur Trade of the Far West*. The Far West and Rockies Historical Series, vol. 7. Glendale, CA: Arthur H. Clark, 1969.

Hall, Thomas B., Jr., and Thomas B. Hall III. *Dr. John Sappington of Saline County, Missouri 1776–1856*. Arrow Rock, MO: Friends of Arrow Rock, 1975.

Hardeman, Nicholas Perkins. *Wilderness Calling*. Knoxville: University of Tennessee Press, 1977.

Harris, John R., III, Rohini Sankaran, and Anthony F. Kardis, comps. *Descriptive Recruitment Lists of Volunteers for the United States Colored Troops for the State of Missouri, 1863–1865*. Julius K. Hunter and Friends African American Research Collection, St. Louis County Library Special Collections, 2002.

Harris, Matthew, and Jay Buckley, eds. *Zebulon Pike, Thomas Jefferson, and the Opening of the American West*. Norman: University of Oklahoma Press, 2012.

Headley, Robert K., Jr. *Genealogical Abstracts from 18th-Century Virginia Newspapers*. Baltimore: Genealogical Publishing, 1987.

———. *Married Well and Often: Marriages of the Northern Neck of Virginia 1649–1800*. Baltimore: Genealogical Publishing, 2003.

Hebard, Grace Raymond, and E. A. Brininstool. *The Bozeman Trail*. 2 Vols. Lincoln: University of Nebraska Press, 1990, c1922.

Historical, Pictorial and Biographical Record of Chariton County, Missouri. Salisbury MO: Pictorial and Biographical Publishing, 1896.

History of Clay and Platte Counties, Missouri. St. Louis: National Historical Co., 1885.

History of Henry and St. Clair Counties, Missouri. St. Joseph, MO: National Historical Co., 1883.

History of Howard and Chariton Counties, Missouri. St. Louis: National Historical Co., 1883.

History of Lafayette County, Missouri. St. Louis: Missouri Historical Co., 1881.

History of Marion County, Missouri. St. Louis: E. F. Perkins, 1884.

History of Monroe and Shelby Counties, Missouri. St. Louis: National Historical Co., 1884.

History of Pike County, Missouri. Des Moines, IA: Mills, 1883.

History of Saline County, Missouri. St. Louis: Missouri Historical Co., 1881.

Hooper, Robert, M. D. *New Medical Dictionary*. Philadelphia: M. Carey & Son, Benjamin Warner, and Edward Parker, 1817.

Houck, Louis, ed. *A History of Missouri: From the Earliest Explorations and Settlements until the Admission of the State into the Union*. Vol. 1. Chicago: R. R. Donnelley & Sons, 1908.

———. *The Spanish Regime in Missouri*. Chicago: R. R. Donnelley & Sons, 1909.

Hughes, Nathaniel C., Jr. *Yale's Confederates: A Biographical Dictionary*. Knoxville: University of Tennessee Press, 2008.

Hulbert, Archer B. *The Cumberland Road*. Historic Highways of America, vol. 10. Cleveland: Arthur H. Clark, 1904.

Hurt, R. Douglas. *Agriculture and Slavery in Missouri's Little Dixie*. Columbia: University of Missouri Press, 1992.

Hyde, William, and Howard L. Conard, eds. *Encyclopedia of the History of St. Louis: A Compendium of History and Biography for Ready Reference*. Vol. 4. St. Louis: Southern History Co., 1899.

Ives, Charles. *Statistics of the Class of 1852, of Yale College*. New Haven, CT: Ezekiel Hayes, 1855.

Jackson, Wm. Rufus. *Missouri Democracy: A History of the Party and its Representative Members, Past and Present*. 3 vols. St. Louis: S. J. Clark, 1935.

Johnson, W. F. *History of Cooper County, Missouri*. Topeka, KS: Historical Publishing, 1919.

To Make a Fortune in Missouri

Journal and Proceedings of the Missouri State Convention, Held at Jefferson City and St. Louis, March 1861; July 1861; October 1861; June 1862; June 1863. 4 Vols. St. Louis: George Knapp, 1861–1863.

Journal of the Senate of the State of Missouri, First Session of the Fifteenth General Assembly; Journal of the House of Representatives of the State of Missouri, First Session of the Fifteenth General Assembly. Jefferson City, MO: Hampton L. Boon, Public Printer, 1848.

Kane, Adam Isaac. *The Western Steamboat: Structure and Machinery, 1811 to 1860.* MA thesis. College Station, TX: Texas A& M University, 2001.

Katz-Hyman, Martha B., and Kym S. Rice, eds. *World of a Slave: Encyclopedia of the Material Life of Slaves in the United States.* 2 vols. Santa Barbara, CA: Greenwood, 2011.

Kellogg, Louis P., ed. "The Mississippi Voyage of Joliet and Marquette." In *Early Narratives of the Northwest, 1634–1699.* New York: Charles Scribner's Sons, 1917.

Larkin, Lew. *Bingham, Fighting Artist.* St. Louis: State Publishing Co., 1955.

Lavender, David. *Bent's Fort,* Gloucester, MA: Peter Smith, 1968.

Laws of A Public and General Nature, of the District of Louisiana, of the Territory of Louisiana, of the Territory of Missouri, and of the State of Missouri, up to the Year 1824. Vol. 1. Jefferson City, MO: W. Lusk & Son, 1842.

Leopard, Buel, and Floyd C. Shoemaker, eds. *The Messages and Proclamations of the Governors of the State of Missouri.* Vol 3. Columbia, MO: State Historical Society of Missouri, 1922.

Lewis, Virgil A. *The Soldiery of West Virginia: Third Biennial Report of the Department of Archives and History.* Charleston: State of West Virginia, 1911.

Local Laws and Private Acts of the State of Missouri, Passed at the Adjourned Session of the 18th General Assembly. Jefferson City, MO: James Lusk, public printer, 1855.

Linklater, Andro. *Measuring America; How an Untamed Wilderness Shaped the United States and Fulfilled the Promise of Democracy.* New York: Walker, 2002.

Lyman, Myron E., and William W. Hankins. *Encounters with the British in Virginia During the War of 1812.* n.p.: The Society of the War of 1812 in the Commonwealth of Virginia, 2008.

Maddocks, Melvin. *The Seafarers: The Atlantic Crossing.* Alexandria, VA: Time-Life Books, 1981.

McCandless, Perry. *A History of Missouri, Volume II, 1820 to 1860.* Columbia: University of Missouri Press, 1972.

McDermott, John F. *George Caleb Bingham: River Portraitist.* Norman: University of Oklahoma Press, 1959.

McElroy, John. *The Struggle for Missouri.* Washington, DC: National Tribune Publishing, 1909.

Meyer, Duane. *The Heritage of Missouri.* rev. ed. St. Louis: State Publishing Co., 1965.

Miller, Joseph. *New Mexico: A Guide to the Colorful State.* rev. ed. New York: Hastings House, 1953.

Morgan, Robert. *Boone.* Chapel Hill NC: Algonquin Books, 2007.

Morton, Charles. "Third Regiment of Cavalry." In *Army of the US Historical Sketches of Staff and Line with Portraits of Generals-in-Chief,* edited by T. F. Rodenbough and W. L. Haskin. New York: Maynard, Merrill, 1896.

Napton, William Barclay, Jr. *Over The Santa Fe Trail, 1857.* Santa Fe: Stagecoach Press, 1964. Reprinted from the original 1905 edition.

———. *Past and Present of Saline County, Missouri.* Indianapolis: B. F. Bowen, 1910.

Nugent, Nell M., comp. *Cavaliers and Pioneers: Abstracts of Virginia Land Patents and Grants 1623–1666.* Books 1, 2, 5. Baltimore: Genealogical Publishing, 1983.

O'Bryan-Lawson, Robert A. *Chapel Hill, Missouri: Lost Visions of America's Vanguard on the Western Frontier, 1820–1865.* MA thesis. Kansas City: University of Missouri , 2014.

Bibliography

Ohman, Marian M. *A History of Missouri's Counties, County Seats, and Courthouse Squares.* Columbia: University of Missouri Extension, 1983.

Park, Eleanora G., and Kate S. Morrow. *Women of the Mansion: Missouri, 1821–1936.* Jefferson City, MO: Midland Printing Company, 1936.

Parker, Nathan H. *Missouri As It Is in 1867: An Illustrated Gazetteer of Missouri.* Philadelphia: J. B. Lippincott, 1867.

Peters, J. T., and H. B. Carden. *History of Fayette County, West Virginia.* Charleston, SC: Jarrett Printing, 1926.

Phillips, Christopher. *Missouri's Confederate: Claiborne Fox Jackson and the Creation of Southern Identity in the Border West.* Columbia: University of Missouri Press, 2000.

Phillips, Christopher, and Jason L. Pendleton, eds. *The Union on Trial: The Political Journals of Judge William Barclay Napton 1829–1883.* Columbia: University of Missouri Press, 2005.

Phillips, Claude A. *A History of Education in Missouri.* Jefferson City, MO: Hugh Stephens Printing, 1911.

Pickard, Madge E., and R. Carlyle Buley. *The Midwest Pioneer, His Ills, Cures, & Doctors.* New York: Henry Schuman, 1946.

Preston, Samuel H., and Michael R. Haines. *Fatal Years: Child Mortality in Late Nineteenth-Century America.* Princeton, NJ: Princeton University Press, 1991.

Quarstein, John V. *The CSS Virginia: Sink Before Surrender.* Charleston, SC: History Press, 2012.

Register of Graduates and Former Cadets, United States Military Academy 1802–1963. West Point, NY: West Point Alumni Foundation, 1963.

Shoemaker, Floyd C. *Missouri and Missourians; Land of Contrasts and People of Achievements.* 5 vols. Chicago: Lewis, 1943.

———. *Missouri, Day by Day.* 2 vols. Columbia, MO: State Historical Society of Missouri, 1942–1943.

Skogen, Larry C. *Indian Depredation Claims, 1796–1920.* Norman: University of Oklahoma Press, 1996.

Smith, Page. *Trial by Fire, A People's History of the Civil War and Reconstruction.* New York: McGraw-Hill, 1982.

Sparacio, Ruth, and Sam Sparacio, eds. *Deed and Will Abstracts of Westmoreland County, Virginia, 1751–1756.* McLean, VA: Antient Press, 1995.

———. *Westmoreland County, Virginia, Court Record Order Book 1712–1716,* Virginia County Court Records. McLean, VA: Antient Press, 1998.

Spencer, Warren F. *The Confederate Navy in Europe.* Tuscaloosa: University of Alabama Press, 1997.

Stark, Rodney. *For the Glory of God: How Monotheism Led to Reformations, Science, Witch-hunts, and the End of Slavery.* Princeton, NJ: Princeton University Press, 2004.

State Historical Society of Missouri, comp. *This Week in Missouri History,* 5 vols. Columbia, MO: State Historical Society of Missouri, 1989.

Stevens, Walter B. *Centennial History of Missouri (The Center State): one hundred years in the Union 1820–1921.* 6 vols. St. Louis: S. J. Clarke, 1921.

Sunder, John E. *Joshua Pilcher: Fur Trader and Indian Agent.* Norman: University of Oklahoma, 1968.

Switzler, William F., et al. *Illustrated History of Missouri, from 1541 to 1877.* St. Louis: C. R. Barns, 1879.

Thrapp, Dan L. *Encyclopedia of Frontier Biography.* 3 vols. Lincoln: University of Nebraska Press, 1991.

Torok, George D. *From the Pass to the Pueblos.* Santa Fe, NM: Sunstone Press, 2012.

Trexler, Harrison A. *Slavery in Missouri 1804–1865.* Baltimore: Johns Hopkins Press, 1914.

Weber, David J. *The Taos Trappers: The Fur Trade in the Far Southwest, 1540–1846.* Norman: University of Oklahoma Press, 1971.

Welsh, Jack D. *Medical Histories of Confederate Generals*. Kent, OH: Kent State University Press, 1995.

Wetmore, Alphonzo, comp. *Gazetteer of the State of Missouri* Reprint. New York: Arno Press, 1975, c1837.

White, David A., comp. *News of the Plains and Rockies 1803–1865*. Vol. 2. Spokane, WA: Arthur H. Clark, 1996.

Willet, Jarrett M. *The Missouri State Guard: Culture, Politics, and the Confederacy's Loss of Missouri in 1861*. MA thesis. Maryville, MO: Northwest Missouri State University, 2015.

Williams, Walter, and Floyd C. Shoemaker, et al. *Missouri, Mother of the West*. Vol. 1. Chicago: American Historical Society, 1930.

Wills, Garry. *Inventing America*. Garden City, NY: Doubleday, 1978.

Wilstach, Paul. *Tidewater Virginia*. New York: Tudor, 1945, c1929.

Wood, W. Raymond, comp. *An Atlas of Early Maps of the American Midwest*. Vol. 18. Springfield, IL: Illinois State Museum, 1983.

Wright, Holly G., and F. Edward Wright. *Colonial Families of the Northern Neck of Virginia*. Vol. 1. Lewes, DE: Colonial Roots, 2005.

Wright, Thomas R. B., *Westmoreland County, Virginia 1653–1912, A Short Chapter and Bright Day in its History, Parts I & II*. Richmond, VA: Whittet & Shepperson, 1912.

Young, William. *Young's History of Lafayette County, Missouri*. Indianapolis: B. F. Bowen, 1910.

NEWSPAPERS

State Historical Society of Missouri Newspaper Collection

A search for "Marmaduke" in the index of the newspaper collection belonging to the State Historical Society of Missouri produced numerous returns in publications on microfilm. With the exception of those containing obvious duplicate articles, all newspapers were reviewed by the author. Those used in developing the manuscript are referenced by name, date, and microfilm reel in the chapter notes. Other newspapers in the collection used in writing the book are similarly referenced.

Other Newspaper Articles

"The Army at Camp Floyd." *The New York Times*, January 17, 1860.

"Trade between Mexico and Missouri." *Niles' Weekly Register*, Vol. 27, January 15, 1825.

"The West." *Niles' Weekly Register*, Vol. 25, December 13, 1823.

PERIODICALS

Atherton, Lewis E. "The Pioneer Merchant in Mid-America." *University of Missouri Studies Quarterly of Research* 14, no. 2 (April 1939).

Atwood, Albert W. "Tidewater Virginia, Where History Lives." *National Geographic* 81, no. 5 (May 1942).

Baumann, Timothy E. "African American Archaeology: A Missouri Perspective." *The Missouri Archaeologist* 59 (December 1998).

Chappell, Phil E. "Missouri River Steamboats." *Transactions of the Kansas State Historical Society* 9 (1906).

Diamond, William. "Imports of the Confederate Government from Europe and Mexico." *The Journal of Southern History* 6, no. 4 (November 1940).

Dickey, Michael. "Specie, Sweat and Survival: The Impact of the Santa Fe Trail on Missouri's Economy." *Boone's Lick Heritage Quarterly* 12, no. 4 (Winter 2013–14).

Dollarhide, William. "Wagon Roads to the Ohio Country, 1787–1820." *Genealogy Bulletin, American Genealogical Lending Library Newsletter*, no. 23 (July, August, September 1994).

Dyer, Robert L. "A Brief History of Steamboating on the Missouri River With Emphasis on the Boonslick Region." *Boone's Lick Heritage Quarterly* 5, no. 2 (June 1997).

Bibliography

Foster, Kevin J. "The Diplomats Who Sank a Fleet." *Prologue, Quarterly of the National Archives and Records Administration* 33, no. 3 (Fall 2001).

Judah, Samuel Bernard. "A Journal of Travel from New York to Indiana in 1827." *Indiana Magazine of History* 17, no. 4 (December 1921).

Lee, John F. "John Sappington Marmaduke." *Missouri Historical Society Collections* 2, no. 6 (July 1906).

Lemmer, George F. "The Early Agricultural Fairs of Missouri." *Agricultural History* 17, no. 3 (July 1943).

Myers, Harry C., ed. "Meredith Miles Marmaduke's Journal of a Tour to New Mexico, 1824–1825." *Wagon Tracks: Santa Fe Trail Association Quarterly* 12, no.1 (November 1997).

"Old Franklin: A Frontier Town of the Twenties." *The Mississippi Valley Historical Review* 9, no. 4 (March 1923). Paper read at the association's 15th annual meeting, May 12, 1922.

Schafer, Joseph. "Jesse Applegate: Pioneer, Statesman and Philosopher." *The Washington Historical Quarterly* 1, no. 4 (July 1907).

Sharp, Grace M. "The Marmadukes and Some Allied Families." *William and Mary College Quarterly* 15, no. 2 (April 1935).

Shaw, Madelyn. "Slave Cloth and Clothing Slaves: Craftsmanship, Commerce, and Industry." *Journal of Early Southern Decorative Arts* 33 (2012).

Waldo, William. "Reflections of a Septuagenarian." *Glimpses of the Past*, Missouri Historical Society V, nos. 4–6 (April–June 1938) (1880).

Weber, David J. "Señor Escudero Goes to Washington: Diplomacy, Indians, and the Santa Fe Trail." *Western Historical Quarterly* 43, no. 4 (Winter 2012).

MISSOURI HISTORICAL REVIEW ARTICLES

Atherton, Lewis E. "Business Techniques in the Santa Fe Trail." Vol. 34, No. 3 (April 1940).

"The Birch-Jackson Encounter of 1838." Vol 28, no. 3 (April 1934); reprinted from the Smithville *Star*, September 20, 1906.

Broadhead, G. C. "The Santa Fe Trail." Vol. 4, no. 4 (July 1910).

Bullard, Loring. "Missouri Salt: The Rise and Fall of a Frontier Industry." Vol. 106, no. 2 (January 2012).

Christisen, Don. "A Vignette of Missouri's Native Prairie." Vol. 61, no. 2 (January 1967).

Cox, Isaac Joslin. "Opening the Santa Fe Trail." Vol. 25, no. 1 (October 1930).

Eaton, Miles W. "The Development and Later Decline of the Hemp Industry in Missouri." Vol. 43, no. 4 (July 1949).

Goodrich, James W. "In the Earnest Pursuit of Wealth: David Waldo in Missouri and the Southwest, 1820–1878." Vol. 66, no. 2 (January 1972).

Goodrich, James W., and Lynn Wolf Gentzler, eds. "I Well Remember: David Holmes Conrad's Recollections of St. Louis, 1819–1822." Vol. 90, no. 1 (October 1995); no. 2 (January 1996).

Gregg, Kate L. "Major Alphonso Wetmore." Vol. 35, no. 3 (April 1941).

Hurt, R. Douglas. "Planters and Slavery in Little Dixie." Vol. 88, no. 4 (July 1994).

Kirkpatrick, Arthur R. "Missouri on the Eve of the Civil War." Vol. 55, no. 2 (January 1961).

Lanser, Roland. "The Pioneer Physician in Missouri 1820–1850." Vol. 44, no. 1 (October 1949).

Lemmer, George F. "Agitation for Agricultural Improvement in Central Missouri Newspapers prior to the Civil War." Vol. 37, no. 4 (July 1943).

———. "Early Leaders in Livestock Improvement in Missouri." Vol. 37, no. 1 (October 1942).

———. "Missouri Agriculture as Revealed in the Eastern Agricultural Press, 1823–1869, Part 1." Vol. 42, no. 3 (April 1948).

McClure, C. H. "Early Opposition to Thomas Hart Benton." Vol. 10, no. 3 (April 1916).

McLarty, Vivian K., ed. "The First Steamboats on the Missouri; Reminiscences of Captain W. D. Hubbell." Vol. 51, no. 4 (July 1957).

Merkel, Benjamin C. "The Slavery Issue and the Political Decline of Thomas Hart Benton, 1846–1856." Vol. 38, no. 4 (July 1944).

"Missouriana: Advertisements in the Pioneer Press: Post Roads in 1827." Vol. 28, no. 3 (April 1934).

"Missouri History Not Found in Textbooks: Osage River Commerce in the 1870s." Vol. 51, no. 4 (July 1957).

Morrow, Lynn. "Dr. John Sappington: Southern Patriarch in the New West." Vol. 90, no. 1 (October 1995).

Richardson, Lemont K. "Private Land Claims in Missouri, Part III: The Era of Increasing Liberality." Vol.50, no.4 (July 1956).

Sampson, Francis A., ed. "The Journals of Capt. Thomas Becknell from Boone's Lick to Santa Fe, and from Santa Cruz to Green River." Vol. 4, no. 2 (January 1910).

Sayles, Stephen. "Thomas Hart Benton and the Santa Fe Trail." Vol. 69, no. 1 (October 1974).

Sharp, Grace H. "Letters from a Missouri 'Forty-Niner,' Col. William Daniel Marmaduke." Vol. 20, no. 1 (October 1925).

Scarpino, Philip V. "Slavery in Callaway County, Missouri: 1845–1855." Vol. 71, nos. 1, 3, (October 1976, April 1977).

Schroeder, Walter A. "Spread of Settlement in Howard County, Missouri, 1810–1859." Vol. 63, no. 1 (October 1968).

Schultz, Gerard. "Steamboat Navigation on the Osage River before the Civil War." Vol. 29, no. 3 (April 1935).

Shoemaker, Floyd C. "Osceola, Land of Osage River Lore." Vol. 54, no. 4 (July 1960).

Shortridge, James R. "The Expansion of the Settlement Frontier in Missouri." Vol. 75, no. 1 (October 1980).

Stephens, F. F., ed. "Major Alphonso Wetmore's Diary of a Journey to Santa Fe, 1828." Vol. 8, no. 4, (July 1914).

———. "Missouri and the Santa Fe Trail." Vol. 10, no. 4 (July 1916); Vol. 11, nos. 3 and 4 (April and July 1917).

Strickland, Arvarh E. "Aspects of Slavery in Missouri, 1821." Vol. 65, no. 4 (July 1971).

Thomas, Raymond D. "Missouri Valley Settlement — St. Louis to Independence." Vol. 21, no. 1 (October 1926).

Trexler, Harrison A. "Slavery in Missouri Territory." Vol. 3, no. 3 (April 1909).

———, "The Value and the Sale of the Missouri Slave," Vol. 8, no. 2 (January 1914).

"The Underground Railroad in Boonville." Vol. 30, no. 2 (January 1936). Reprinted from the *Boonville Observer* by the Glasgow *Weekly Times*, December 1, 1853.

Welsh, Donald H., ed. "Travel by Stage on the Boonslick Road." Vol. 54. no. 4 (July 1960).

Windell, Marie George, ed. "Westward Along the Boone's Lick Trail in 1826, the Diary of Colonel John Glover." Vol. 39, no. 2, (January 1945).

ARCHIVE COLLECTIONS

Audsley, Francis Fairbank and Harriet Elizabeth Papers 1861–1912, C2374: State Historical Society of Missouri, Columbia.

Bills and Resolutions, House of Representatives, 35th Congress, 1st Session, H.R. 505 (Report No. 293). Library of Congress.

Bibliography

Capitol Fire Documents, Election returns 1860, Folder 16424, Reel CFD-187, Missouri State Archives.

Congressional Series of United States Public Documents, Vol. 869, Kansas Affairs; Special Committee to investigate the troubles in the Territory of Kansas, 34th Congress, 1st Session, U.S. House of Representatives, (Report No. 200). Library of Congress.

Glasgow Insurance Company Books 1855–1870: C2313, State Historical Society of Missouri, Columbia.

Hardeman, Glen O. Collection C3655: State Historical Society of Missouri, Columbia.

Index of Patentees for Military Bounty Land Warrants Issued under the Act of 1812 Located in Missouri; Military Bounty Land Warrants under the Act of 1812. Record Group 49, Records of the Bureau of Land Management 1865–2006. Microfilm Publication M848. National Archives and Records Administration (NARA).

Marmaduke Collection C1021: State Historical Society of Missouri, Columbia.

Marmaduke Family File: Mary Ball Washington Museum and Library, Lancaster, Va.

Marmaduke, Meredith M. Will: inventory and appraisal, settlement and distribution of the M. M. Marmaduke Estate: Missouri State Archives, Saline County Probate Estate Files, Microfilm Reel C-8250, Estate CE-1710.

McRoberts, A. J. Papers 1859–1876, C0375: State Historical Society of Missouri, Columbia.

Records of Governor Meredith Miles Marmaduke: Missouri State Archives, Jefferson City.

Records of Governor Thomas Reynolds: Missouri State Archives, Jefferson City.

Register of Enlistments in the United States Army, compiled 1798–1914. Record Group 94, Records of the Adjutant General's Office, 1780s–1917. Microfilm Publication M233. National Archives and Records Administration (NARA).

Sappington Family Papers C159: State Historical Society of Missouri, Columbia.

Sappington, John Papers C1027: State Historical Society of Missouri, Columbia.

Sappington-Marmaduke Family Papers: Missouri Historical Society, St. Louis.

Smith, Thomas Adams Collection C1029: State Historical Society of Missouri, Columbia.

U.S. Superintendency of Indian Affairs, St. Louis, Records 1807–1855. State Historical Society of Missouri Manuscript Collection C2960.

Virginia Militia, War of 1812 Muster and Payrolls, 1812–1815. Library of Virginia, Record Group 46, Box 1, folder 5, 118th Regiment.

ELECTRONIC DOCUMENTS

American Heritage Science Dictionary. "Scrofula." dictionary.com/browse/scrofula

Ancestry.com (online database). "U.S., Union Provost Marshal's Papers, 1861–1867. Provo, UT." From National Archives: Union Provost Marshal's File of Papers Relating to Individual Civilians, 1861–1867. Microfilm Publication MO345, Record Group 109.

Avalon Project: United States Statutes at Large. "An Act to Regulate Trade and Intercourse with the Indian Tribes, and to Preserve Peace on the Frontiers, May 19, 1796." avalon.law.yale.edu/18th_century/na030.asp

Black Past. "The Black Laws of Oregon, 1844–1857." blackpast.org/perspectives/black-laws-oregon

Economic History Association. "Fertility and Mortality in the United States." Michael Haines, Colgate University. eh.net/encyclopedia/fertility-and-mortality-in-the-united-states

Harrison County Genealogical Society. "Early Trails and Roads into Western Virginia." John R. Ice, compiler. wvhcgs.com

Kansas City Public Library: Civil War on the Western Border: The Missouri-Kansas Conflict, 1854–1865 (website). "Shadow War: Federal Military Authority and Loyalty Oaths in Civil War Missouri."

To Make a Fortune in Missouri

Christopher Phillips. civilwaronthewesternborder.org/essay/shadow-war-federal-military-authority-and-loyalty-oaths-civil-war-missouri

Kingdom of Callaway Historical Society. "History of Steamboating on the Missouri River." Phillip E. Chappell. kchsoc.callawegian.org/steamboat.html

Latin Library. "William Wing Loring 1818–1886." thelatinlibrary.com/chron/civilwarnotes/loring.html

Library of Congress. "About Jefferson Inquirer (Jefferson City, Mo.) 1838–1854." chroniclingamerica.loc.gov/lccn/sn84020038

———: "The Records of the Virginia Company of London." Vol. 3. loc.gov/item/06035006

Louisiana Endowment for the Humanities, 64 Parishes. "French Colonial Louisiana." Michael T. Pasquier. 64parishes.org/entry/french-colonial-louisiana

———. "Slavery in Spanish Colonial Louisiana." John C. Rodrigue. 64parishes.org/entry/slavery-in-spanish-colonial-louisiana

Measuring Worth Foundation. Seven Ways to Compute the Relative Value of a U.S. Dollar Amount, 1774 to Present. Samuel H. William. measuringworth.com/calculators/uscompare3

Missouri State Archives. "Missouri's Early Slave Laws: A History in Documents." https://www.sos.mo.gov/archives/education/aahi/earlyslavelaws

———. U.S. Census, Schedule 5. "Products of Industry in the County of St. Clair during the year ending June 1, 1850" on CD: Census, Industrial Schedules 1850/1860/1870. sos.mo.gov/archives

National Endowment for the Humanities. "Christianity in 18th Century America." edsitement.neh.gov/curriculum-unit/religion-18th-century-america

National Institutes of Health. "Decennial Life Tables for the White Population of the United States, 1790–1900." Table 1. J. David Hacker. ncbi.nlm.nih.gov/pmc/articles/PMC2885717

National Park Service Historic Jamestowne. "Tobacco: Colonial Cultivation Methods." nps.gov/jame/historyculture

Society of the War of 1812 in the Commonwealth of Virginia. "1812 chronological list of encounters during the of the War of 1812 in Virginia, revised December 7, 2010." Myron E. Lyman Sr. and William W. Hankins. 1812va.org

Spotsylvania (Virginia) District for the Superior Court of Chancery Abstracts. Barry L. McGhee, archivist. historiccourtrecords.org

Steamboat Times. "Steamboats 1811–1861: Western Engineer." steamboattimes.com/steamboats_1811-61_p1.html

Stoddard County, MOGenWeb. "Amos Stoddard and the Territory of Missouri." sites.rootsweb.com/~mostodd2/history/stod-settlers/amos-stod.htm

Texas State Library and Archives Commission. "Hard Road to Texas, Texas Annexation 1836–1845." www.tsl.texas.gov/exhibits/annexation

Tobacco News (website). "Economic Aspects of Tobacco during the Colonial Period 1612–1776." archive.tobacco.org/History/colonialtobacco.html

U.S. Census. "Agricultural Schedules 1850 to 1900." census.gov/history/pdf/agcensusschedules.pdf

Virginia Places (website). "The Origins of Slavery in Virginia." virginiaplaces.org/population/slaveorigin.html

Westmoreland County Chancery Court Records. ADMR of John Hunter vs. James Hunter and Vincent Marmaduke. Index No. 1825-002. lva.virginia.gov/chancery/default.asp#res

———. ADMX of Vincent Marmaduke vs Thomas Sanford, etc. Index No. 1797-013 & ADMX of Vincent Marmaduke vs Charles Sanford. Index No. 1805-012. lva.virginia.gov/chancery/default.asp#res

Wikipedia. "First Principal Meridian," "Fifth Principal Meridian," "Seven Ranges. en.wikipedia.org/wiki/First_principal_meridian, en.wikipedia.org/wiki/Fifth_principal_meridian, en.wikipedia.org/wiki/Seven_Ranges

Bibliography

———. "Old Point Comfort." en.wikipedia.org/wiki/Old_Point_Comfort

CORRESPONDENCE

Letter, Myron Lyman to Lee Cullimore, January 2, 2012. Accompanied by manuscript, *1812 chronological list of encounters during the War of 1812 in Virginia*, revised December 7, 2010.

Letter, Zoe Hasselbring to Lee Cullimore, March 16, 2016. Identification of figures in painting *Verdict of the People*.

Letter, Elizabeth Burnes to Lee Cullimore, March 23, 2016. Search of NARA tract books for Fayette, Missouri, Land Office July 7, 1832–1849.

Letter, Joan McPeak to Lee Cullimore, April 7, 2016. Information on Marmaduke holdings in St. Clair County.

Letter, Charles Valier to Lee Cullimore, April 12, 2016. Identification of figures in painting *Verdict of the People*.

INDEX

Page numbers in italics refer to illustrations. MM refers to Meredith Marmaduke; JS refers to John Sappington. When ranks are mentioned, generally the highest rank attained is used, regardless of when a specific entry occurred.

1860 presidential race, 259–61

A

Adams, John Quincy (Pres.), 21, 39, 116
Agricultural and Commercial Society of Missouri, 208
Allen, Charles H., 140
Ambler, Charles, 19–20
Applegate, Jesse A., 175, 177
Arrow Rock, Missouri, 28, *194*, 285–86; Civil War activity, 278–79; established, 166; growth, 166–67; stores, 106–07, 111, 247
Atherton, Lewis, 109
Audsley, Francis F., 277

B

Barbour, James, 21
Barbour, Philip Pendleton, 21
Barnes, "Big Jim," 79
Barnes, "Long Jim," 79
Barron, Samuel (Capt.), 273, 274
Barton, David (Sen.), 115–16, 117
Barton, Joshua, 116, 117
Bates, Edward (Rep.), 80, 116, 163, 175–76; letter to MM, 102–03
Bates, Frederick (Gov.), 43
Beale, George William, Rev., 7

Becknell, William, 27–28, 38–39, 49, 54–55, 61, 102; 1821 trip to Santa Fe, 52–53
Bell, John, 260–61
Bentis, J. J., 224
Benton, Thomas Hart (Sen.), 31, 37, 39, 41, 43, 95-96, 115–16, 117–18, 119, 120, 126, 129, 139, 140, 141, *191*, 202, 247–48, 249–51; on annexation of Texas, 250–51; on dueling, 116–18; final days in politics and death, 256–58; on land graduation, 163–64
Bicknell, George T., 153–58, 205–06
Bingham, George Caleb, 88, 118–19, 123, *182*, *183*, *184*, *185*, *194*
Bingham, Mathias, 149
Birch, James H., 117–18, 123
Birch, James H., Jr., 117–18
Birch, Weston F., 274
Blain, Thompkins & Barrett, 202
Blair, Francis (Frank) P., Jr., 255, 257, 262
Bogy, Joseph, 123
Boon, Ratliff, 137
Boone, Baptiste, 71
Boone, Daniel Morgan, 28, 52
Boone, Joseph H., 147, 148–49
Boone, Nathan, 28, 29, 71

Boone's Lick Heritage, 204
Booneslick region, 27, 28, *181*; agriculture in, 200–05, 217–18; connections of MM in, 35–44; livestock breeding in, 206–08; slave trade in, 24, 218, 222–27; suffers economically during Civil War, 276–77
Boone's Lick saltworks, 28, 52
Bound Away, Virginia and the Westward Movement, 22
Bradford, C. M., 146, 157
Breathitt, John. B., 279
Breckinridge, John C., 260
Briscoe, John, 223
Broadhead, James (Col.), 271, 272
Brown, Benjamin Gratz, 117
Brown, Egbert B. (Brig. Gen.), 278
Brown, William Wells, 221, 222
Brownlee, Andrew, 285
Burke, Diane Mutti, 221–22
busting sod, method for, 199–200

C
Calhoun, John, 249
Campbell, John P., 137
Camp Jackson Affair, 262
Carr, William C., 208
Catholicism, frontier attitudes on, 64–65
cattle business, Missouri, 206–08
Central Missouri Stock Importing Company, 208
Chariton County, Missouri, 18, 166
Charless, Joseph, 145
cholera outbreaks, 92, 218
Chouteau, Auguste, 24, 71
Chouteau, Pierre, 24
Clark, John B., 123, 125, 268–69
Clark, Robert P., 223
Clark, William, 22, 29–30, 42, 70–71, 80, 104
Clay, Henry, 115, 166
Cochrane, Alexander, (Vice Adm.), 12
Collins, James L., 79, 81, 82, 107

Concha, Fernando de la (Gov.), 50
Coonce, Jacob, 171–72
Cooper, Benjamin (Col.), 54, 55
Cooper, Stephen, 55
county and state fairs, 208–10
Craddock, Edward, 222
Cravens, Charles M., 119–20, 123
Crow, Phillip, 176
Curtis, Samuel (Maj. Gen.), 271

D
Dickey, Michael, 92
Douglas, Stephen A., 260
Drake, Charles D., 271–72
Dr. Sappington's Anti-Fever Pills, 42, 108, 143–46; Marmaduke and Bicknell, 153–58; Tymony, Francis (agent), 150–53, 159
dueling, 116–19, 248–49, 268–69
Duggins, Frances, 234
Duggins, John, 234
Dyer, Robert, 204–05

E
Eakin, James H., 286–87
Eakin, Julia, 238
Earickson, James, 121, 137
Eaton, John H., 80
Eddins, Layton, 135, 136, 137, 141, 146, 152, 209, 255
Eddins, Susan, 135, 225
E. D. Sappington and Company, 108
education of Marmaduke children, 234–42
Edwards, John C., 140
emigration to America, motivations for, 2
Escudero, Don Manuel Simon de, 68, 70, 75

F
Farrar, Bernard G., 145
Fedric, Francis, 23
Fenwick, William H., 285
fertility, 91–92

Index

Fischer, David H., 22
Fox, Joseph, 21
Franklin, Missouri, 18, 24–25, 30–33
Free Soil Party, 256–57

G

Gamble, Hamilton (Gov.), 271
Garcia, Ramon, 68, 71
Garrett, Laban, 233–34
Gash brothers, 172
Geyer, Henry S., 122, 257
Gilbraith, Alexander, 226
Glascock, George, 206–07
Gordon, James (Capt.), 12
Green, Duff, 120
Greenspan, Ezra, 222
Greenwood, Alfred, 82
Gregg, Josiah, 62
Grisham, John R., 119

H

Hall, Sylvester, 143–44
Hammond, James R., 207
Hanard, John, 13, 14, 21
Hardeman, Bailey, 55, 251
Hardeman, John, 35, 36, 37–38, 55, 111, 222; MM letter to, 66–67
Hardeman, John Locke, 111, *196*, 198, 199, 201, 208, 209–210; letter to Beverley Tucker, 218; letter to MM, 222–23, 251
Hardeman, Nicholas Perkins, 36, 56, 111
Hardeman, Seth, 89–90
Hardeman, Thomas, 31, 35–37, 55, 111
Hardin, Joel, 136
Harris, Nathan, 77, 79
Harris & Scott, 77–78
Harvey, Thomas B., 167
Harvey, Thomas H., 119, 121, 127–28, 201, 220, 250
Harvey, Thomas R. E., 274–75
Harwood, Jane, 234, 235–36, 272, 287
Harwood, Levin, 225, 234, 236, 258, 267, 275–76, 286, 287, 288

Haskell, John G., 224
Hayden, Joel H., 169
headright system of land ownership, 3
Heath, John G., 54
Heathman, James, 150
hemp, as cash crop, 203–04, 205
Hempstead, Thomas, 116
Henderson, John B., 256
Higgerson, Joseph, 224
Hogan, George M., 157, 158
Hough, George W., 256
Huffman, James H., 220
Hughes, Nathaniel, Jr., 237
Hungerford, Henry (uncle to MM), 13, 19, 49; declines to go West, 49–50; letter to MM, 47–48; reporting on family slaves, 23–24
Hungerford, John P. (Brig. Gen.), 7, 12
Hunter, James, 20
Hunter, John (MM brother-in-law), 5, 20
Hunter, Sarah, 87
Hurt, Ossumus, 220
Hurt, R. Douglas, 208–09, 217
Huston, Benjamin, 76–77, 166
Hutchins, Thomas, 164–65

I

indentured servitude, as solution to British economy, 2–3
Indian depredation claims, 80–81
infant mortality rates, 19th century, 92

J

Jackson, Andrew (Pres.), 37, 115–16, 120
Jackson, Claiborne Fox, 117–18, 119, 120, 129, 141, 147, *186*, 258; anti-Union activities of 1861, 261–62, 268–70; background, 247; conspiracy to finance Confederate military activities, 276–77; defeated in 1848 gubernatorial race, 253–55; introduces Jackson Resolutions, 256, 277; land speculation with MM,

168–70, 175, 177, 178, 197; political career, 248–49, 259–62; threatens duel, 248–49
Jackson, Eliza nee Sappington (formerly Pearson), 99, 100, 157, *187*, 248
Jackson, Jane Sappington, 99
Jackson, John P., 158
Jackson, Louisa Sappington, 99, 248
Jackson Resolutions, 256, 277
Jeffersonian Republican, 125–26
Jefferson Inquirer, 257
Jenkins, Thomas, 208
J. & E. Walsh, 202, 203–04, 205–06, 234
Jones, John Beauchamp, 106–07

K
Kansa tribes, 50
Kelly, James C., 22
King, Austin, 137, 141, 253–55, 258
Kirkman, Francis, 3
Korh, Charles (Lt.), 274

L
La Lande, Jean Baptiste, 51
Lane, Joseph, 253
Lankford, Jesse, 41
Lavender, David, 172
Lecompton Constitution, 260
Lee, Henry ("Black Horse Harry"), 37
Lee, Richard Henry, 7
Leonard, Abiel, 117, 121, 123
Letcher, William H., 200–01
Lewis, William, 207
Lexington Proslavery Convention, 258–59
Liberty Weekly Tribune, 258, 259
Littlepage, Hardin B., 273
Loan, Benjamin (Brig. Gen.), 271
Long, John W., 123
Lowry, John J., 119, 250, 252, 253
Lucas, Charles, 31, 43, 116–17
Lucas, James H., 64
Lujan, Jose Maguel, 81
Lusk, James, 257

Luster, T. J., 145
Lyon, Nathaniel (Gen.), 262, 268

M
malaria, 42, 144. *See also* Dr. Sappington's Anti-Fever Pills
Mallet, Paul, 51
Mallet, Pierre, 51
Mallory, Stephen R., 274
Marmaduke, Christopher, 4–5
Marmaduke, Darwin William (son of MM, b. 1840), 92, 95, *193*, 205, 234, 235, 241, 267, 268, 286, 287; in Enrolled Missouri Militia, 270; letter to MM, 101
Marmaduke, Henry Hungerford, (son of MM, b. 1842), 92, *193*, 242, 287; naval career, 272–74
Marmaduke, Jacob (arr. 1663), 3
Marmaduke, James Bragg, 123, 127
Marmaduke, Jane (daughter of MM, b. 1827, m. Harwood), 234
Marmaduke, John Sappington (son of MM, b. 1833), 92, *193*, 236–37; military career, 240–41; switches allegiance, joins Confederate States Army, 270; at West Point, 239–40
Marmaduke, Lavinia ("Bena") (daughter of MM, b. 1838), 235–36, 287
Marmaduke, Lavinia Sappington (wife of MM), 88–91, 95, *183*, 286, 287, 289; as home schooler, 234; repeated childbirths, 92, 242; letters to MM, 95; letter to brother, 93–94; manages plantation affairs, 95–96, 219–20; suffers in MM's General Assembly absence, 133–35
Marmaduke, Layton Price (son of MM, b. 1841), 92, 135, 241
Marmaduke, Leslie, (son of MM, b. 1846), 92, *193*
Marmaduke, Meredith Miles (b. 1791), 4, 5–6, 55, *182*, *192*, *196*, 197; 1823 journey to Franklin, 18–21; 1839 St. Clair County land purchase, 169–73;

1840 manifesto in *Jeffersonian Republican*, 125–27; appointed University curator, 122; appointed Westmoreland Co. Commissioner of Revenue, 13; attempts to collect debt from Joseph Boone, 147, 148–49; Booneslick connections of, 35–44; children, 92; commissioned in Virginia Militia, 10; courtship of Lavinia, 88; death, 285–86; depicted in Bingham's *Stump Speaking*, 118–119; early family life, 94–96; elected Lt. Gov., 1840, 127–29; ends St. Clair County ambitions, 175–178; early political career, 119–25; farming properties, 197–200; hemp income, 203–05; holds Saline County political offices, 43; homestead, *188–89*; letters of introduction, 21–22; letters to Darwin Sappington, 109–10; letter to JS as agent, 147–48; letter to William Sappington, 100; as lifelong networker and correspondent, 120; mercantile ventures, 106–11; appointed Missouri State Agricultural Society president, 209; Missouri Territory land purchase, 17–18; on New Mexicans' morals, 66–67; Oregon, questions moving to, 252–53; real estate, final value of, 288–89; political decline after 1844 elections, 137–41; rises to governorship, 136–37; Saline County land purchase with Claiborne Jackson, 168–69; Santa Fe journal entries, 62–65; gives up Santa Fe retail trips, 82–83; as slaveholder, 24, 217–19, 223–28, 287–88; Texas, brief interest in, 251; tobacco crop, lack of interest in Missouri, 201; wedding, 90–91

Marmaduke, Miles (tobacco planter, d. 1695), 4

Marmaduke, M. M. Jr. (nephew of MM), 136

Marmaduke, Meredith Miles Jr. (son of MM, b. 1835), 92, 136, *193*, 238, 286–87; charged with treason, 274–75

Marmaduke, Molly (sister of MM, m. Hunter), 5

Marmaduke, Richard (arr. 1637), 2

Marmaduke, Richard (arr. 1649), 3

Marmaduke, Robert (purchases land, 1681), 4

Marmaduke, Sarah (mother of MM), 5–6

Marmaduke, Sarah Porter, (daughter of MM, b. 1829, m. Yerby), 92, 235

Marmaduke, Vincent (brother of MM), 20, 21–22

Marmaduke, Vincent (father of MM), 5

Marmaduke, Vincent (son of MM, b. 1831), 92, *193*, 236, 286; in Confederate Secret Service, 272; education, 237–38; letters to MM, 47, 48, 87; marriage, 238; support of Confederacy, 271–72

Marmaduke, William (advertising for runaway servant, 1775), 3–4

Marmaduke, William (arr. 1663), 3

Marmaduke and Sappington, 106–08

Marmaduke homestead, *188–89*, *190*

Marshall Democrat, 259

McCausland, Alexander, 76

McClanahan, Elizabeth (sister of MM), 5; implores MM not to go West, 48–49

McClanahan, John (nephew of MM), 223–24

McClanahan, Vincent (MM nephew), 17, 19, 20; letter to MM, 47, 87

McClure, Samuel (Col.), 39–40, 56, 63, 66, 68, 75, 90, 238

McClure & Marmaduke, 56–57, 65–66; dissolves, 75–76; seek recompense from property lost in ambush, 68–71

McCorkle, Samuel W., 201

McKim, Randolph H., 7

McKnight-Baird expedition, 52

McLanahan, Joseph, 51–52

McMahan, Thomas, 24, 76, 77, 81, 82, 108
McNees, Robert, 78–79
Mead, David, 22
metes and bounds survey, 164
Miller, John G. (Gov.), 42–43, 102, 119, 248
Miller, Robert H., 258, 259
Minor, William G. (Col.), 136
Missouri Compromise: repealed by Kansas-Nebraska Act, 258
Missouri Intelligencer, 38, 52, 61, 69, 119–20
Missouri Intelligencer & Boon's Lick Advertiser, 76, 78
Missouri politics, 115; 1820 Constitutional Convention, 36; 1848 Democratic Party convention, 254–55; 19th century, 115–16; 1840 Whig convention, 123; ticket process of voting, 125
Missouri population growth, 171
Missouri State Agricultural Society, 209–210
Missouri Statesman, 224, 254
Missouri Weekly Democrat, 205
M. M. Marmaduke & Co., 76, 108; reparations attempts for 1828 Pawnee Indian attack, 78–83
Monroe, Daniel, 78–79
Morris, Robert W., 55–56
Morrison, James, 52
Morrison, Jesse, 52
Morrison, William, 51, 52
Morrow, Lynn, 99
Moss, F. H., 221

N
Napton, William Barclay, 199, 259, 277–78
Napton, William Barclay, Jr., 63–64
Niles' Weekly Register, 39
Nowlin, Peyton, 90, 120, 166, 234

O
O'Bryan-Lawson, Robert Anthony, 237
Odell, Jeremiah, 168
O'Fallon, John, 207–08
Oliver, Polly, 201
Oregon Territory established, 251–52
Orr, Sample, 260, 261, 271
Osage River, steamboat traffic on, 170–71

P
Parsons, Augustine aka Alonzo Pearson, 100–04
Parsons, Mary Ann, 100
Patten, Nathaniel, 61–62
Patterson, James, 51–52
Patterson, Thomas, 71
Pawnee tribe, suit against, 79–82
Payne, Richard: letter to MM, 87
Pearson, Alonzo aka Augustine Parsons, 100–104, 106, 120, 146, 237
Pearson, Darwin (nephew to MM), 237
Pearson and Sappington, 100, 106
Penn, George, 92, 119, 120, 121, 123, 140, 167, 225, 226, 242, 249, 253, 256, 269
Pethy, Marilda, 224
Phelps, John S., 81–82, 239
Piersol, Jeremiah, 17–18
Piersol, Samuel, 17, 18
Pike, Zebulon, 49
Pilot Hickory (Sappington farm), 90, *196*, 259
Pitts, George R., 19, 37, 136; letters to MM, 104–06
planter class, Virginia, 7
Porter, Frances: letter to MM, 87
Porter, Samson: letter to MM, 88
Price, Mary Ellen, 92, 99
Price, Sterling, 119, 141, 258, 261, 262, 268, 271, 274
Price, Thomas L., 273
Price, William, 92, 146, 147, 156, 157, 287
public education, early 19th century, 233–34

R

Rector, Thomas, 117
Rector, William C. (Gen.), 42, 117, 165
Reid, Samuel, 91
Reynolds, Eliza Ann, 124, 136
Reynolds, Thomas (Gov.), 119, 121, 123, 248–49; background, 124–25; death, 136; elected governor 1840, 127–29
Robert, Henry M., 240
Robert's Rules of Order, 240
Rollins, James S., 121–22, 123, 141, 208, 209
Roscoe, Missouri, St. Clair County, 172–73, 174–75, 176
Rosegill Plantation, 3

S

Saline County: 1850 census, 200–01; Agriculture and Mechanical Association, 209; determining county seat, 167–68
Santa Fe: Becknell journal, 61–62; McClure & Marmaduke partnership, 56–57; MM expeditions, 38–39, 48–57
Santa Fe Trail: personalities important to, 38–39, 49–51, 61–62
Sappington, Erasmus Darwin (E. D.), 76, 77, 81, 82, 96, 100, 101, 106, 107–08, 109, 110, 118–19, 146, 149, 175, 176–77, 178, 197, 220, 241; favors land purchase over retail, 173–74
Sappington, Jane Breathitt, 41, *185*, 225; children, 91
Sappington, John, 24, 40, 88, 99, *184*, *196*; deals with Parsons bigamy, 100–04; develops quinine pill, 42, 145; early life, 41–42; settles family and practice near Glasgow, 42; *Theory and Treatment of Fevers*, 153
Sappington, Mark, 41
Sappington, Mary Ellen, 92, 99
Sappington, Susan, 99, 225
Sappington, William Breathitt, 93, 100, 118–19, 146, 177, *196*, 258, 276, 286, 287
Sappington and Sons, 42, 108, 144; original formation, territories, and dissolution, 146–47
Sappington/Marmaduke neighborhood, *196*
Scarpino, Philip V., 221
Schofield, John (Maj. Gen.), 278
Scott, William, 77, 79, 81, 82
Scott, William (Judge), 167, 168
Sebastian, William K., 82
Sharp, Grace Marmaduke, 4
Shelby, Jo (Col.), 278–79
Shields, Patrick, 172
Shoemaker, Floyd C., 115, 139, 140
Sibley, George, 70, 77
Simpson, Jane, 221
Skogen, Larry, 81
Slave Narratives, 224
slavery: Lecompton Constitution, 260; Lexington Proslavery Convention, 258–59; Missouri Compromise, 23, 215, 249, 258; Missouri laws governing, 216–17; Missouri population pre-Civil War, 224; Oregon's black exclusionary clauses, 252–53; owner responsibility to shelter and provision, 226–27; traders, 224–25; treatment of, 221; use of overseers for, 220–21
Smith, Cynthia B., 201
Smith, George W., 10
Smith, John, 225–26
Smith, Page, 13
Smith, Reuben, 51–52
Smith, Thomas Adams (Brig. Gen.), 32, 43–44, 111, 122, 197, 199, 201, 208
Spence, Thomas, 20, 22
St. Clair County independence, 174
Stephens, Joseph L., 209–10
Stevenson, Augustus, 169
St. Louis: in 1823, 24; effects of soft

money policy on economy, 139–40; steamboat traffic from, 204–05
St. Louis Merchants Exchange, 202
Storrs, Augustus, 39, 55
Story, James, 198
Stratford Hall plantation, 37
Sublette, Milton, 79
Switzler, William, 254
Sydnor, Washington, 56–57

T
Theory and Treatment of Fevers, 153
The Pioneer Merchant in Mid-America, 109
The Seven Ranges of Townships survey, 165
The Western Merchant, 106–07
Thompson, Philip, 81
Tidewater Virginia, 6; economic depression, 9; marshy atmosphere, 14; Westmoreland County aristocracy, 7–8
tobacco crop, business, 9–10
Todd & Krum, 206
Totten, James (Gen.), 274
Trade and Intercourse Act (1796), 80; (1834), 81
Trexler, Harrison, 228
Trigg, William H., 209–10
Tucker, Nathaniel Beverley, 100–02, 198; background, 104; Pitts on, 104–06
Turley, Jesse, 79, 82
Tyler, John (Pres.), 249, 251
Tymony, Francis (agent for Sappington and Sons), 150–53, 159, 206, 253–54

U
University of Missouri established, 121–22

V
Valdenar, James M., 220
Van Meter, Abraham, 201

Vial, Pedro, 50

W
Waldo, David, 172
Waldo, William, 79
Waldo family, 172
Walsh, Edward, 202
Walsh, James, 202
War of 1812, 10–13; land warrant system, 18
Washington *National Intelligencer*, 37
Watkins, Joel, 20
Watson, James L., 203
Welborn, James Curtis, 235
Wells, Carty, 256
Wetmore, Alphonso (Capt.), 44
Wetmore, Johnson, 24, 44
White, John R., 224
Wilcocks, James "Santiago" S., 65
Wild, Daniel, 3
Wilderness Calling, 56, 111
Wilkinson, James (Gen.), 49
Willard, J. P., 203
Williams, H. L., 251
Williams, P., 137
Wilson, James, 176
Wilson, W. A., 167
Wilson, W. S., 198
Wilstach, Paul, 6
Woodson, Samuel, 82
Wormeley, Christopher, 1–3
Wormeley, Ralph, 3

Y
Yale's Confederates: A Biographical Dictionary, 238
Yeatman, Pittman & Co. (Yeatman, Robinson & Co.), 202–03
Yerby, Thomas J., 235, 286